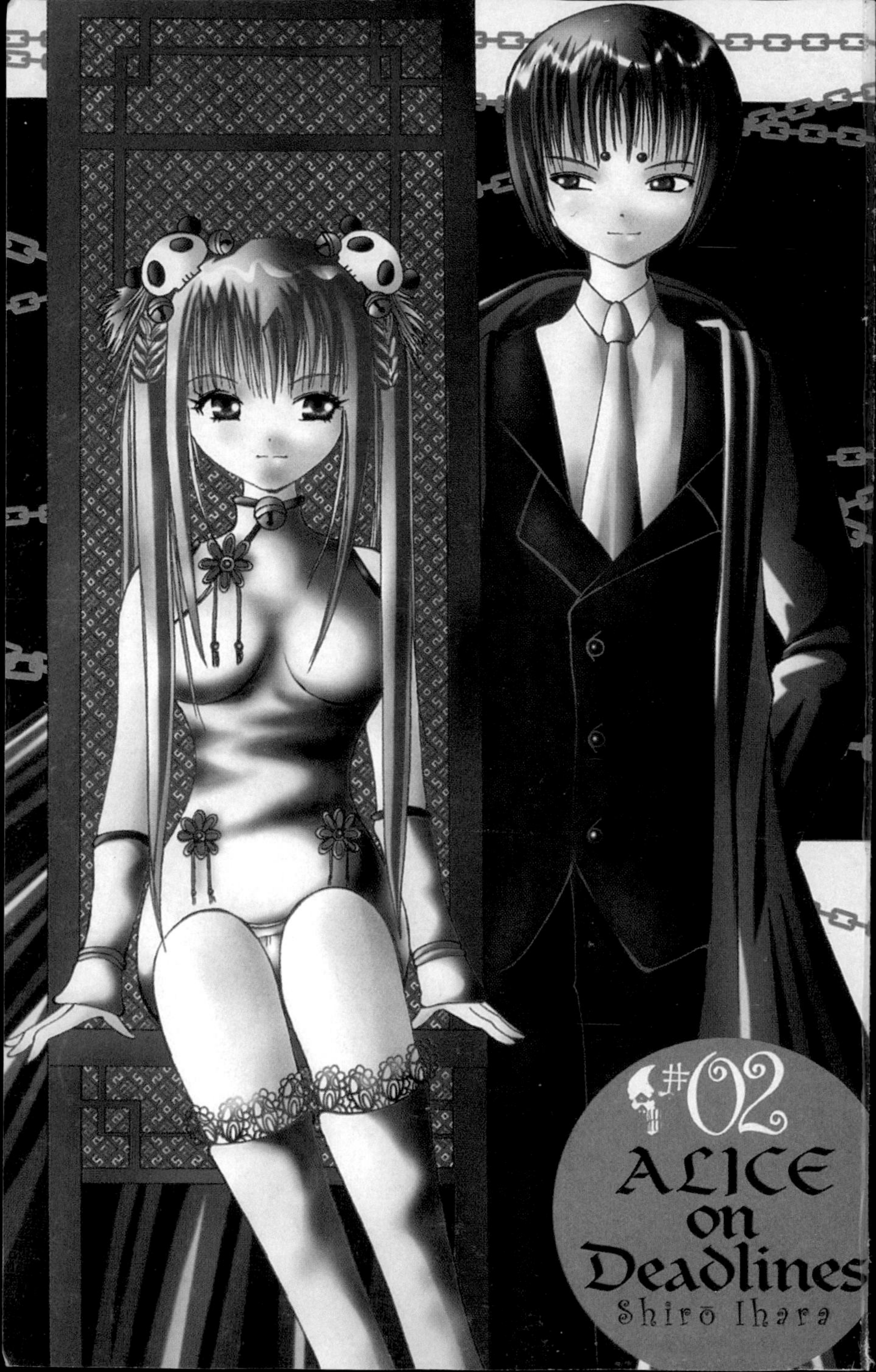
#02
ALICE on Deadlines
Shirō Ihara

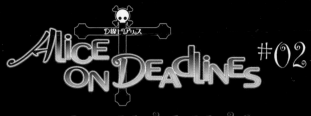

ALICE ON DEADLINES #02

CONTENTS

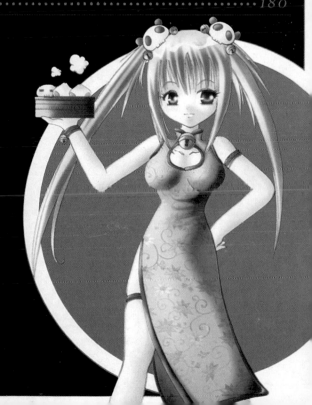

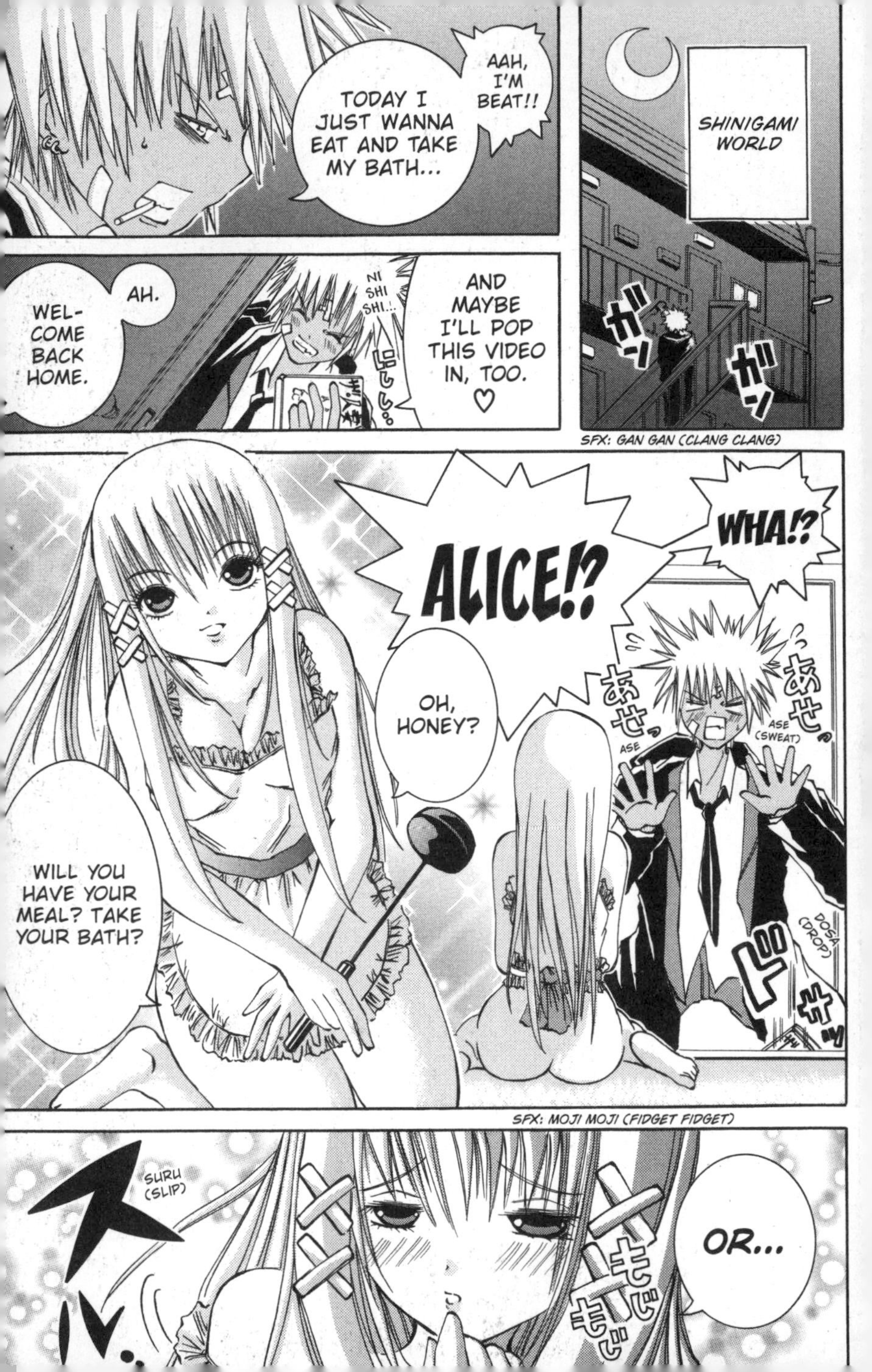
SHINIGAMI WORLD
SFX: GAN GAN (CLANG CLANG)
AAH, I'M BEAT!!
TODAY I JUST WANNA EAT AND TAKE MY BATH...
NI SHI SHI..
AND MAYBE I'LL POP THIS VIDEO IN, TOO. ♡
AH.
WEL-COME BACK HOME.
WHA!?
ALICE!?
ASE (SWEAT)
ASE
DOSA (DROP)
OH, HONEY?
WILL YOU HAVE YOUR MEAL? TAKE YOUR BATH?
SFX: MOJI MOJI (FIDGET FIDGET)
OR...
SURU (SLIP)

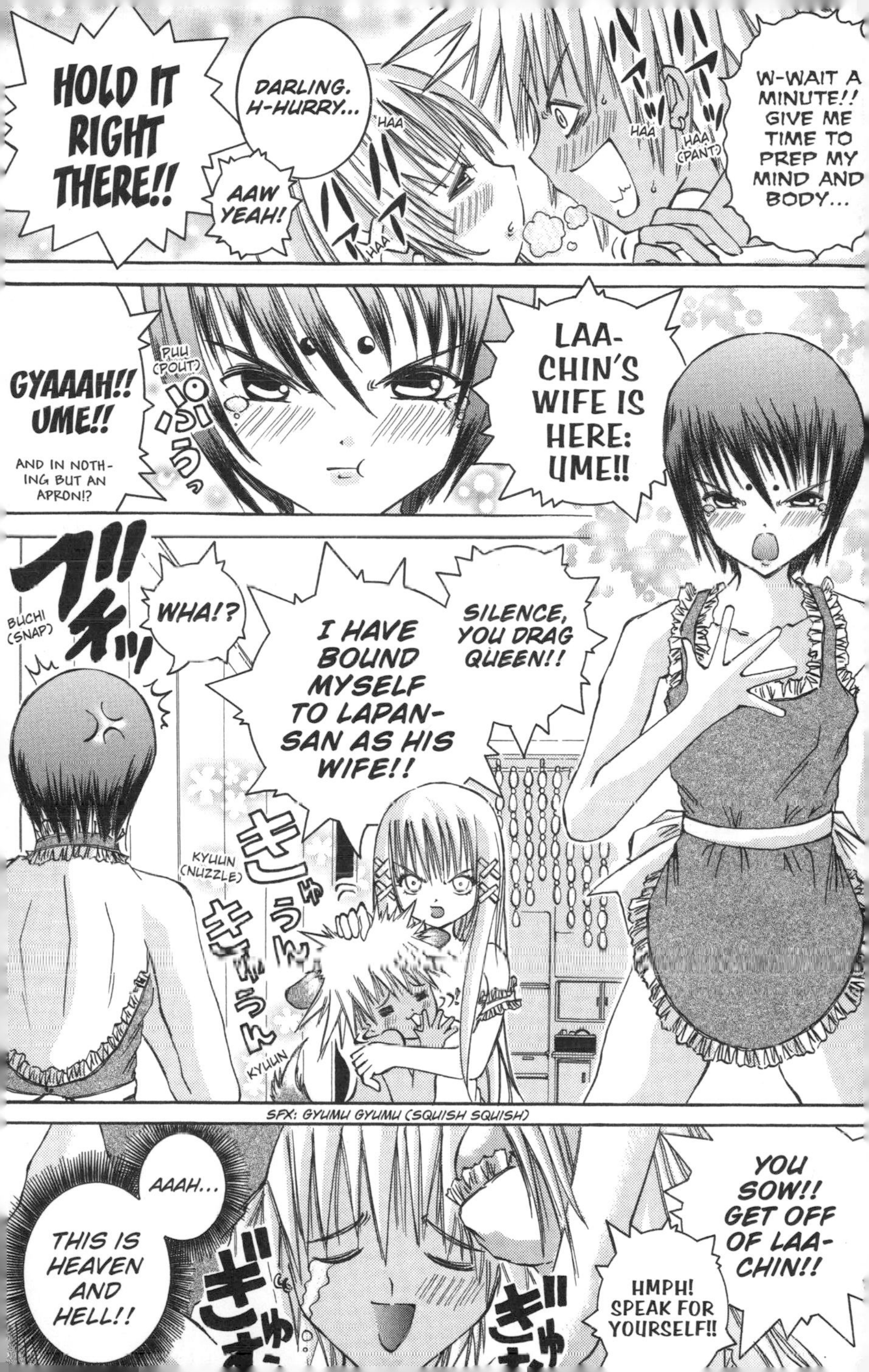
W-WAIT A MINUTE!! GIVE ME TIME TO PREP MY MIND AND BODY...
HAA (PANT)
HAA
DARLING. H-HURRY...
HAA
AAW YEAH!
HAA
HOLD IT RIGHT THERE!!
LAA-CHIN'S WIFE IS HERE: UME!!
PUU (POUT)
GYAAAH!! UME!!
AND IN NOTHING BUT AN APRON!?
SILENCE, YOU DRAG QUEEN!!
I HAVE BOUND MYSELF TO LAPAN-SAN AS HIS WIFE!!
WHA!?
BUCHI (SNAP)
KYUUN (NUZZLE)
KYUUN
SFX: GYUMU GYUMU (SQUISH SQUISH)
YOU SOW!! GET OFF OF LAA-CHIN!!
HMPH! SPEAK FOR YOURSELF!!
AAAH...
THIS IS HEAVEN AND HELL!!

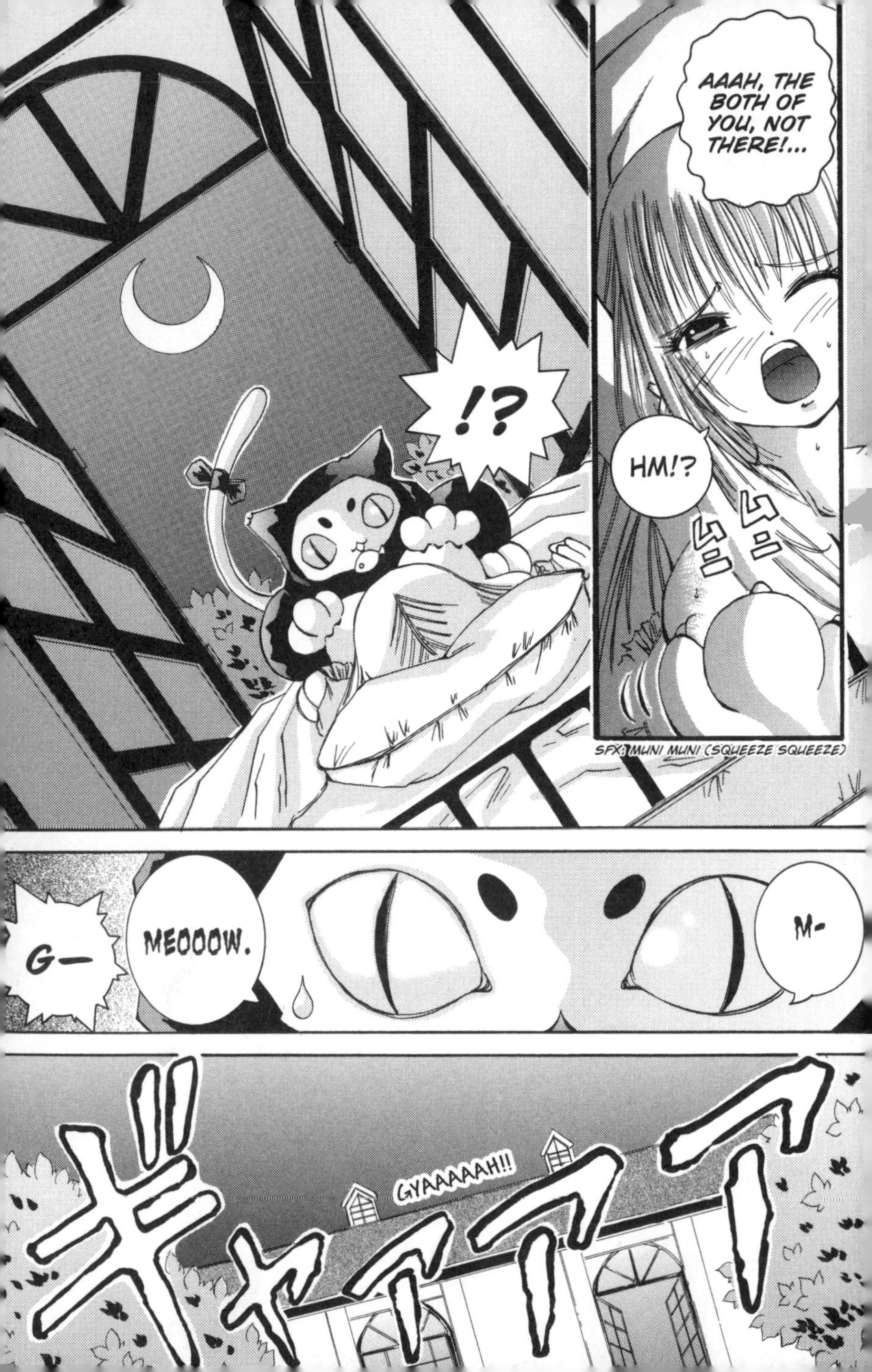
AAAH, THE BOTH OF YOU, NOT THERE!...
HM!?
SFX: MUNI MUNI (SQUEEZE SQUEEZE)
!?
M-
MEOOOW.
G—
GYAAAAAH!!

Line 5: The Cat Burglar & the Black Butterfly

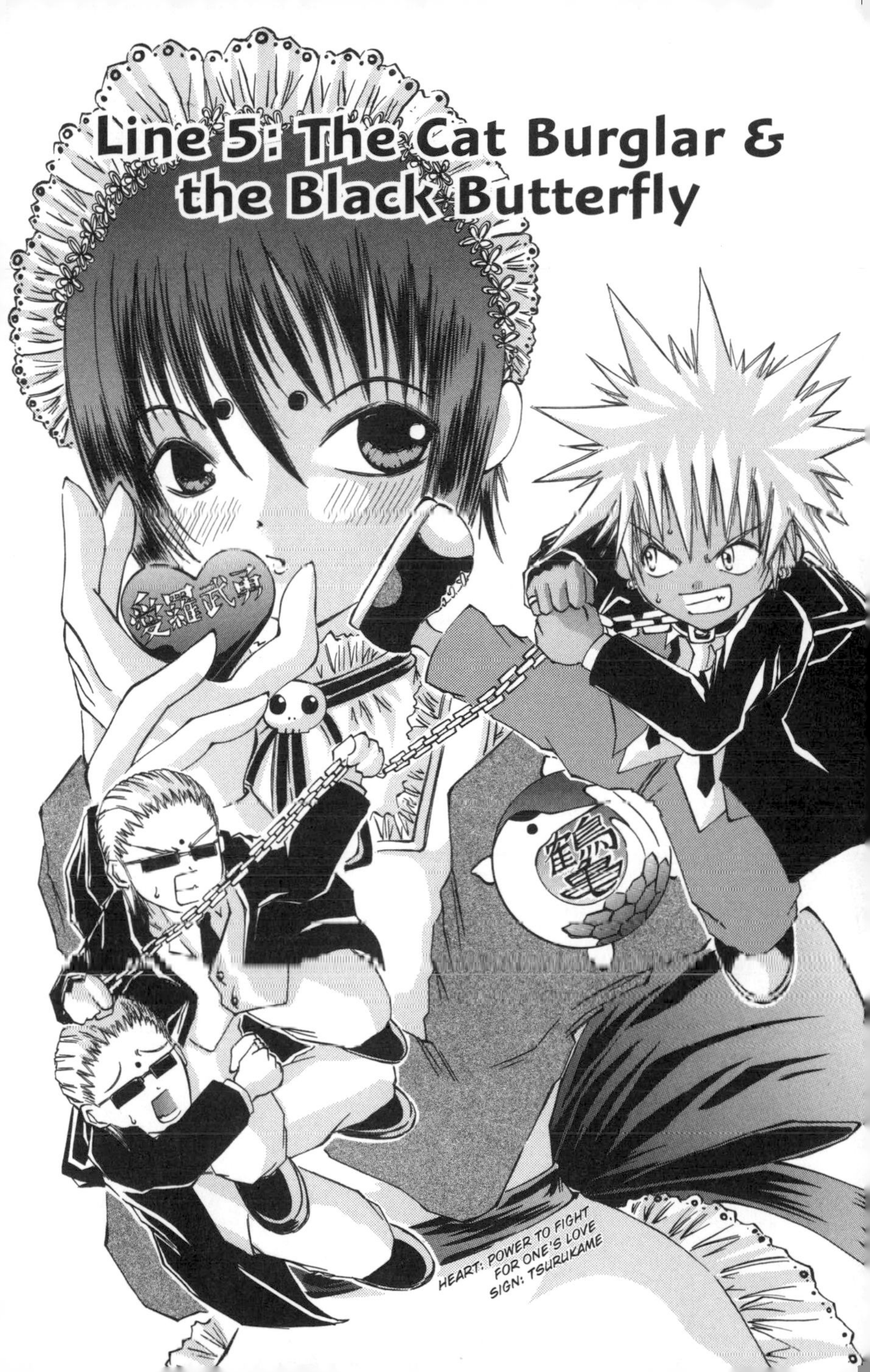

愛羅武勇
HEART: POWER TO FIGHT FOR ONE'S LOVE
SIGN: TSURUKAME

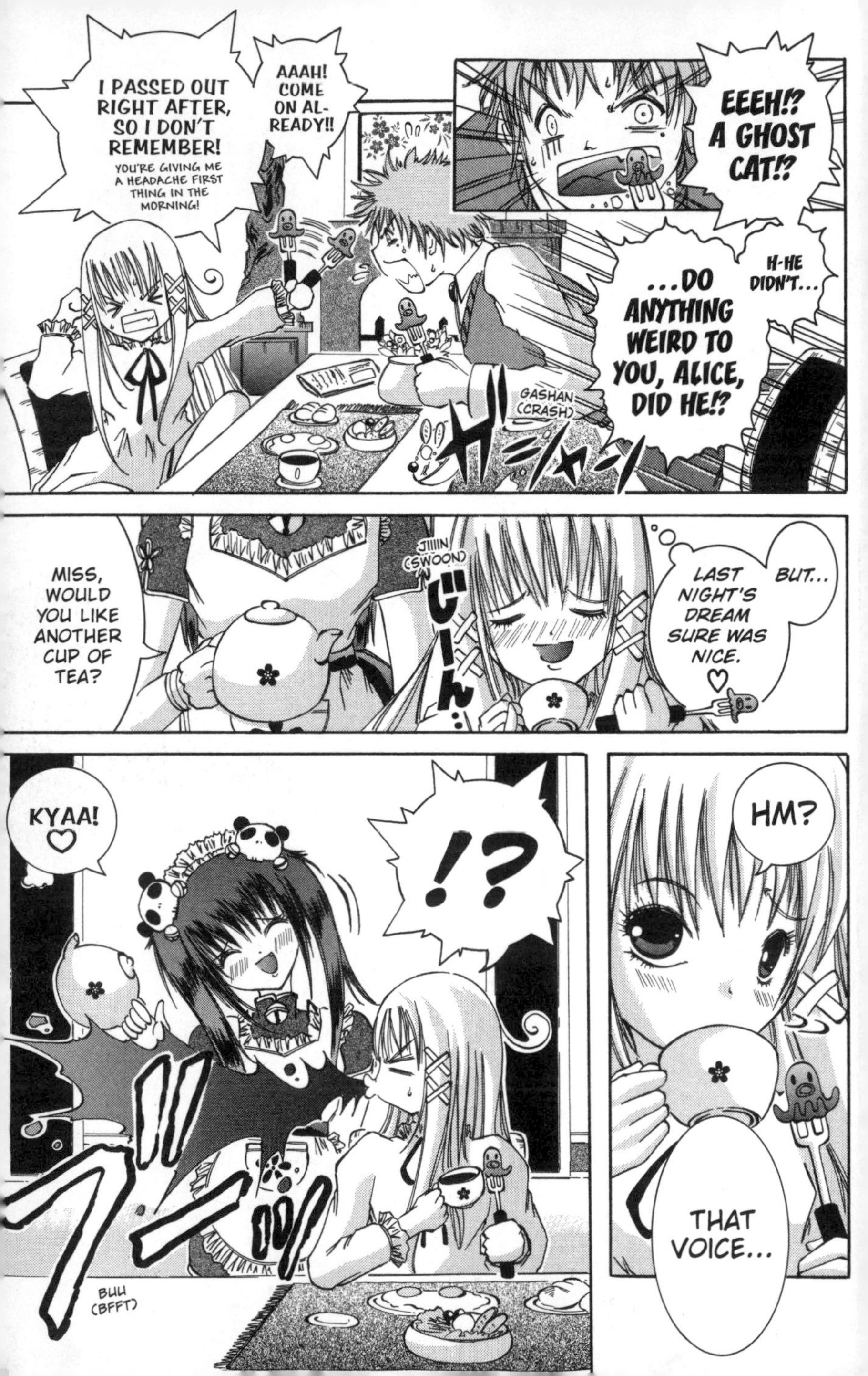
EEEH!? A GHOST CAT!?
H-HE DIDN'T...
...DO ANYTHING WEIRD TO YOU, ALICE, DID HE!?
AAAH! COME ON AL-READY!!
I PASSED OUT RIGHT AFTER, SO I DON'T REMEMBER!
YOU'RE GIVING ME A HEADACHE FIRST THING IN THE MORNING!
GASHAN (CRASH)
BUT...
LAST NIGHT'S DREAM SURE WAS NICE. ♡
JIIIN (SWOON)
MISS, WOULD YOU LIKE ANOTHER CUP OF TEA?
HM?
THAT VOICE...
!?
KYAA! ♡
BUU (BFFT)

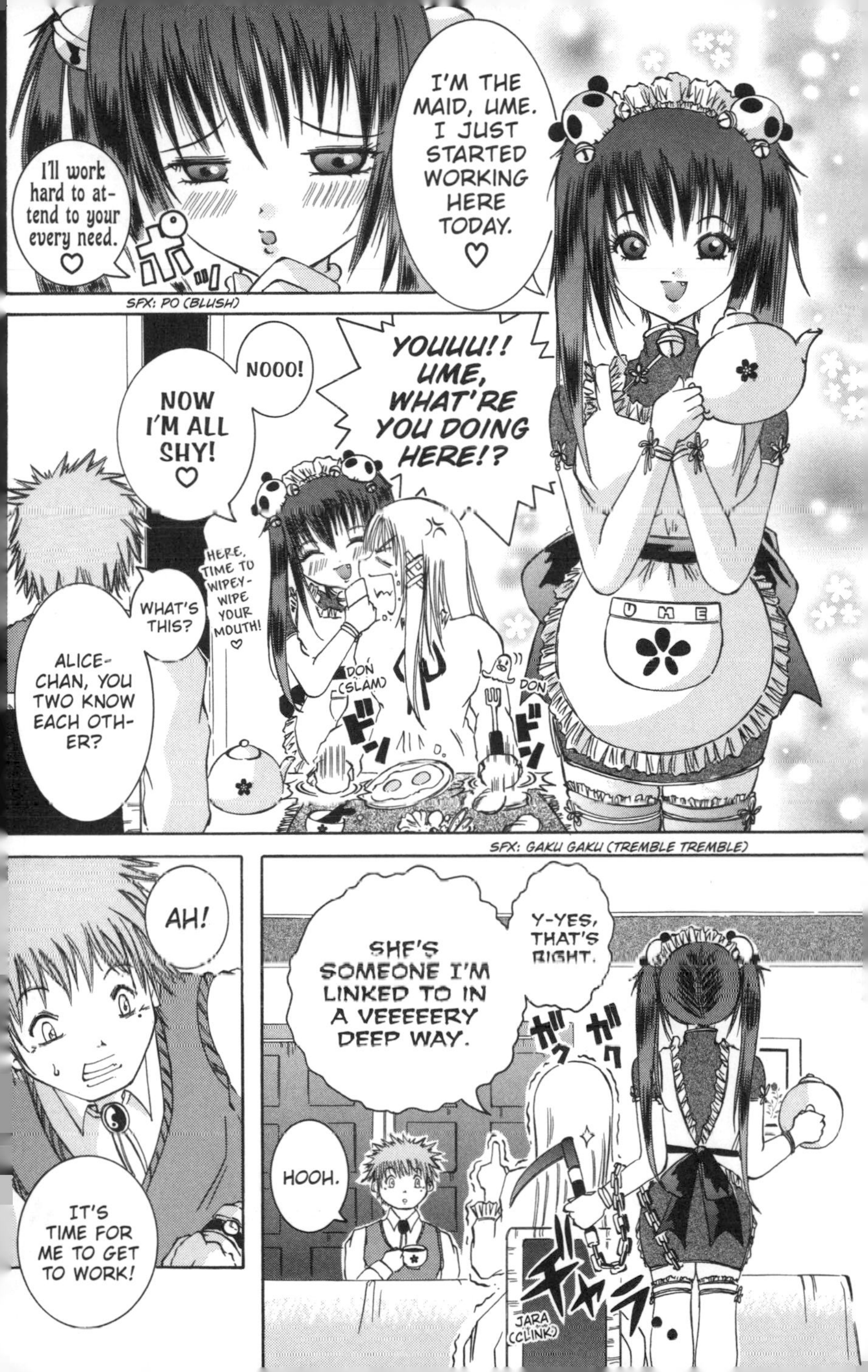
I'M THE MAID, UME. I JUST STARTED WORKING HERE TODAY. ♡
I'll work hard to attend to your every need. ♡
SFX: PO (BLUSH)
YOUUU!! UME, WHAT'RE YOU DOING HERE!?
NOOO!
NOW I'M ALL SHY! ♡
HERE, TIME TO WIPEY-WIPE YOUR MOUTH! ♡
DON
DON (SLAM)
WHAT'S THIS?
ALICE-CHAN, YOU TWO KNOW EACH OTHER?
SFX: GAKU GAKU (TREMBLE TREMBLE)
Y-YES, THAT'S RIGHT.
SHE'S SOMEONE I'M LINKED TO IN A VEEEEERY DEEP WAY.
HOOH.
JARA (CLINK)
AH!
IT'S TIME FOR ME TO GET TO WORK!

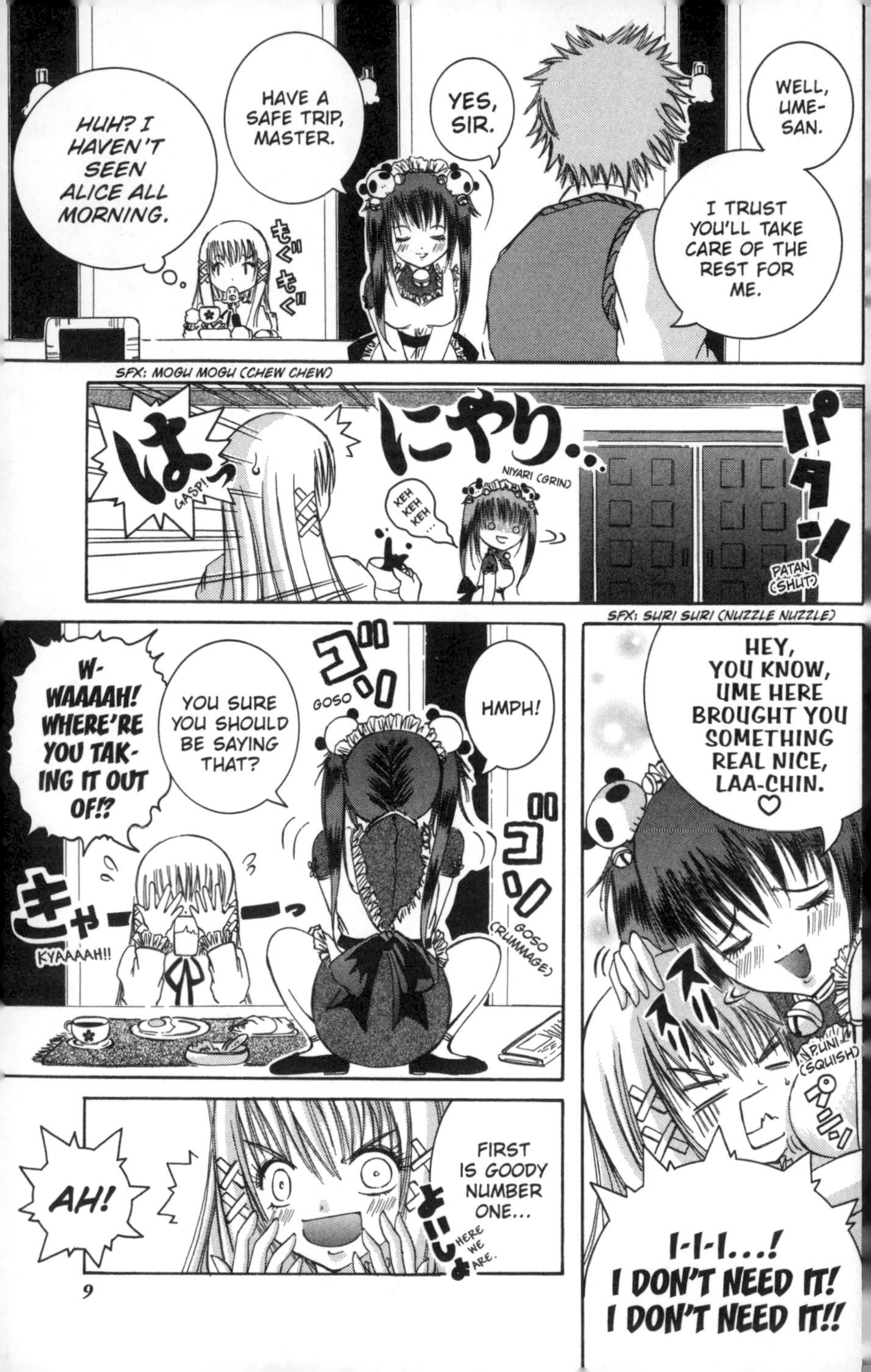

WELL, UME-SAN.
I TRUST YOU'LL TAKE CARE OF THE REST FOR ME.
YES, SIR.
HAVE A SAFE TRIP, MASTER.
HUH? I HAVEN'T SEEN ALICE ALL MORNING.
もぐもぐ
SFX: MOGU MOGU (CHEW CHEW)
パタン
PATAN (SHUT)
にやり
NIYARI (GRIN)
KEH KEH KEH...
はっ
GASP!
SFX: SURI SURI (NUZZLE NUZZLE)
HEY, YOU KNOW, UME HERE BROUGHT YOU SOMETHING REAL NICE, LAA-CHIN. ♡
PUNI (SQUISH)
I-I-I...! I DON'T NEED IT! I DON'T NEED IT!!
HMPH!
ゴソ
GOSO
YOU SURE YOU SHOULD BE SAYING THAT?
W-WAAAAH! WHERE'RE YOU TAKING IT OUT OF!?
ゴソ
GOSO (RUMMAGE)
きゃーーっ
KYAAAAH!!
FIRST IS GOODY NUMBER ONE...
よいしょ
HERE WE ARE.
AH!

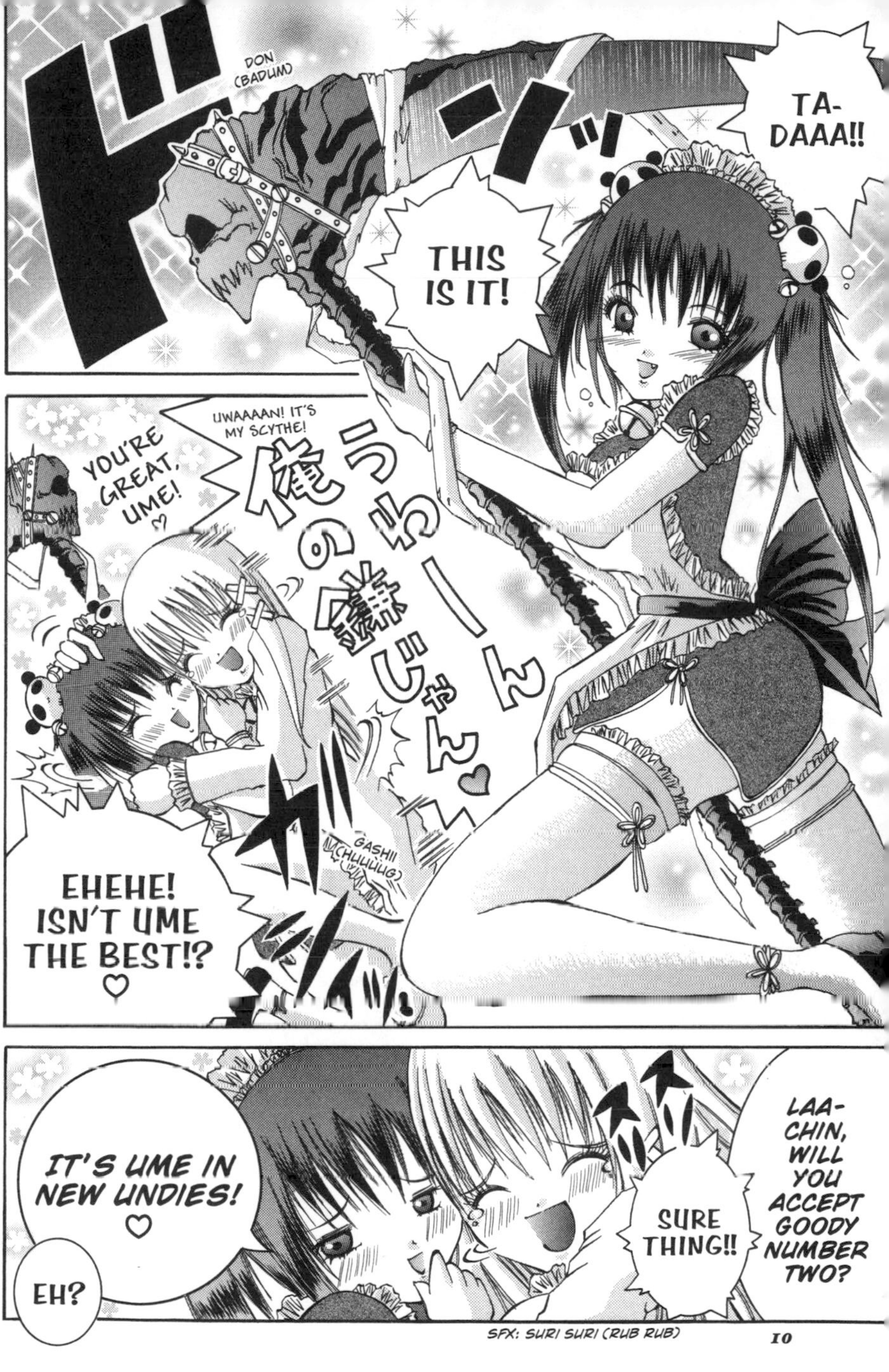
TA-DAAA!!
THIS IS IT!
DON (BADUM)
うわーん
俺の鎌じゃん♥
UWAAAAN! IT'S MY SCYTHE!
YOU'RE GREAT, UME! ♡
GASHII (CHUUUUNG)
EHEHE! ISN'T UME THE BEST!? ♡
LAA-CHIN, WILL YOU ACCEPT GOODY NUMBER TWO?
SURE THING!!
IT'S UME IN NEW UNDIES! ♡
EH?

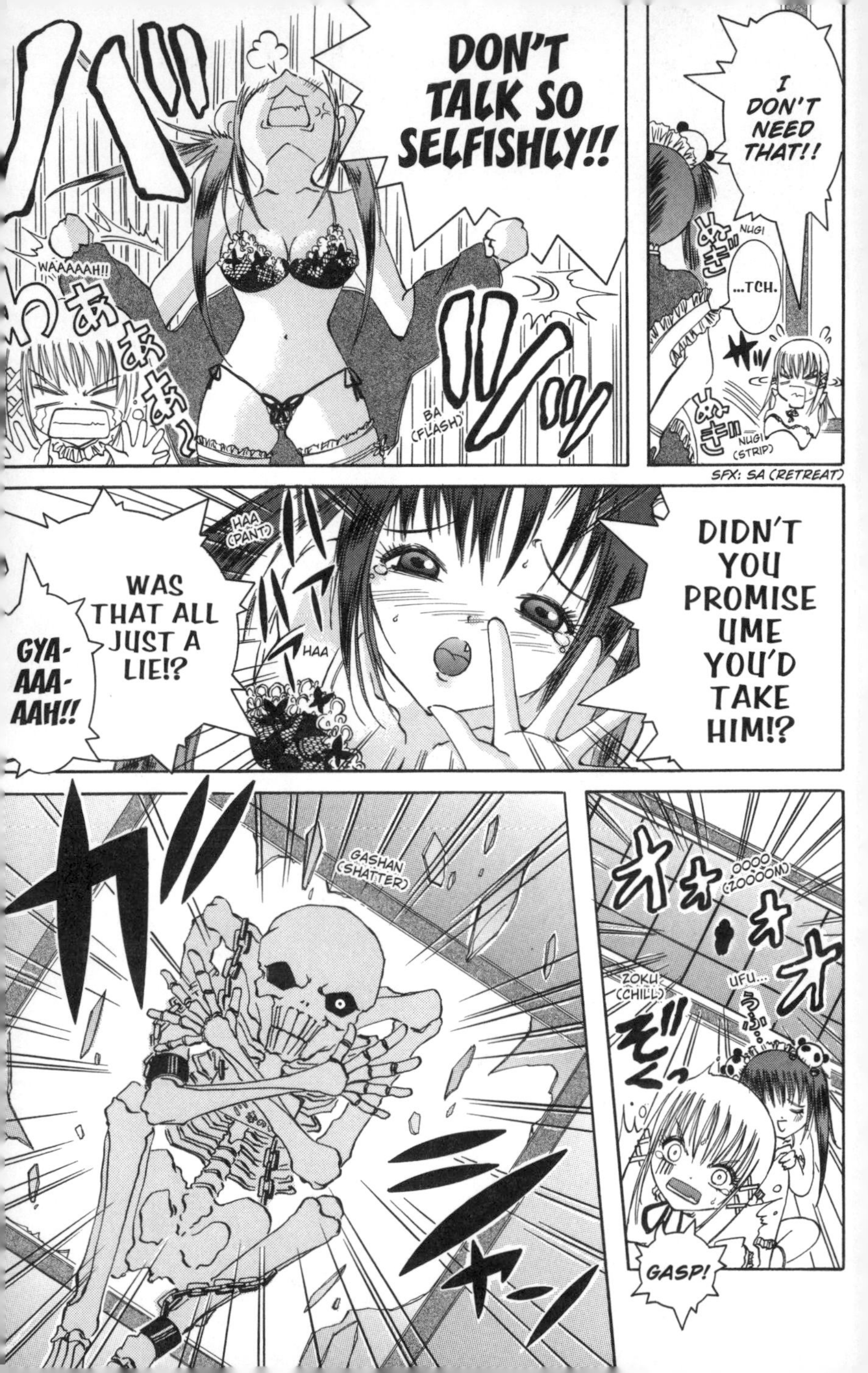
I DON'T NEED THAT!!
NUGI
...TCH.
NUGI (STRIP)
SFX: SA (RETREAT)
DON'T TALK SO SELFISHLY!!
BA (FLASH)
WAAAAAH!!
DIDN'T YOU PROMISE UME YOU'D TAKE HIM!?
HAA (PANT)
HAA
WAS THAT ALL JUST A LIE!?
GYA-AAA-AAH!!
OOOO (ZOOOOM)
UFU...
ZOKU (CHILL)
GASP!
GASHAN (SHATTER)

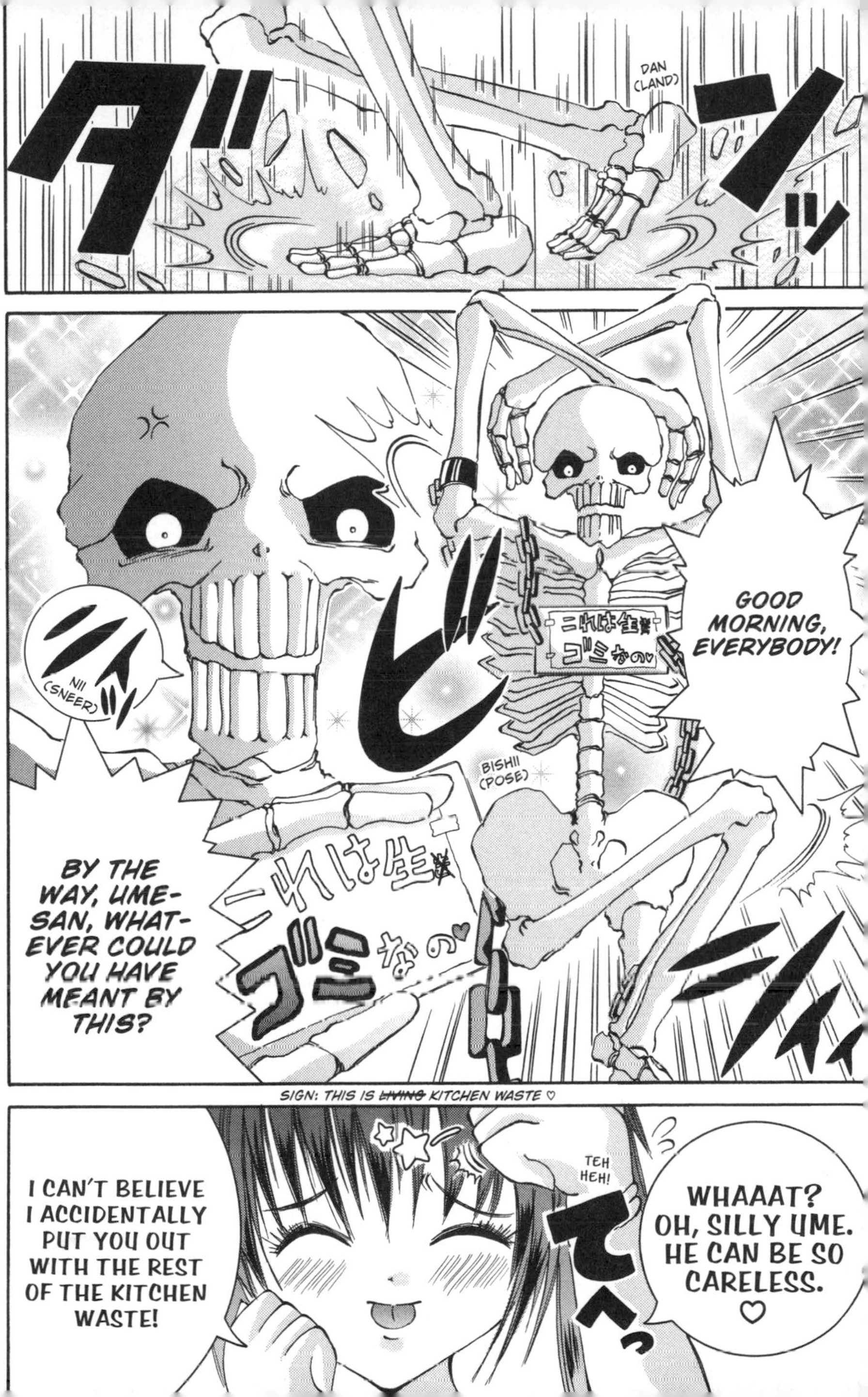
DAN (LAND)
GOOD MORNING, EVERYBODY!
BISHII (POSE)
NII (SNEER)
BY THE WAY, UME-SAN, WHATEVER COULD YOU HAVE MEANT BY THIS?
SIGN: THIS IS ~~LIVING~~ KITCHEN WASTE ♡
WHAAAT? OH, SILLY UME. HE CAN BE SO CARELESS. ♡
TEH HEH!
I CAN'T BELIEVE I ACCIDENTALLY PUT YOU OUT WITH THE REST OF THE KITCHEN WASTE!

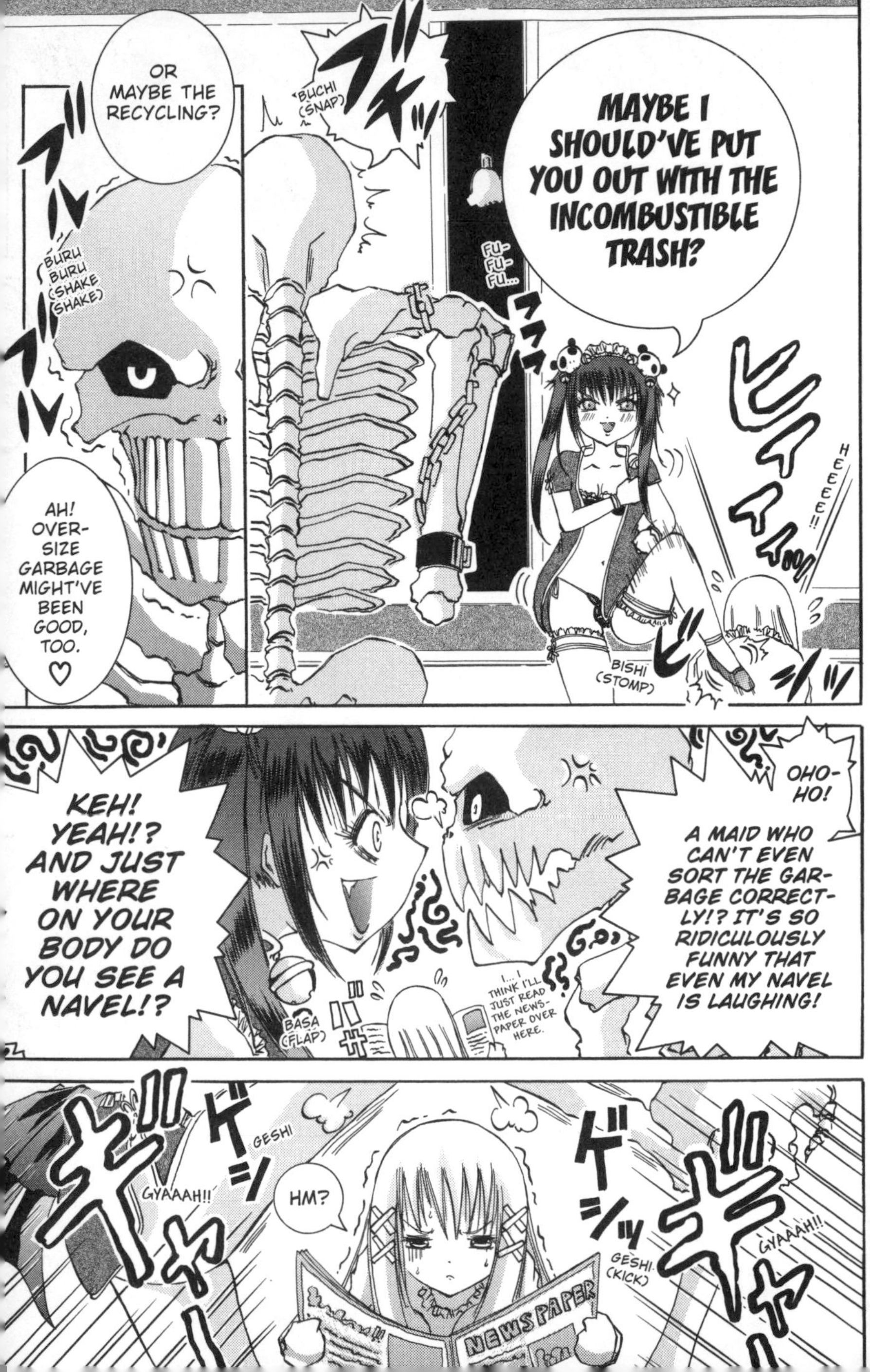
MAYBE I SHOULD'VE PUT YOU OUT WITH THE INCOMBUSTIBLE TRASH?
FU-FU-FU...
HEEEEE!!
BISHI (STOMP)
BUCHI (SNAP)
OR MAYBE THE RECYCLING?
BURU BURU (SHAKE SHAKE)
AH! OVER-SIZE GARBAGE MIGHT'VE BEEN GOOD, TOO. ♡
OHO-HO!
A MAID WHO CAN'T EVEN SORT THE GAR-BAGE CORRECT-LY!? IT'S SO RIDICULOUSLY FUNNY THAT EVEN MY NAVEL IS LAUGHING!
I... I THINK I'LL JUST READ THE NEWS-PAPER OVER HERE.
BASA (FLAP)
KEH! YEAH!? AND JUST WHERE ON YOUR BODY DO YOU SEE A NAVEL!?
GYAAAH!!
GESHI (KICK)
HM?
NEWSPAPER
GESHI
GYAAAH!!

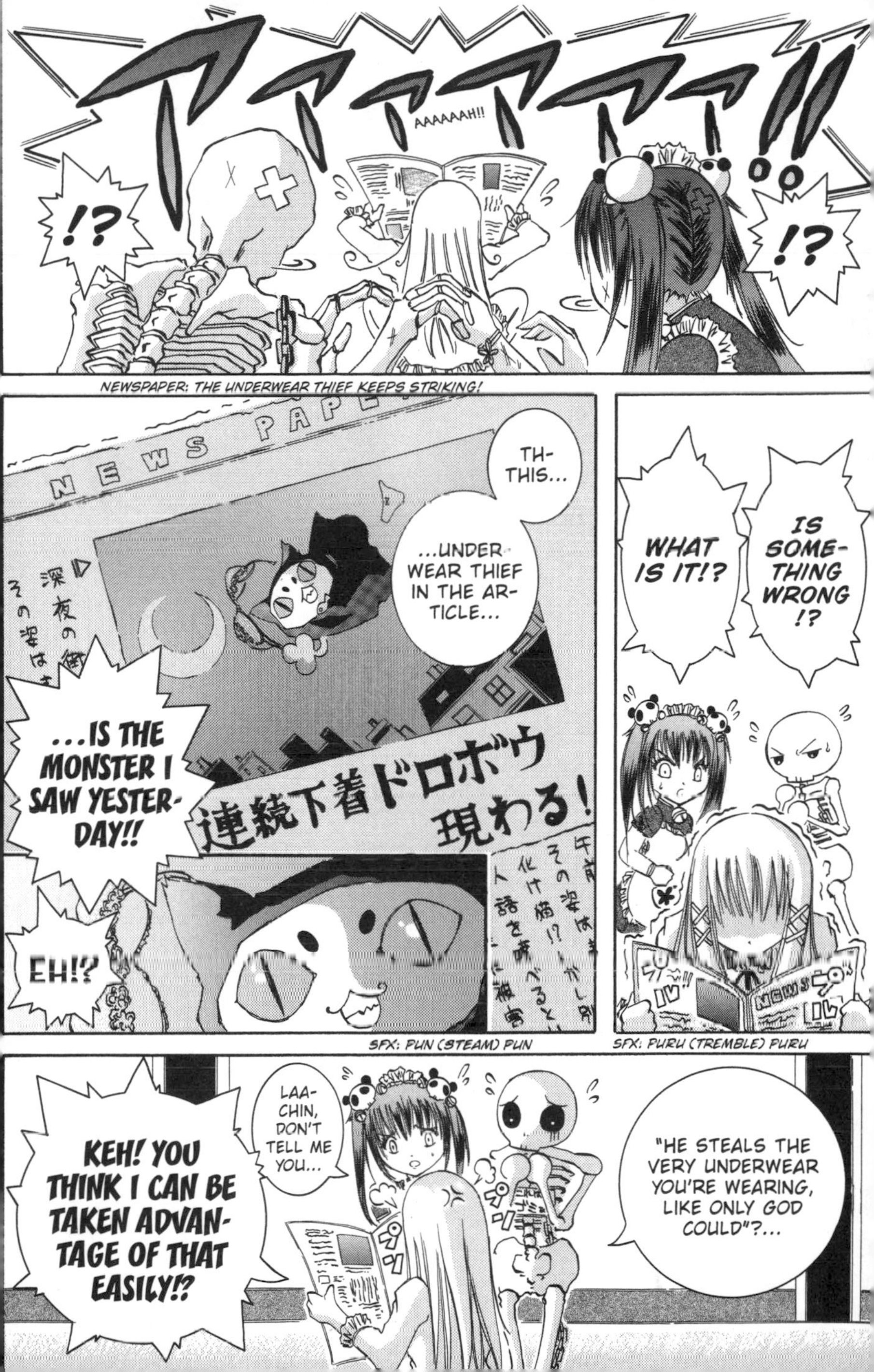
AAAAAAH!!
!?
!?
NEWSPAPER: THE UNDERWEAR THIEF KEEPS STRIKING!
IS SOMETHING WRONG!?
WHAT IS IT!?
SFX: PURU (TREMBLE) PURU
TH-THIS...
...UNDERWEAR THIEF IN THE ARTICLE...
...IS THE MONSTER I SAW YESTERDAY!!
連続下着ドロボウ現わる！
EH!?
SFX: PUN (STEAM) PUN
"HE STEALS THE VERY UNDERWEAR YOU'RE WEARING, LIKE ONLY GOD COULD"?...
LAA-CHIN, DON'T TELL ME YOU...
KEH! YOU THINK I CAN BE TAKEN ADVANTAGE OF THAT EASILY!?

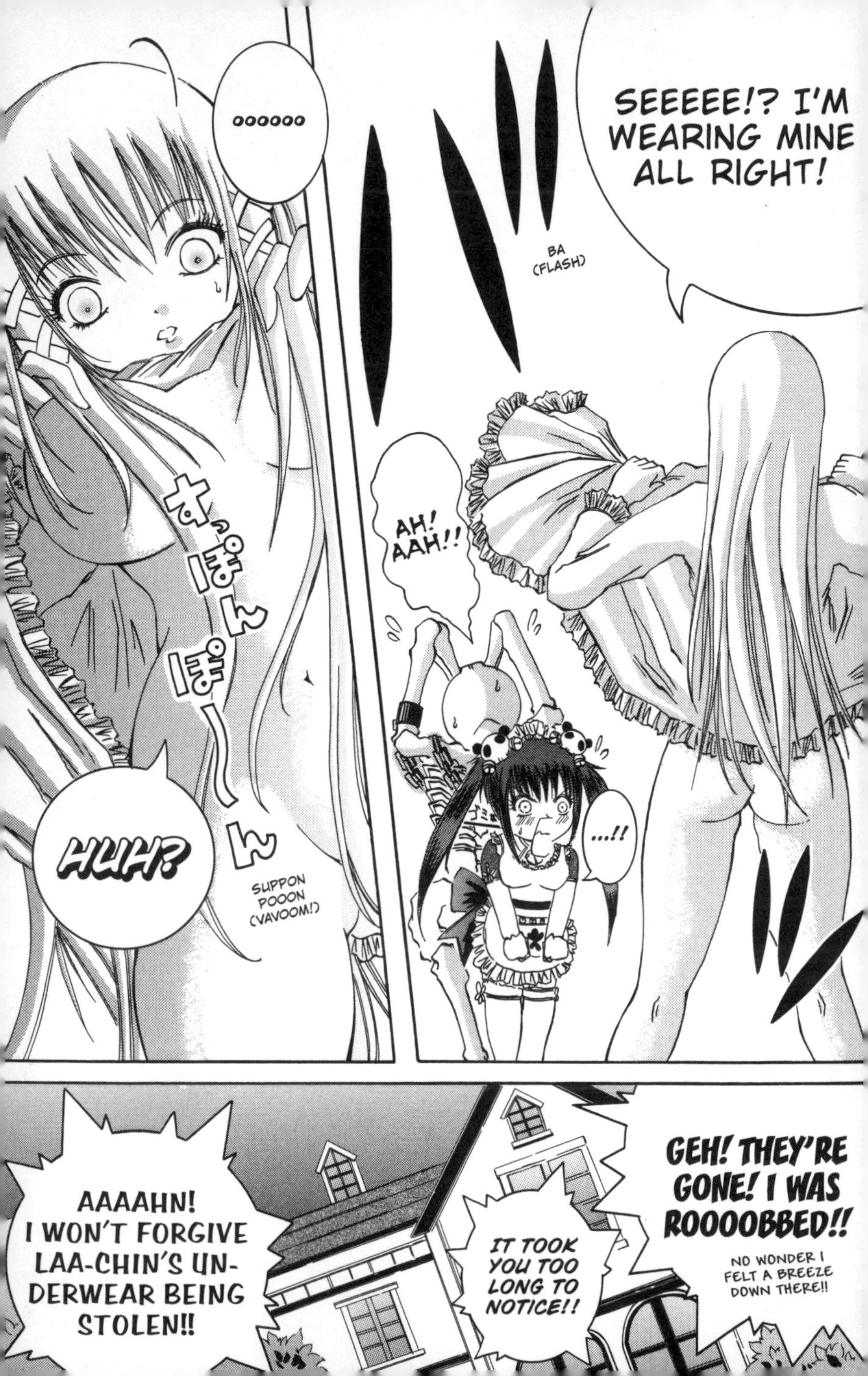

SEEEEE!? I'M WEARING MINE ALL RIGHT!
BA (FLASH)
AH! AAH!!
...!!
oooooo
すっぽんぽーん
HUH?
SUPPON POOON (VAVOOM!)
GEH! THEY'RE GONE! I WAS ROOOOBBED!!
NO WONDER I FELT A BREEZE DOWN THERE!!
IT TOOK YOU TOO LONG TO NOTICE!!
AAAAHN! I WON'T FORGIVE LAA-CHIN'S UN-DERWEAR BEING STOLEN!!

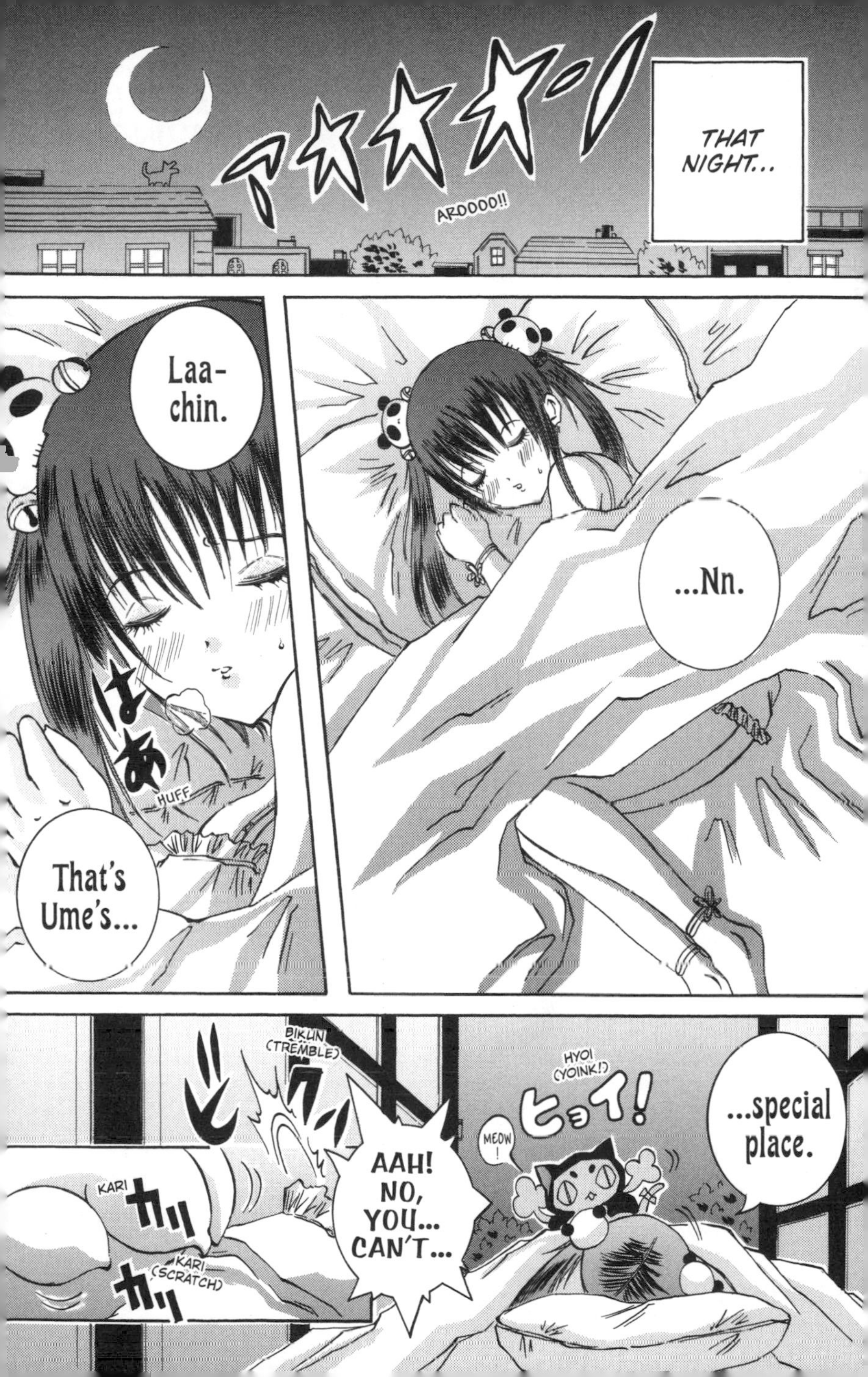
THAT NIGHT...
AROOOO!!
...Nn.
Laa-chin.
はぁ
HUFF
That's Ume's...
...special place.
ヒョイ!
HYOI (YOINK!)
MEOW!
AAH! NO, YOU... CAN'T...
BIKUN (TREMBLE)
KARI
カリ
KARI (SCRATCH)
カリ

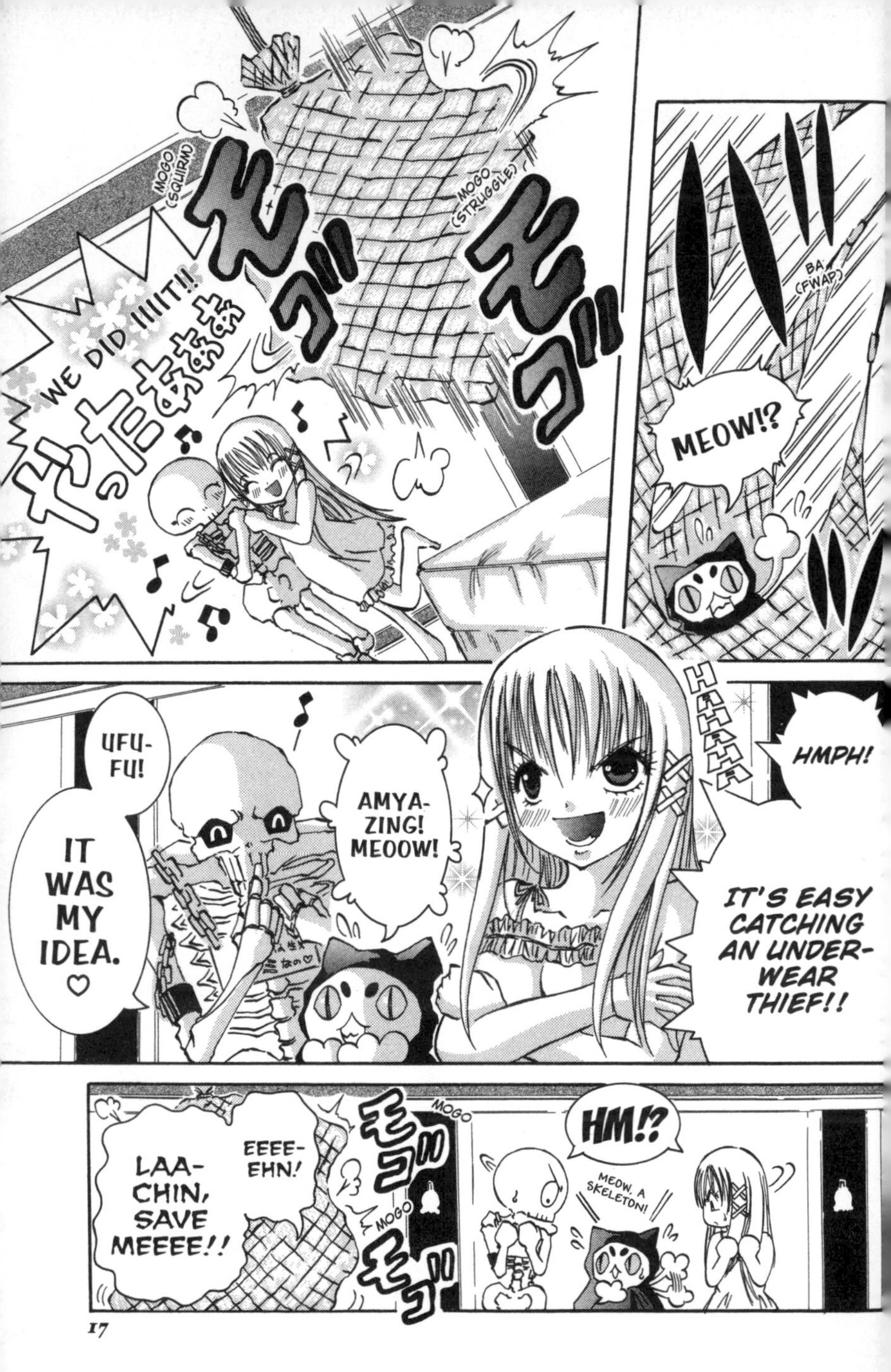

BA (FWAP)
MEOW!?
MOGO (STRUGGLE)
MOGO (SQUIRM)
WE DID IIIIT!!
HMPH!
IT'S EASY CATCHING AN UNDER-WEAR THIEF!!
AMYA-ZING! MEOOW!
UFU-FU!
IT WAS MY IDEA. ♡
HM!?
MEOW, A SKELETON!
MOGO
MOGO
EEEE-EHN!
LAA-CHIN, SAVE MEEEE!!

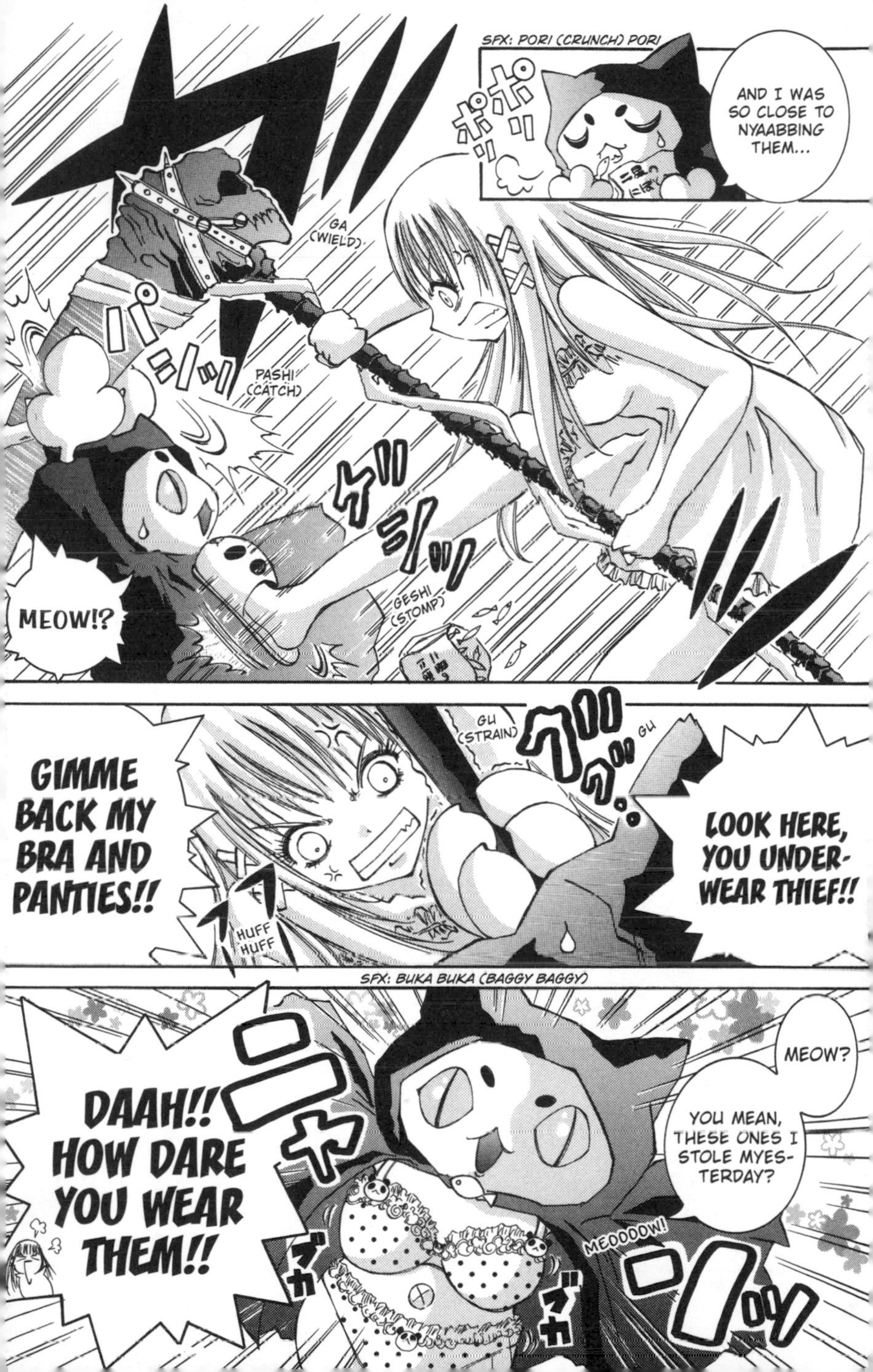
SFX: PORI (CRUNCH) PORI
AND I WAS SO CLOSE TO NYAABBING THEM...
GA (WIELD)
PASHI (CATCH)
GESHI (STOMP)
MEOW!?
GU (STRAIN)
GU
LOOK HERE, YOU UNDER-WEAR THIEF!!
GIMME BACK MY BRA AND PANTIES!!
HUFF HUFF
SFX: BUKA BUKA (BAGGY BAGGY)
MEOW?
YOU MEAN, THESE ONES I STOLE MYES-TERDAY?
MEOOOOW!
DAAH!! HOW DARE YOU WEAR THEM!!

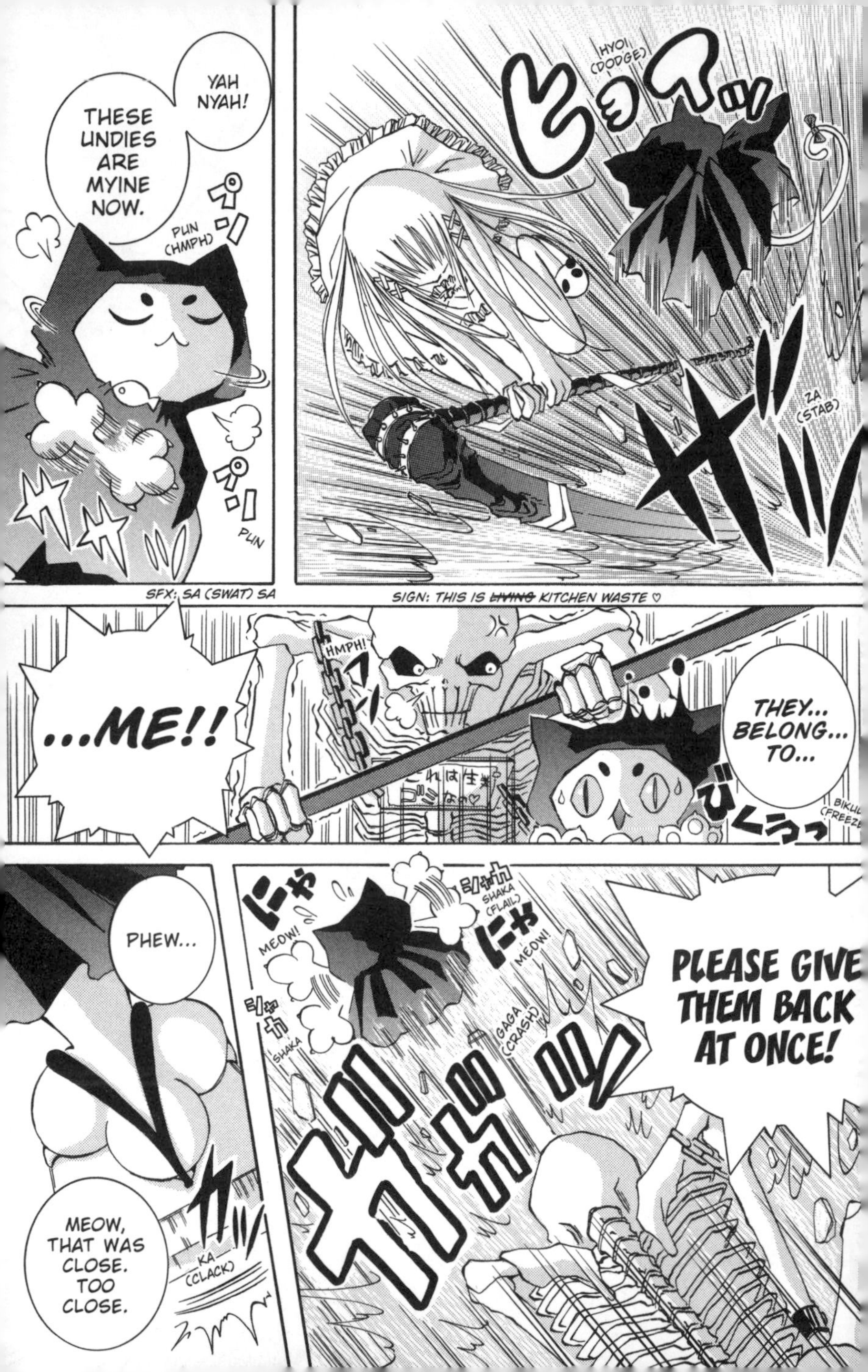
HYOI (DODGE)
ZA (STAB)
YAH NYAH!
THESE UNDIES ARE MYINE NOW.
PUN (HMPH)
PUN
SIGN: THIS IS ~~LIVING~~ KITCHEN WASTE ♡
SFX: SA (SWAT) SA
THEY... BELONG... TO...
BIKU! (FREEZE)
HMPH!
...ME!!
PLEASE GIVE THEM BACK AT ONCE!
SHAKA (FLAIL)
MEOW!
MEOW!
SHAKA
GAGA (CRASH)
PHEW...
MEOW, THAT WAS CLOSE. TOO CLOSE.
KA (CLACK)

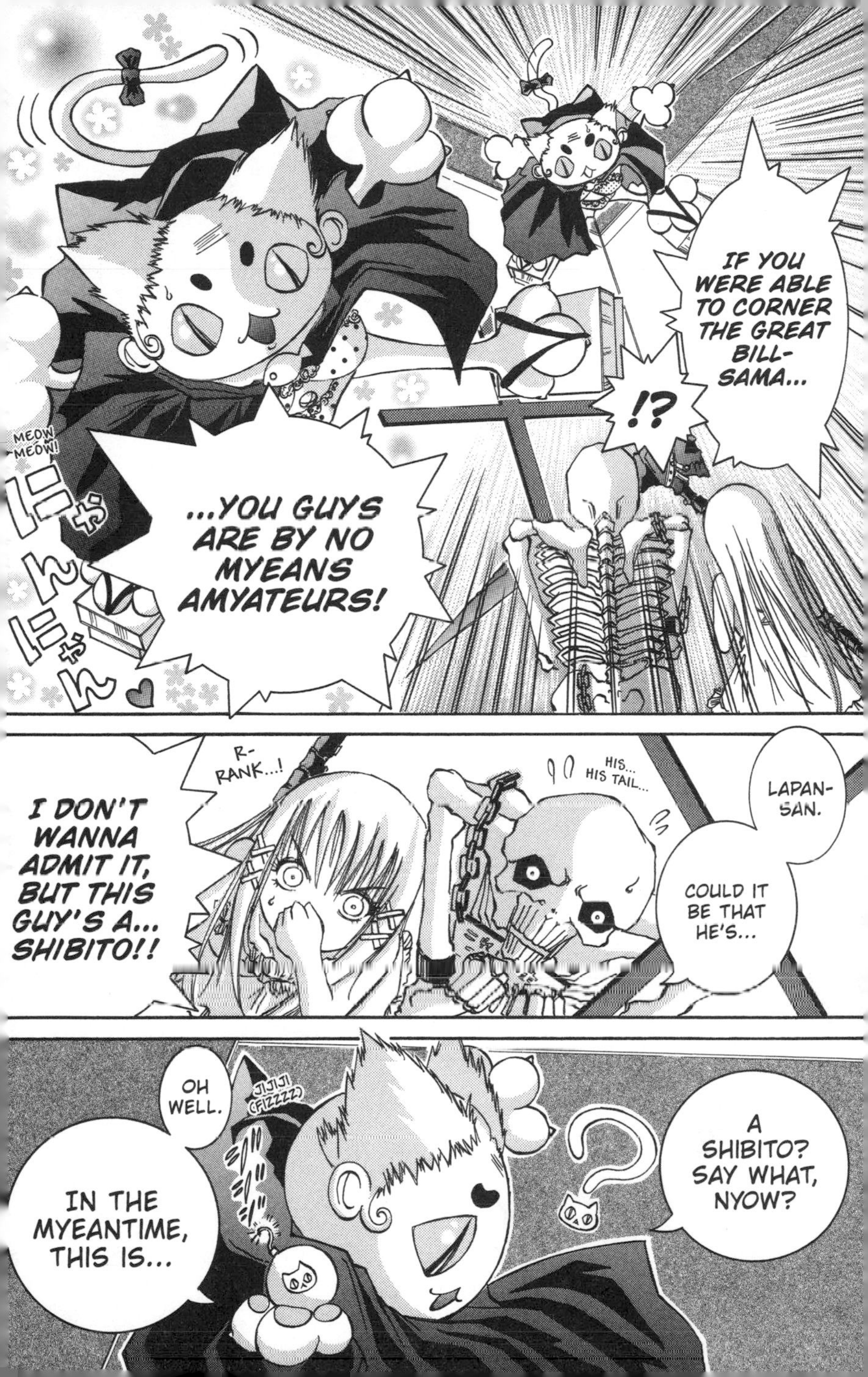

IF YOU WERE ABLE TO CORNER THE GREAT BILL-SAMA...
!?
...YOU GUYS ARE BY NO MYEANS AMYATEURS!
MEOW MEOW!
にゃんにゃん
LAPAN-SAN.
COULD IT BE THAT HE'S...
HIS... HIS TAIL...
R-RANK...!
I DON'T WANNA ADMIT IT, BUT THIS GUY'S A... SHIBITO!!
A SHIBITO? SAY WHAT, NYOW?
OH WELL.
JIJIJI (FIZZZZ)
IN THE MYEANTIME, THIS IS...

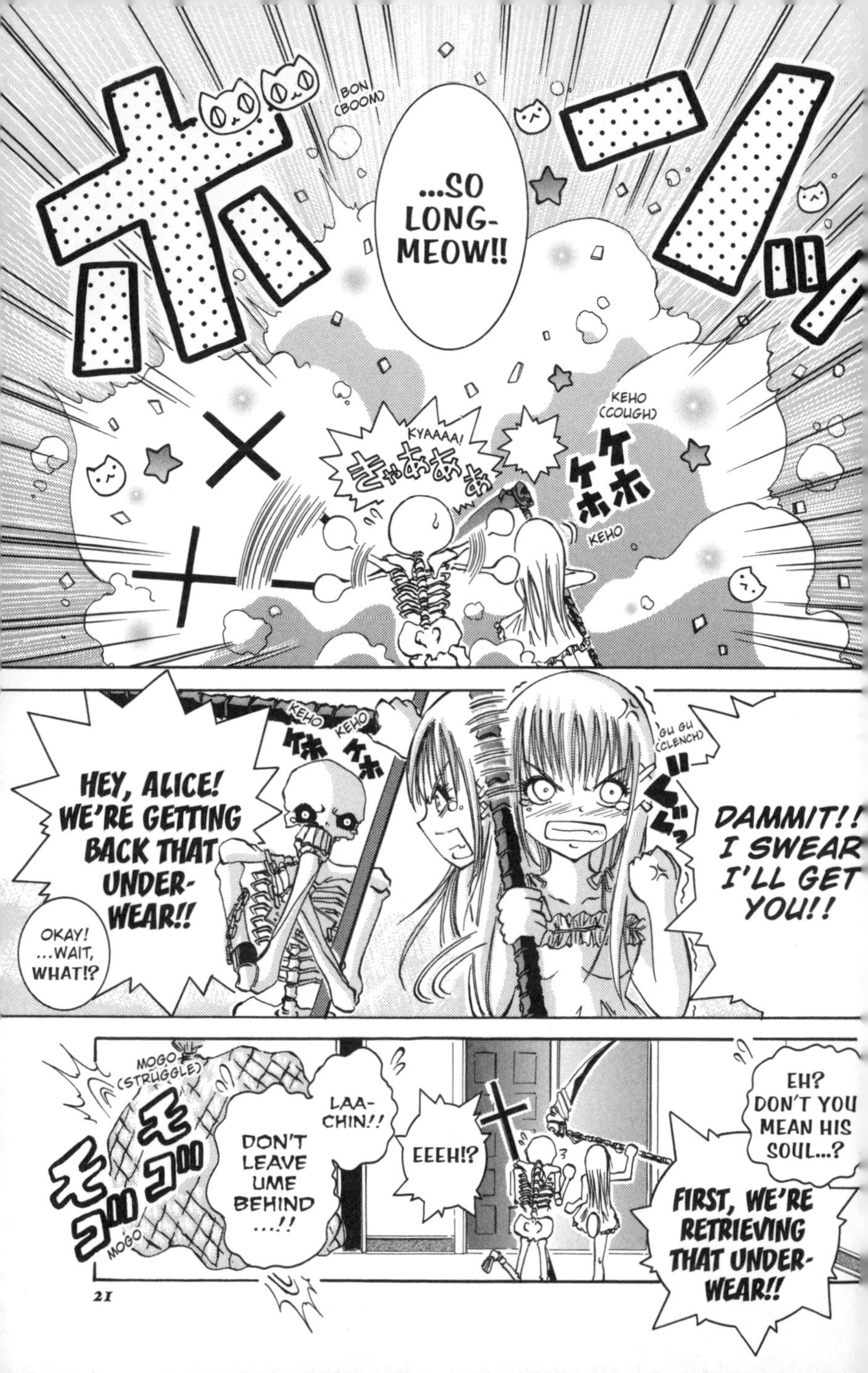
BON (BOOM)
...SO LONG-MEOW!!
KYAAAA!
KEHO (COUGH)
KEHO
GU GU (CLENCH)
DAMMIT!! I SWEAR I'LL GET YOU!!
KEHO KEHO
HEY, ALICE! WE'RE GETTING BACK THAT UNDER-WEAR!!
OKAY! ...WAIT, WHAT!?
EH? DON'T YOU MEAN HIS SOUL...?
FIRST, WE'RE RETRIEVING THAT UNDER-WEAR!!
EEEH!?
LAA-CHIN!!
DON'T LEAVE UME BEHIND ...!!
MOGO (STRUGGLE)
MOGO

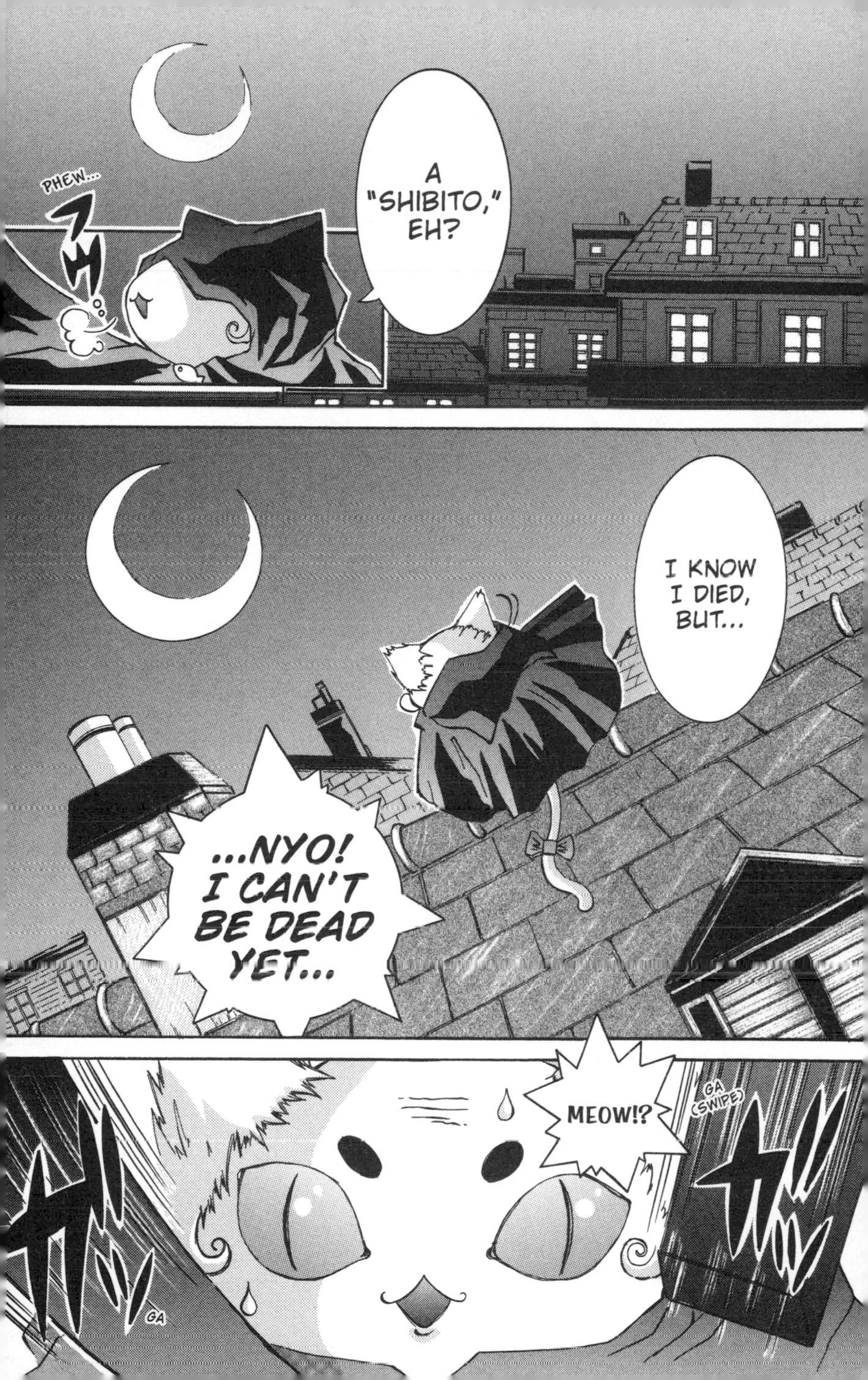
A "SHIBITO," EH?
PHEW...
I KNOW I DIED, BUT...
...NYO! I CAN'T BE DEAD YET...
GA (SWIPE)
MEOW!?
GA

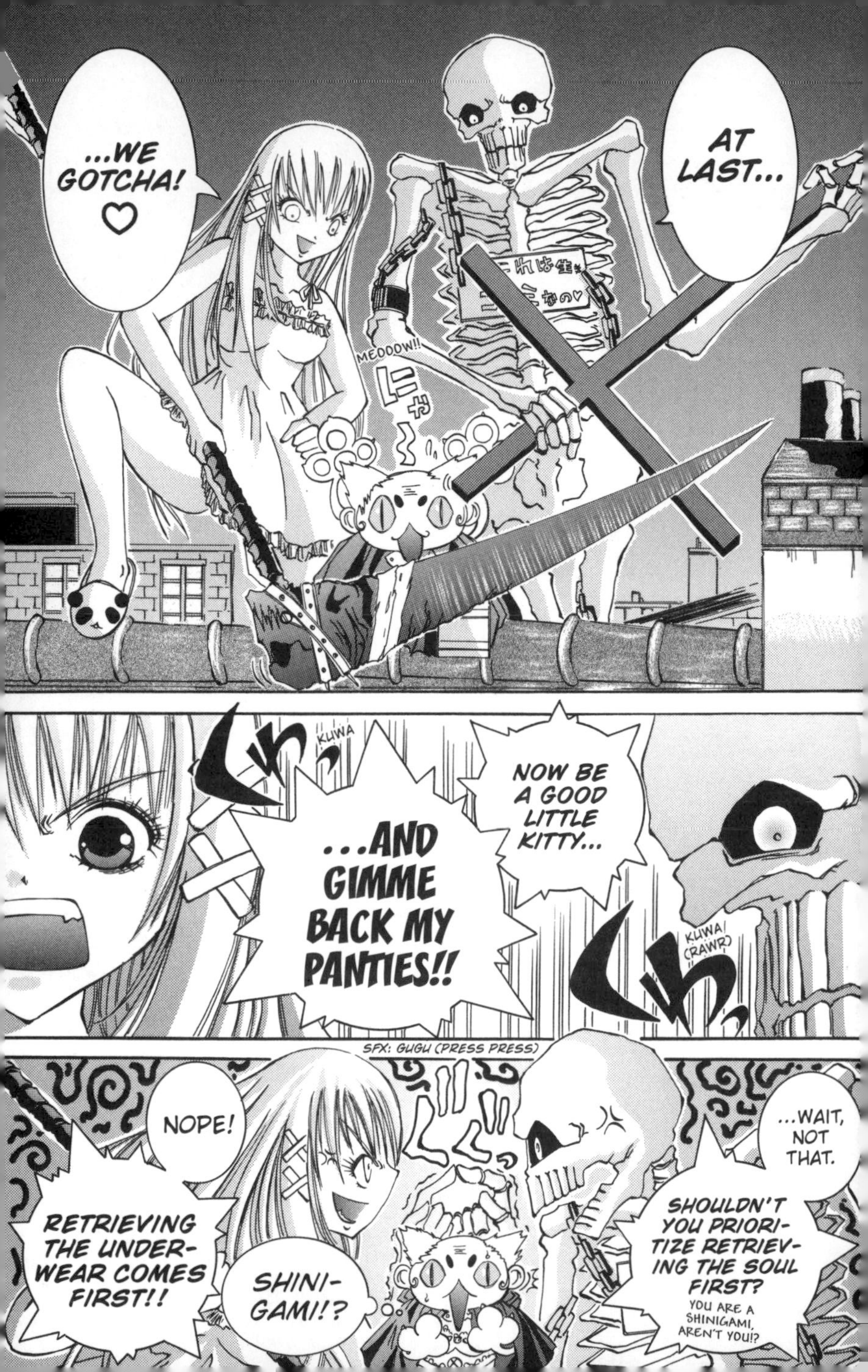
AT LAST...
...WE GOTCHA! ♡
MEOOOW!!
NOW BE A GOOD LITTLE KITTY...
KUWA
...AND GIMME BACK MY PANTIES!!
KUWA (RAWR)
SFX: GUGU (PRESS PRESS)
...WAIT, NOT THAT.
NOPE!
SHOULDN'T YOU PRIORI-TIZE RETRIEV-ING THE SOUL FIRST?
YOU ARE A SHINIGAMI, AREN'T YOU!?
SHINI-GAMI!?
RETRIEVING THE UNDER-WEAR COMES FIRST!!

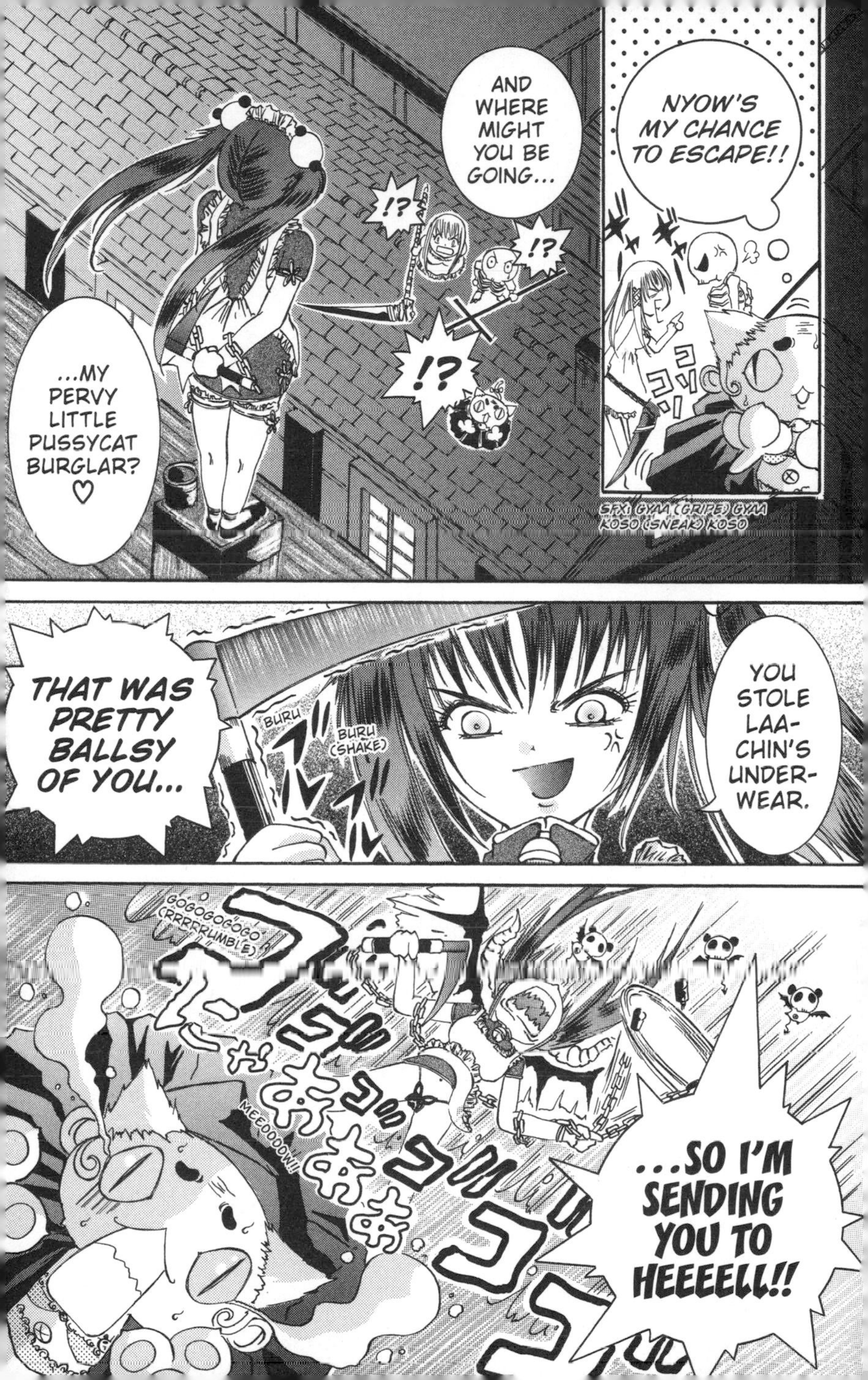
NYOW'S MY CHANCE TO ESCAPE!!
SFX: GYAA (GRIPE) GYAA
KOSO (SNEAK) KOSO
AND WHERE MIGHT YOU BE GOING...
!?
!?
!?
...MY PERVY LITTLE PUSSYCAT BURGLAR? ♡
YOU STOLE LAA-CHIN'S UNDER-WEAR.
BURU BURU (SHAKE)
THAT WAS PRETTY BALLSY OF YOU...
GOGOGOGOGO (RRRRRUMBLE)
...SO I'M SENDING YOU TO HEEEELL!!
MEEOOOOW!!

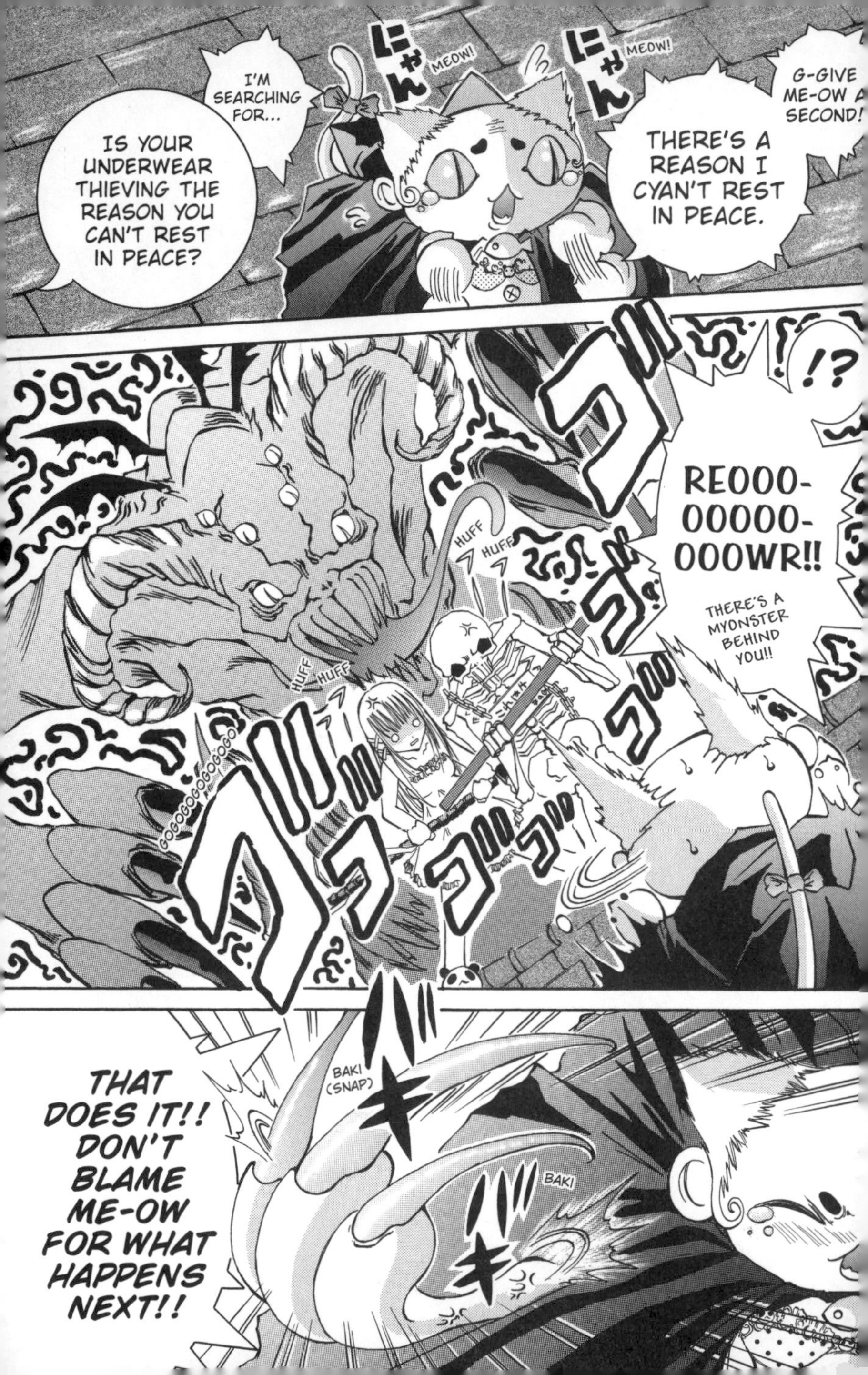
G-GIVE ME-OW A SECOND!
にゃん
MEOW!
THERE'S A REASON I CYAN'T REST IN PEACE.
にゃん
MEOW!
I'M SEARCHING FOR...
IS YOUR UNDERWEAR THIEVING THE REASON YOU CAN'T REST IN PEACE?
!?
REOOO-OOOOO-OOOWR!!
THERE'S A MYONSTER BEHIND YOU!!
HUFF HUFF
HUFF HUFF
GOGOGOGOGOGO
BAKI (SNAP)
BAKI
THAT DOES IT!! DON'T BLAME ME-OW FOR WHAT HAPPENS NEXT!!

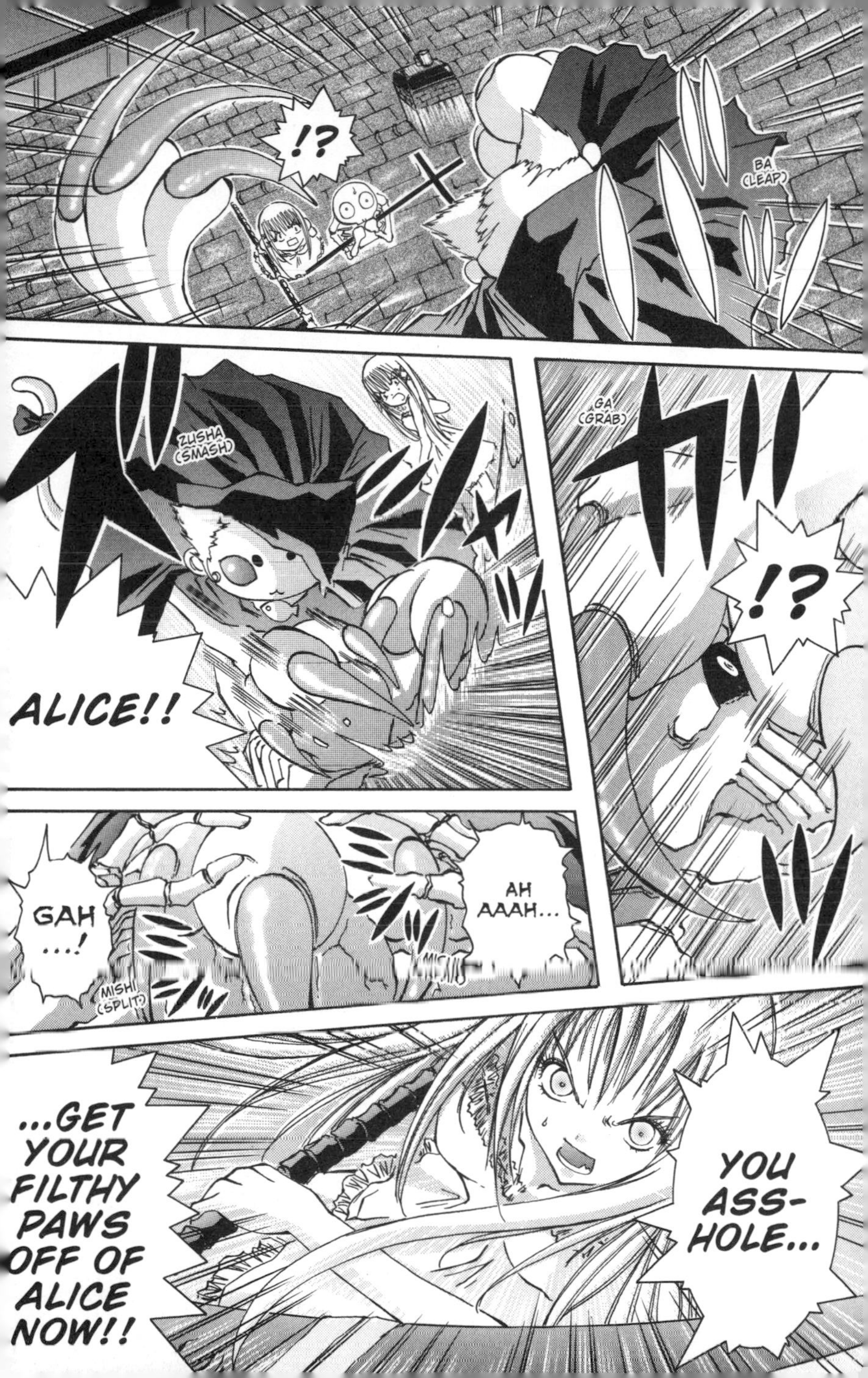
BA (LEAP)
!?
GA (GRAB)
!?
ZUSHA (SMASH)
ALICE!!
AH AAAH...
GAH ...!
MISHI (SPLIT)
YOU ASS-HOLE...
...GET YOUR FILTHY PAWS OFF OF ALICE NOW!!

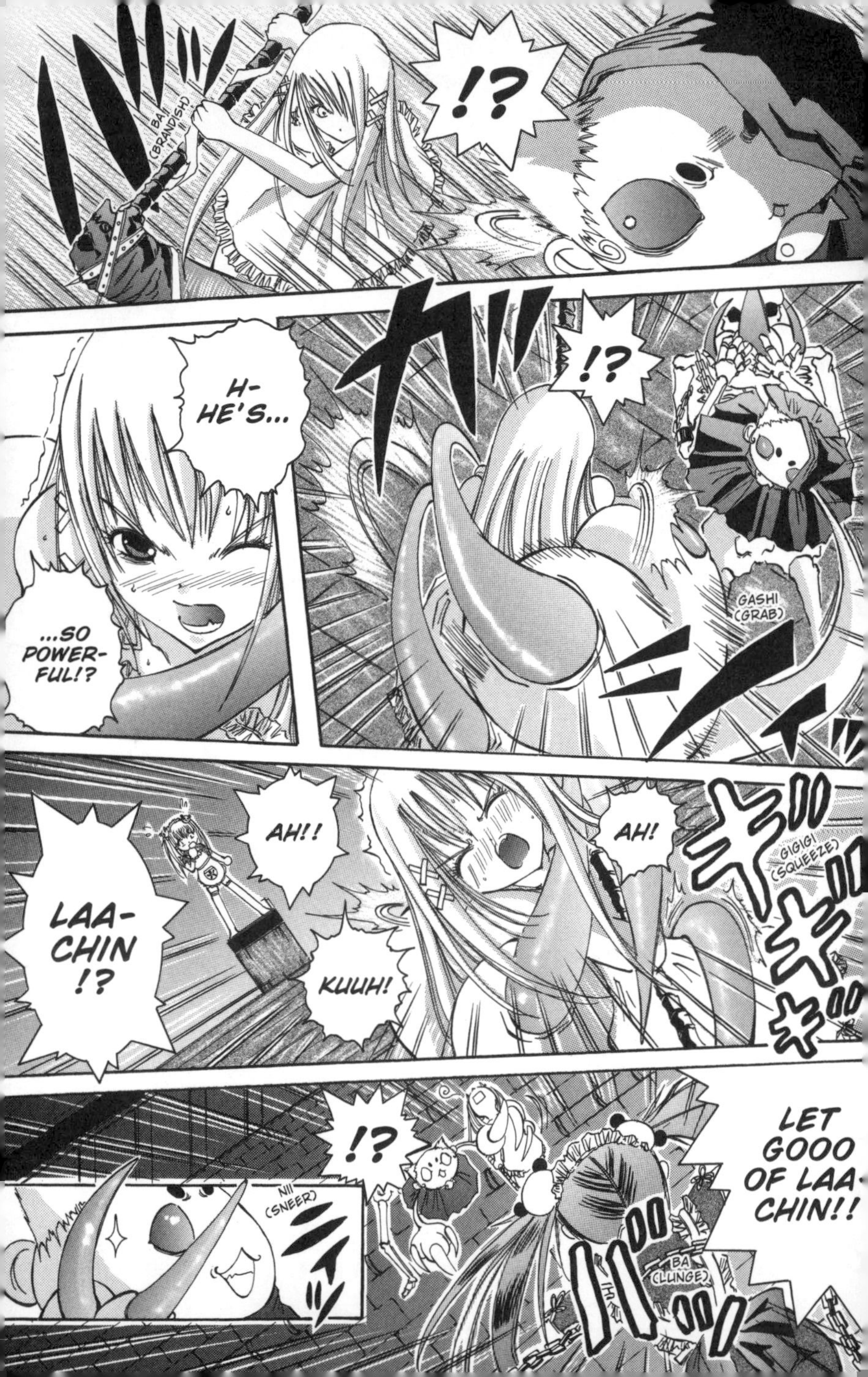
!?
BA (BRANDISH)
!?
GASHI (GRAB)
H- HE'S...
...SO POWER-FUL!?
GIGIGI (SQUEEZE)
AH!
AH!!
KUUH!
LAA-CHIN!?
LET GOOO OF LAA-CHIN!!
BA (LUNGE)
!?
NII (SNEER)

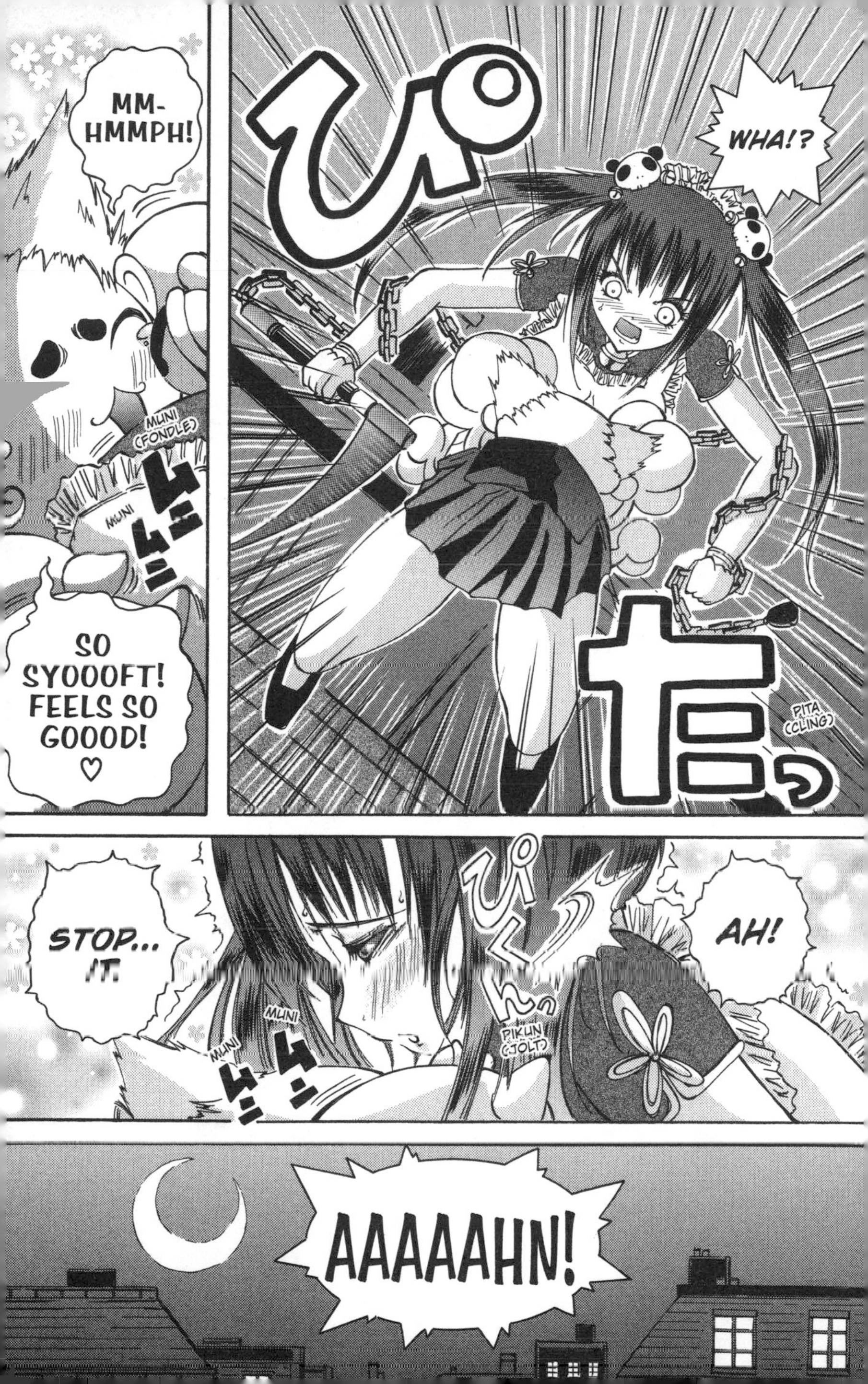

WHA!?
ぴ
PITA (CLING)
MM-HMMPH!
MUNI (FONDLE)
MUNI
SO SYOOOFT! FEELS SO GOOOD! ♡
AH!
PIKUN (JOLT)
MUNI
MUNI
STOP... IT.
AAAAAHN!

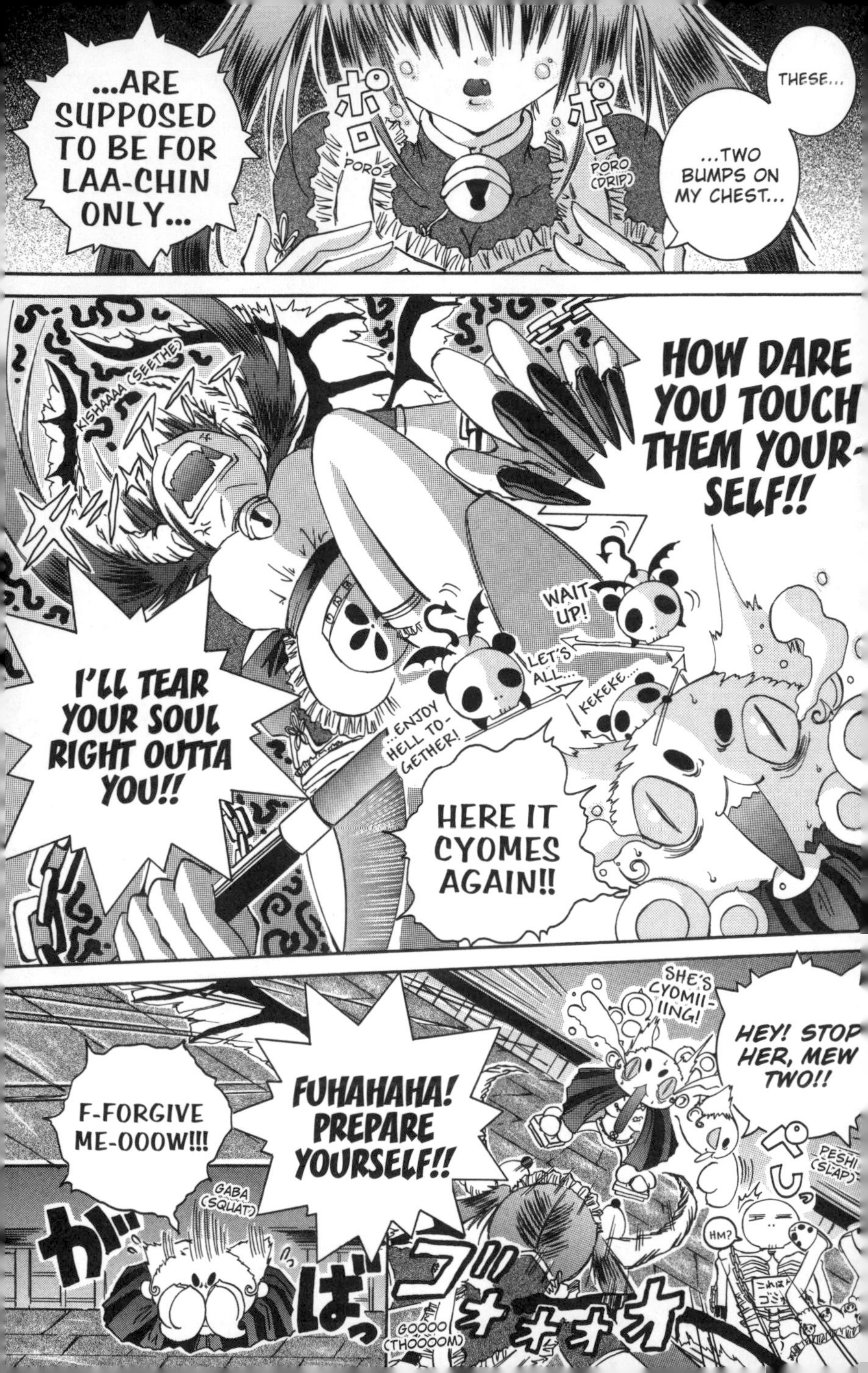
THESE...
...TWO BUMPS ON MY CHEST...
PORO (DRIP)
PORO
...ARE SUPPOSED TO BE FOR LAA-CHIN ONLY...
HOW DARE YOU TOUCH THEM YOUR-SELF!!
WAIT UP!
LET'S ALL...
KEKEKE...
...ENJOY HELL TO-GETHER!
HERE IT CYOMES AGAIN!!
KISHAAAA (SEETHE)
I'LL TEAR YOUR SOUL RIGHT OUTTA YOU!!
SHE'S CYOMIIIING!
HEY! STOP HER, MEW TWO!!
PESHI (SLAP)
HM?
FUHAHAHA! PREPARE YOURSELF!!
GOOOO (THOOOOM)
F-FORGIVE ME-OOOW!!!
GABA (SQUAT)

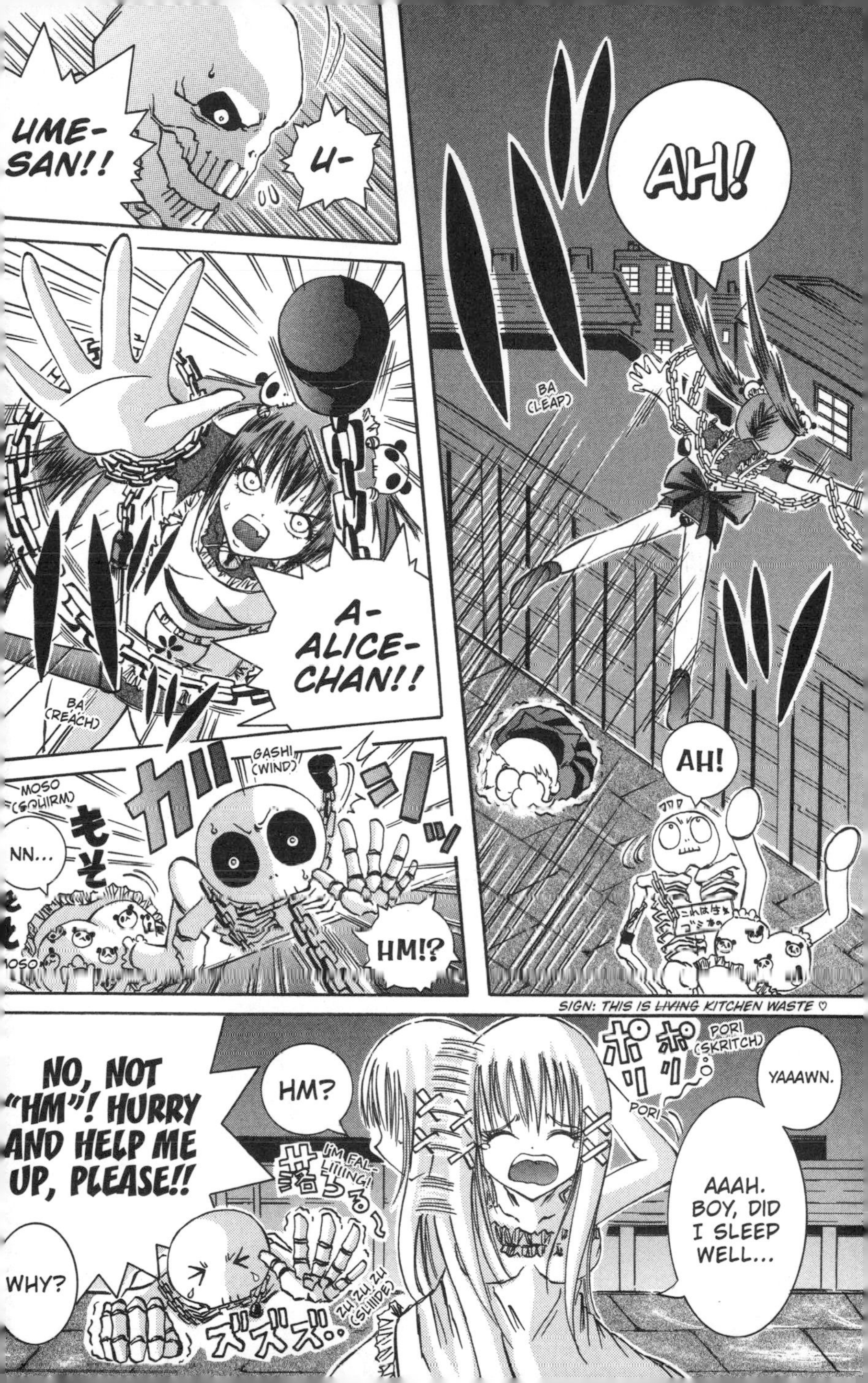
AH!
BA (LEAP)
AH!
SIGN: THIS IS LIVING KITCHEN WASTE ♡
U-
UME-SAN!!
A-ALICE-CHAN!!
BA (REACH)
ガッ
GASHI (WIND)
もそもそ
MOSO (SQUIRM)
MOSO
NN...
HM!?
YAAAWN.
ポリポリ
PORI (SKRITCH)
PORI
AAAH. BOY, DID I SLEEP WELL...
HM?
NO, NOT "HM"! HURRY AND HELP ME UP, PLEASE!!
落ちる～
I'M FAL-LIIIING!
ズズズ..
ZU ZU ZU (SLIIIDE)
WHY?

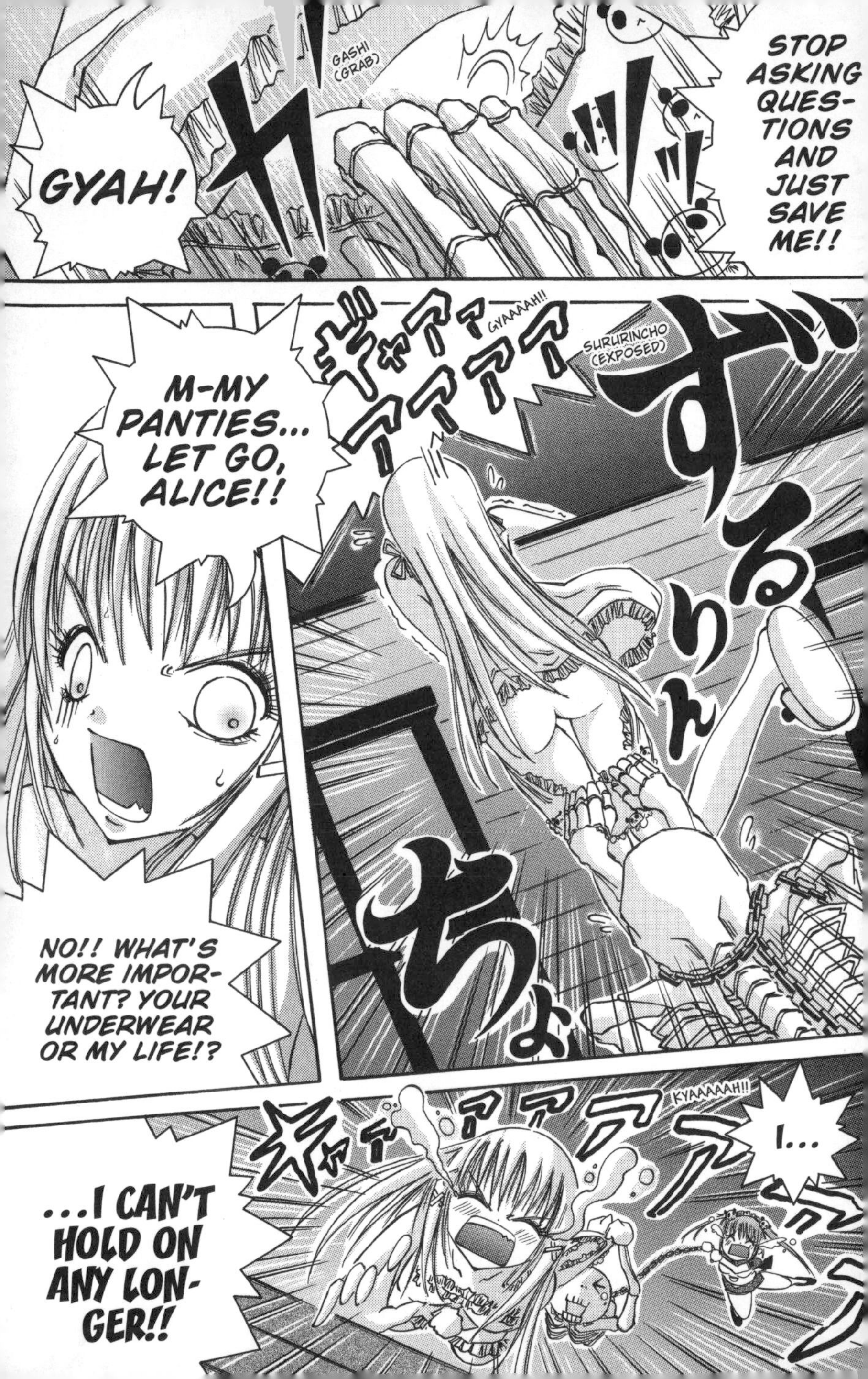
STOP ASKING QUESTIONS AND JUST SAVE ME!!
GASHI (GRAB)
GYAH!
SURURINCHO (EXPOSED)
GYAAAAH!!
M-MY PANTIES... LET GO, ALICE!!
NO!! WHAT'S MORE IMPORTANT? YOUR UNDERWEAR OR MY LIFE!?
I...
KYAAAAAH!!
...I CAN'T HOLD ON ANY LONGER!!

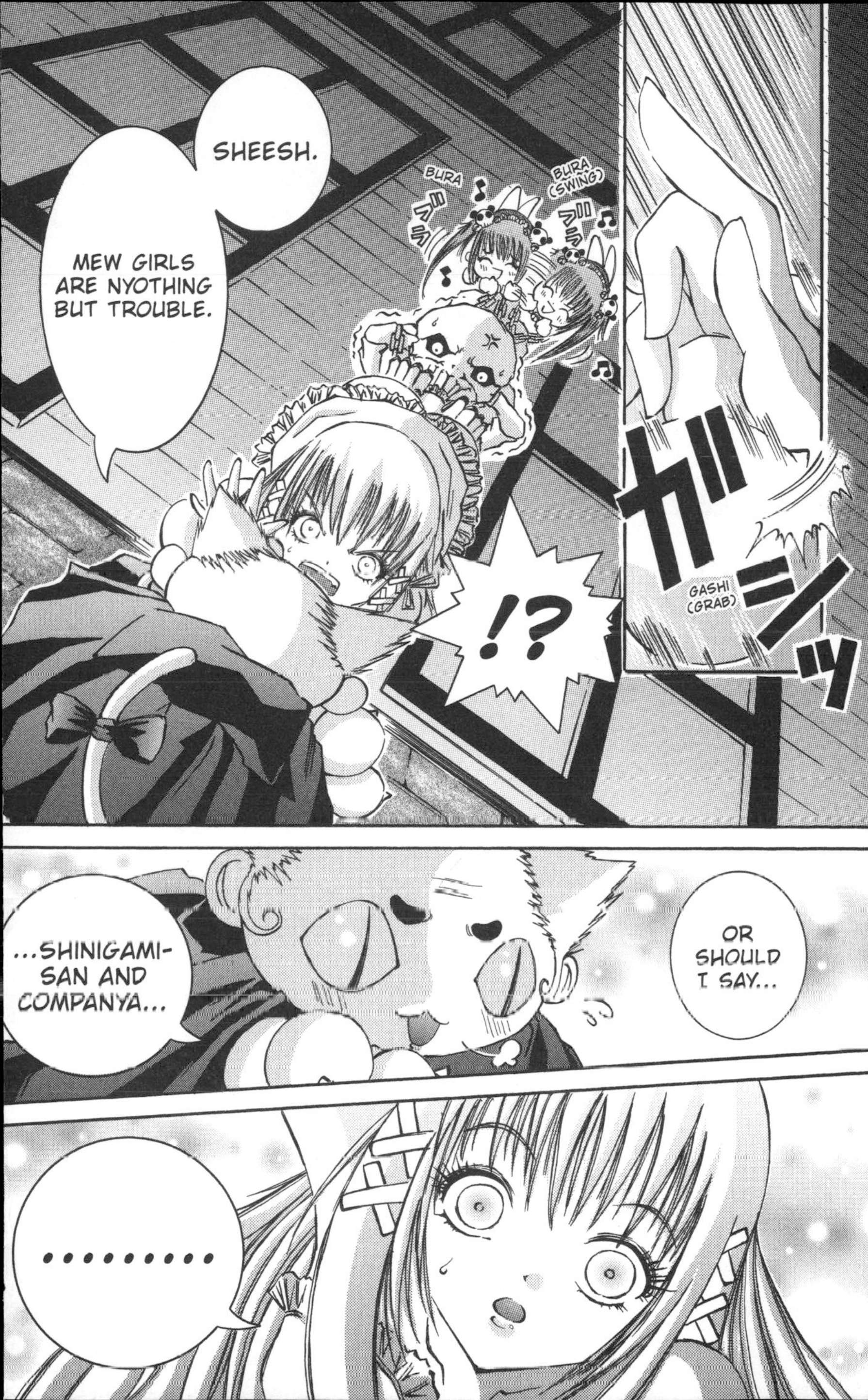
GASHI (GRAB)
BURA (SWING)
BURA
SHEESH.
MEW GIRLS ARE NYOTHING BUT TROUBLE.
!?
OR SHOULD I SAY...
...SHINIGAMI-SAN AND COMPANYA...
....

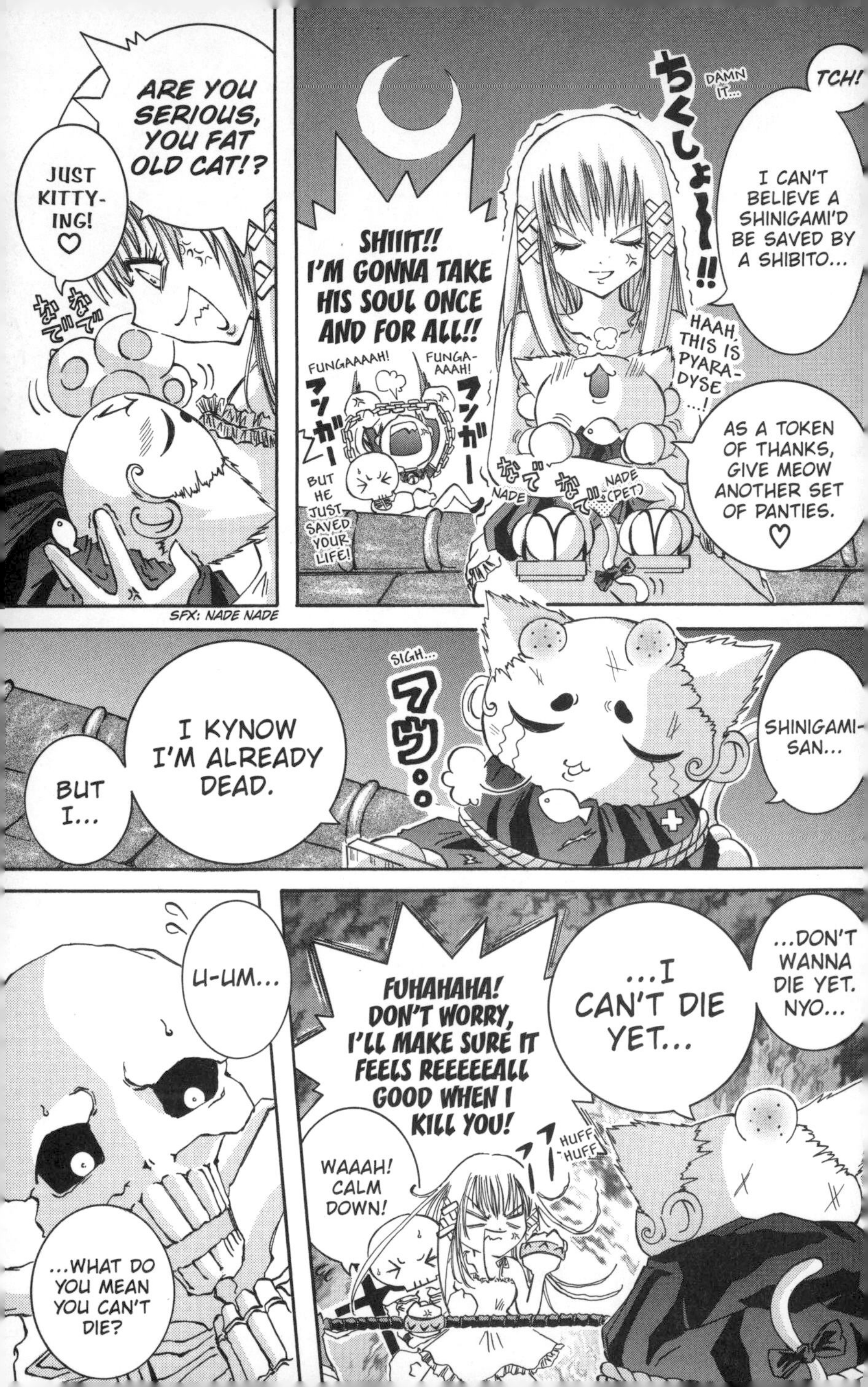
TCH!
DAMN IT...
ちくしょ〜!!
I CAN'T BELIEVE A SHINIGAMI'D BE SAVED BY A SHIBITO...
HAAH, THIS IS PYARA-DYSE...!
AS A TOKEN OF THANKS, GIVE MEOW ANOTHER SET OF PANTIES. ♡
NADE (PET)
なでなで
NADE
SHIIIT!! I'M GONNA TAKE HIS SOUL ONCE AND FOR ALL!!
FUNGA-AAAH!
フンガー
FUNGAAAAH!
フンガー
BUT HE JUST SAVED YOUR LIFE!
ARE YOU SERIOUS, YOU FAT OLD CAT!?
JUST KITTY-ING! ♡
なでなで
SFX: NADE NADE
SHINIGAMI-SAN...
SIGH...
マヴ。。
I KYNOW I'M ALREADY DEAD.
BUT I...
...DON'T WANNA DIE YET. NYO...
...I CAN'T DIE YET...
FUHAHAHA! DON'T WORRY, I'LL MAKE SURE IT FEELS REEEEEALL GOOD WHEN I KILL YOU!
HUFF HUFF
WAAAH! CALM DOWN!
U-UM...
...WHAT DO YOU MEAN YOU CAN'T DIE?

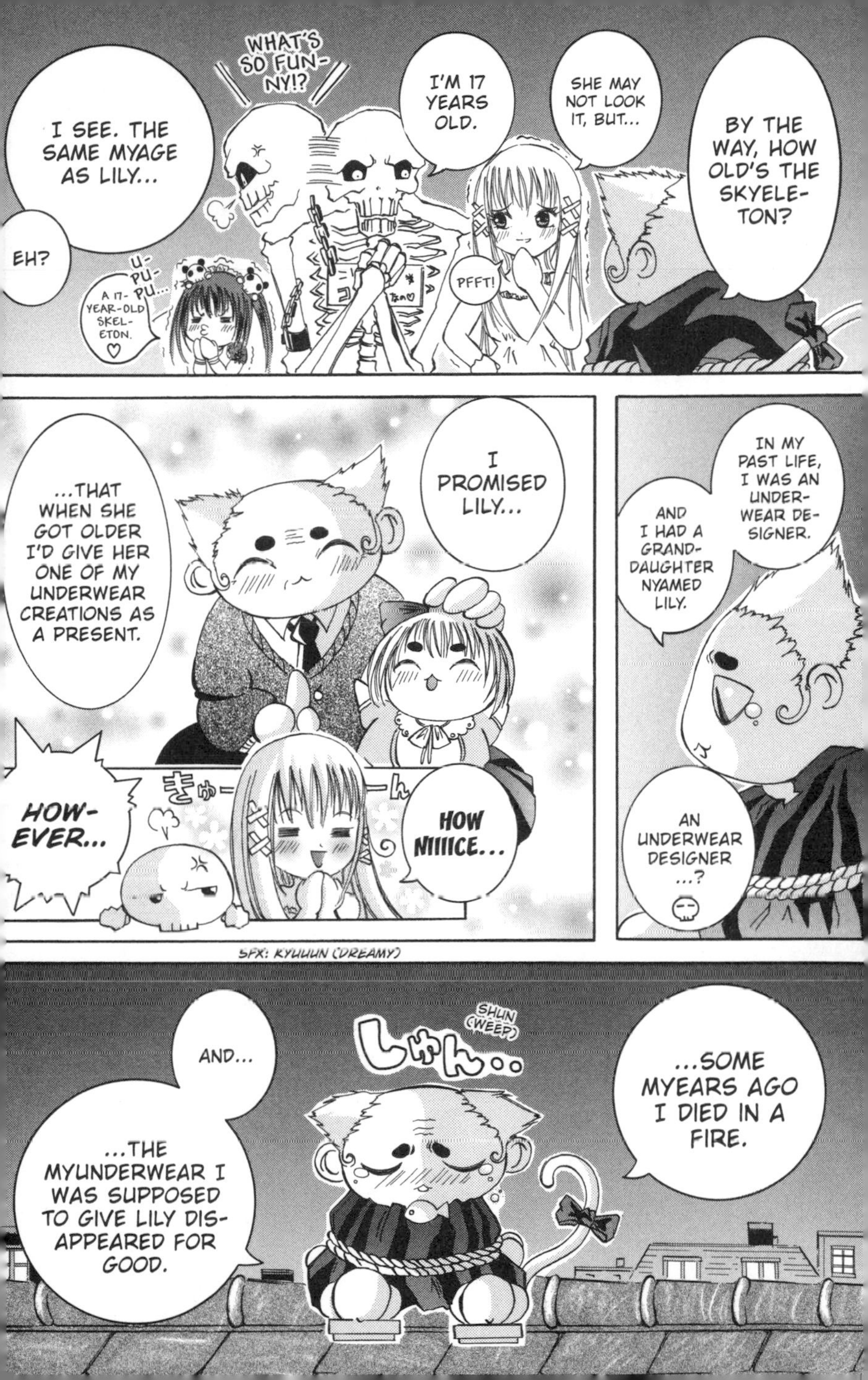
BY THE WAY, HOW OLD'S THE SKYELETON?
SHE MAY NOT LOOK IT, BUT...
I'M 17 YEARS OLD.
WHAT'S SO FUNNY!?
PFFT!
I SEE. THE SAME MYAGE AS LILY...
U-PU-PU...
A 17-YEAR-OLD SKELETON. ♡
EH?
IN MY PAST LIFE, I WAS AN UNDERWEAR DESIGNER.
AND I HAD A GRANDDAUGHTER NYAMED LILY.
AN UNDERWEAR DESIGNER ...?
I PROMISED LILY...
...THAT WHEN SHE GOT OLDER I'D GIVE HER ONE OF MY UNDERWEAR CREATIONS AS A PRESENT.
HOW NIIIICE...
HOWEVER...
SFX: KYUUUN (DREAMY)
...SOME MYEARS AGO I DIED IN A FIRE.
しゅん。。
SHUN (WEEP)
AND...
...THE MYUNDERWEAR I WAS SUPPOSED TO GIVE LILY DISAPPEARED FOR GOOD.

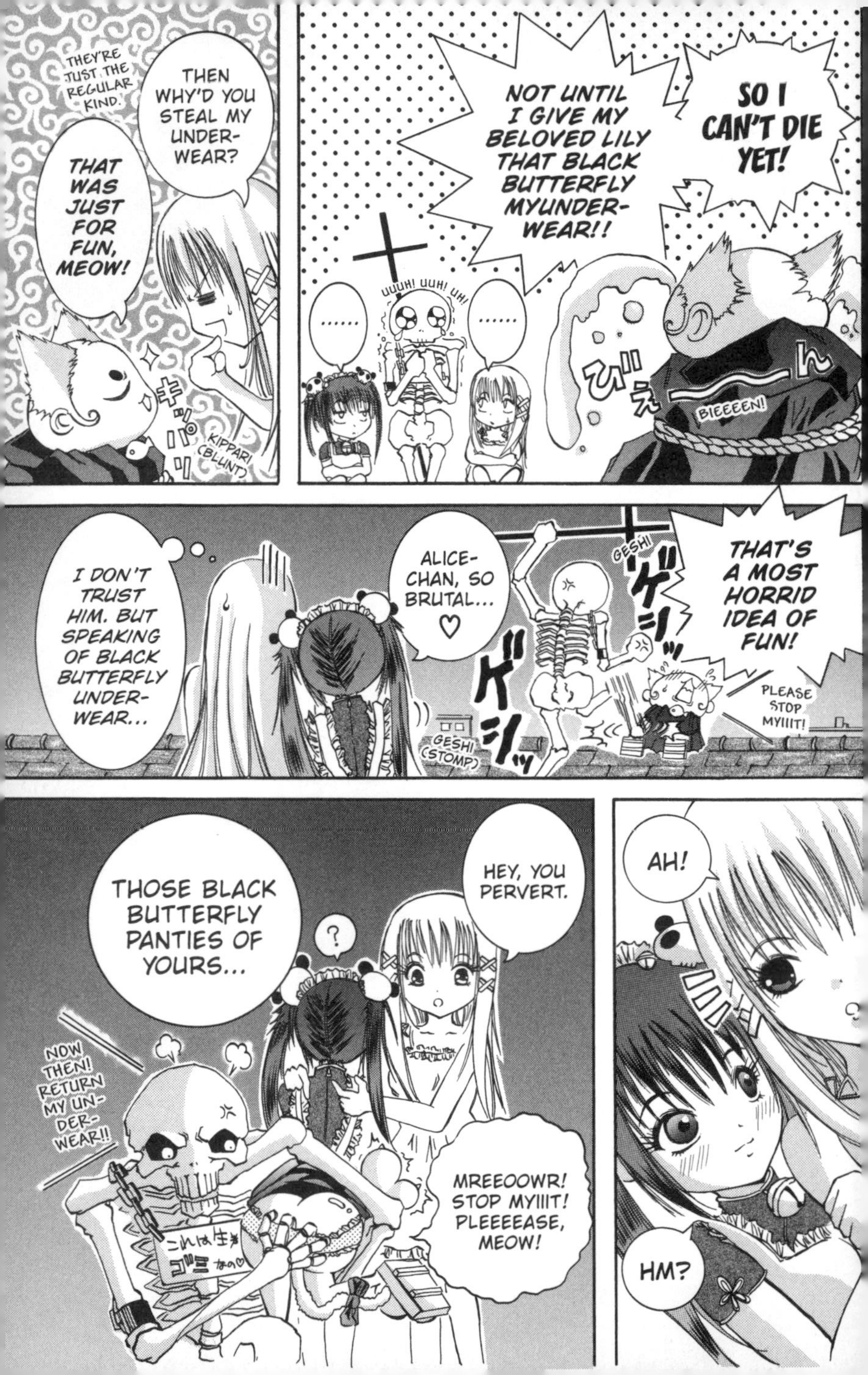
SO I CAN'T DIE YET!
NOT UNTIL I GIVE MY BELOVED LILY THAT BLACK BUTTERFLY MYUNDER-WEAR!!
BIEEEEN!
......
UUUH! UUH! UH!
......
THEY'RE JUST THE REGULAR KIND.
THEN WHY'D YOU STEAL MY UNDER-WEAR?
THAT WAS JUST FOR FUN, MEOW!
KIPPARI (BLUNT)
THAT'S A MOST HORRID IDEA OF FUN!
GESHI
PLEASE STOP MYIIIT!
GESHI (STOMP)
ALICE-CHAN, SO BRUTAL... ♡
I DON'T TRUST HIM. BUT SPEAKING OF BLACK BUTTERFLY UNDER-WEAR...
AH!
HM?
HEY, YOU PERVERT.
?
THOSE BLACK BUTTERFLY PANTIES OF YOURS...
MREEOOWR! STOP MYIIIT! PLEEEEASE, MEOW!
NOW THEN! RETURN MY UN-DER-WEAR!!
これは生ゴミなの♡

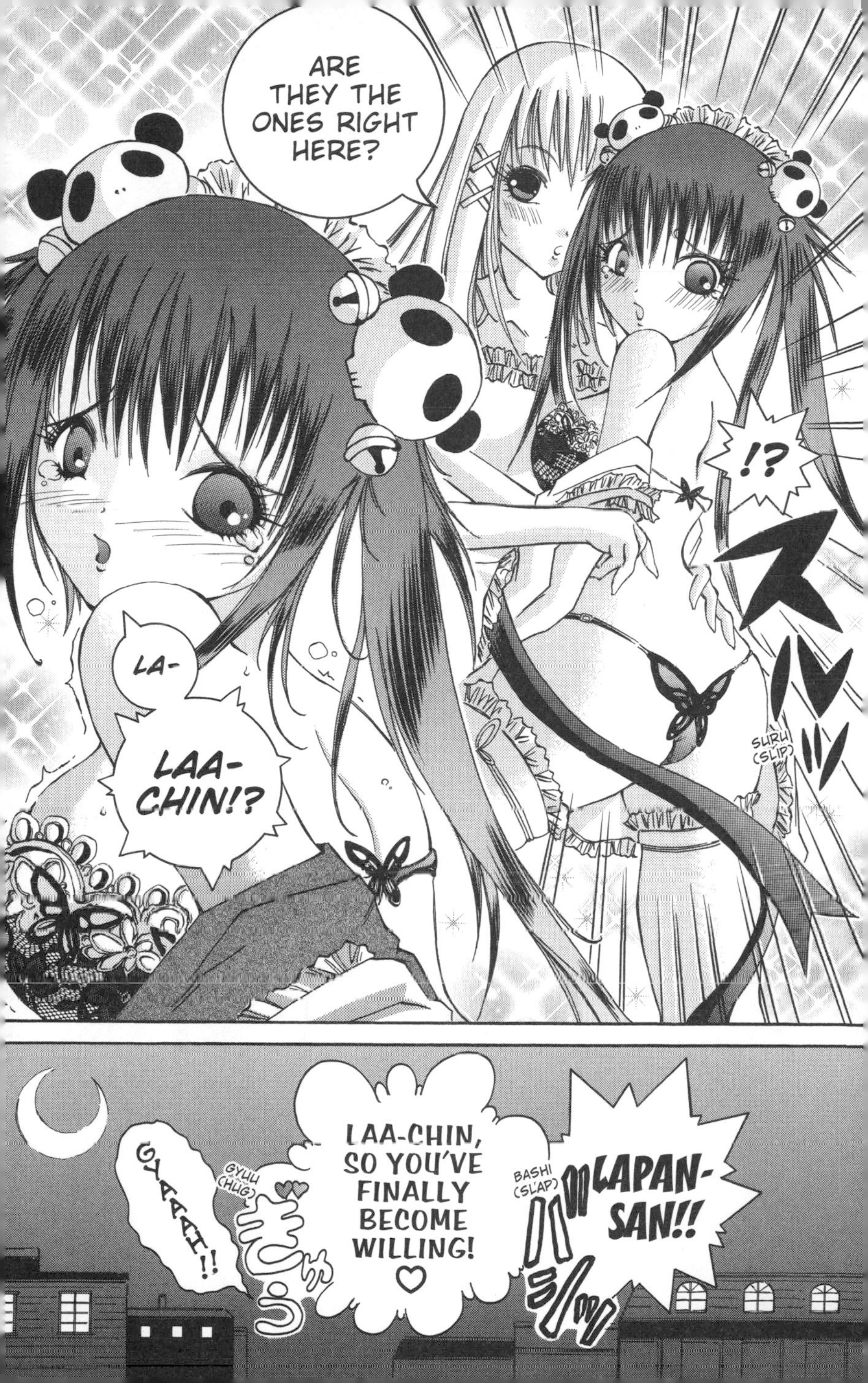
ARE THEY THE ONES RIGHT HERE?
!?
SURU (SLIP)
LA-
LAA-CHIN!?
LAPAN-SAN!!
BASHI (SLAP)
LAA-CHIN, SO YOU'VE FINALLY BECOME WILLING! ♡
GYUU (HUG)
GYAAAH!!

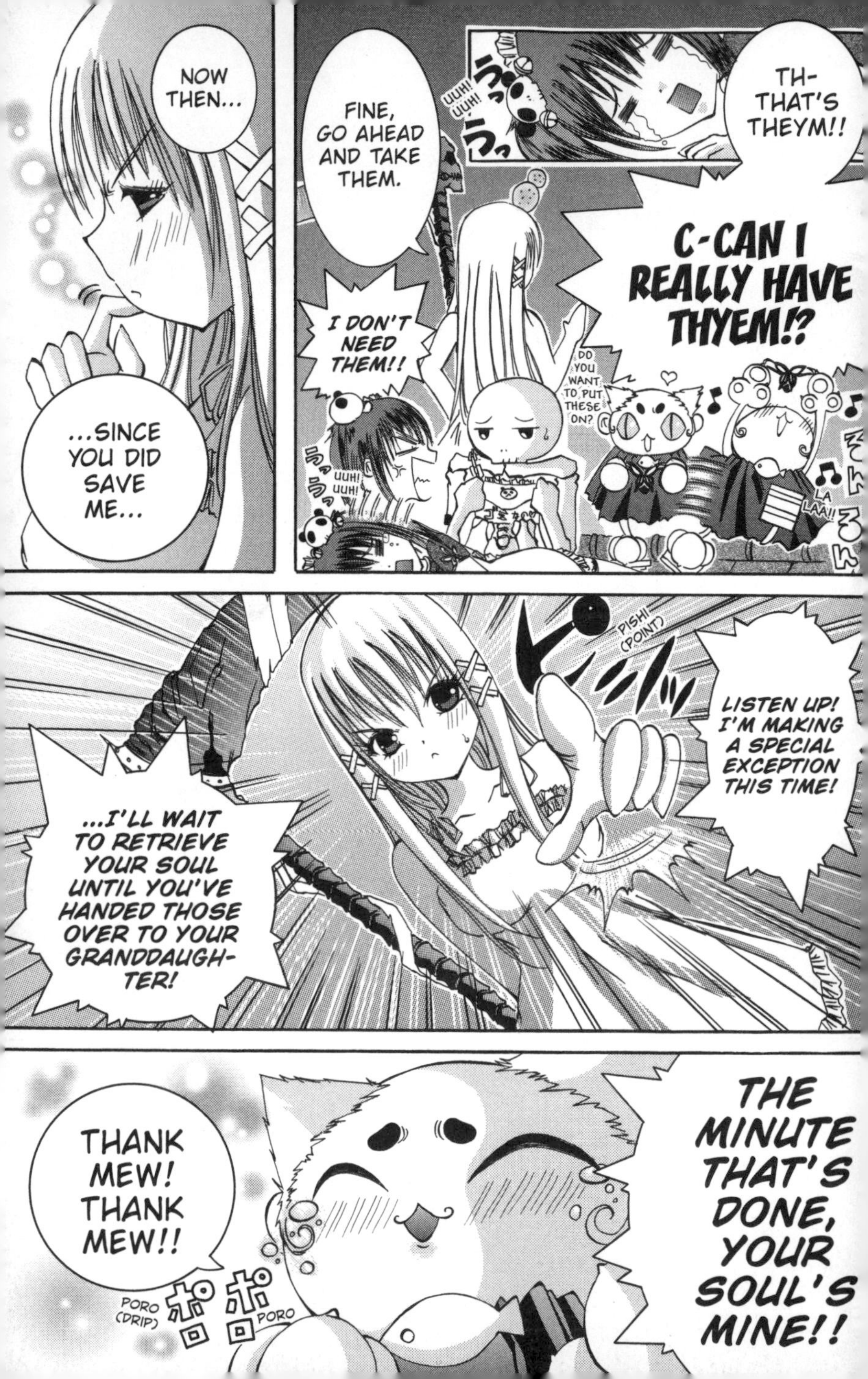
TH- THAT'S THEYM!!
UUH! UUH!
FINE, GO AHEAD AND TAKE THEM.
C-CAN I REALLY HAVE THYEM!?
DO YOU WANT TO PUT THESE ON?
LA LAAA!!
I DON'T NEED THEM!!
UUH! UUH!
NOW THEN...
...SINCE YOU DID SAVE ME...
PISHI (POINT)
LISTEN UP! I'M MAKING A SPECIAL EXCEPTION THIS TIME!
...I'LL WAIT TO RETRIEVE YOUR SOUL UNTIL YOU'VE HANDED THOSE OVER TO YOUR GRANDDAUGH-TER!
THE MINUTE THAT'S DONE, YOUR SOUL'S MINE!!
THANK MEW! THANK MEW!!
PORO PORO (DRIP)

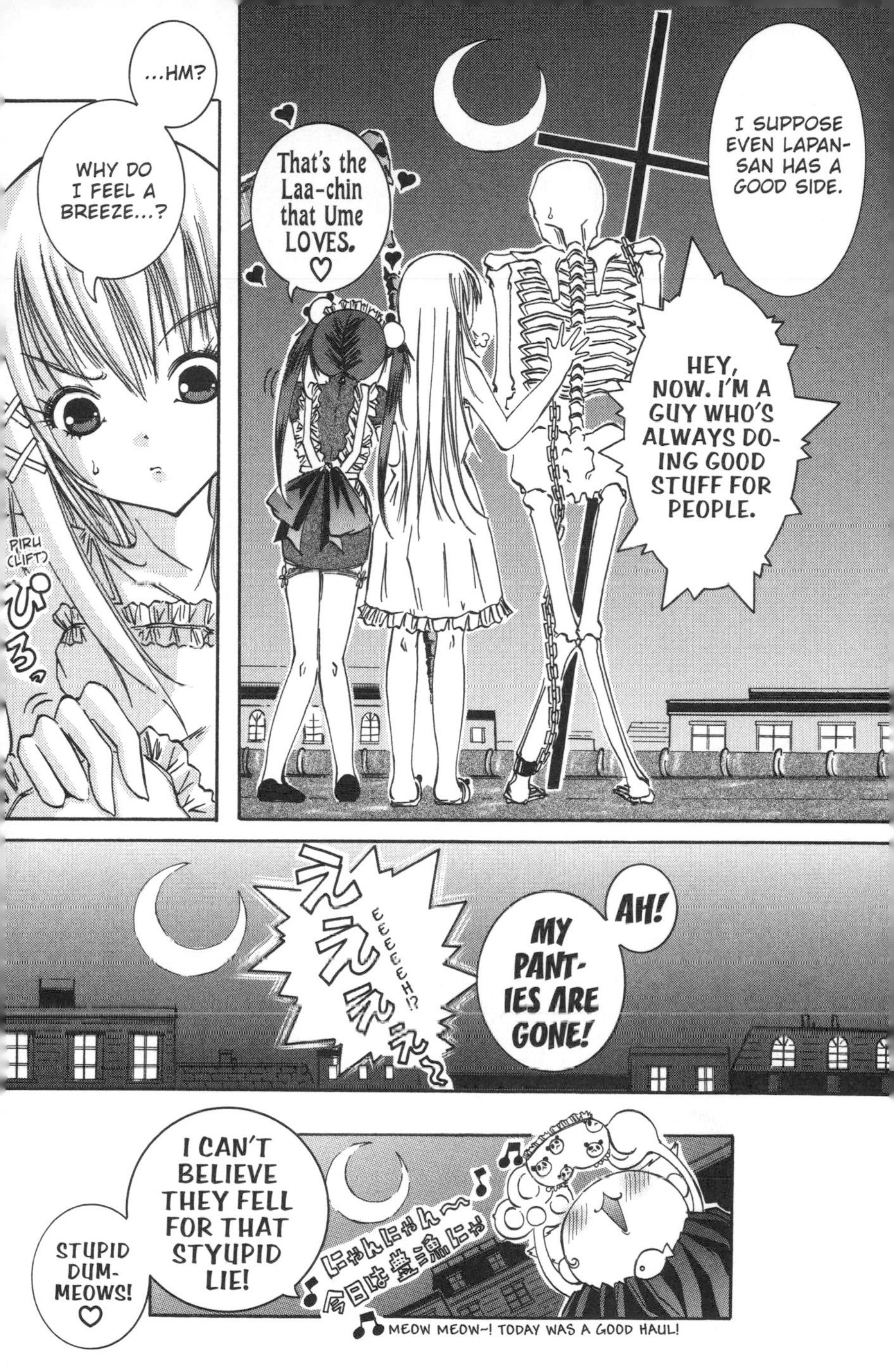
I SUPPOSE EVEN LAPAN-SAN HAS A GOOD SIDE.
That's the Laa-chin that Ume LOVES. ♡
HEY, NOW. I'M A GUY WHO'S ALWAYS DOING GOOD STUFF FOR PEOPLE.
...HM?
WHY DO I FEEL A BREEZE...?
PIRU (LIFT)
AH!
MY PANTIES ARE GONE!
えええええ~
EEEEEEH!?
にゃんにゃん~♪
今日は豊漁にゃ♪
MEOW MEOW~! TODAY WAS A GOOD HAUL!
I CAN'T BELIEVE THEY FELL FOR THAT STYUPID LIE!
STUPID DUM-MEOWS! ♡

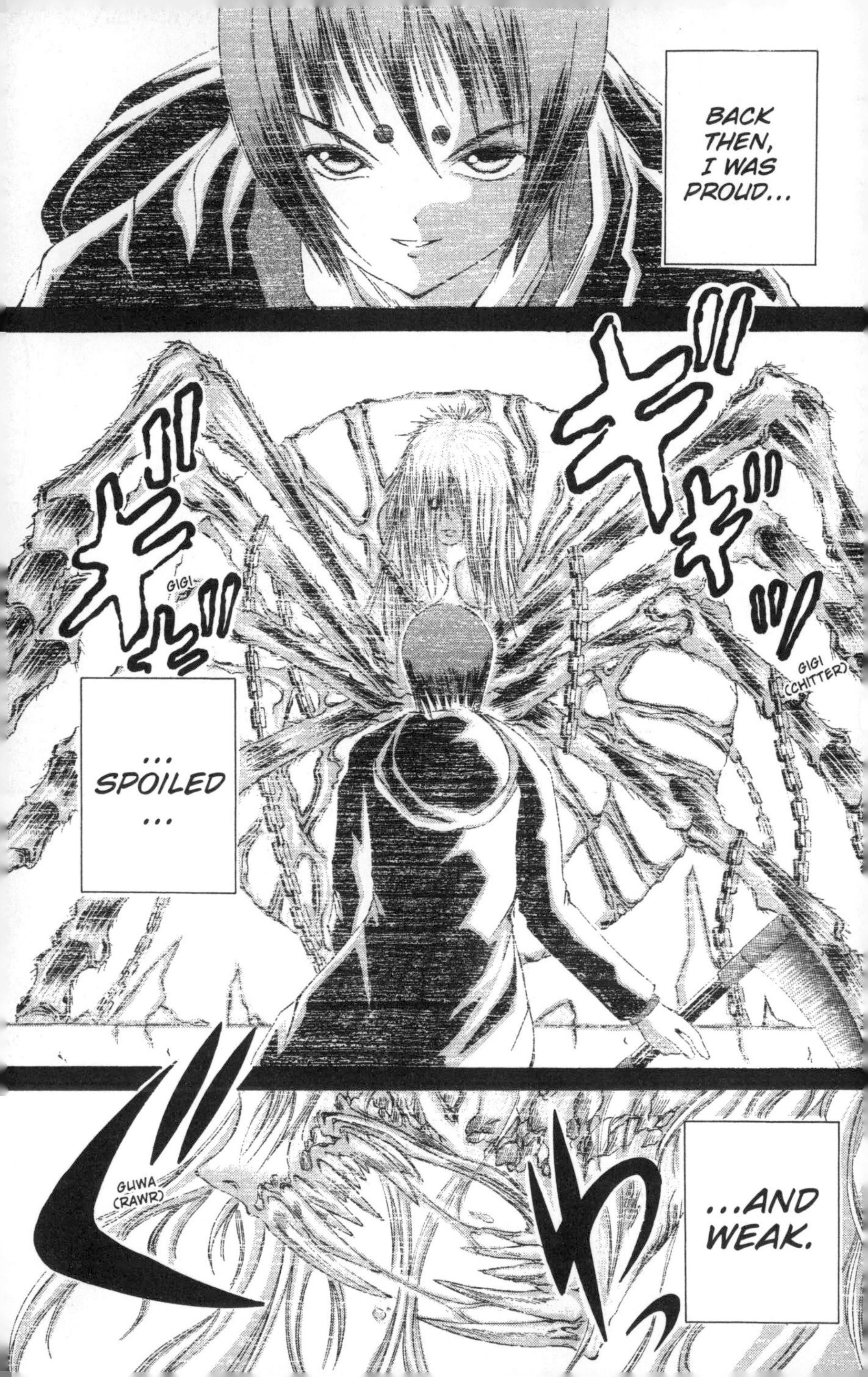
BACK THEN, I WAS PROUD...
GIGI (CHITTER)
GIGI
...SPOILED...
...AND WEAK.
GUWA (RAWR)

Line 6: The Doll & the Ume of Yore

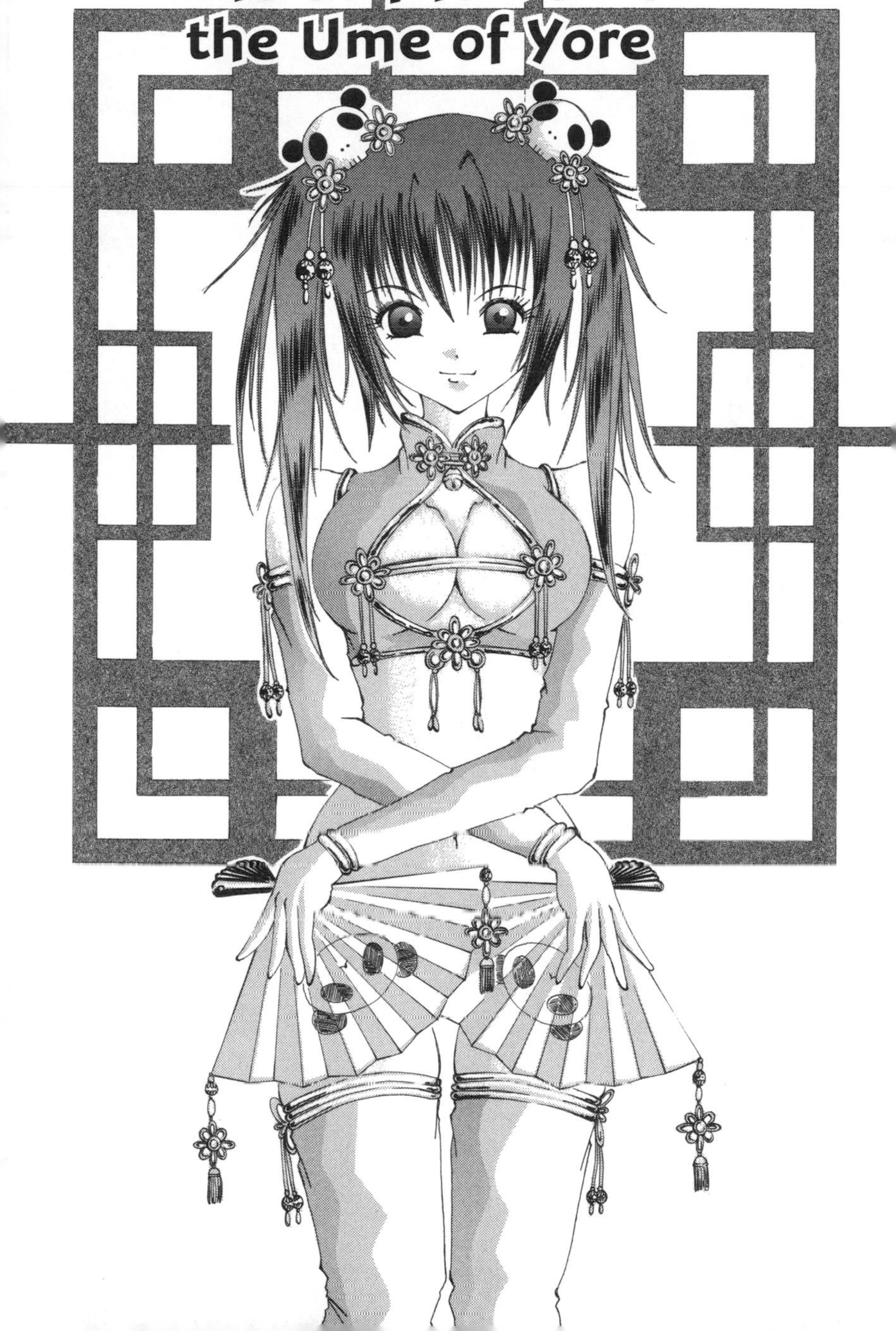

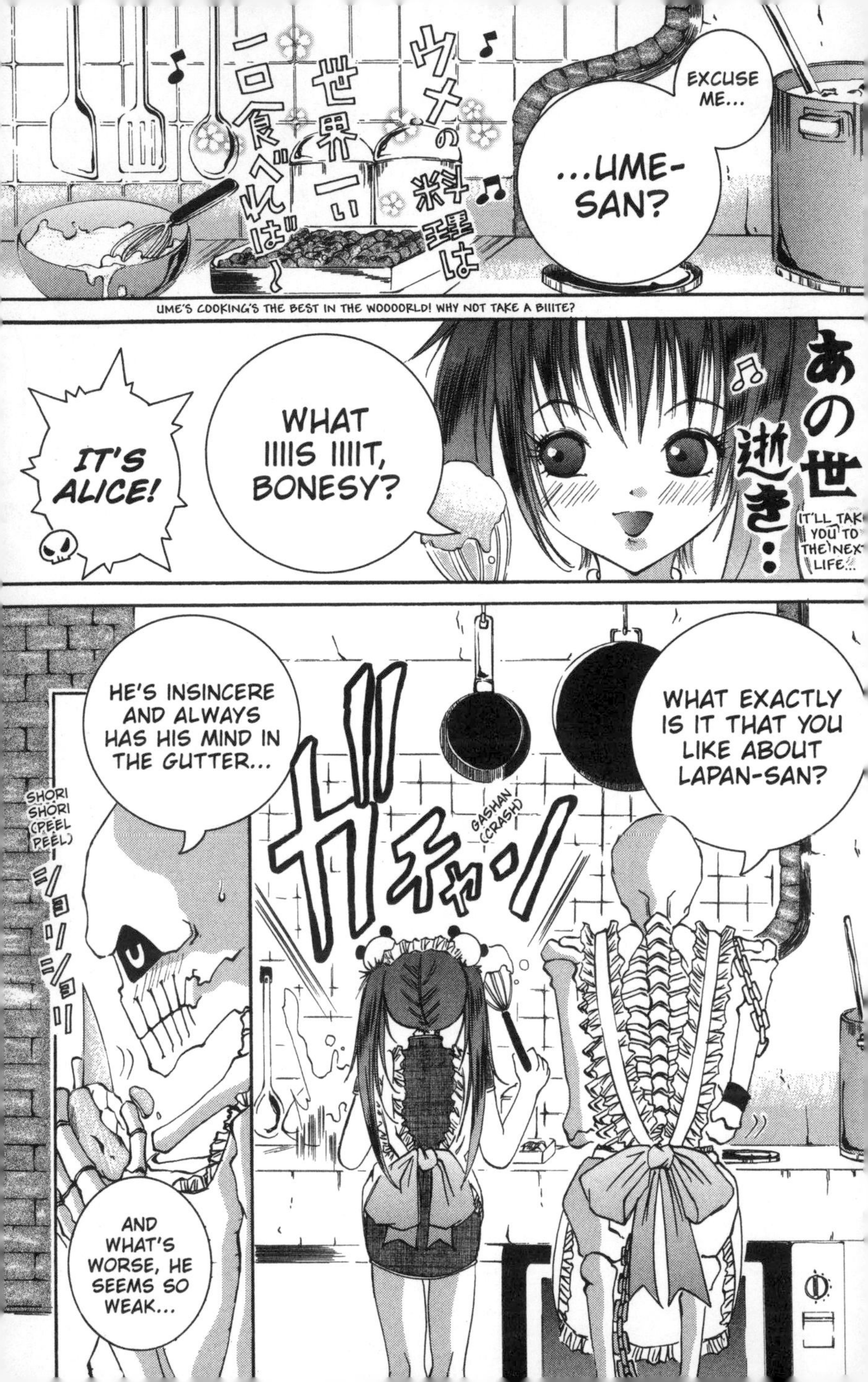
EXCUSE ME...
...UME-SAN?
ウメの料理は
世界一い
一口食べれば〜
UME'S COOKING'S THE BEST IN THE WOOOORLD! WHY NOT TAKE A BIIITE?
あの世逝き・・
IT'LL TAKE YOU TO THE NEXT LIFE...
WHAT IIIIS IIIIT, BONESY?
IT'S ALICE!
WHAT EXACTLY IS IT THAT YOU LIKE ABOUT LAPAN-SAN?
ガチャッ
GASHAN (CRASH)
HE'S INSINCERE AND ALWAYS HAS HIS MIND IN THE GUTTER...
ショリショリ
SHORI SHORI (PEEL PEEL)
AND WHAT'S WORSE, HE SEEMS SO WEAK...

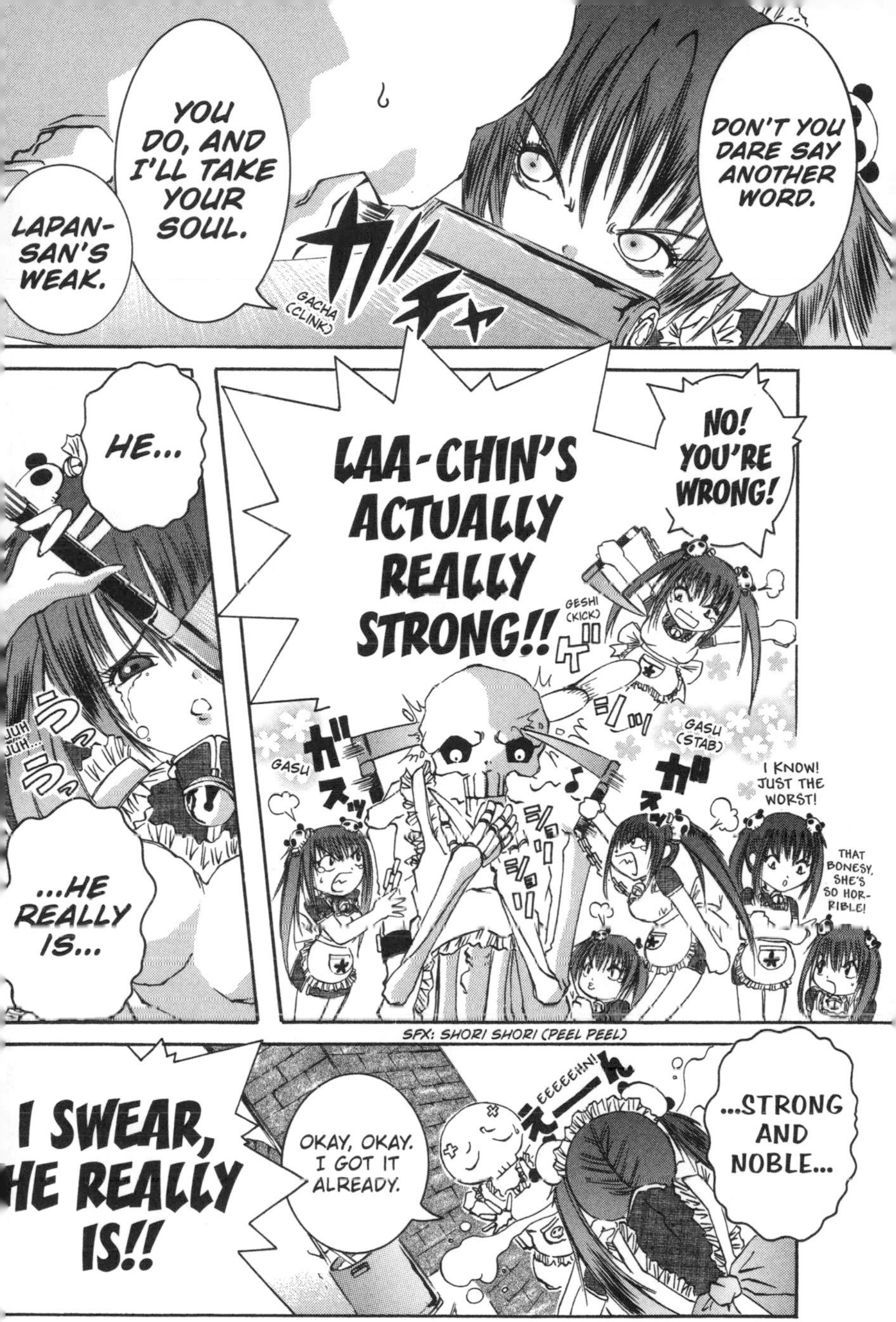
DON'T YOU DARE SAY ANOTHER WORD.
GACHA (CLINK)
YOU DO, AND I'LL TAKE YOUR SOUL.
LAPAN-SAN'S WEAK.
NO! YOU'RE WRONG!
LAA-CHIN'S ACTUALLY REALLY STRONG!!
GESHI (KICK)
GASU (STAB)
I KNOW! JUST THE WORST!
THAT BONESY, SHE'S SO HORRIBLE!
GASU
HE...
JUH JUH...
...HE REALLY IS...
SFX: SHORI SHORI (PEEL PEEL)
...STRONG AND NOBLE...
EEEEEHN!
OKAY, OKAY. I GOT IT ALREADY.
I SWEAR, HE REALLY IS!!

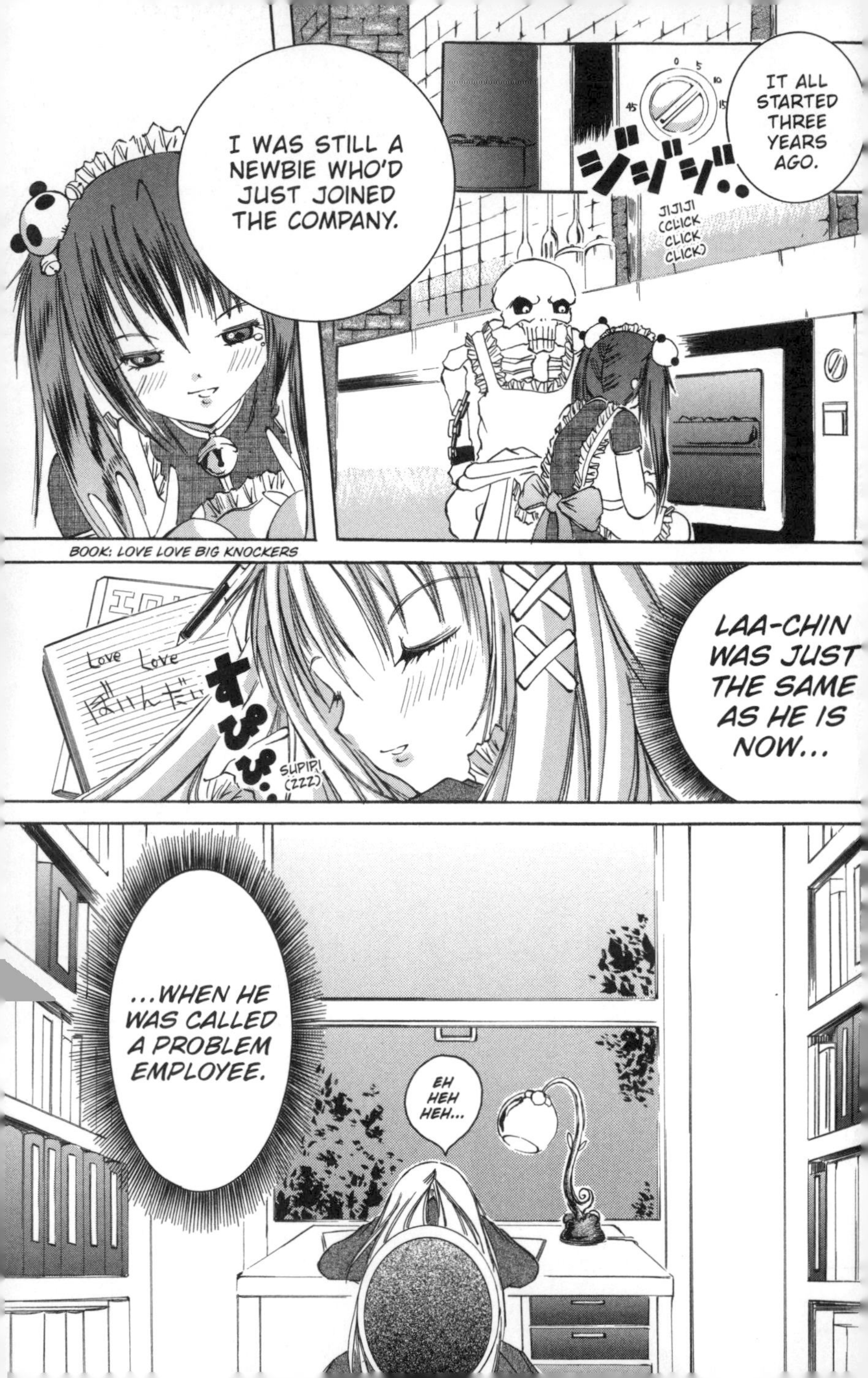
IT ALL STARTED THREE YEARS AGO.
JIJIJI (CLICK CLICK CLICK)
I WAS STILL A NEWBIE WHO'D JUST JOINED THE COMPANY.
BOOK: LOVE LOVE BIG KNOCKERS
LAA-CHIN WAS JUST THE SAME AS HE IS NOW...
Love Love
SUPIPI (ZZZ)
...WHEN HE WAS CALLED A PROBLEM EMPLOYEE.
EH HEH HEH...

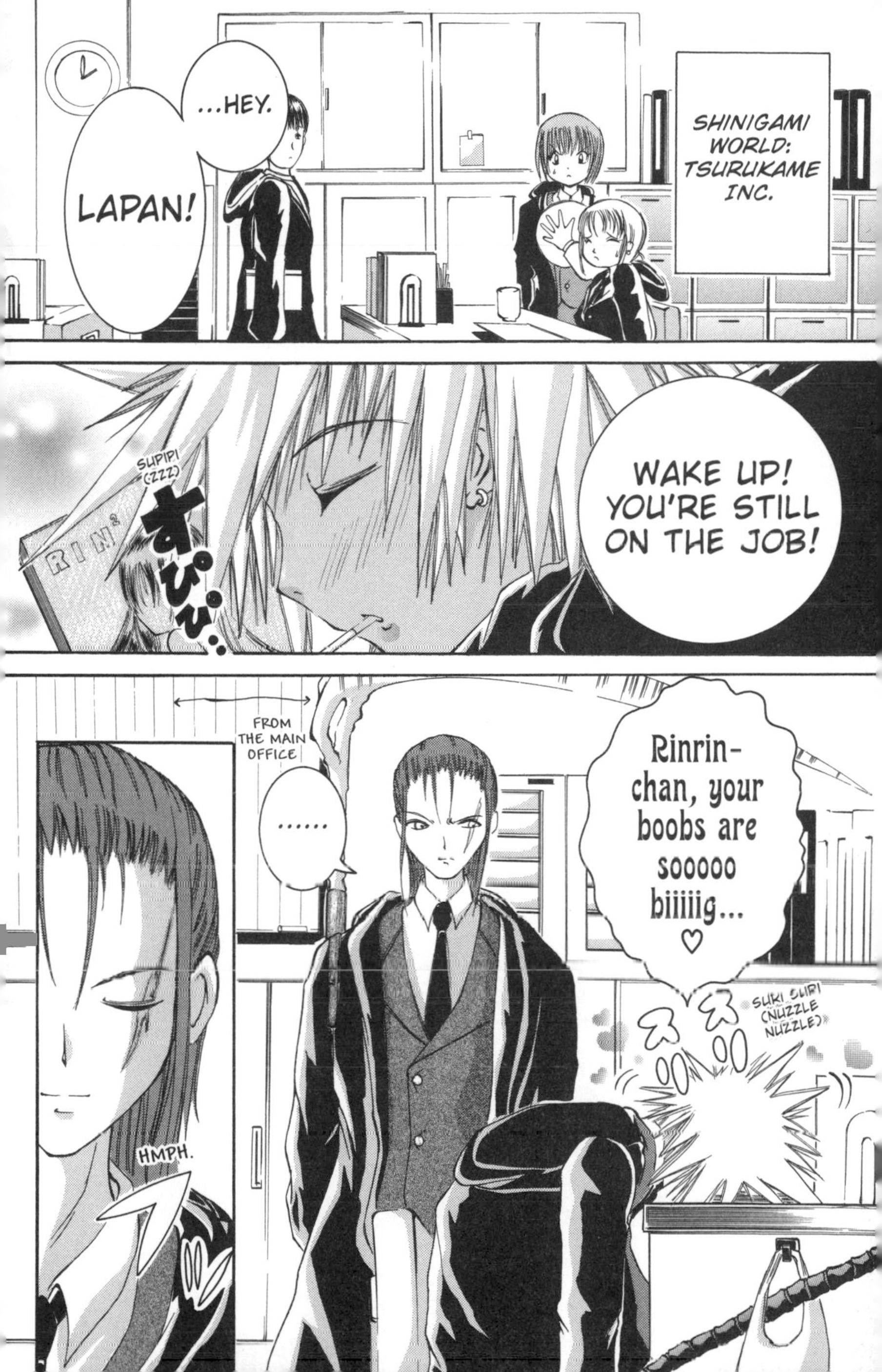
SHINIGAMI WORLD: TSURUKAME INC.
...HEY.
LAPAN!
WAKE UP! YOU'RE STILL ON THE JOB!
SUPIPI (ZZZ)
RIN
Rinrin-chan, your boobs are sooooo biiiiig... ♡
SURI SURI (NUZZLE NUZZLE)
FROM THE MAIN OFFICE
......
HMPH.

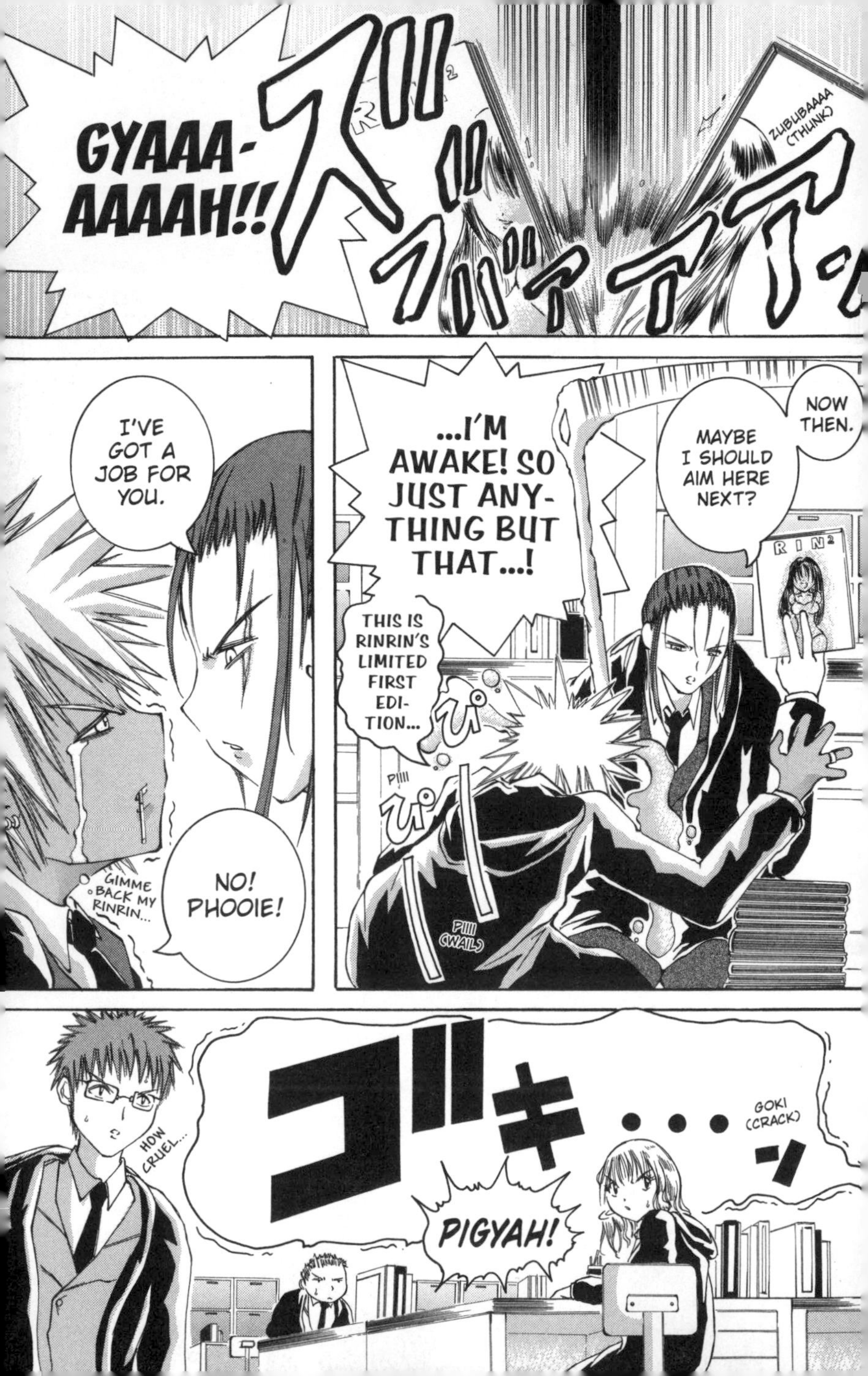
ZUBUBAAAA (THUNK)
GYAAA-AAAAH!!
NOW THEN.
MAYBE I SHOULD AIM HERE NEXT?
...I'M AWAKE! SO JUST ANY-THING BUT THAT...!
THIS IS RINRIN'S LIMITED FIRST EDI-TION...
PIIII
PIIII (WAIL)
I'VE GOT A JOB FOR YOU.
NO! PHOOIE!
GIMME BACK MY RINRIN...
GOKI (CRACK)
PIGYAH!
HOW CRUEL...

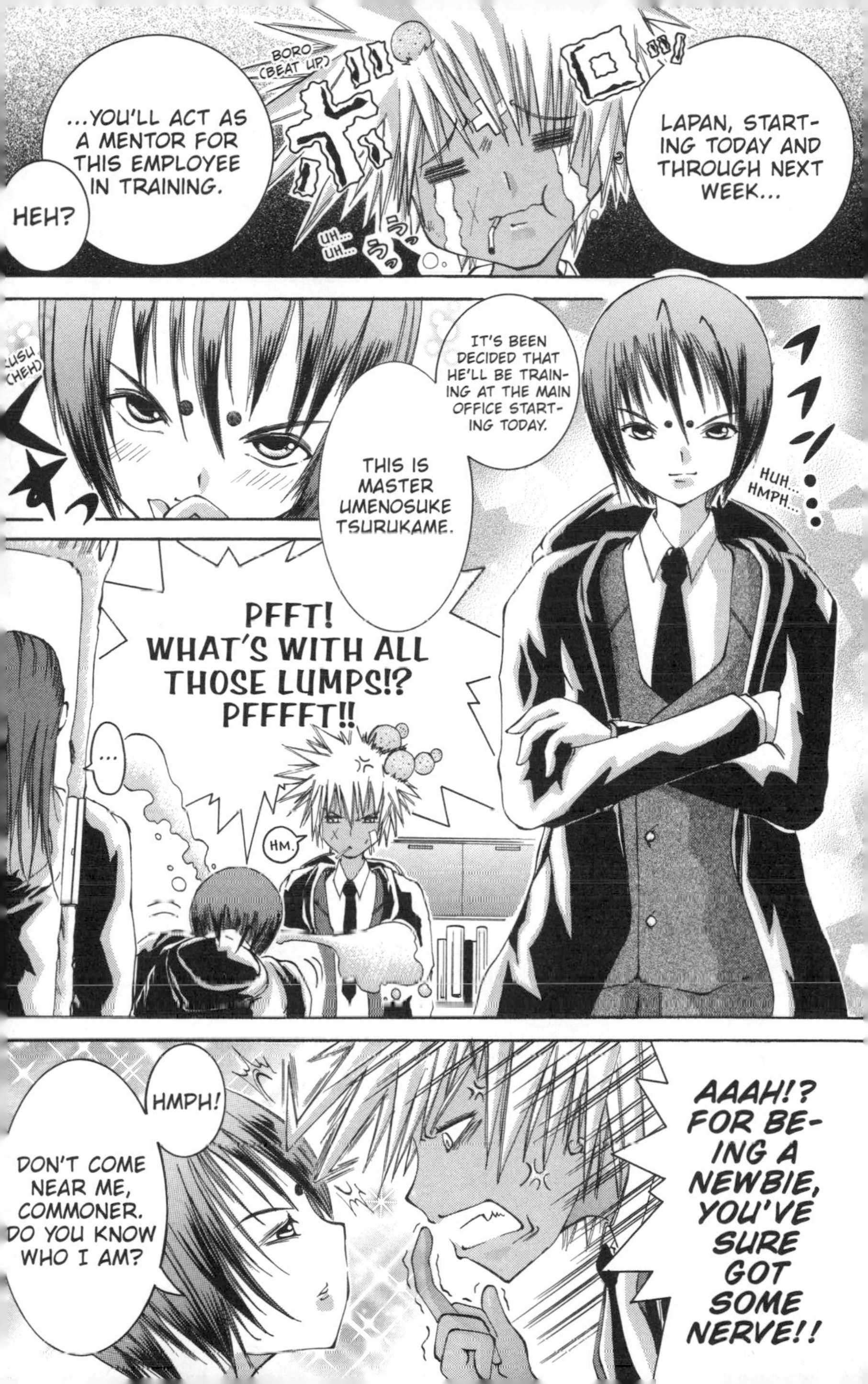
LAPAN, STARTING TODAY AND THROUGH NEXT WEEK...
BORO (BEAT UP)
...YOU'LL ACT AS A MENTOR FOR THIS EMPLOYEE IN TRAINING.
UH... UH...
HEH?
IT'S BEEN DECIDED THAT HE'LL BE TRAINING AT THE MAIN OFFICE STARTING TODAY.
HUH... HMPH...
THIS IS MASTER UMENOSUKE TSURUKAME.
KUSU (HEH)
PFFT! WHAT'S WITH ALL THOSE LUMPS!? PFFFFT!!
HM.
...
AAAH!? FOR BEING A NEWBIE, YOU'VE SURE GOT SOME NERVE!!
HMPH!
DON'T COME NEAR ME, COMMONER. DO YOU KNOW WHO I AM?

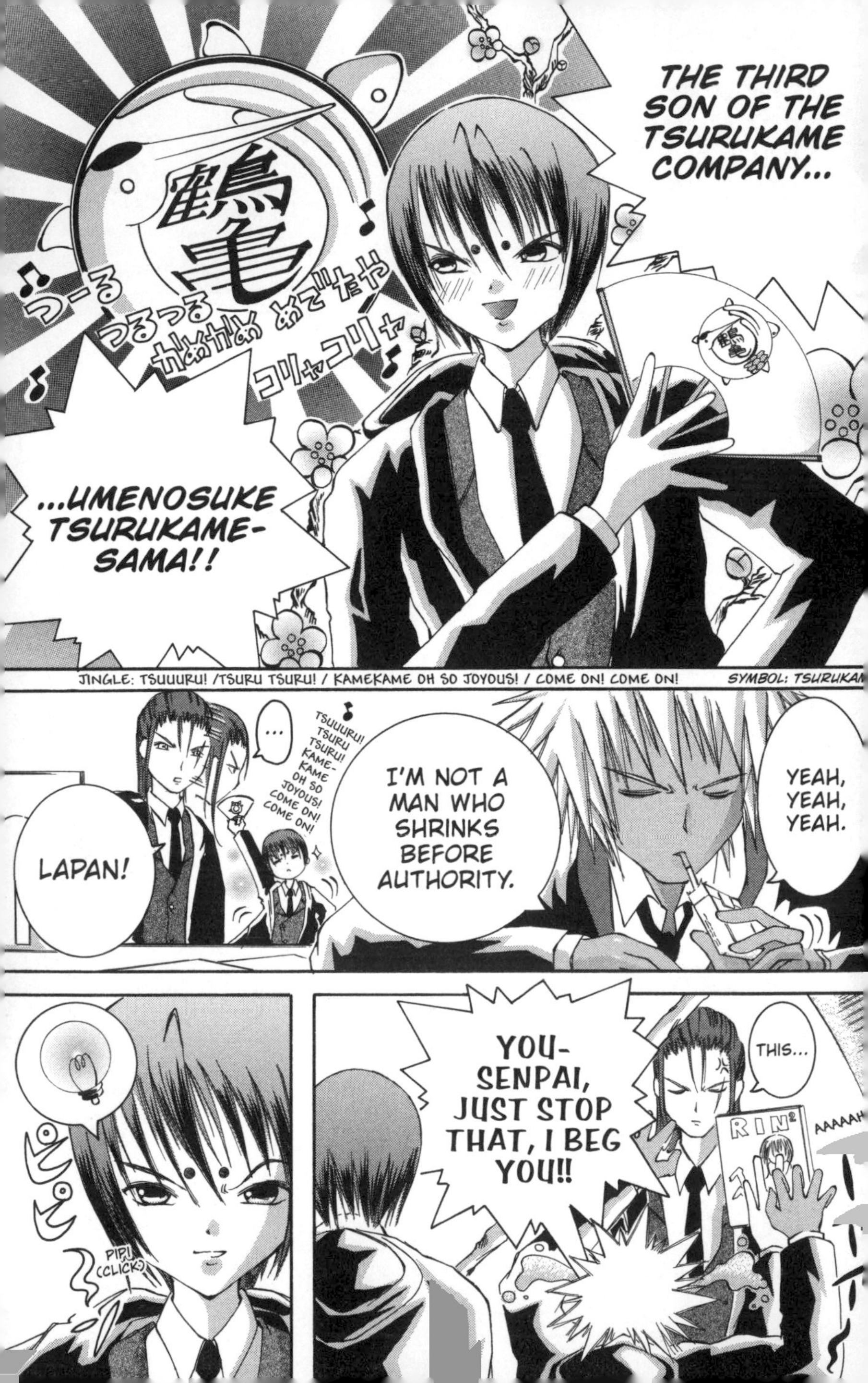

THE THIRD SON OF THE TSURUKAME COMPANY...
鶴亀
つーる つるつる かめかめ めでたや コリャコリャ
...UMENOSUKE TSURUKAME-SAMA!!
JINGLE: TSUUURU! /TSURU TSURU! / KAMEKAME OH SO JOYOUS! / COME ON! COME ON!
SYMBOL: TSURUKAM
YEAH, YEAH, YEAH.
I'M NOT A MAN WHO SHRINKS BEFORE AUTHORITY.
TSUUURU! TSURU TSURU! KAME-KAME OH SO JOYOUS! COME ON! COME ON!
...
LAPAN!
THIS...
AAAAAH
YOU-SENPAI, JUST STOP THAT, I BEG YOU!!
PIP! (CLICK)

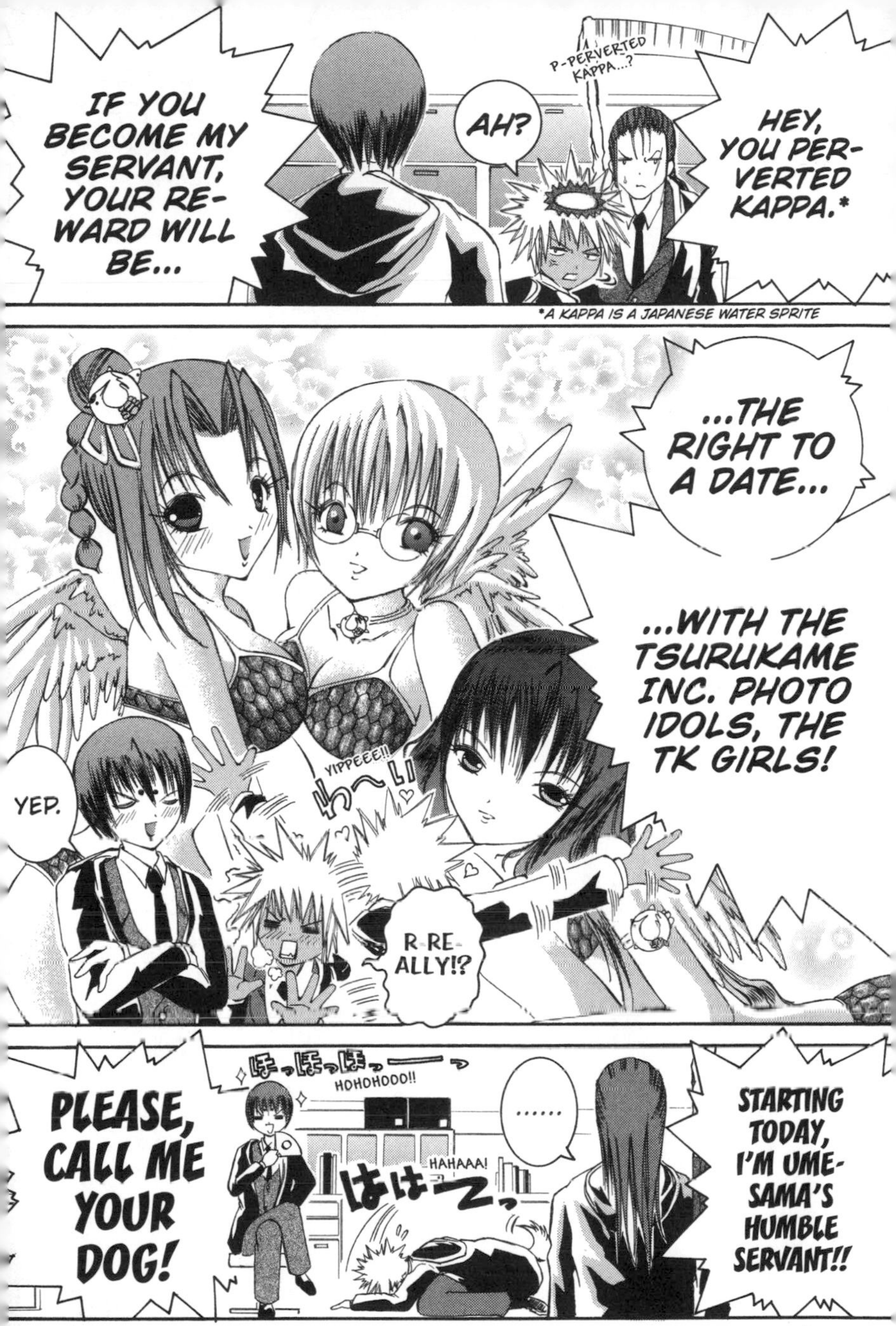
HEY, YOU PER-VERTED KAPPA.*
P-PERVERTED KAPPA...?
AH?
IF YOU BECOME MY SERVANT, YOUR RE-WARD WILL BE...
*A KAPPA IS A JAPANESE WATER SPRITE
...THE RIGHT TO A DATE...
...WITH THE TSURUKAME INC. PHOTO IDOLS, THE TK GIRLS!
YIPPEEE!!
わ〜い!
R-RE-ALLY!?
YEP.
STARTING TODAY, I'M UME-SAMA'S HUMBLE SERVANT!!
......
ははーっ
HAHAAA!
ほっほっほっーーっ
HOHOHOO!!
PLEASE, CALL ME YOUR DOG!

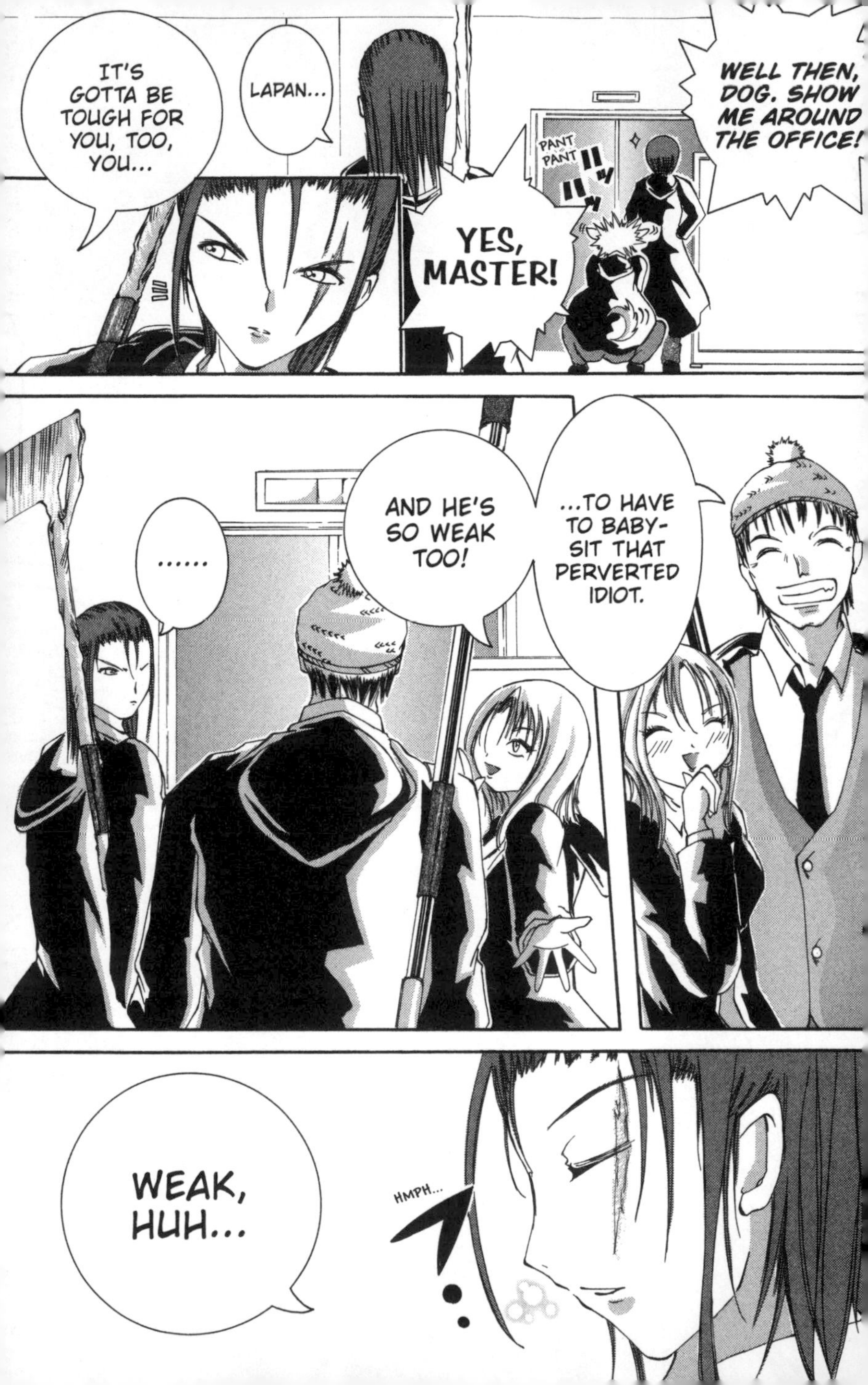
WELL THEN, DOG. SHOW ME AROUND THE OFFICE!
PANT PANT
YES, MASTER!
LAPAN...
IT'S GOTTA BE TOUGH FOR YOU, TOO, YOU...
...TO HAVE TO BABY-SIT THAT PERVERTED IDIOT.
AND HE'S SO WEAK TOO!
......
HMPH...
WEAK, HUH...

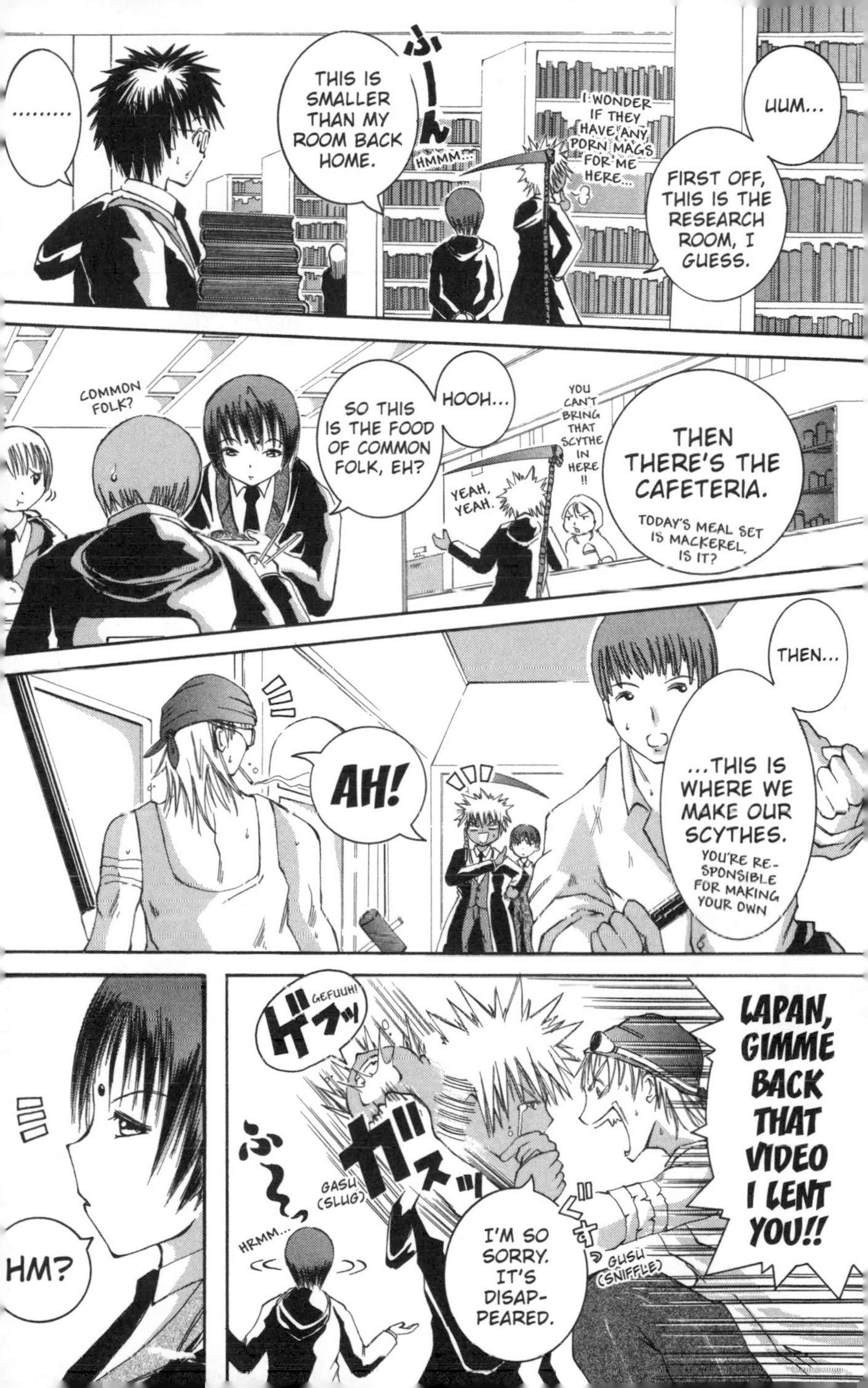
UUM...
FIRST OFF, THIS IS THE RESEARCH ROOM, I GUESS.
I WONDER IF THEY HAVE ANY PORN MAGS FOR ME HERE...
ふーん
HMMM...
THIS IS SMALLER THAN MY ROOM BACK HOME.
....
THEN THERE'S THE CAFETERIA.
TODAY'S MEAL SET IS MACKEREL, IS IT?
YOU CAN'T BRING THAT SCYTHE IN HERE!!
YEAH, YEAH.
HOOH...
SO THIS IS THE FOOD OF COMMON FOLK, EH?
COMMON FOLK?
THEN...
...THIS IS WHERE WE MAKE OUR SCYTHES.
YOU'RE RE-SPONSIBLE FOR MAKING YOUR OWN
AH!
LAPAN, GIMME BACK THAT VIDEO I LENT YOU!!
ゲフッ
GEFUUH!
ガスッ
GASU (SLUG)
ぐす
GUSU (SNIFFLE)
I'M SO SORRY. IT'S DISAP-PEARED.
ふ～～
HRMM...
HM?

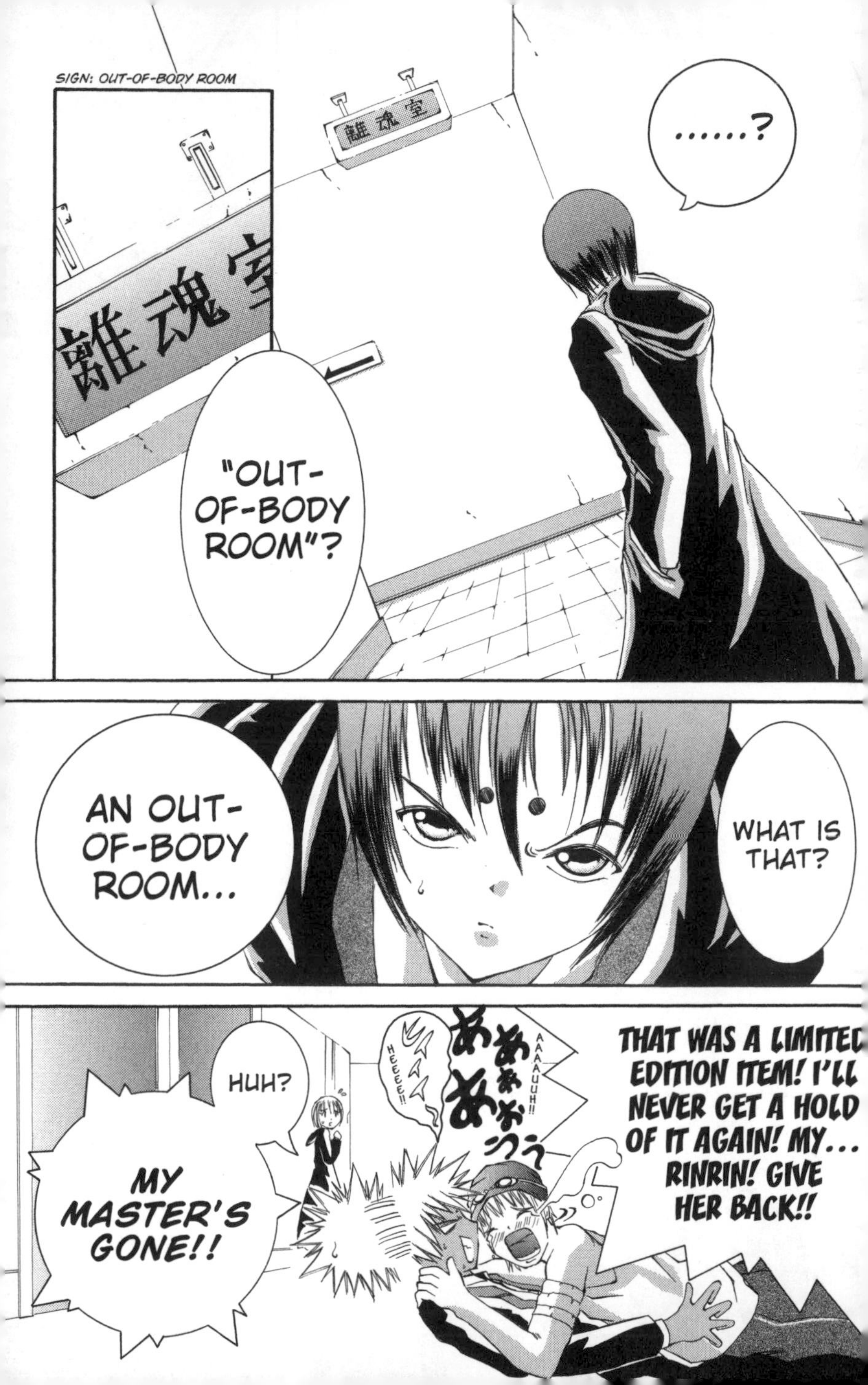
SIGN: OUT-OF-BODY ROOM
......?
"OUT-OF-BODY ROOM"?
WHAT IS THAT?
AN OUT-OF-BODY ROOM...
THAT WAS A LIMITED EDITION ITEM! I'LL NEVER GET A HOLD OF IT AGAIN! MY... RINRIN! GIVE HER BACK!!
AAAAUUH!!
HEEEE!!
HUH?
MY MASTER'S GONE!!

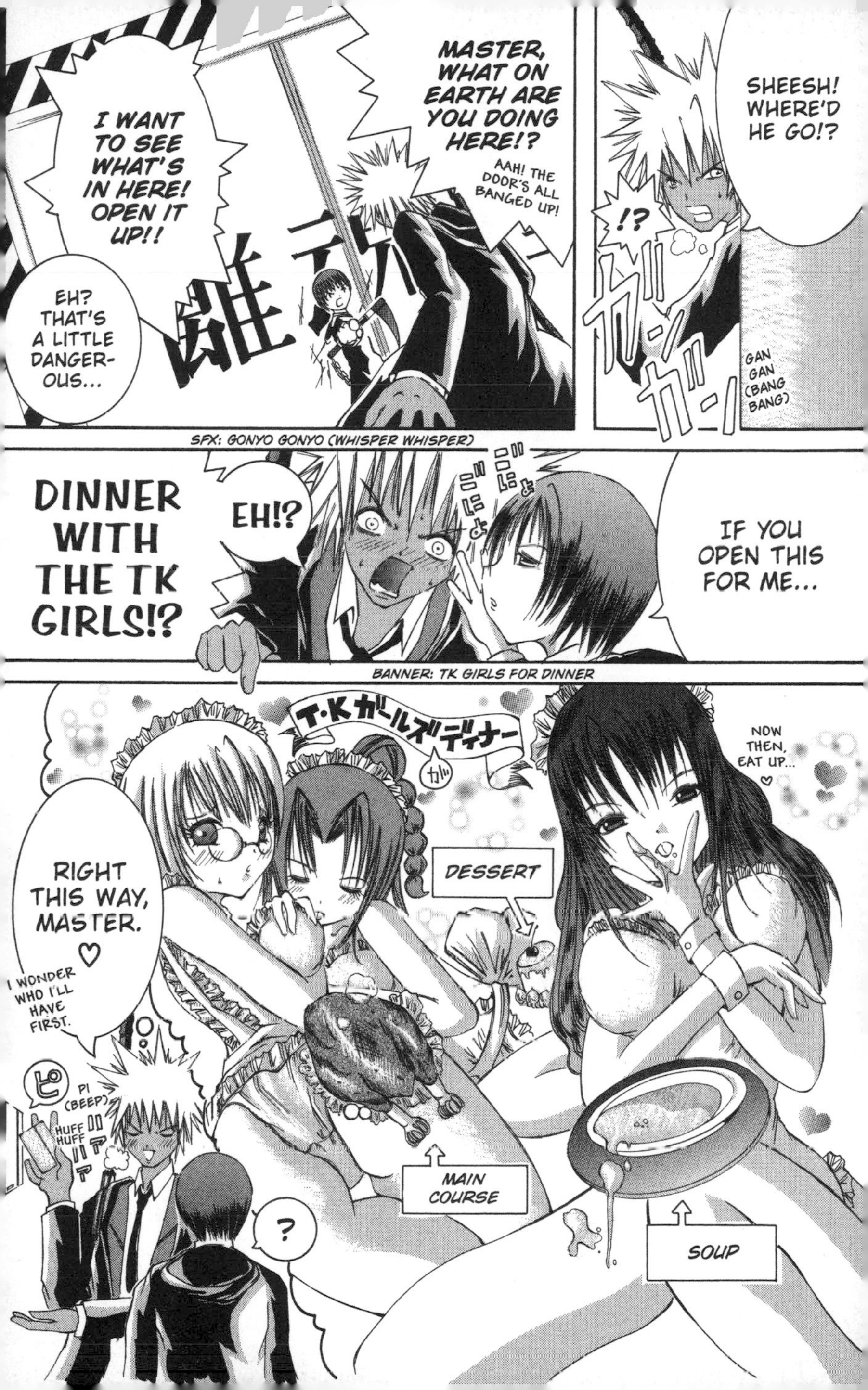
SHEESH! WHERE'D HE GO!?
!?
GAN GAN (BANG BANG)
MASTER, WHAT ON EARTH ARE YOU DOING HERE!?
AAH! THE DOOR'S ALL BANGED UP!
I WANT TO SEE WHAT'S IN HERE! OPEN IT UP!!
EH? THAT'S A LITTLE DANGER-OUS...
SFX: GONYO GONYO (WHISPER WHISPER)
IF YOU OPEN THIS FOR ME...
EH!?
DINNER WITH THE TK GIRLS!?
BANNER: TK GIRLS FOR DINNER
NOW THEN, EAT UP... ♡
T·Kガールズディナー
DESSERT
RIGHT THIS WAY, MASTER. ♡
I WONDER WHO I'LL HAVE FIRST.
SOUP
MAIN COURSE
PI (BEEP)
HUFF HUFF
?

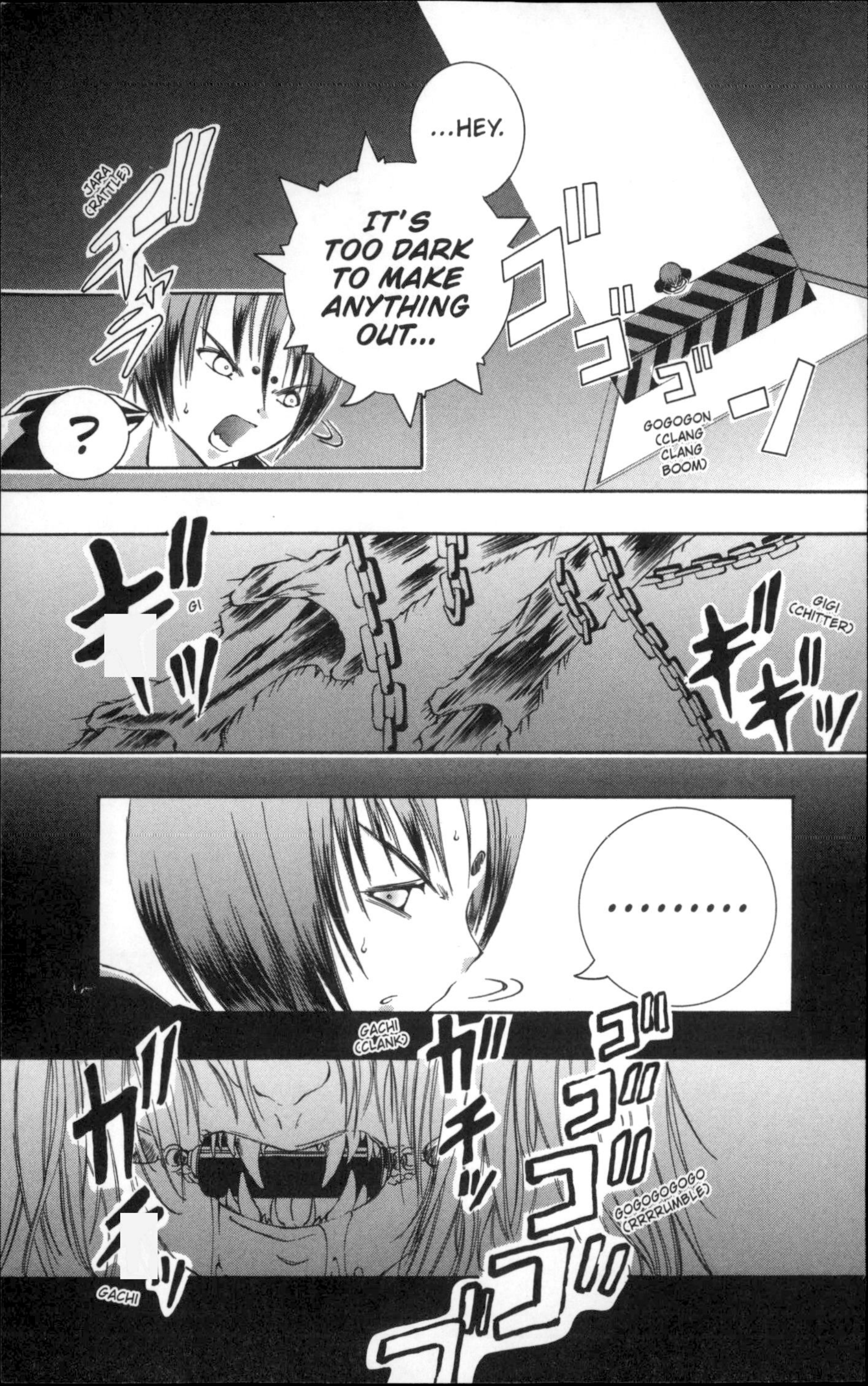
...HEY.
GOGOGON (CLANG CLANG BOOM)
IT'S TOO DARK TO MAKE ANYTHING OUT...
JARA (RATTLE)
?
GIGI (CHITTER)
GI
....
GOGOGOGOGO (RRRRUMBLE)
GACHI (CLANK)
GACHI

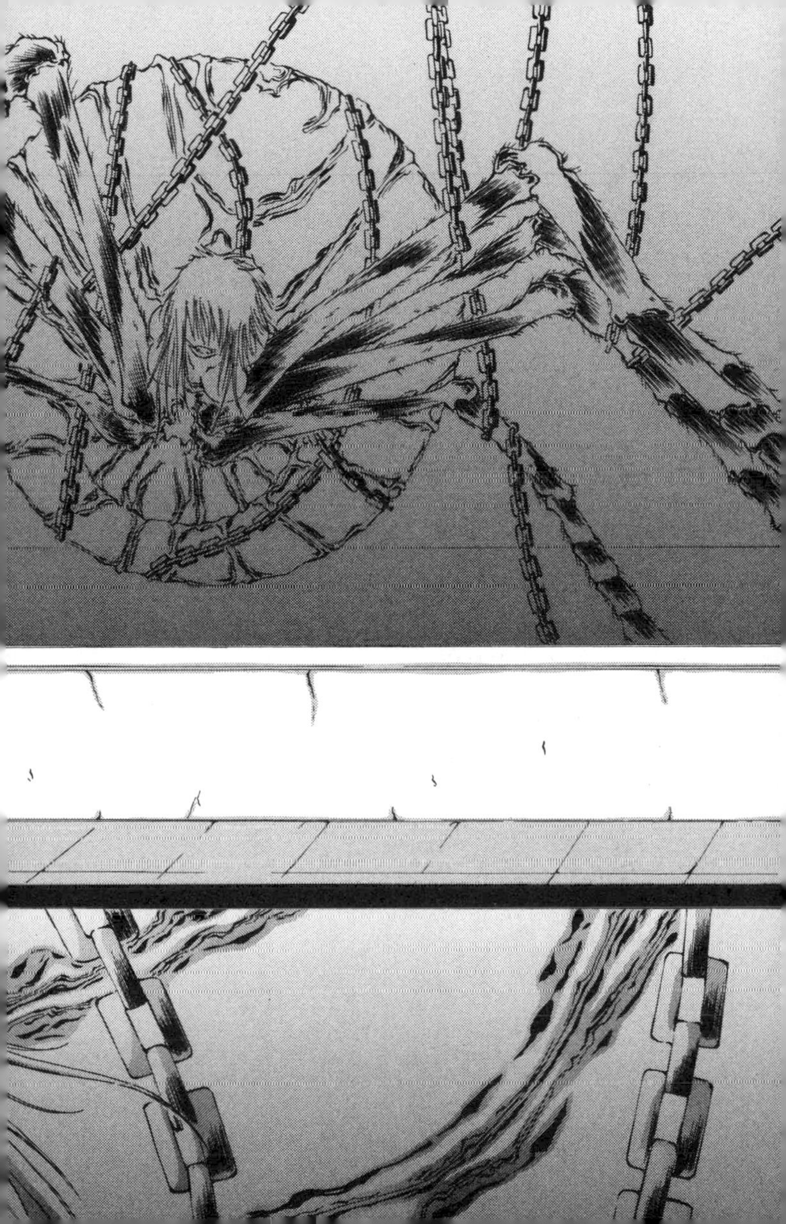

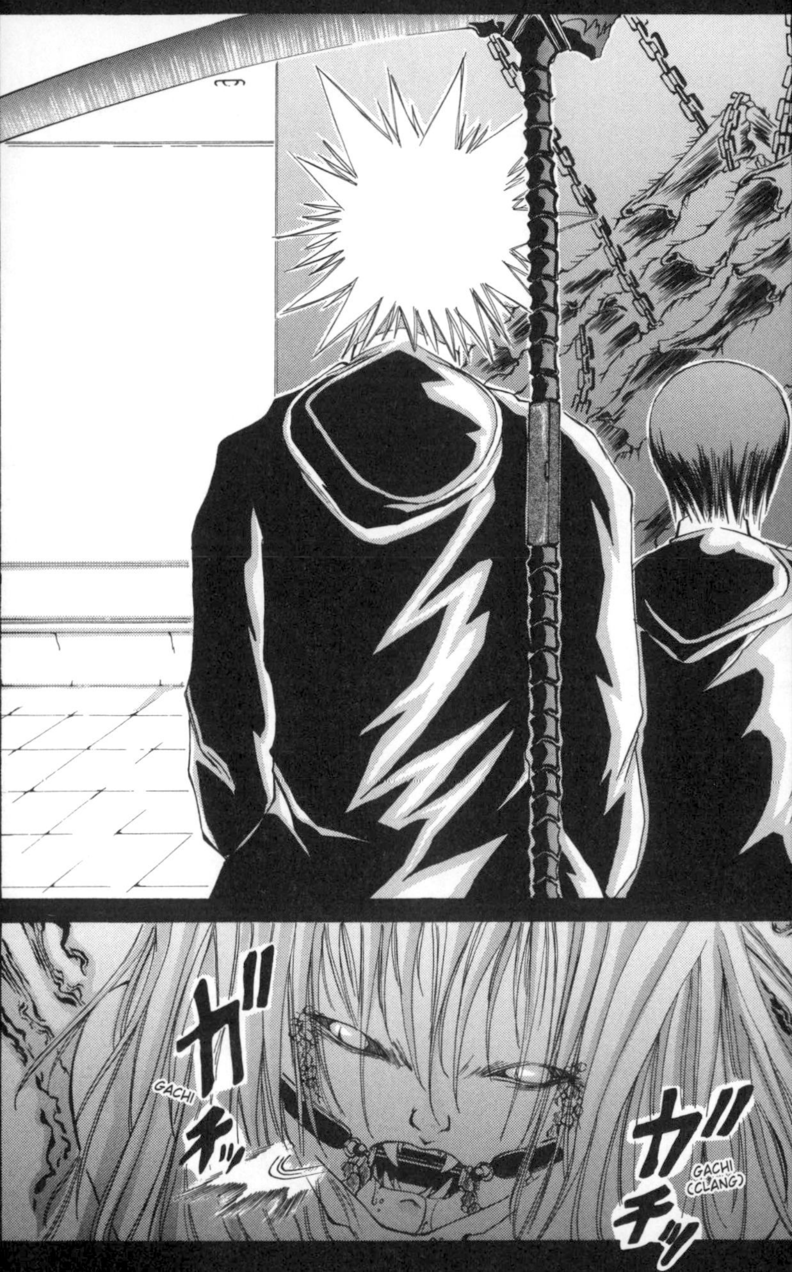
ガチッ
GACHI (CLANG)
ガチッ
GACHI

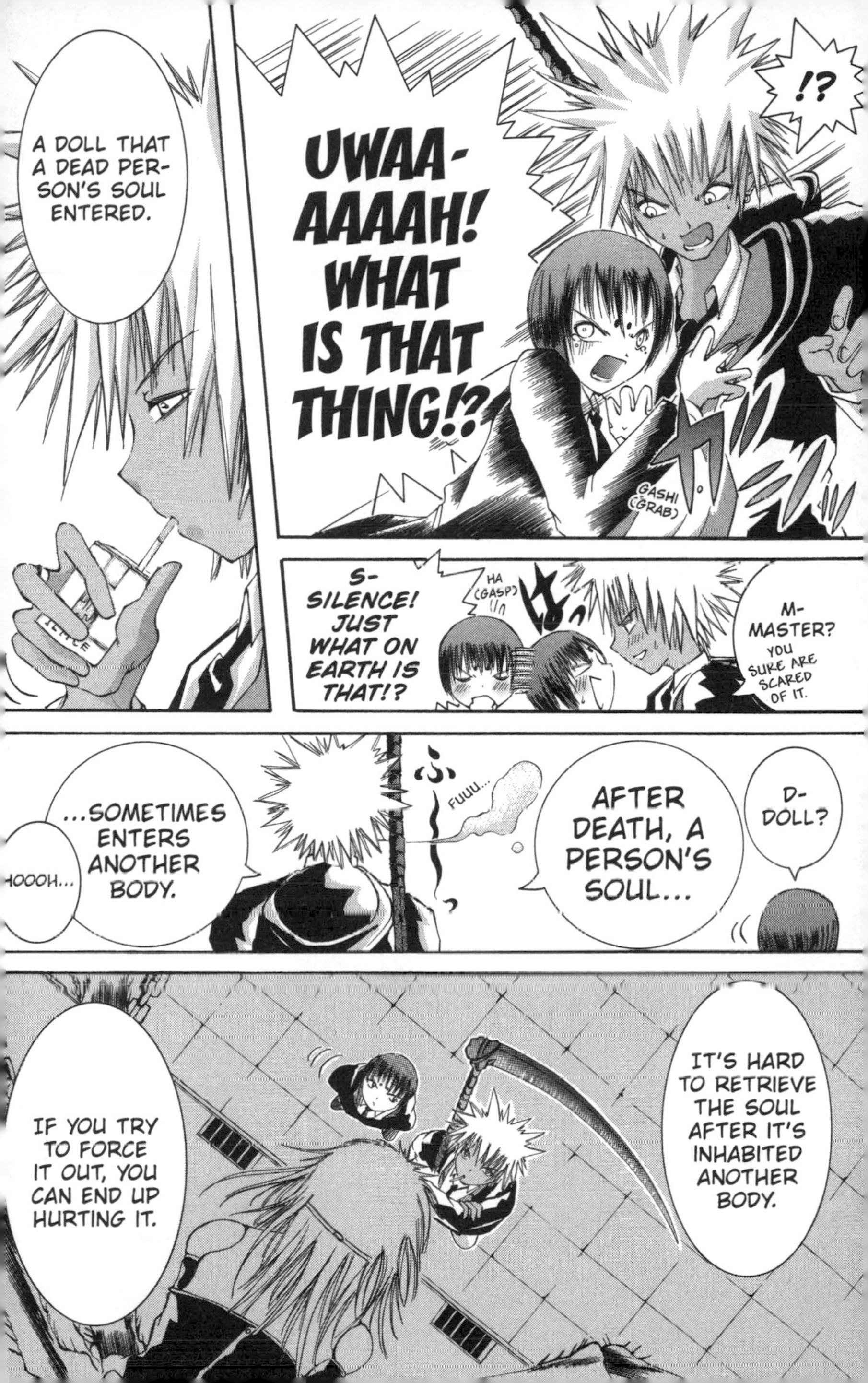
!?
UWAAA-AAAAH! WHAT IS THAT THING!?
GASHI (GRAB)
M-MASTER? YOU SURE ARE SCARED OF IT.
HA (GASP)
S-SILENCE! JUST WHAT ON EARTH IS THAT!?
A DOLL THAT A DEAD PERSON'S SOUL ENTERED.
D-DOLL?
AFTER DEATH, A PERSON'S SOUL...
FUUU...
...SOMETIMES ENTERS ANOTHER BODY.
HOOOH...
IT'S HARD TO RETRIEVE THE SOUL AFTER IT'S INHABITED ANOTHER BODY.
IF YOU TRY TO FORCE IT OUT, YOU CAN END UP HURTING IT.

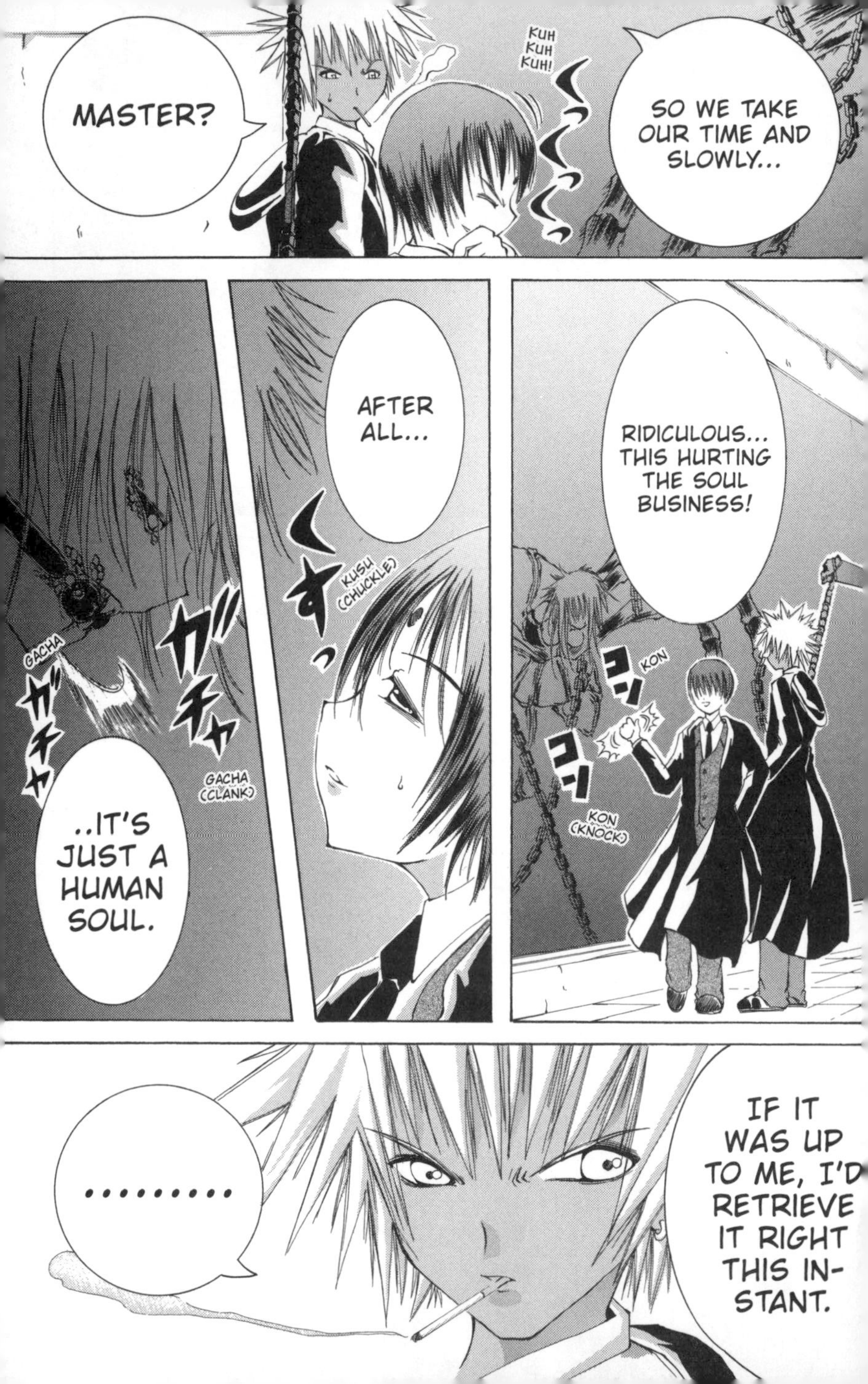
SO WE TAKE OUR TIME AND SLOWLY...
KUH KUH KUH!
MASTER?
RIDICULOUS... THIS HURTING THE SOUL BUSINESS!
KON
KON (KNOCK)
AFTER ALL...
KUSU (CHUCKLE)
GACHA
GACHA (CLANK)
..IT'S JUST A HUMAN SOUL.
IF IT WAS UP TO ME, I'D RETRIEVE IT RIGHT THIS IN-STANT.
....

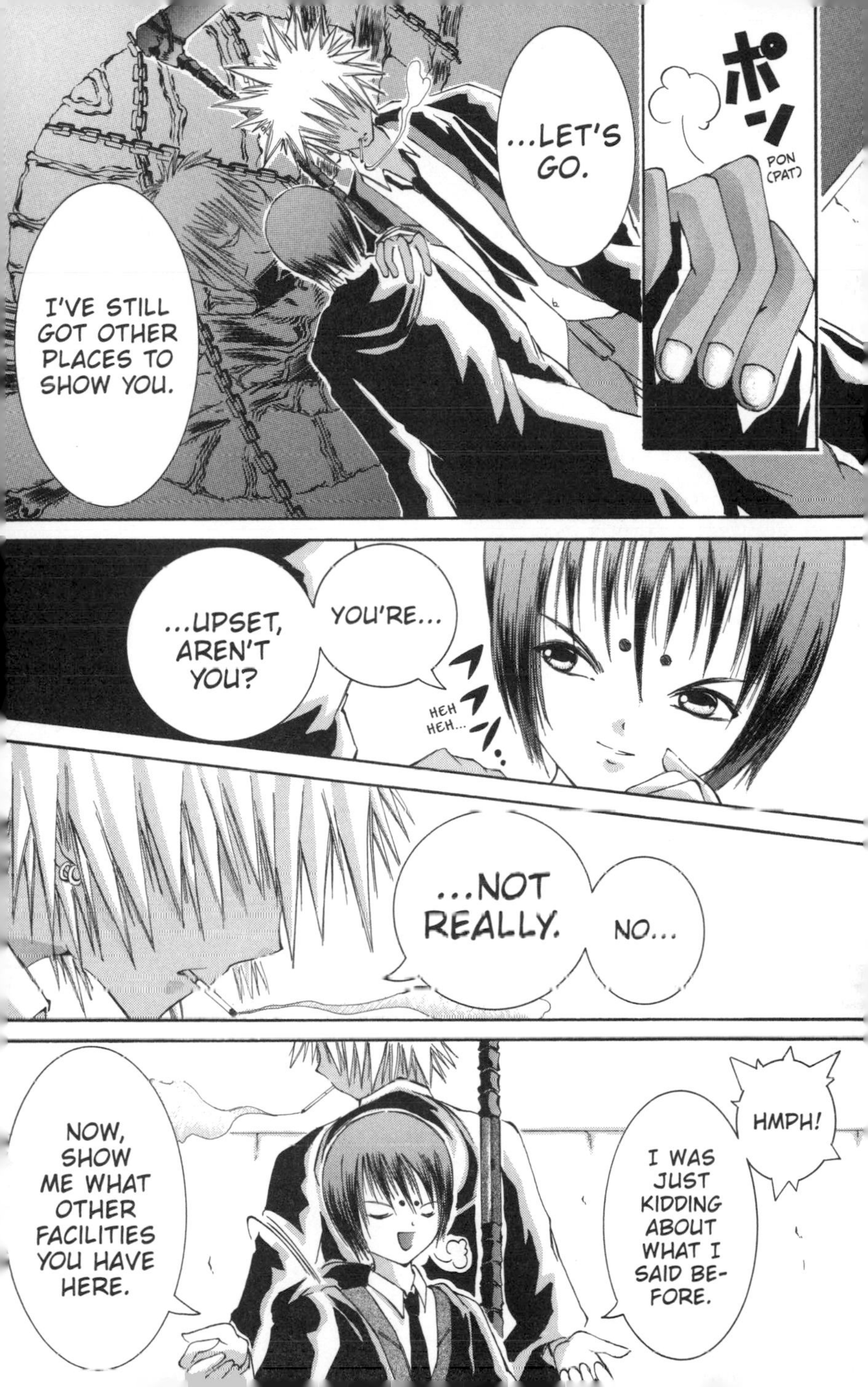
ポン
PON (PAT)
...LET'S GO.
I'VE STILL GOT OTHER PLACES TO SHOW YOU.
YOU'RE...
...UPSET, AREN'T YOU?
HEH HEH...
NO...
...NOT REALLY.
HMPH!
I WAS JUST KIDDING ABOUT WHAT I SAID BEFORE.
NOW, SHOW ME WHAT OTHER FACILITIES YOU HAVE HERE.

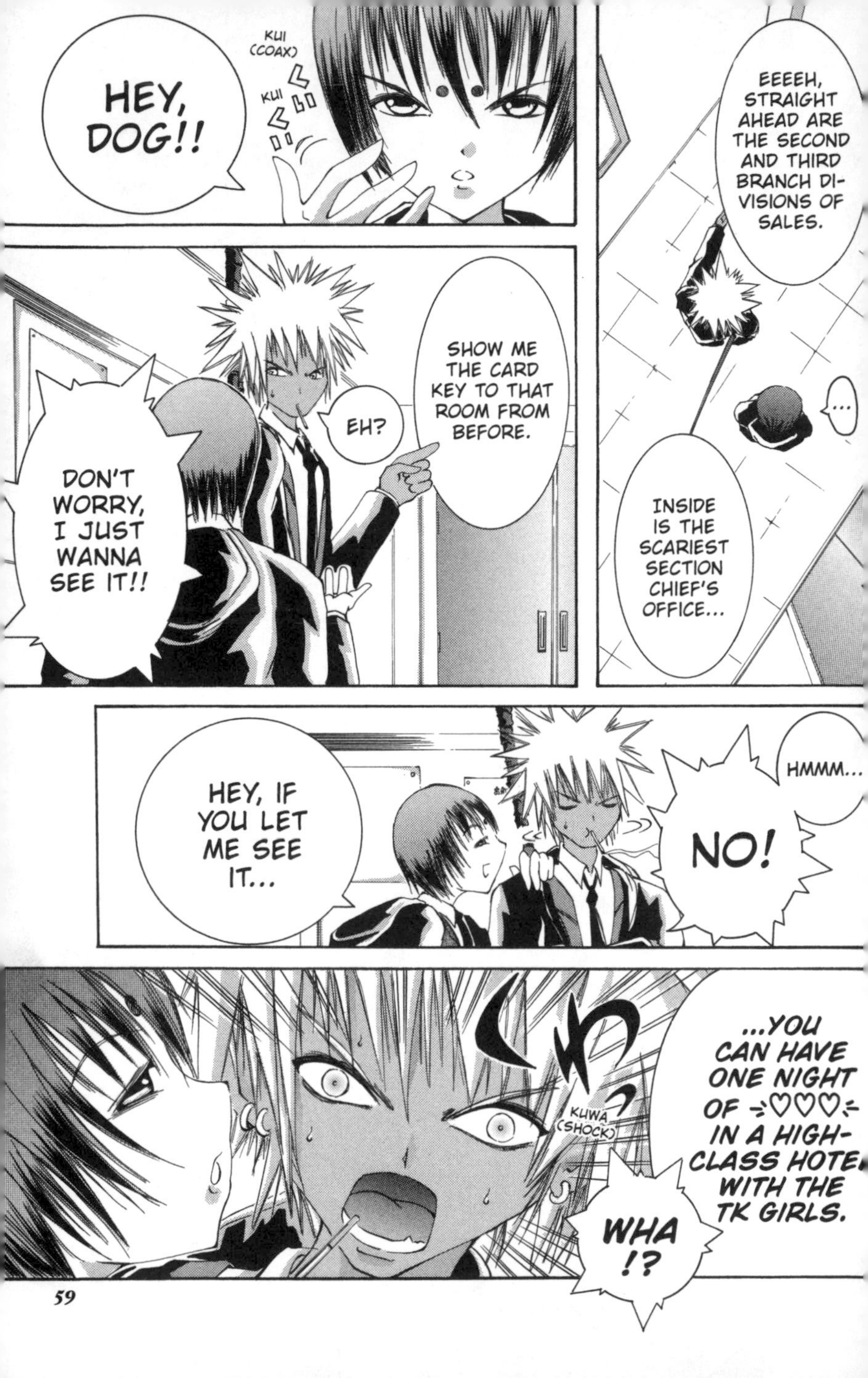
EEEEH, STRAIGHT AHEAD ARE THE SECOND AND THIRD BRANCH DI-VISIONS OF SALES.
...
INSIDE IS THE SCARIEST SECTION CHIEF'S OFFICE...
KUI (COAX) KUI
HEY, DOG!!
SHOW ME THE CARD KEY TO THAT ROOM FROM BEFORE.
EH?
DON'T WORRY, I JUST WANNA SEE IT!!
HMMM...
NO!
HEY, IF YOU LET ME SEE IT...
...YOU CAN HAVE ONE NIGHT OF ♡♡♡ IN A HIGH-CLASS HOTE WITH THE TK GIRLS.
KUWA (SHOCK)
WHA!?

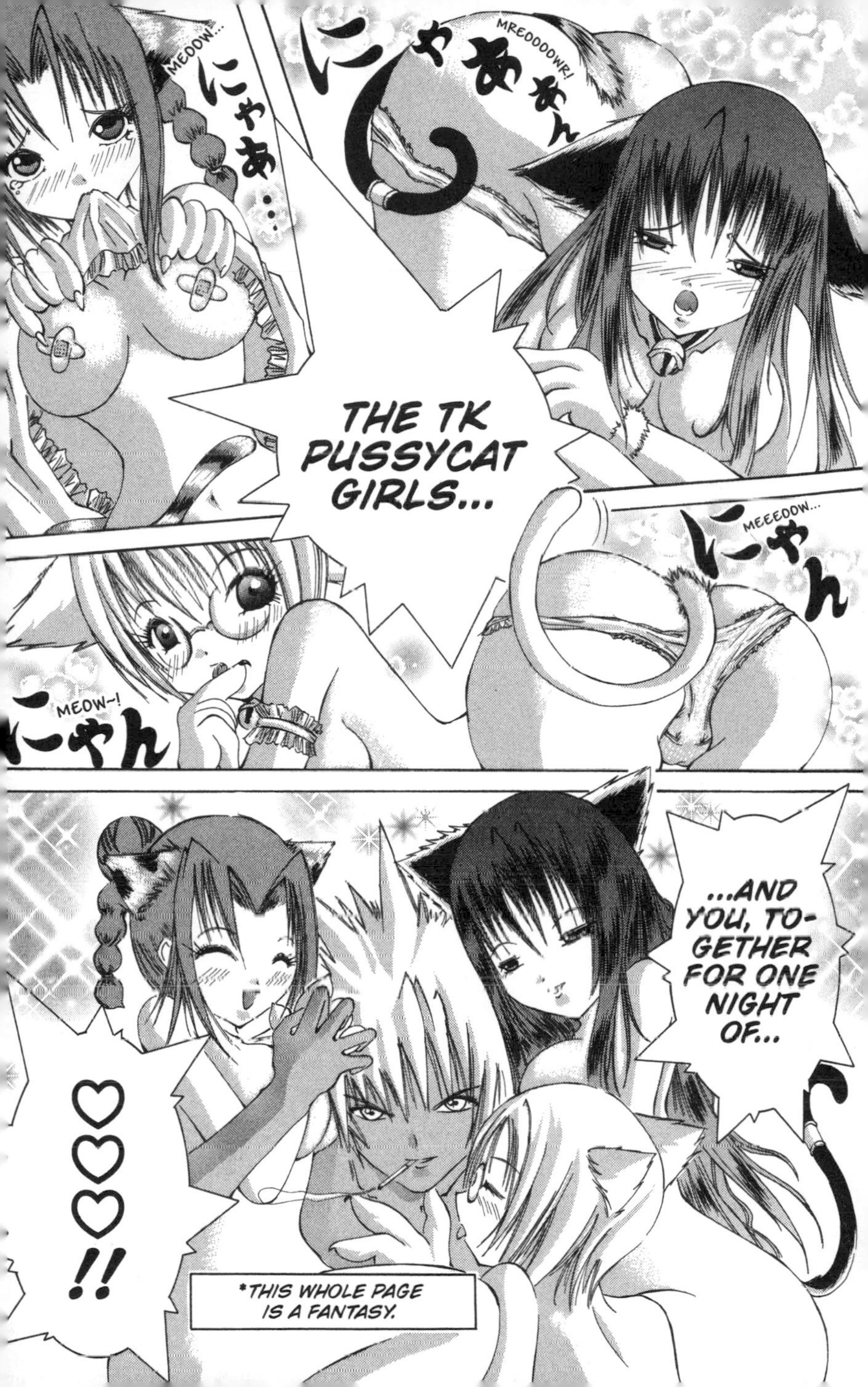
MREOOOOWR!
にゃあぁん
MEOOW...
にゃあ...
THE TK PUSSYCAT GIRLS...
MEEEOW...
にゃん
MEOW~!
にゃん
...AND YOU, TOGETHER FOR ONE NIGHT OF...
♡♡♡!!
*THIS WHOLE PAGE IS A FANTASY.

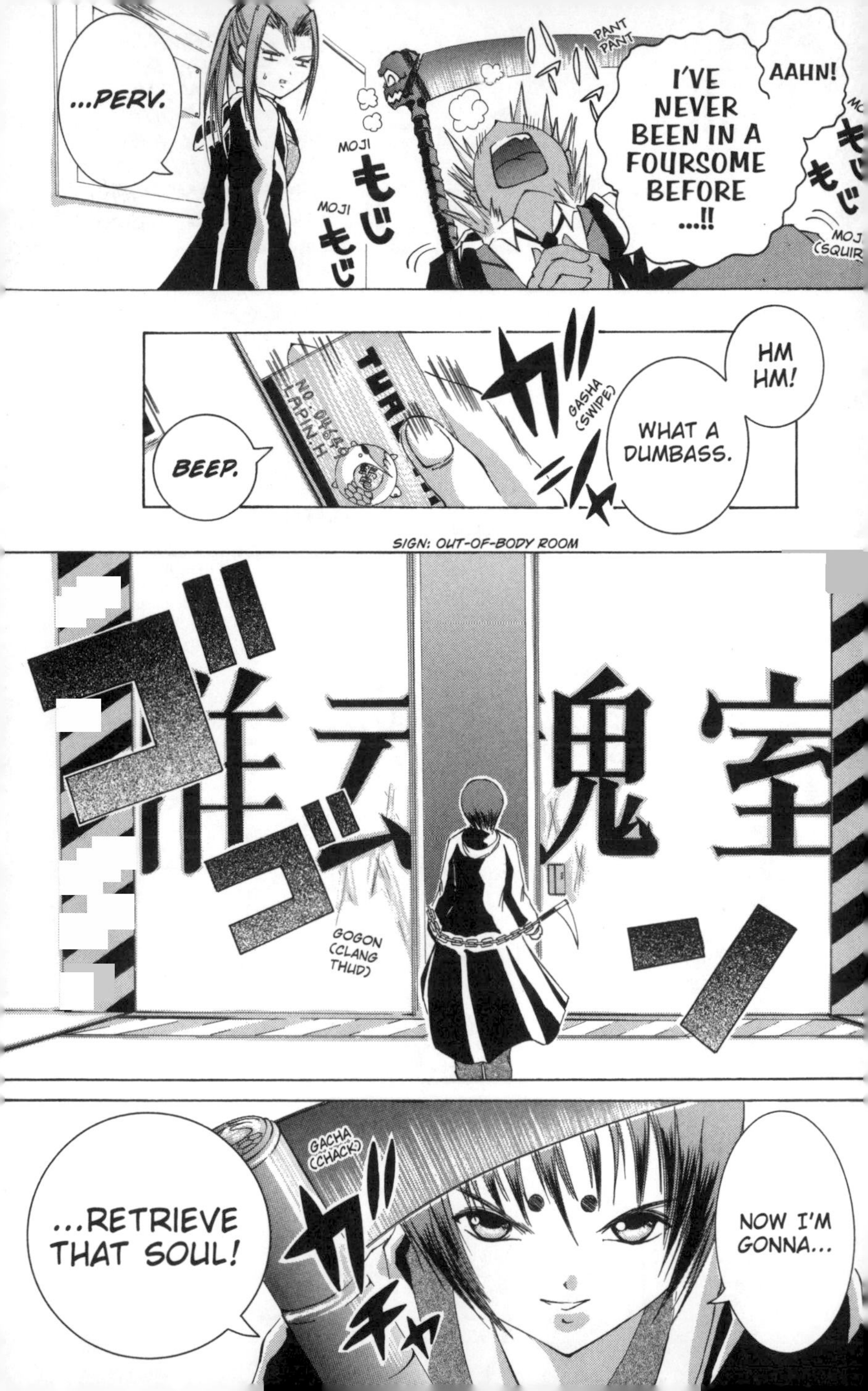
AAHN!
I'VE NEVER BEEN IN A FOURSOME BEFORE ...!!
PANT PANT
MOJI MOJI
...PERV.
HM HM!
WHAT A DUMBASS.
GASHA (SWIPE)
NO. 04649
LAPIN.H
BEEP.
SIGN: OUT-OF-BODY ROOM
GOGON (CLANG THUD)
NOW I'M GONNA...
GACHA (CHACK)
...RETRIEVE THAT SOUL!

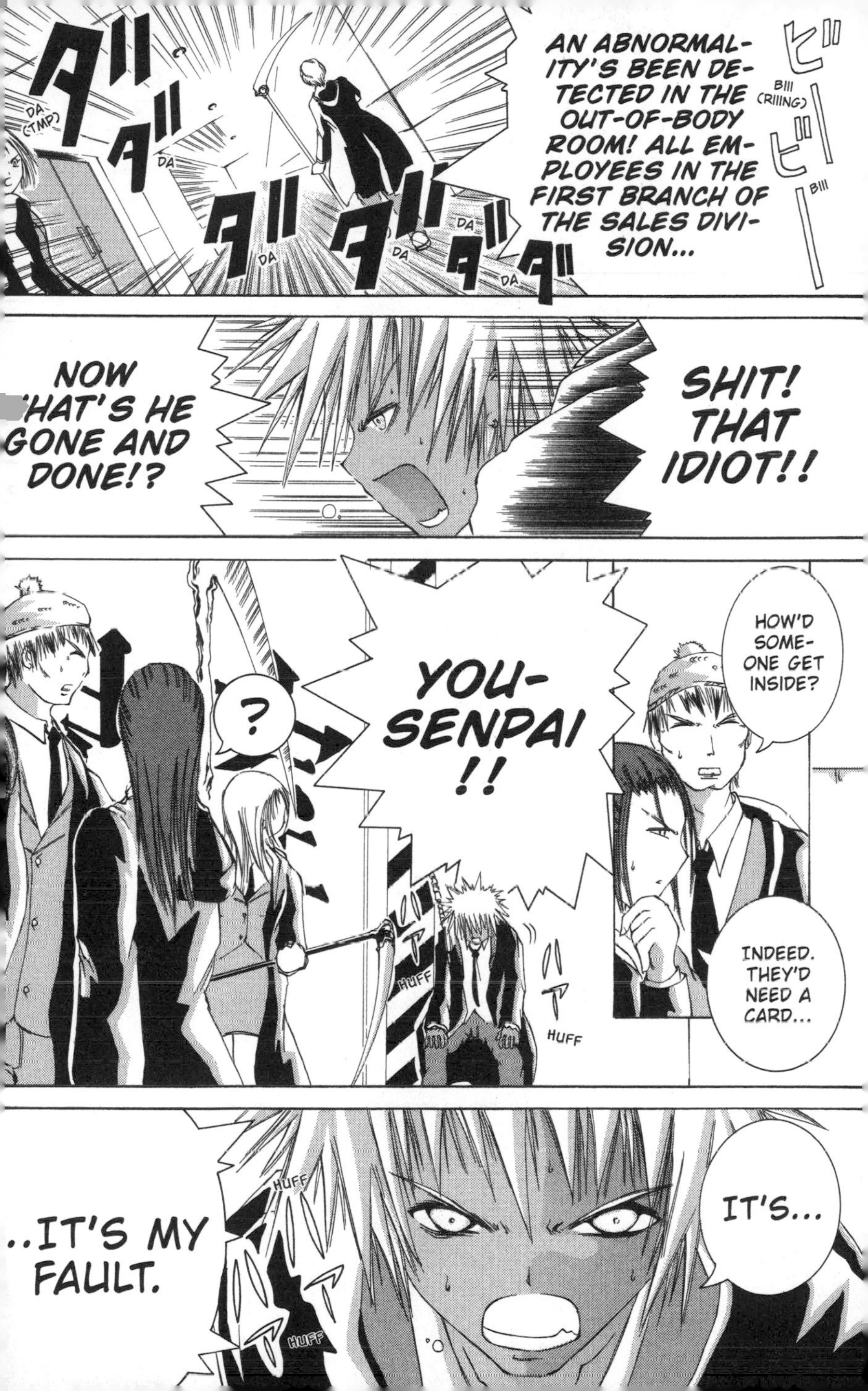
BIII (RIIING)
BIII
AN ABNORMALITY'S BEEN DETECTED IN THE OUT-OF-BODY ROOM! ALL EMPLOYEES IN THE FIRST BRANCH OF THE SALES DIVISION...
DA
DA
DA
DA
DA (TMP)
SHIT! THAT IDIOT!!
NOW 'HAT'S HE GONE AND DONE!?
HOW'D SOMEONE GET INSIDE?
INDEED. THEY'D NEED A CARD...
HUFF
YOU-SENPAI!!
HUFF
?
IT'S...
HUFF
..IT'S MY FAULT.
HUFF

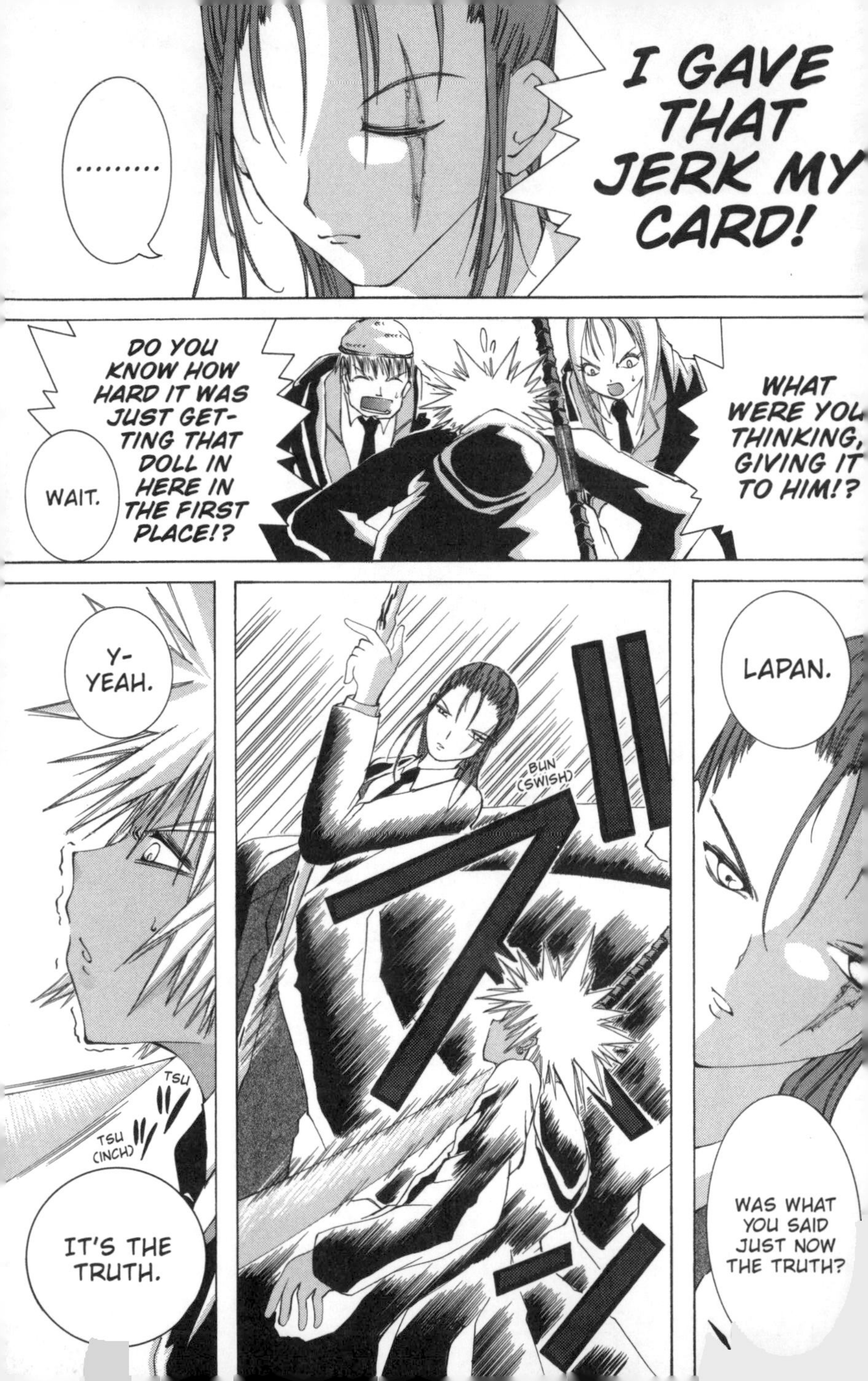

I GAVE THAT JERK MY CARD!
....
WHAT WERE YOU THINKING, GIVING IT TO HIM!?
DO YOU KNOW HOW HARD IT WAS JUST GET-TING THAT DOLL IN HERE IN THE FIRST PLACE!?
WAIT.
LAPAN.
WAS WHAT YOU SAID JUST NOW THE TRUTH?
BUN (SWISH)
Y-YEAH.
TSU
TSU (INCH)
IT'S THE TRUTH.

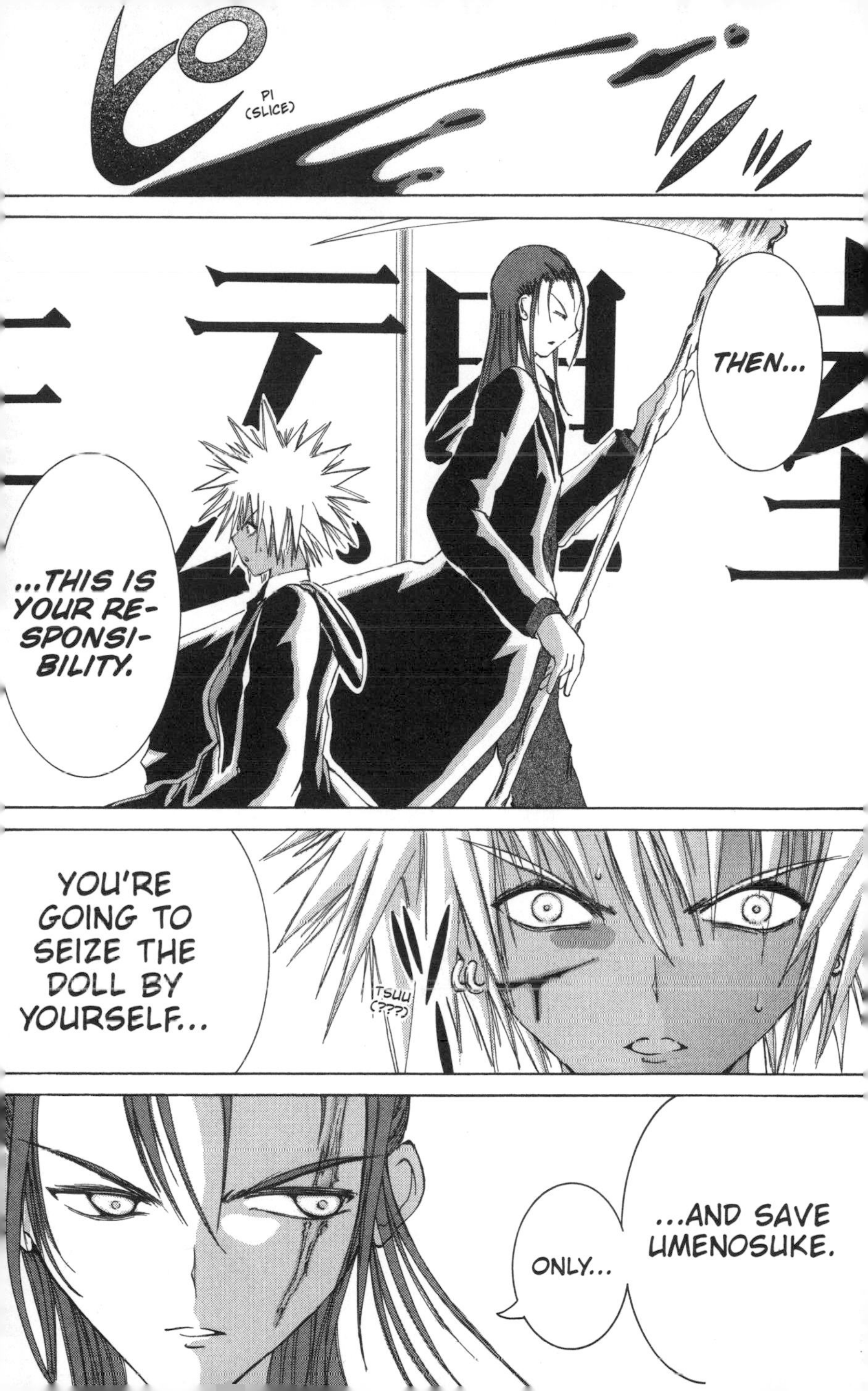
PI
(SLICE)
THEN...
...THIS IS YOUR RE-SPONSI-BILITY.
TSUU
(???)
YOU'RE GOING TO SEIZE THE DOLL BY YOURSELF...
...AND SAVE UMENOSUKE.
ONLY...

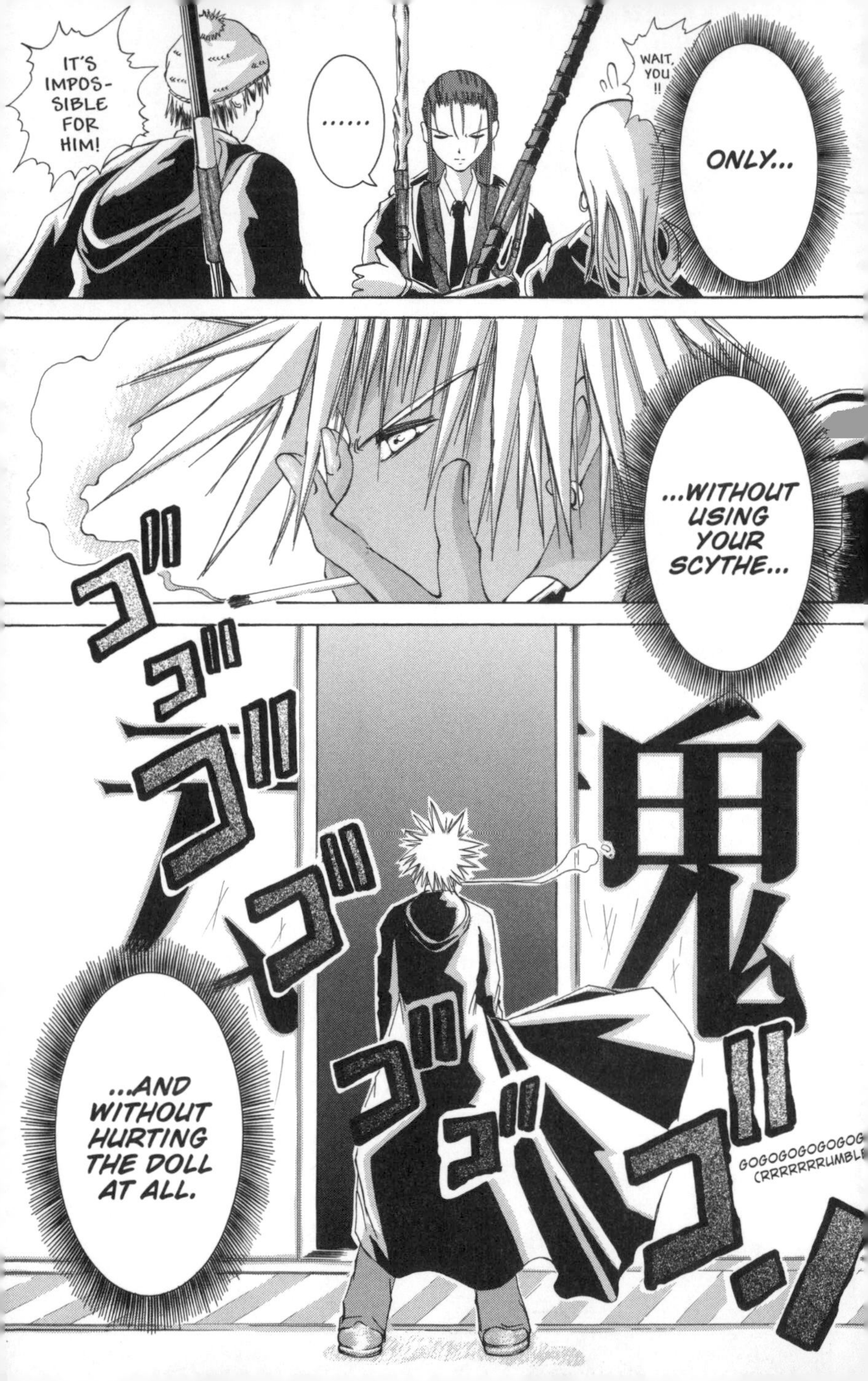
ONLY...
WAIT, YOU !!
......
IT'S IMPOS-SIBLE FOR HIM!
...WITHOUT USING YOUR SCYTHE...
GOGOGOGOGOGOG (RRRRRRRUMBLE
...AND WITHOUT HURTING THE DOLL AT ALL.

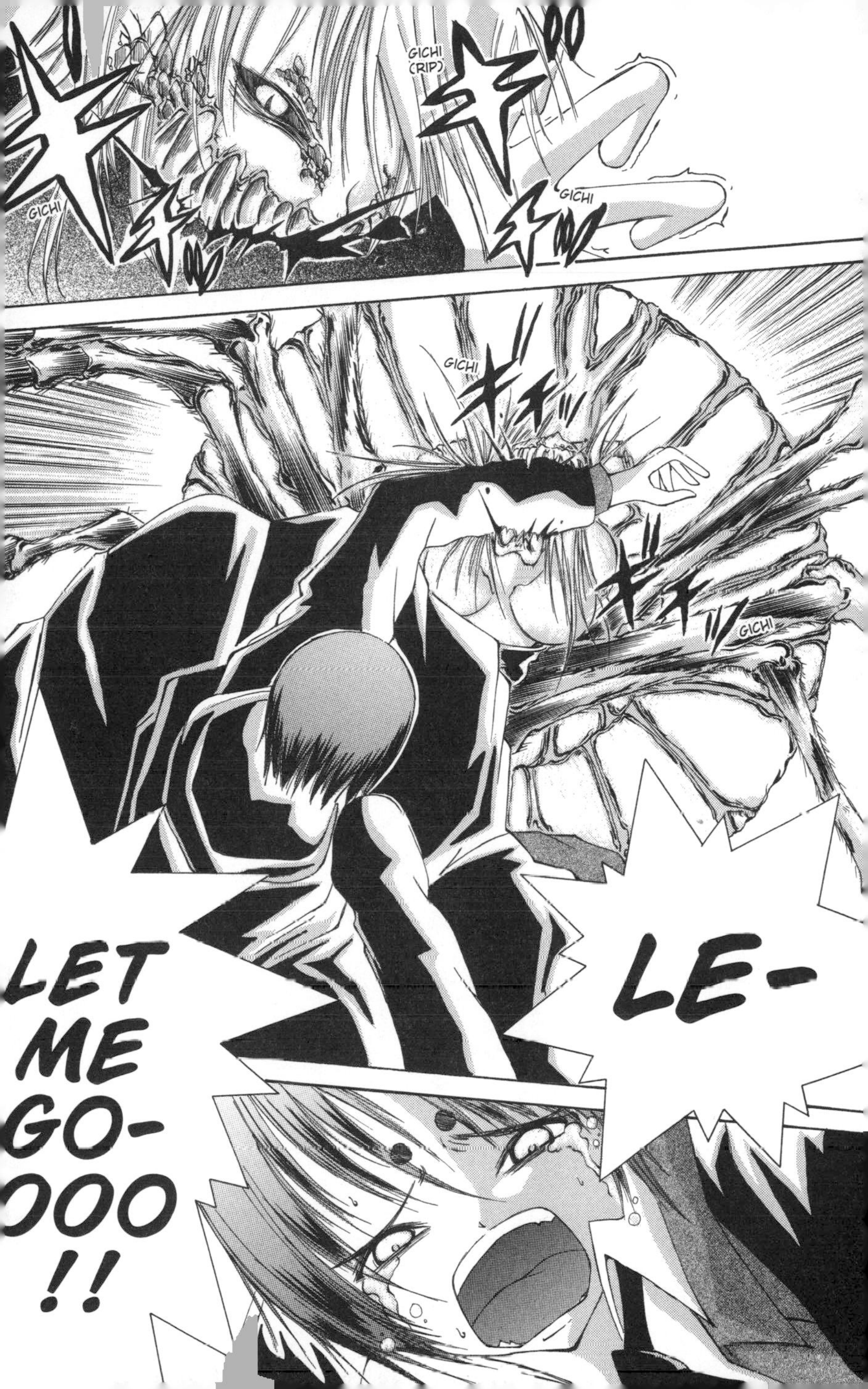
GICHI (RIP)
GICHI
GICHI
GICHI
GICHI
LE-
LET ME GO-OOO!!

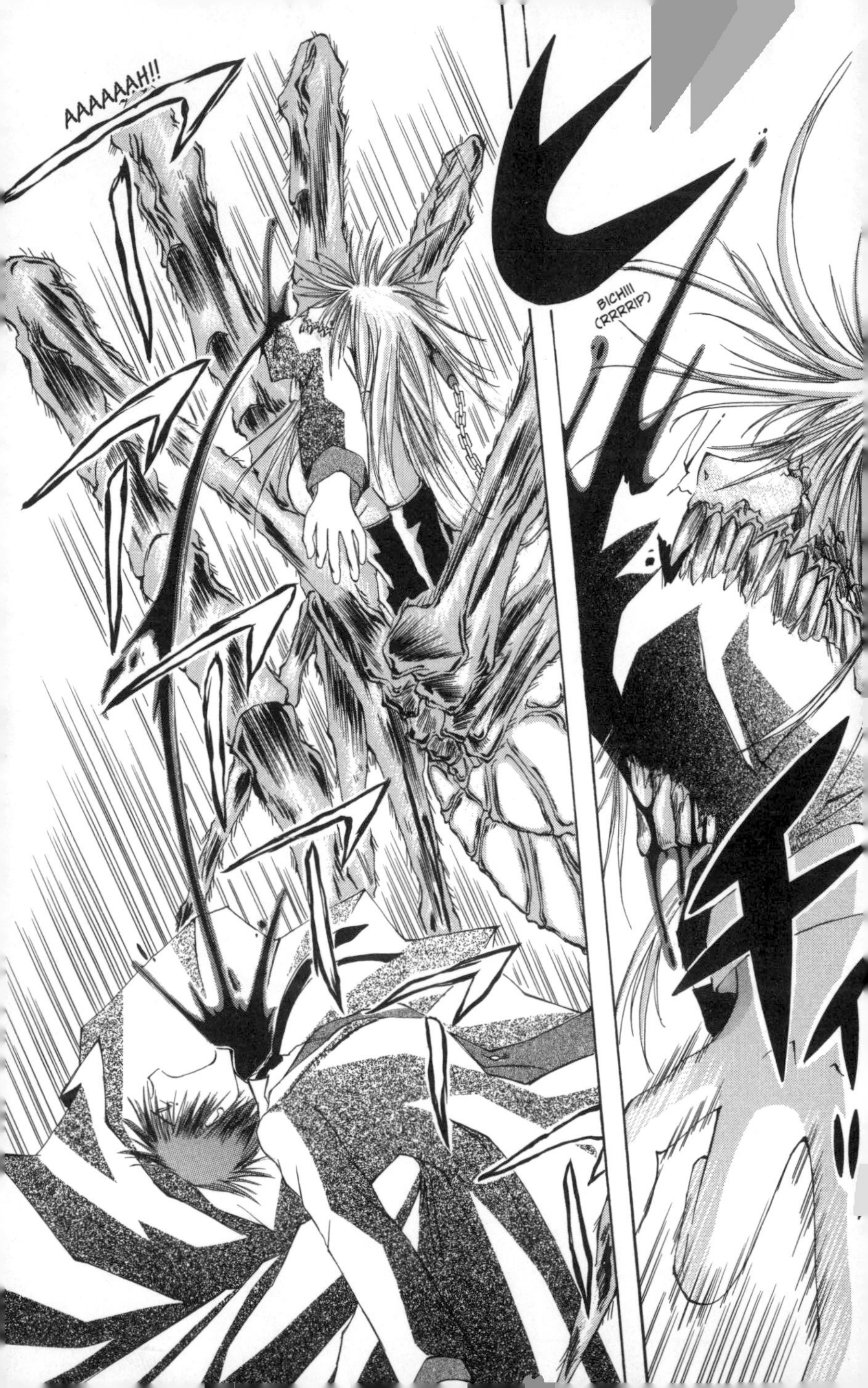
BICHIII
(RRRRIP)
AAAAAAH!!

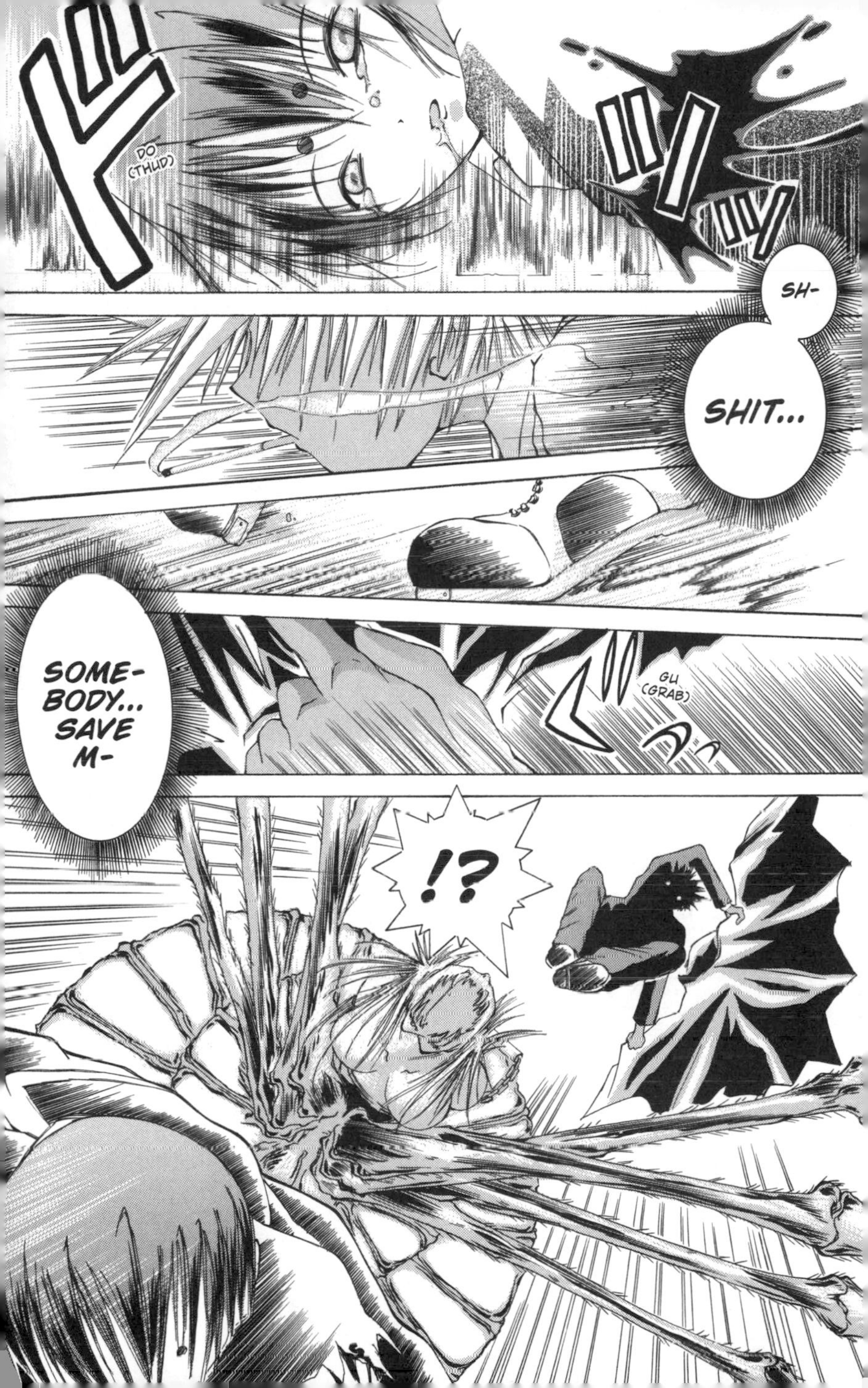
DO (THUD)
SH-
SHIT...
GU (GRAB)
SOME-BODY... SAVE M-
!?

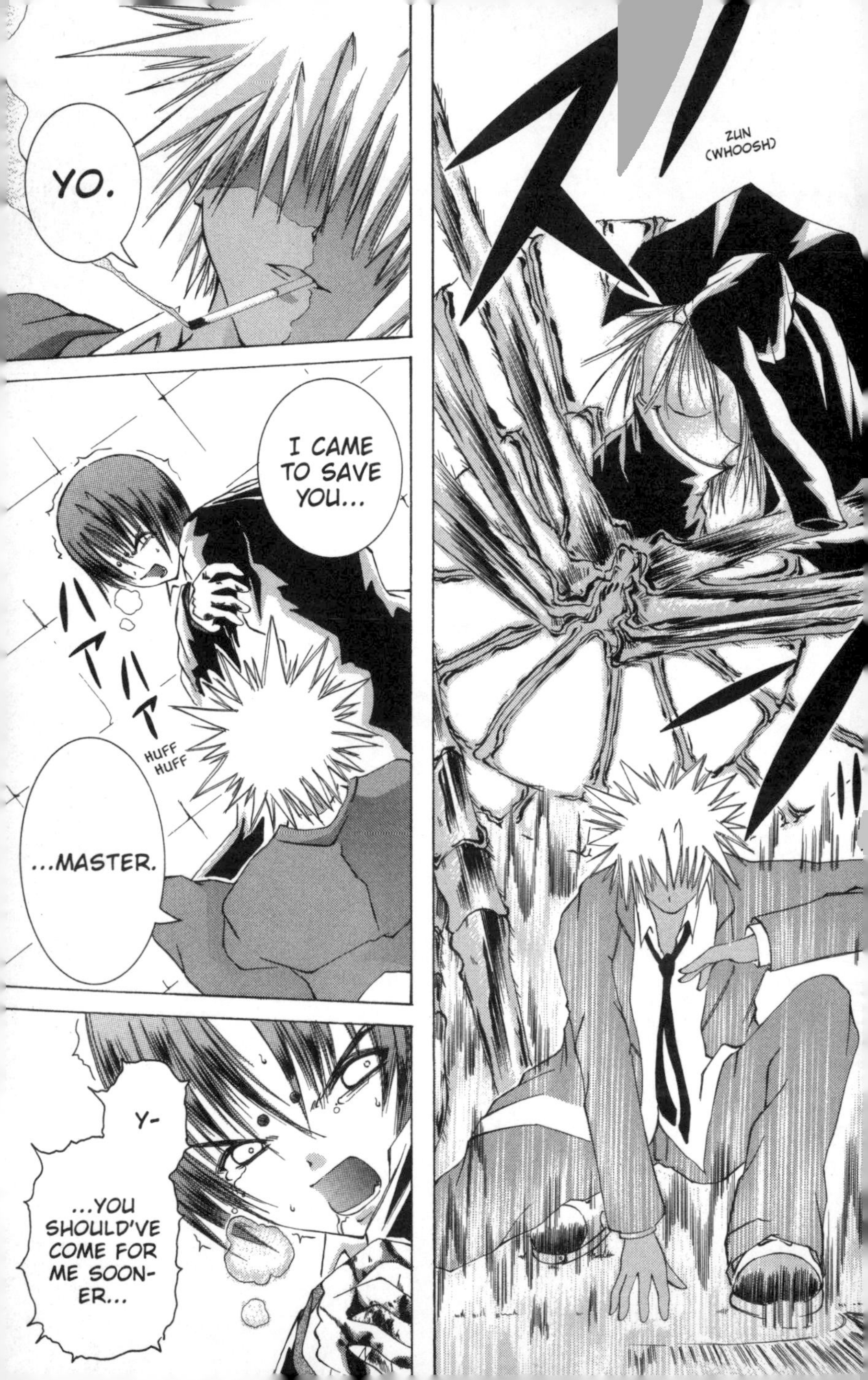
ZUN
(WHOOSH)
YO.
I CAME TO SAVE YOU...
HUFF HUFF
...MASTER.
Y-
...YOU SHOULD'VE COME FOR ME SOON-ER...

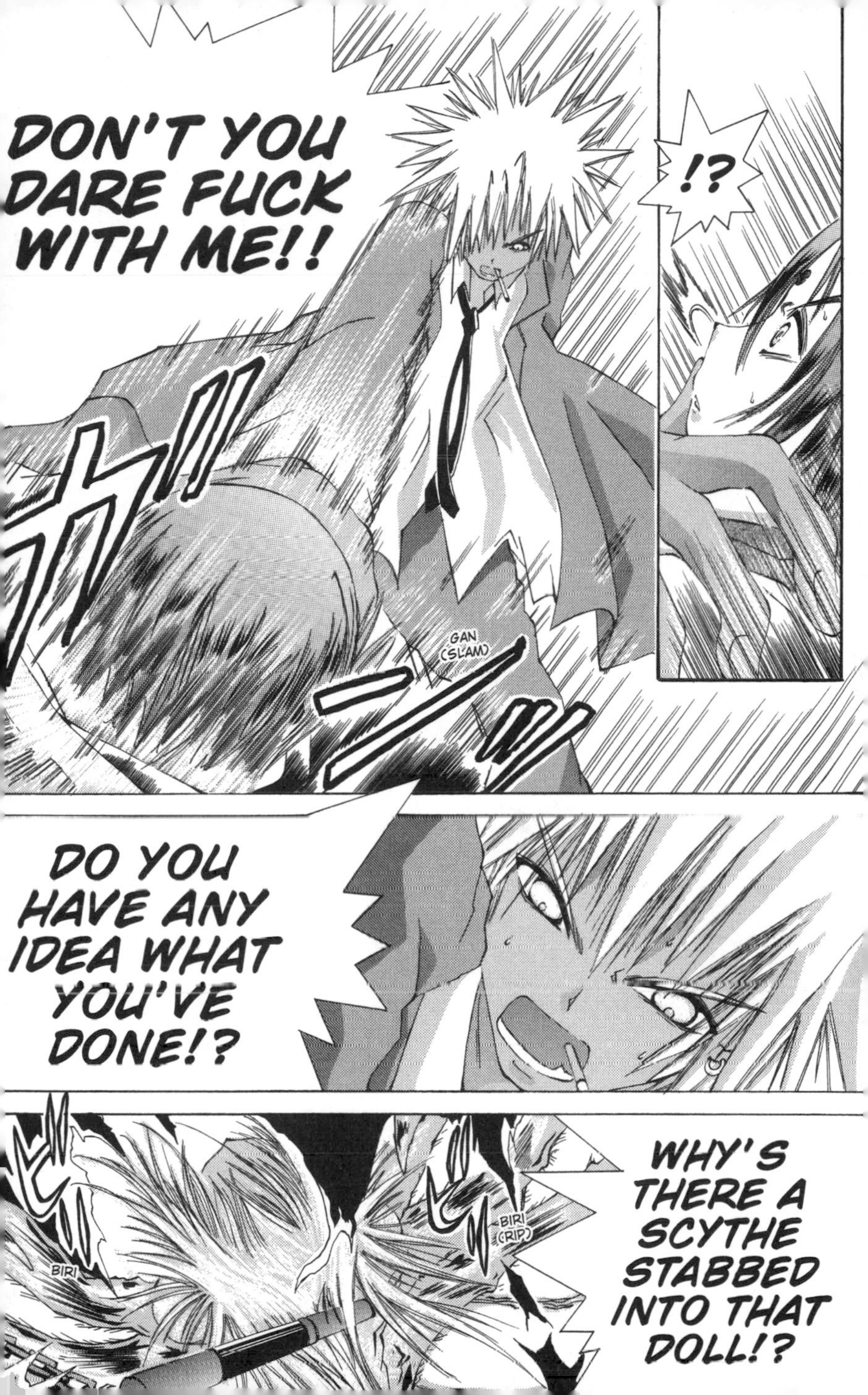
DON'T YOU DARE FUCK WITH ME!!
GAN (SLAM)
!?
DO YOU HAVE ANY IDEA WHAT YOU'VE DONE!?
WHY'S THERE A SCYTHE STABBED INTO THAT DOLL!?
BIRI (RIP)
BIRI

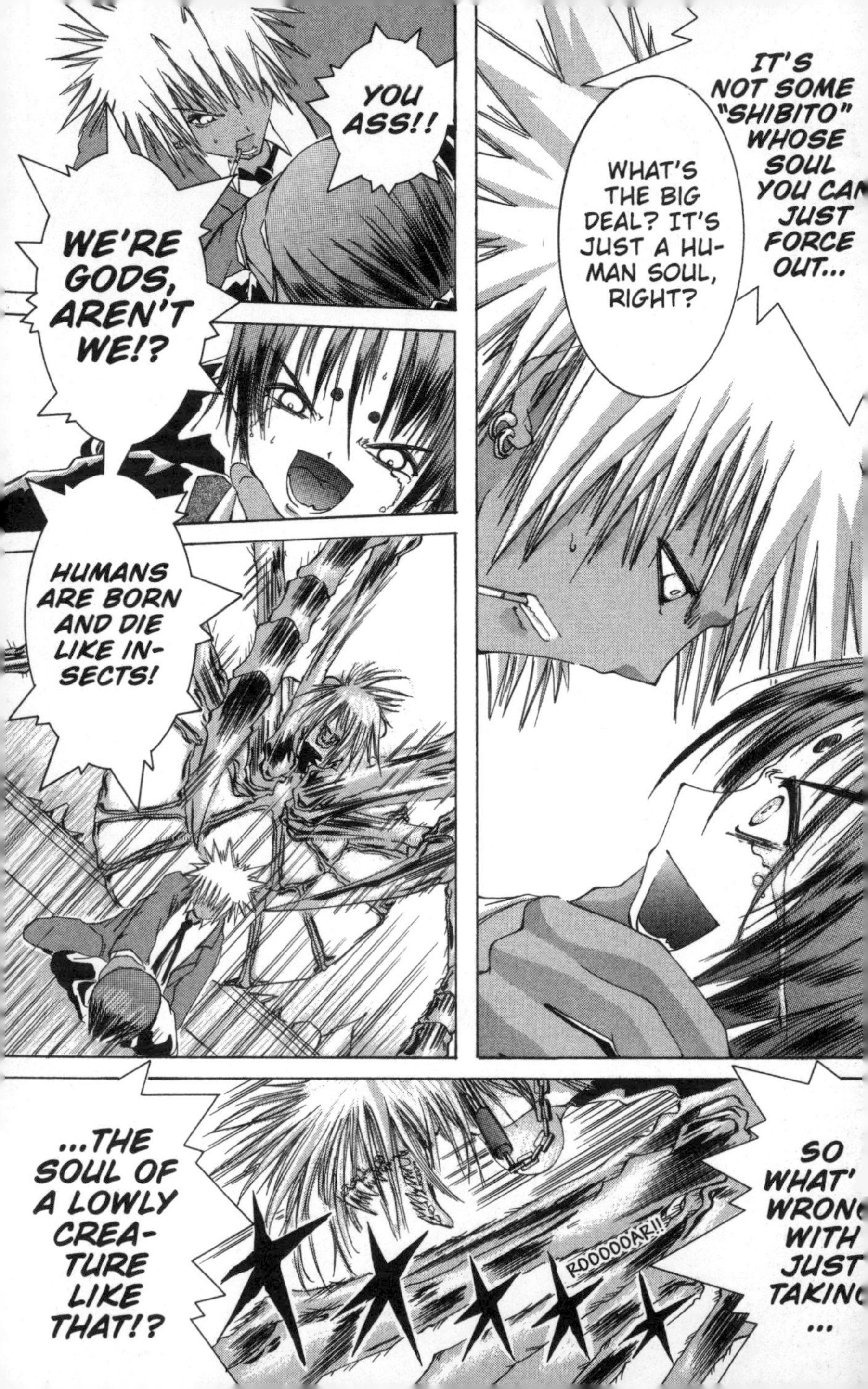
IT'S NOT SOME "SHIBITO" WHOSE SOUL YOU CAN JUST FORCE OUT...
WHAT'S THE BIG DEAL? IT'S JUST A HU-MAN SOUL, RIGHT?
YOU ASS!!
WE'RE GODS, AREN'T WE!?
HUMANS ARE BORN AND DIE LIKE IN-SECTS!
SO WHAT' WRONG WITH JUST TAKING ...
ROOOOOAR!!
...THE SOUL OF A LOWLY CREA-TURE LIKE THAT!?

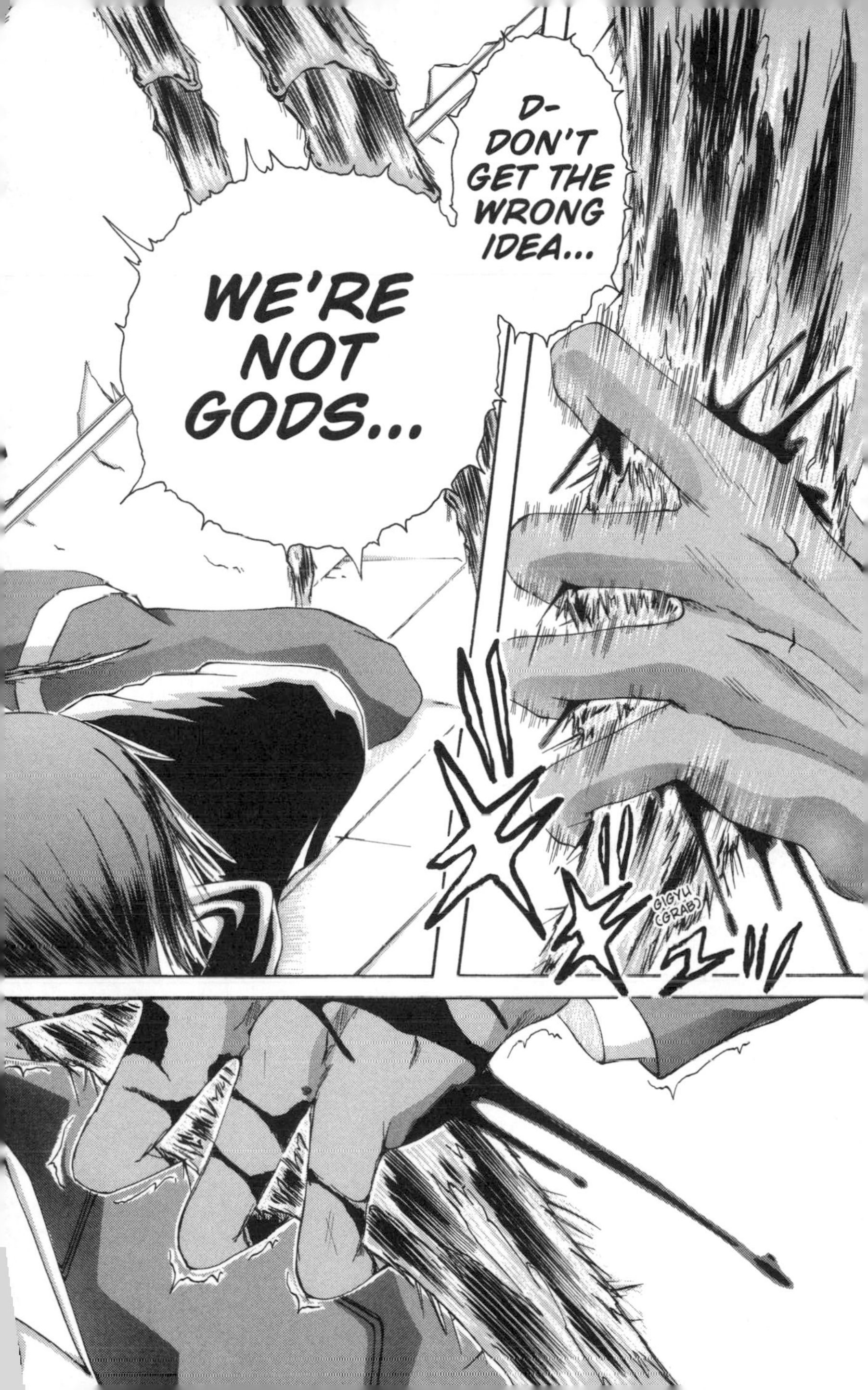
D-
DON'T
GET THE
WRONG
IDEA...
WE'RE
NOT
GODS...
GIGYU
(GRAB)

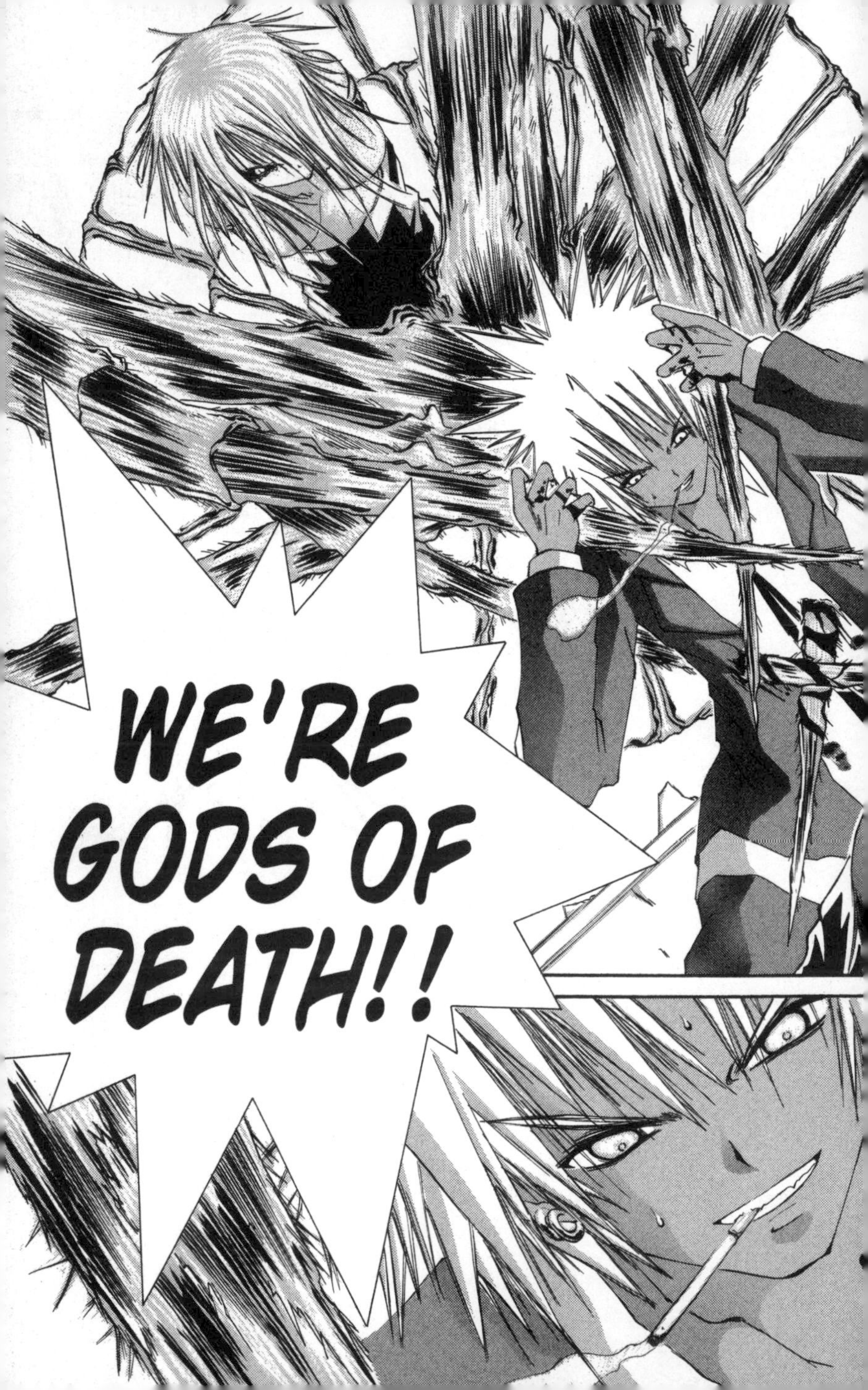
WE'RE GODS OF DEATH!!

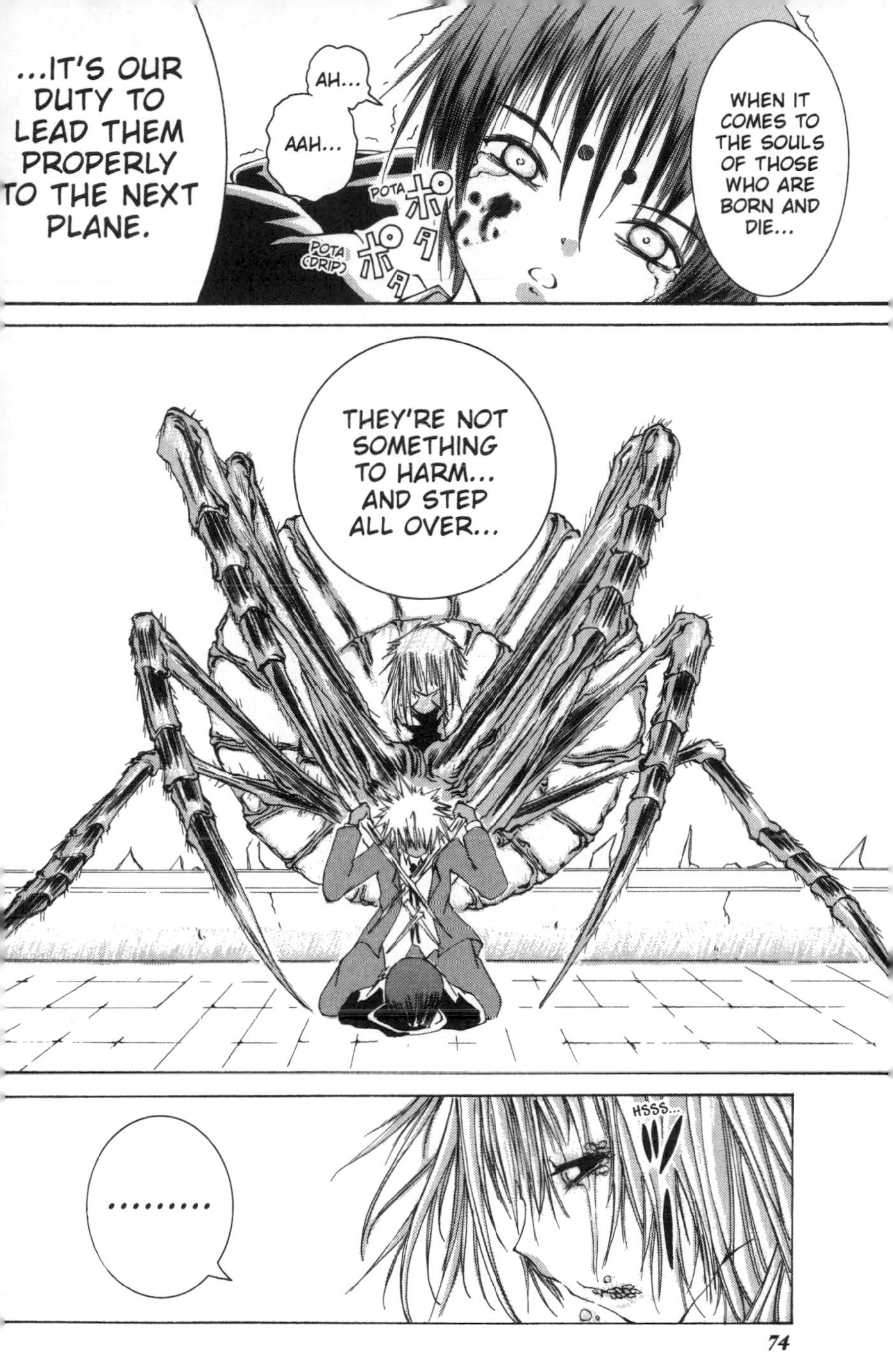

WHEN IT COMES TO THE SOULS OF THOSE WHO ARE BORN AND DIE...
POTA
POTA (DRIP)
AH...
AAH...
...IT'S OUR DUTY TO LEAD THEM PROPERLY TO THE NEXT PLANE.
THEY'RE NOT SOMETHING TO HARM... AND STEP ALL OVER...
HSSS...
....

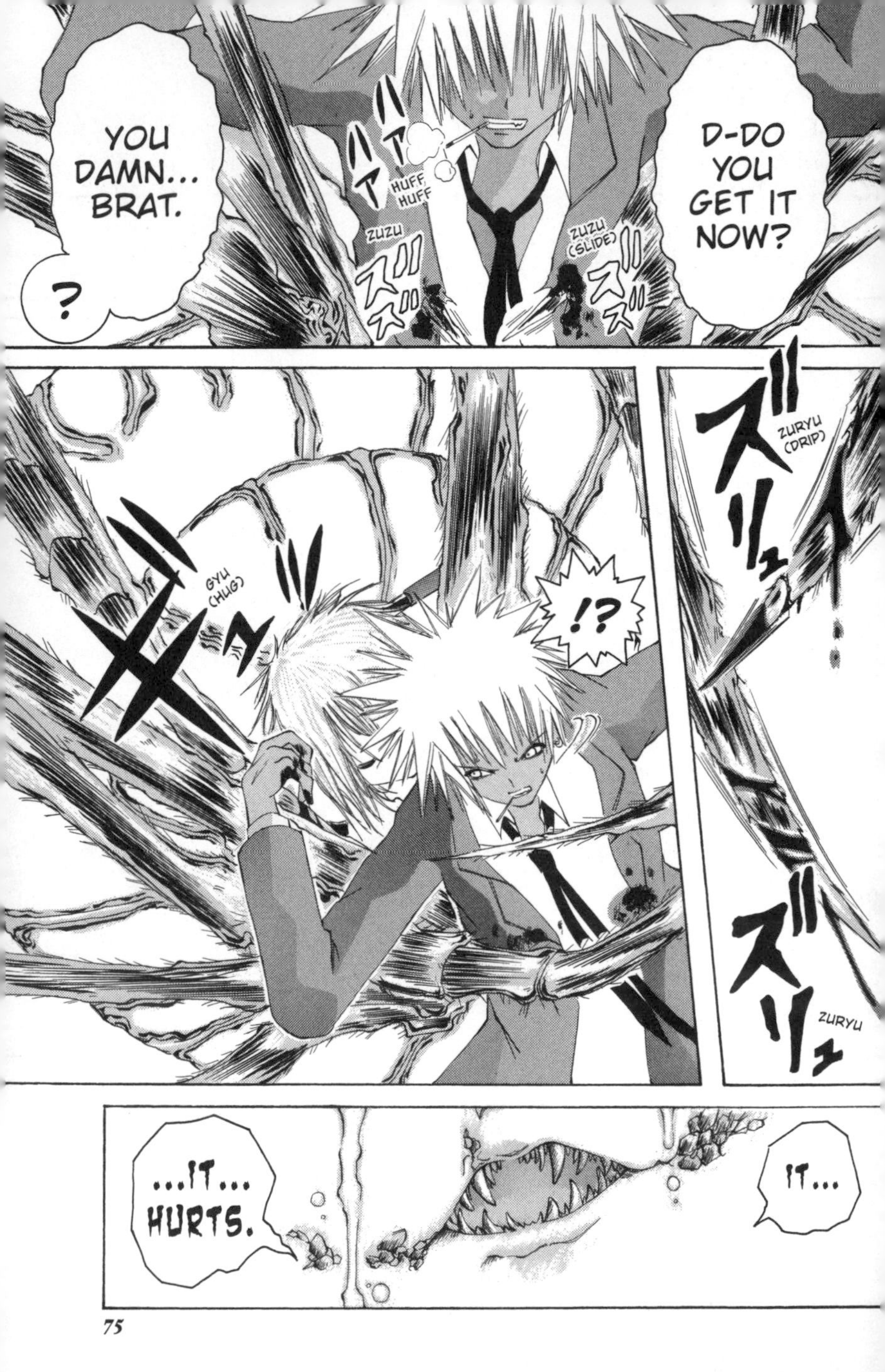
D-DO YOU GET IT NOW?
HUFF HUFF
YOU DAMN... BRAT.
ZUZU (SLIDE)
ZUZU
?
ZURYU (DRIP)
ZURYU
!?
GYU (HUG)
IT...
...IT... HURTS.

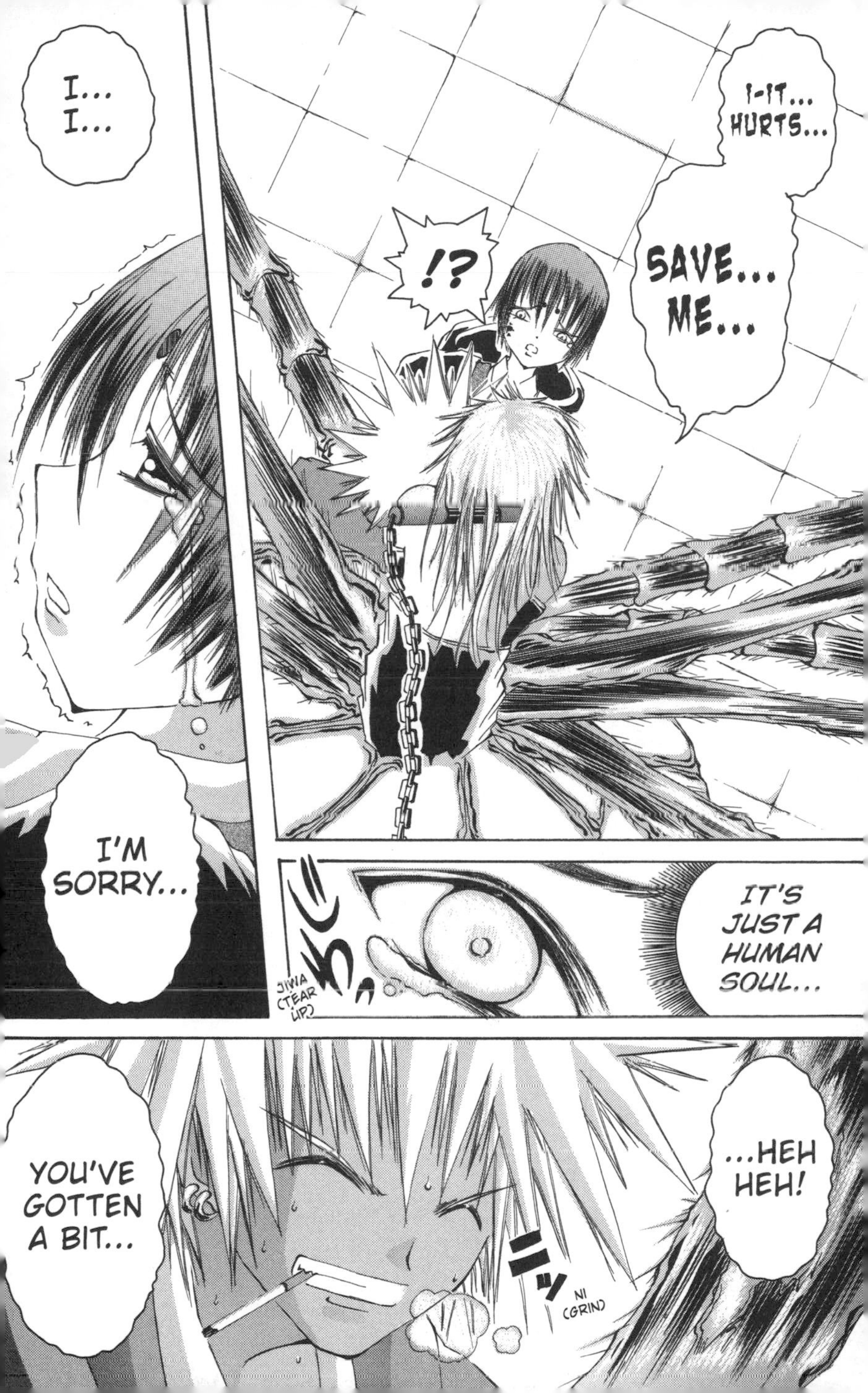
I-IT... HURTS...
SAVE... ME...
!?
IT'S JUST A HUMAN SOUL...
JIWA (TEAR UP)
I... I...
I'M SORRY...
...HEH HEH!
NI (GRIN)
YOU'VE GOTTEN A BIT...

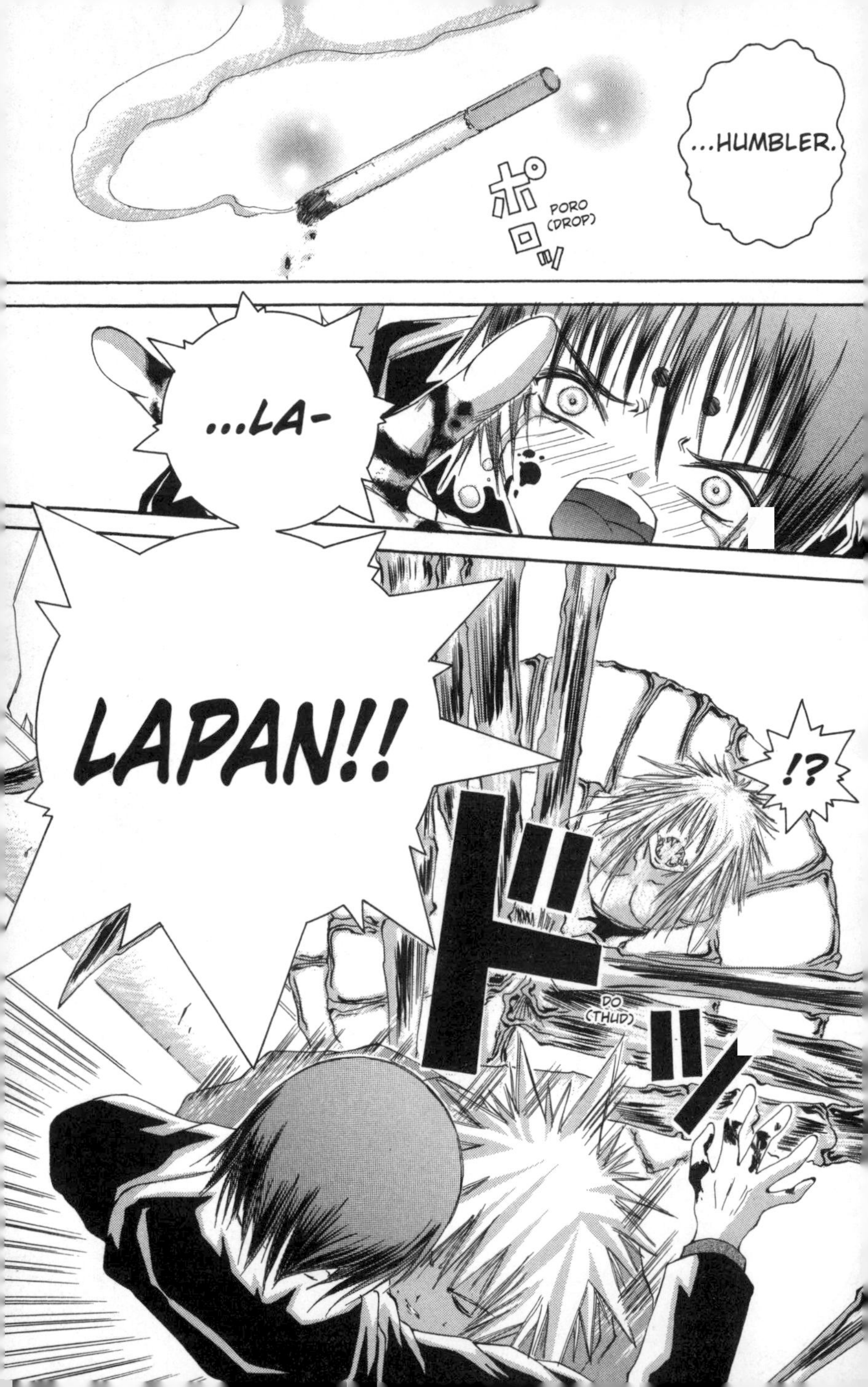
...HUMBLER.
ポロッ
PORO (DROP)
...LA-
LAPAN!!
!?
ドッ
DO (THUD)

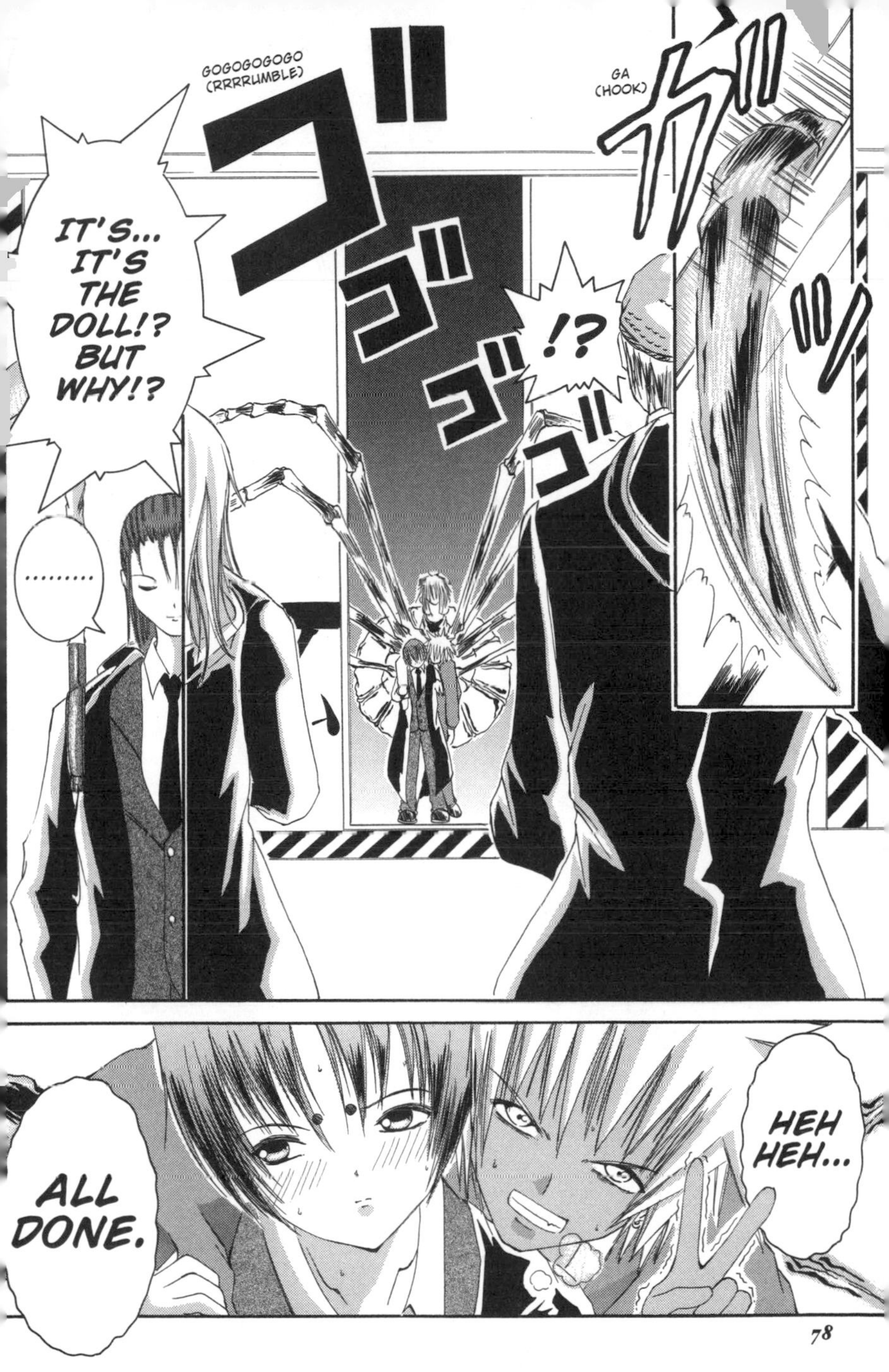
GA (HOOK)
!?
GOGOGOGOGO (RRRRUMBLE)
IT'S... IT'S THE DOLL!? BUT WHY!?
....
HEH HEH...
ALL DONE.

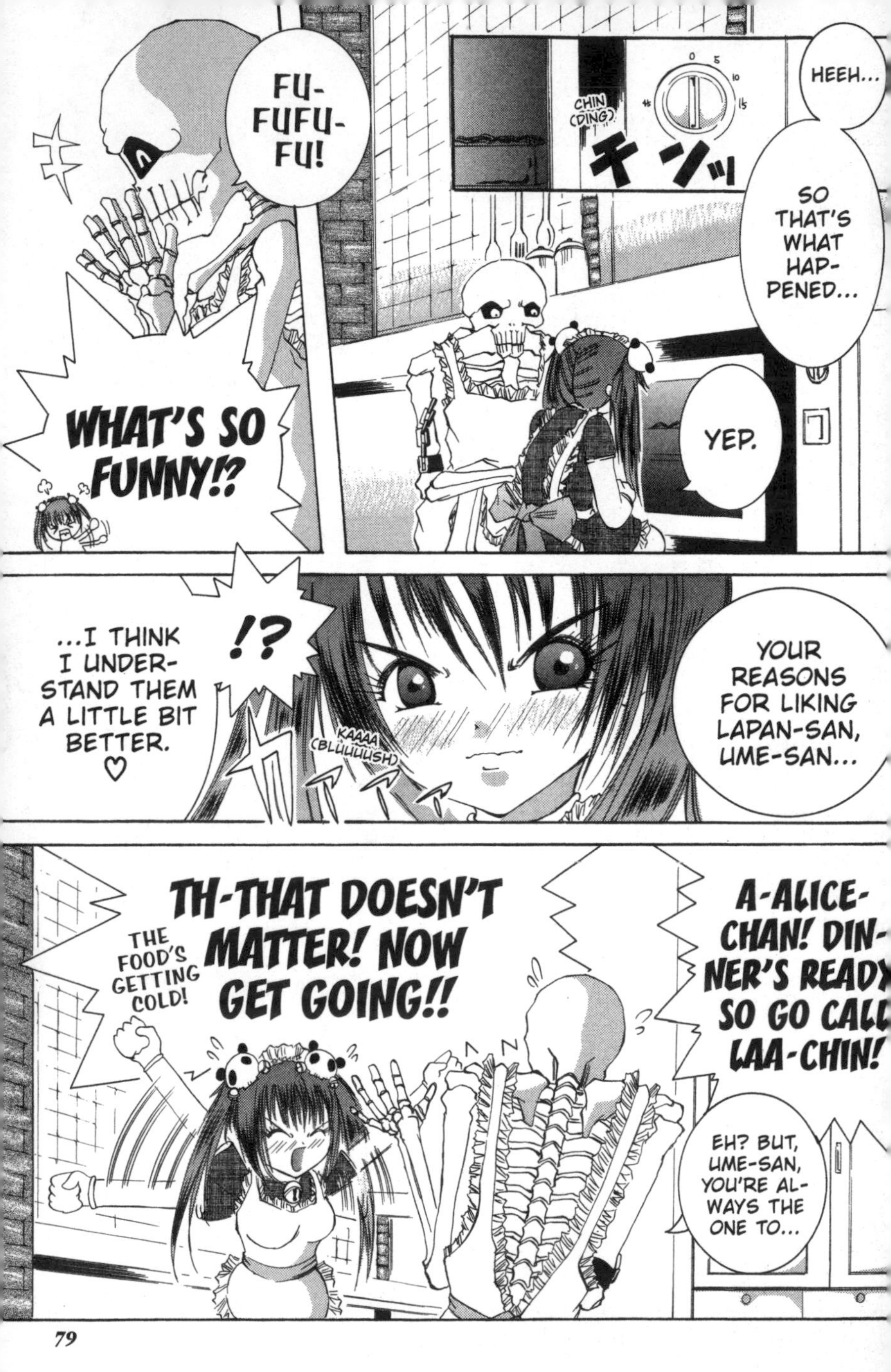
HEEH...
SO THAT'S WHAT HAP-PENED...
CHIN (DING)
チンッ
YEP.
FU-FUFU-FU!
WHAT'S SO FUNNY!?
YOUR REASONS FOR LIKING LAPAN-SAN, UME-SAN...
...I THINK I UNDER-STAND THEM A LITTLE BIT BETTER. ♡
!?
KAAAA (BLUUUUSH)
A-ALICE-CHAN! DIN-NER'S READY SO GO CALL LAA-CHIN!
EH? BUT, UME-SAN, YOU'RE AL-WAYS THE ONE TO...
TH-THAT DOESN'T MATTER! NOW GET GOING!!
THE FOOD'S GETTING COLD!

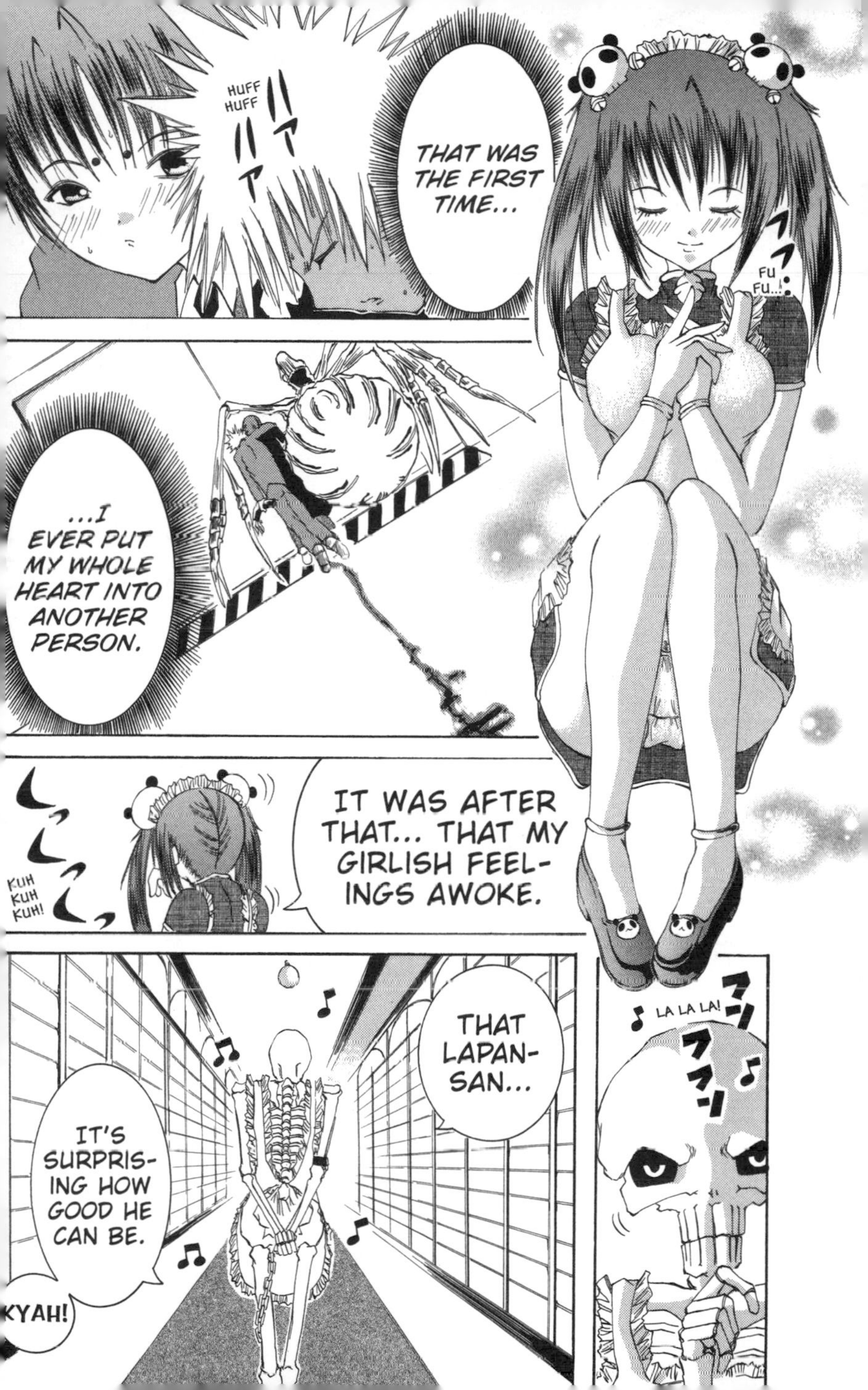
FU FU...
HUFF HUFF
THAT WAS THE FIRST TIME...
...I EVER PUT MY WHOLE HEART INTO ANOTHER PERSON.
IT WAS AFTER THAT... THAT MY GIRLISH FEEL-INGS AWOKE.
KUH KUH KUH!
LA LA LA!
THAT LAPAN-SAN...
IT'S SURPRIS-ING HOW GOOD HE CAN BE.
KYAH!

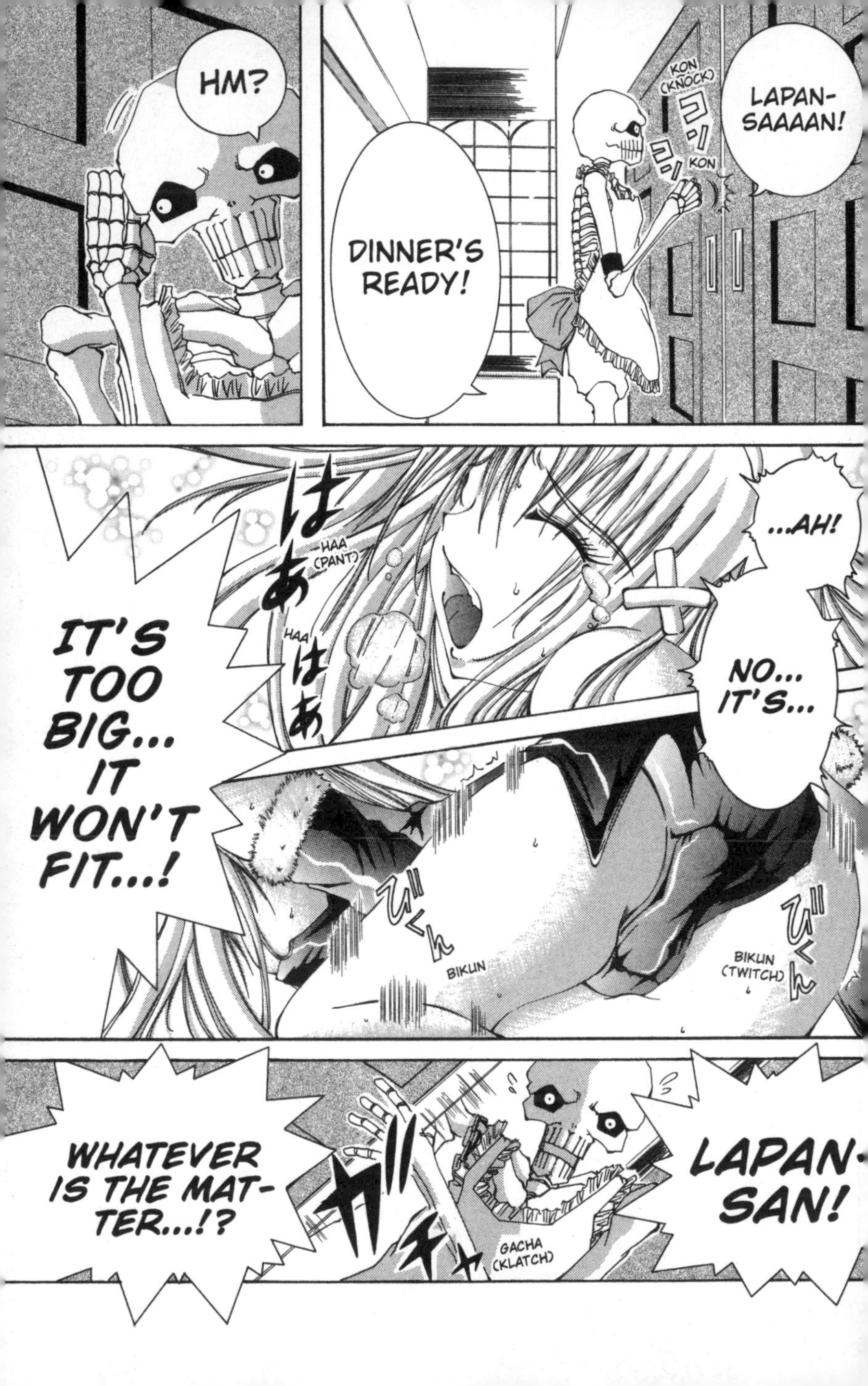
LAPAN-SAAAAN!
KON (KNOCK)
KON
DINNER'S READY!
HM?
...AH!
NO... IT'S...
HAA (PANT)
HAA
IT'S TOO BIG... IT WON'T FIT...!
BIKUN (TWITCH)
BIKUN
LAPAN-SAN!
GACHA (KLATCH)
WHATEVER IS THE MAT-TER...!?

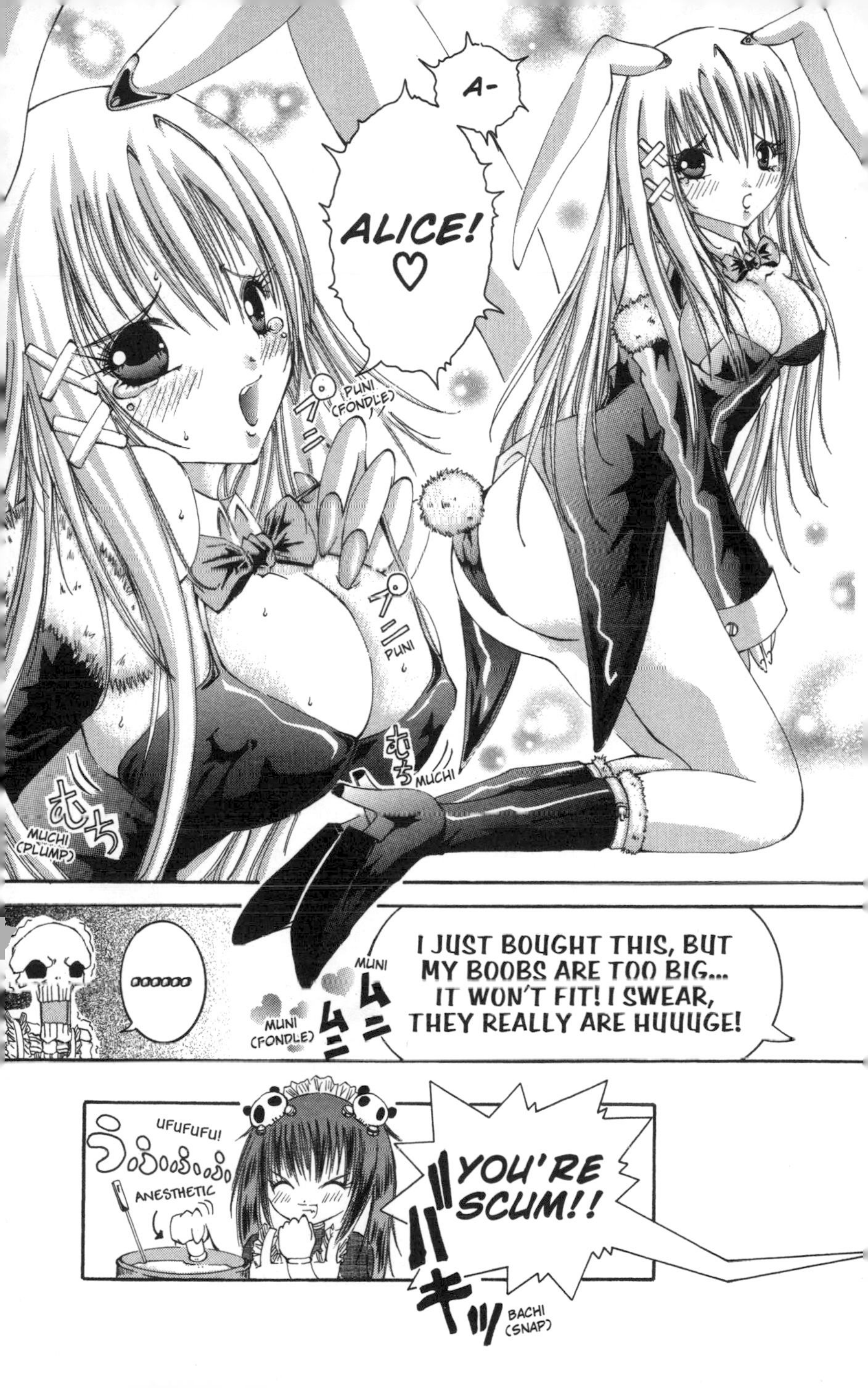
A-
ALICE! ♡
PUNI (FONDLE)
PUNI
むち
MUCHI
むち
MUCHI (PLUMP)
I JUST BOUGHT THIS, BUT MY BOOBS ARE TOO BIG... IT WON'T FIT! I SWEAR, THEY REALLY ARE HUUUGE!
ムニ
MUNI
ムニ
MUNI (FONDLE)
......
YOU'RE SCUM!!
BACHI (SNAP)
UFUFUFU!
ANESTHETIC

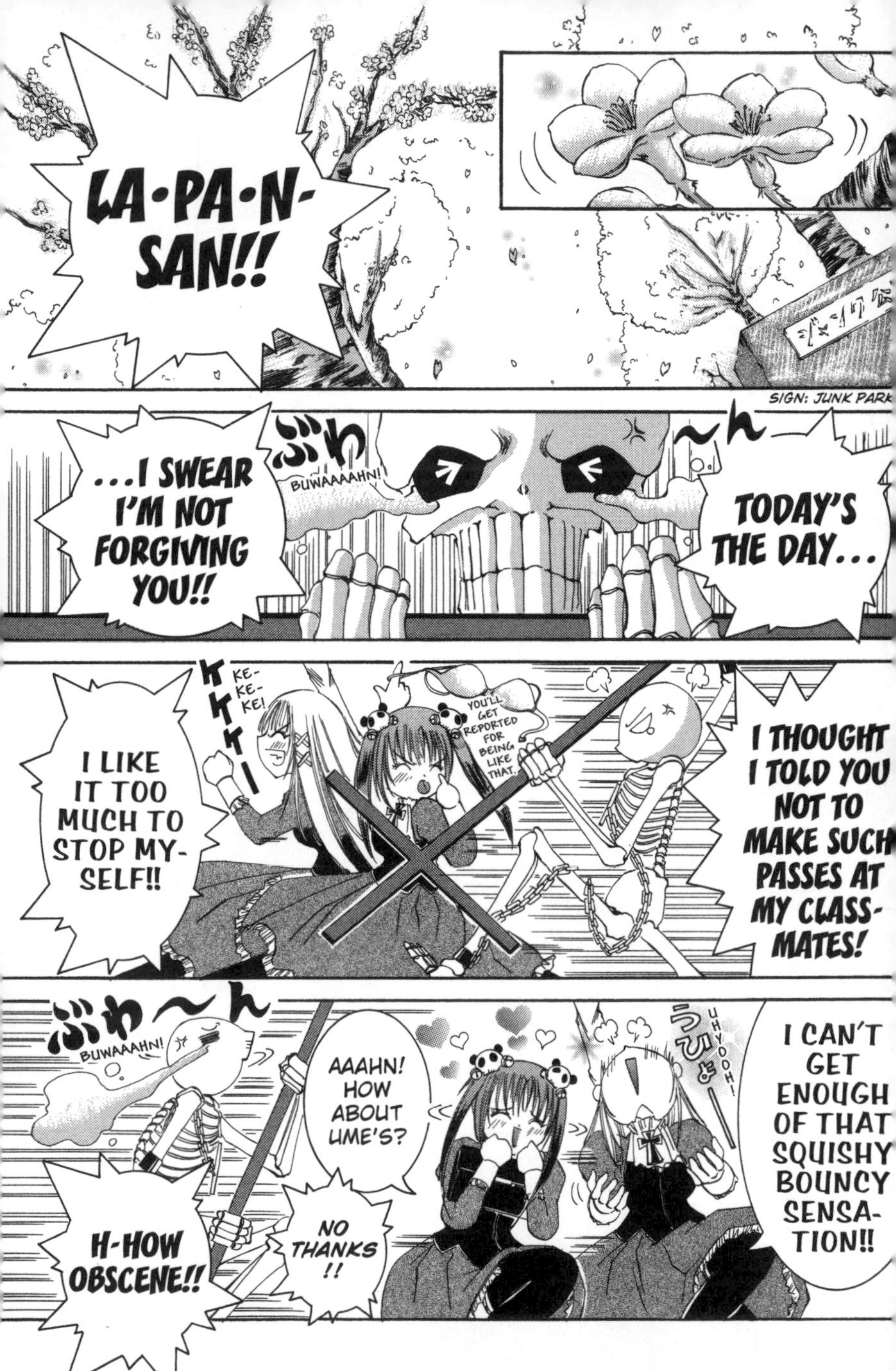
SIGN: JUNK PARK
LA·PA·N-SAN!!
TODAY'S THE DAY...
ぶわ~ん
BUWAAAAHN!
...I SWEAR I'M NOT FORGIVING YOU!!
I THOUGHT I TOLD YOU NOT TO MAKE SUCH PASSES AT MY CLASSMATES!
YOU'LL GET REPORTED FOR BEING LIKE THAT.
KE-KE-KE!
I LIKE IT TOO MUCH TO STOP MYSELF!!
I CAN'T GET ENOUGH OF THAT SQUISHY BOUNCY SENSATION!!
うひょ
UHYOOOH!
AAAHN! HOW ABOUT UME'S?
NO THANKS!!
ぶわ~ん
BUWAAAHN!
H-HOW OBSCENE!!

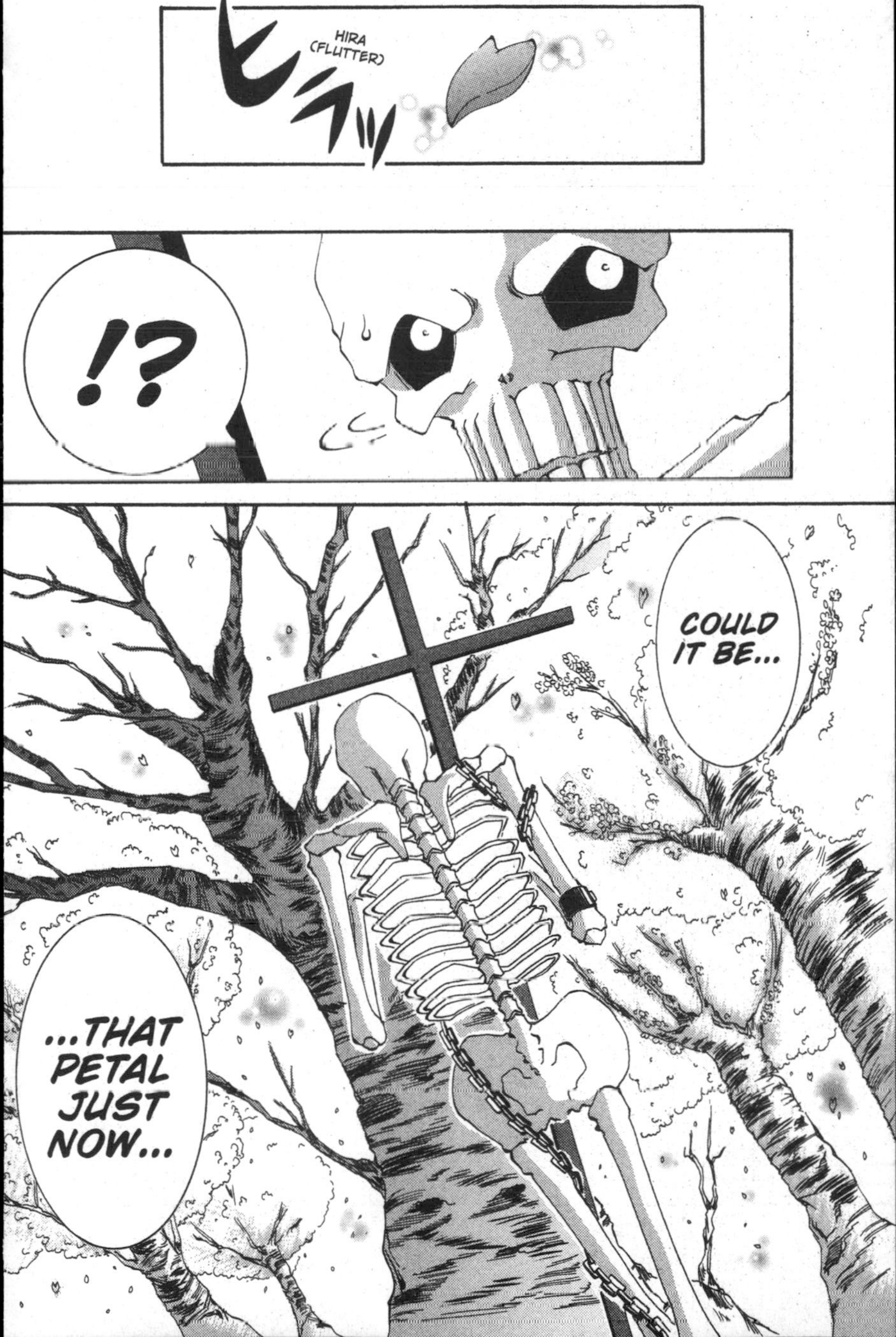
ヒラッ
HIRA (FLUTTER)
!?
COULD IT BE...
...THAT PETAL JUST NOW...

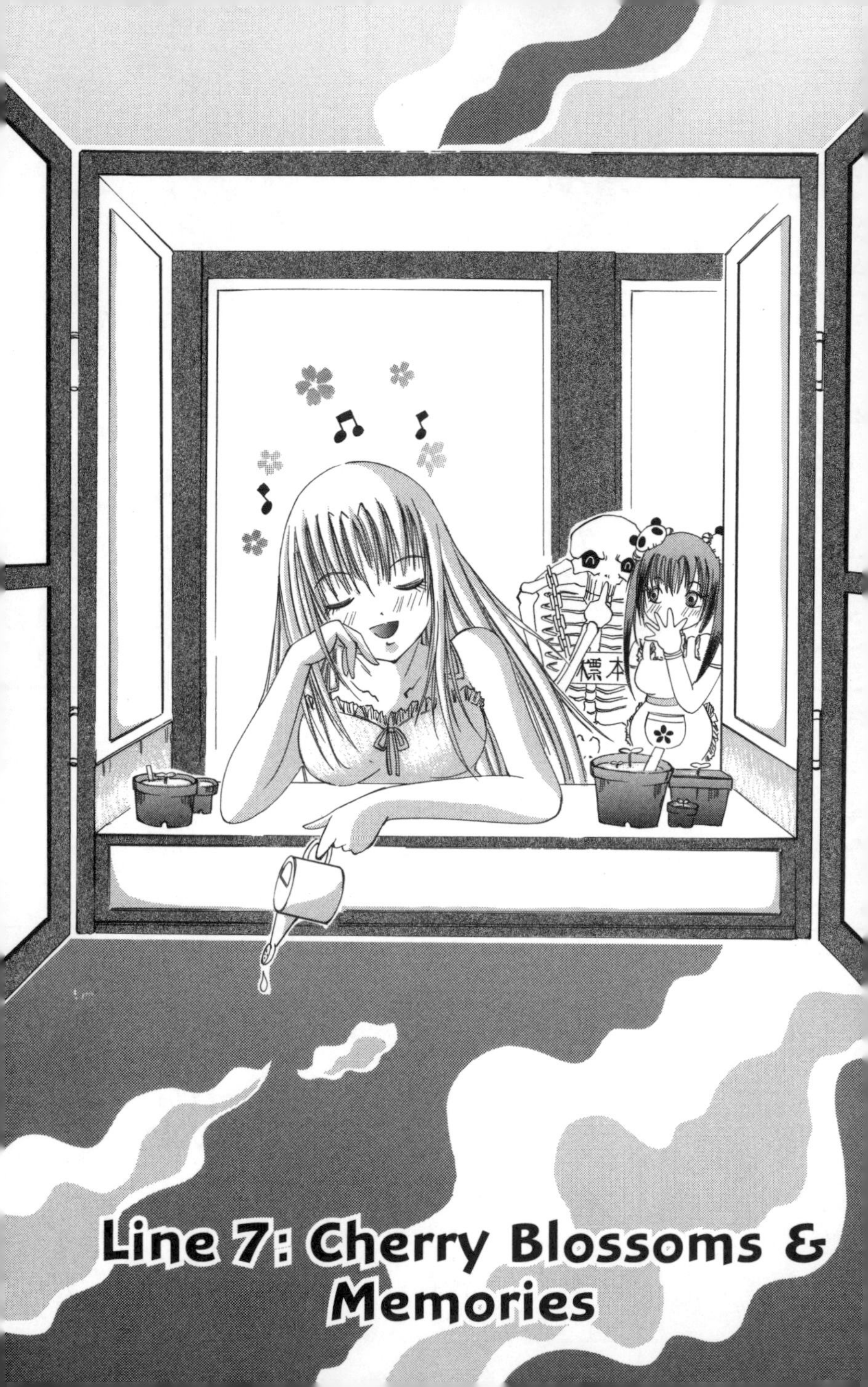
標本

Line 7: Cherry Blossoms & Memories

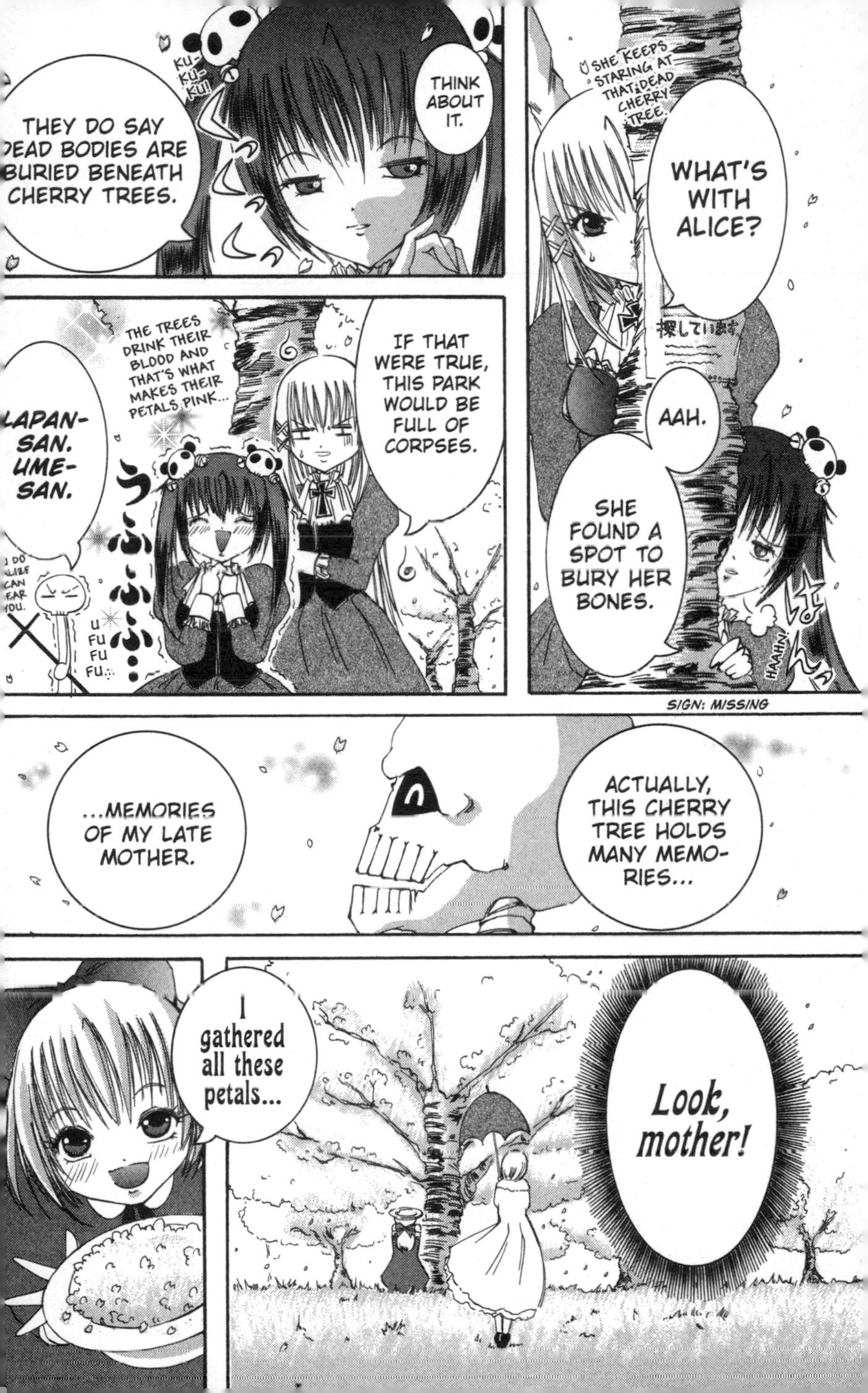
WHAT'S WITH ALICE?
SHE KEEPS STARING AT THAT DEAD CHERRY TREE.
探しています
AAH.
SHE FOUND A SPOT TO BURY HER BONES.
HAAHN
SIGN: MISSING
THINK ABOUT IT.
KU-KU-KU!
THEY DO SAY DEAD BODIES ARE BURIED BENEATH CHERRY TREES.
IF THAT WERE TRUE, THIS PARK WOULD BE FULL OF CORPSES.
THE TREES DRINK THEIR BLOOD AND THAT'S WHAT MAKES THEIR PETALS PINK...
LAPAN-SAN. UME-SAN.
U FU FU FU
ACTUALLY, THIS CHERRY TREE HOLDS MANY MEMORIES...
...MEMORIES OF MY LATE MOTHER.
Look, mother!
I gathered all these petals...

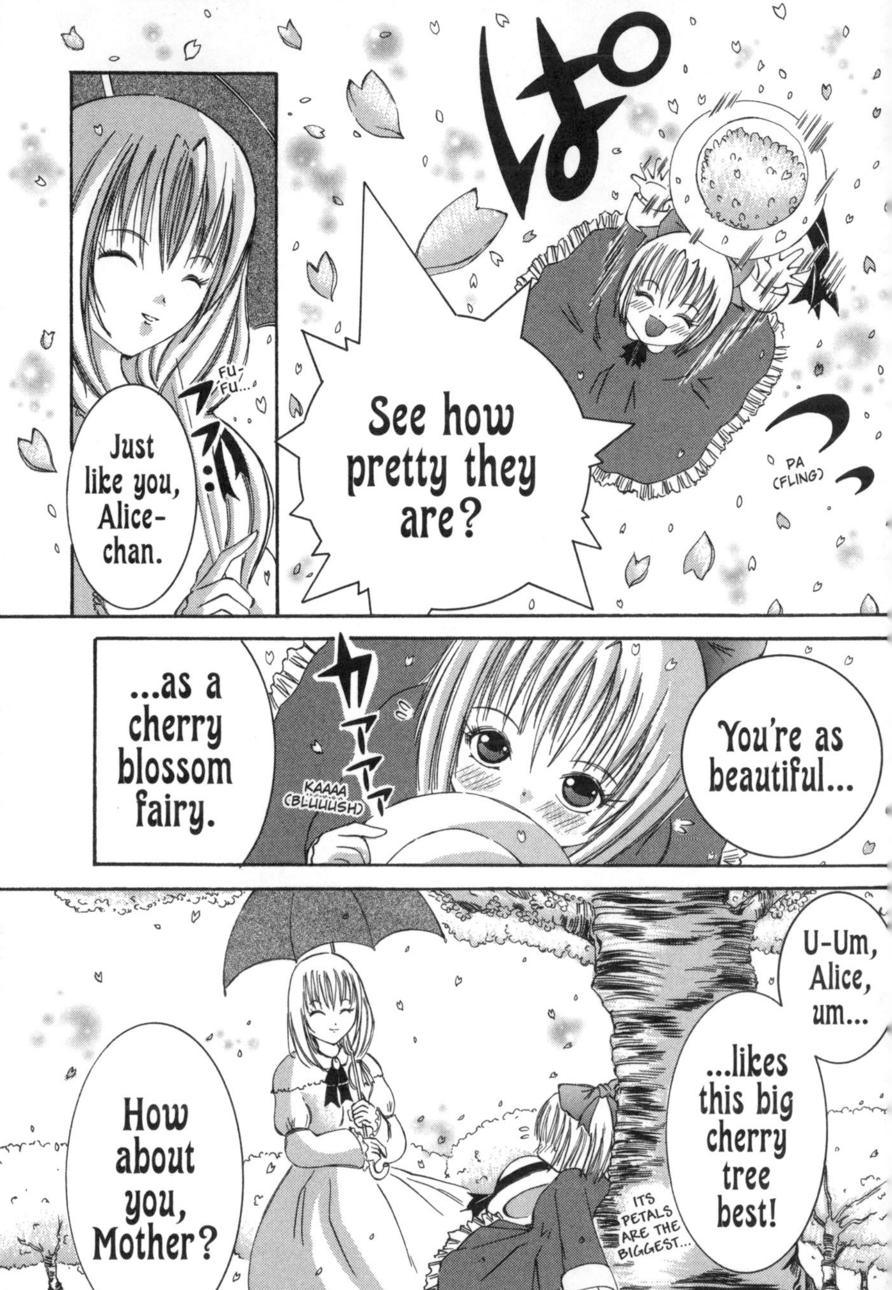
See how pretty they are?
PA (FLING)
FU-FU...
Just like you, Alice-chan.
You're as beautiful...
KAAAA (BLUUUSH)
...as a cherry blossom fairy.
U-Um, Alice, um...
...likes this big cherry tree best!
ITS PETALS ARE THE BIGGEST...
How about you, Mother?

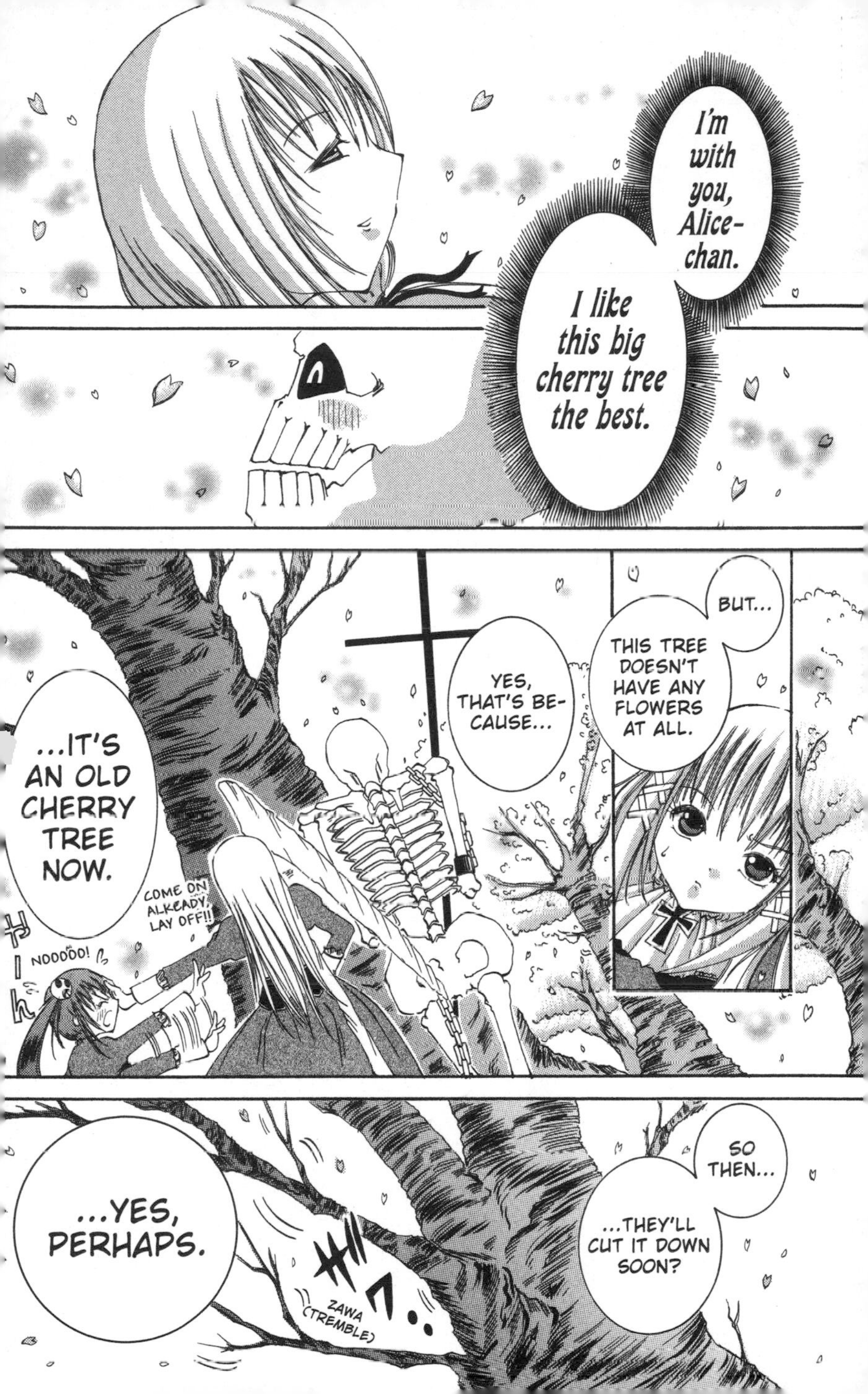
I'm with you, Alice-chan.
I like this big cherry tree the best.
BUT...
THIS TREE DOESN'T HAVE ANY FLOWERS AT ALL.
YES, THAT'S BE-CAUSE...
...IT'S AN OLD CHERRY TREE NOW.
COME ON ALKEADY, LAY OFF!!
NOOOOO!
SO THEN...
...THEY'LL CUT IT DOWN SOON?
ZAWA (TREMBLE)
...YES, PERHAPS.

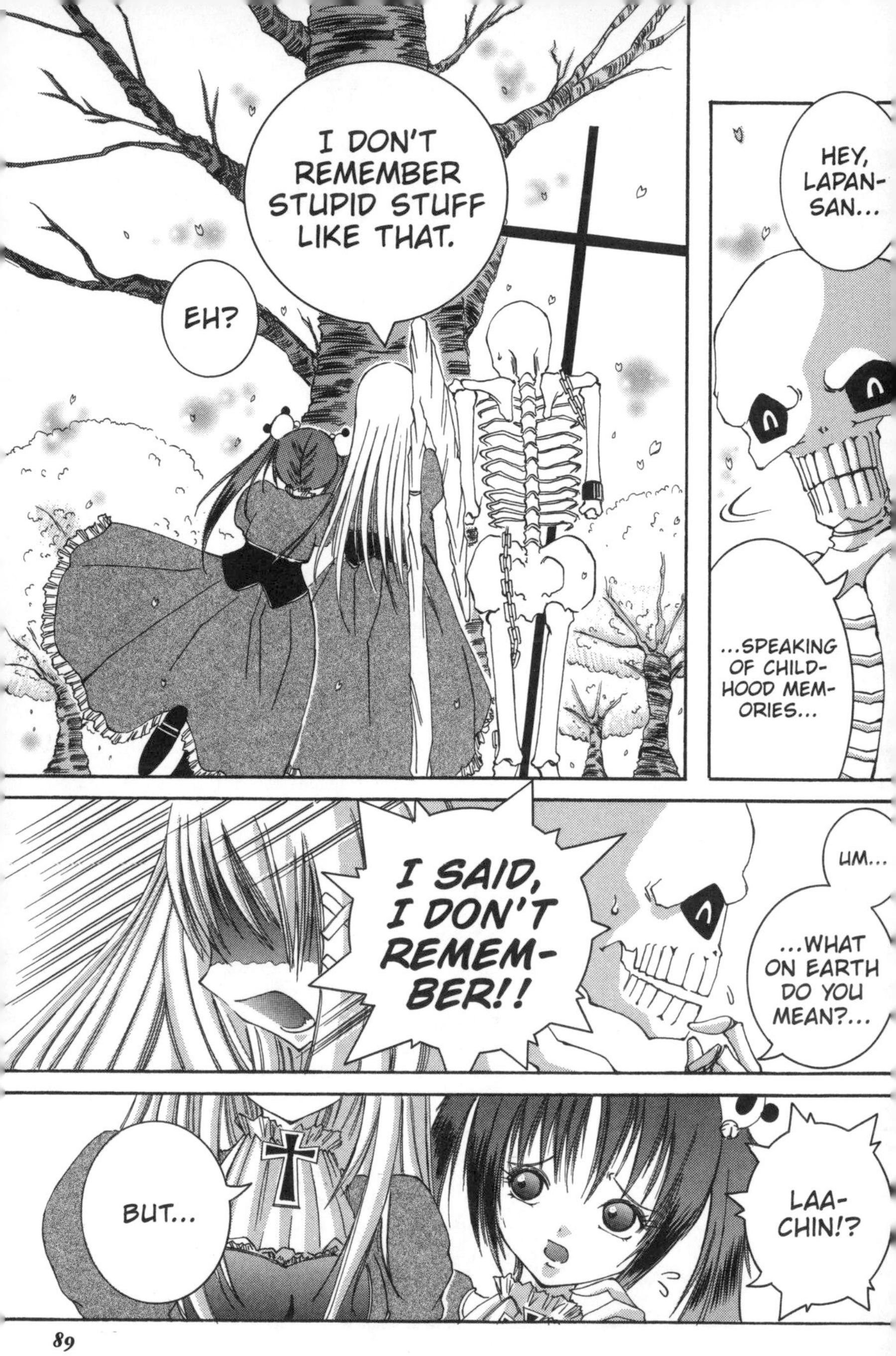
HEY, LAPAN-SAN...
...SPEAKING OF CHILD-HOOD MEM-ORIES...
I DON'T REMEMBER STUPID STUFF LIKE THAT.
EH?
UM...
...WHAT ON EARTH DO YOU MEAN?...
I SAID, I DON'T REMEM-BER!!
LAA-CHIN!?
BUT...

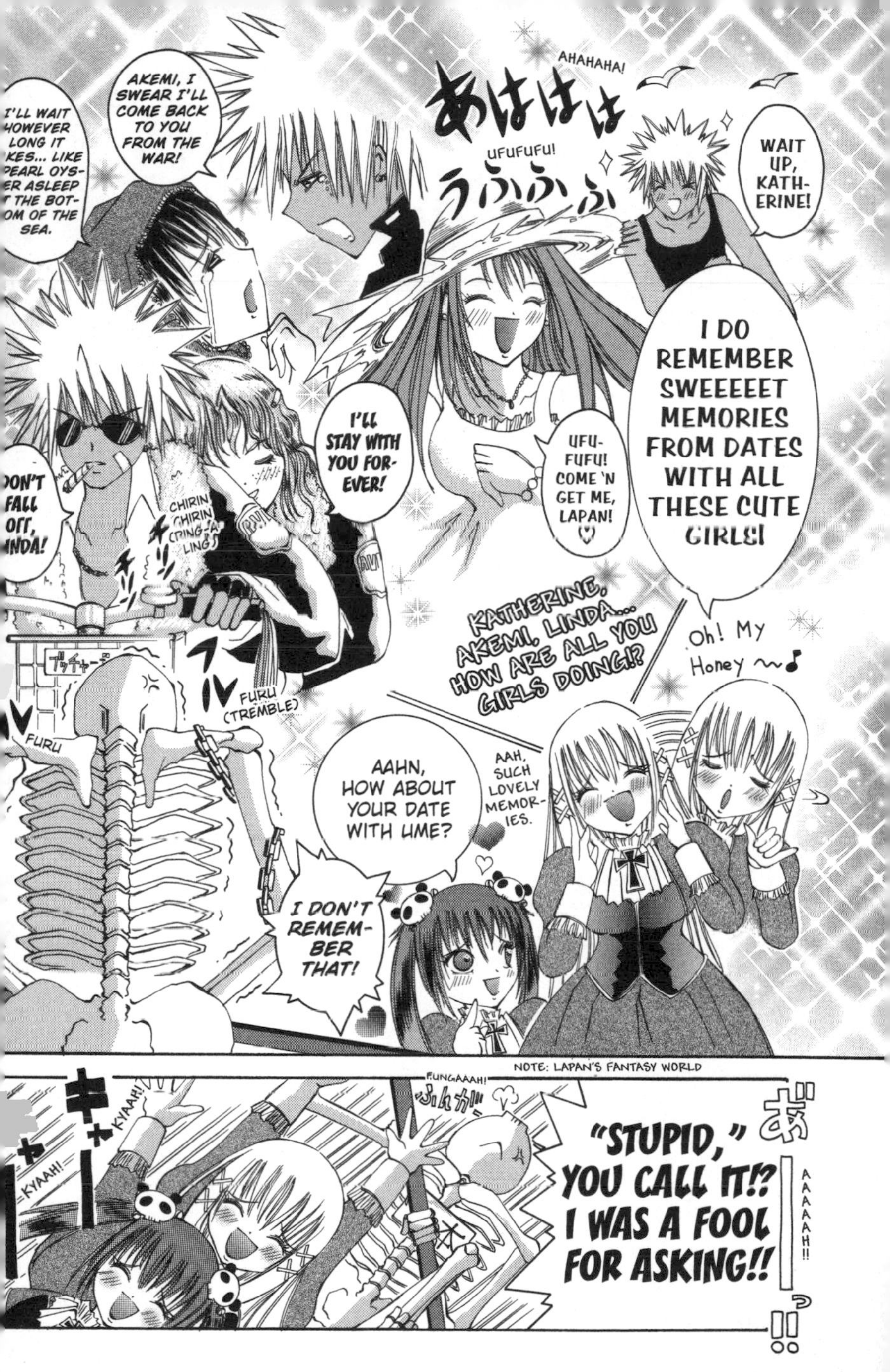
WAIT UP, KATHERINE!
AHAHAHA!
あははは
UFUFUFU!
うふふふ
AKEMI, I SWEAR I'LL COME BACK TO YOU FROM THE WAR!
I'LL WAIT HOWEVER LONG IT KES... LIKE PEARL OYSTER ASLEEP T THE BOTTOM OF THE SEA.
I DO REMEMBER SWEEEEET MEMORIES FROM DATES WITH ALL THESE CUTE GIRLS!
UFU-FUFU! COME 'N GET ME, LAPAN! ♡
I'LL STAY WITH YOU FOREVER!
CHIRIN CHIRIN (CHING-A-LING)
ON'T FALL OFF, INDA!
Oh! My Honey ~♪
KATHERINE, AKEMI, LINDA... HOW ARE ALL YOU GIRLS DOING!?
FURU (TREMBLE)
FURU
AAH, SUCH LOVELY MEMORIES.
AAHN, HOW ABOUT YOUR DATE WITH UME?
I DON'T REMEMBER THAT!
NOTE: LAPAN'S FANTASY WORLD
あっ!!
AAAAAAH!!
"STUPID," YOU CALL IT!? I WAS A FOOL FOR ASKING!!
FUNGAAAH!
ふんが
KYAAH!
KYAAH!

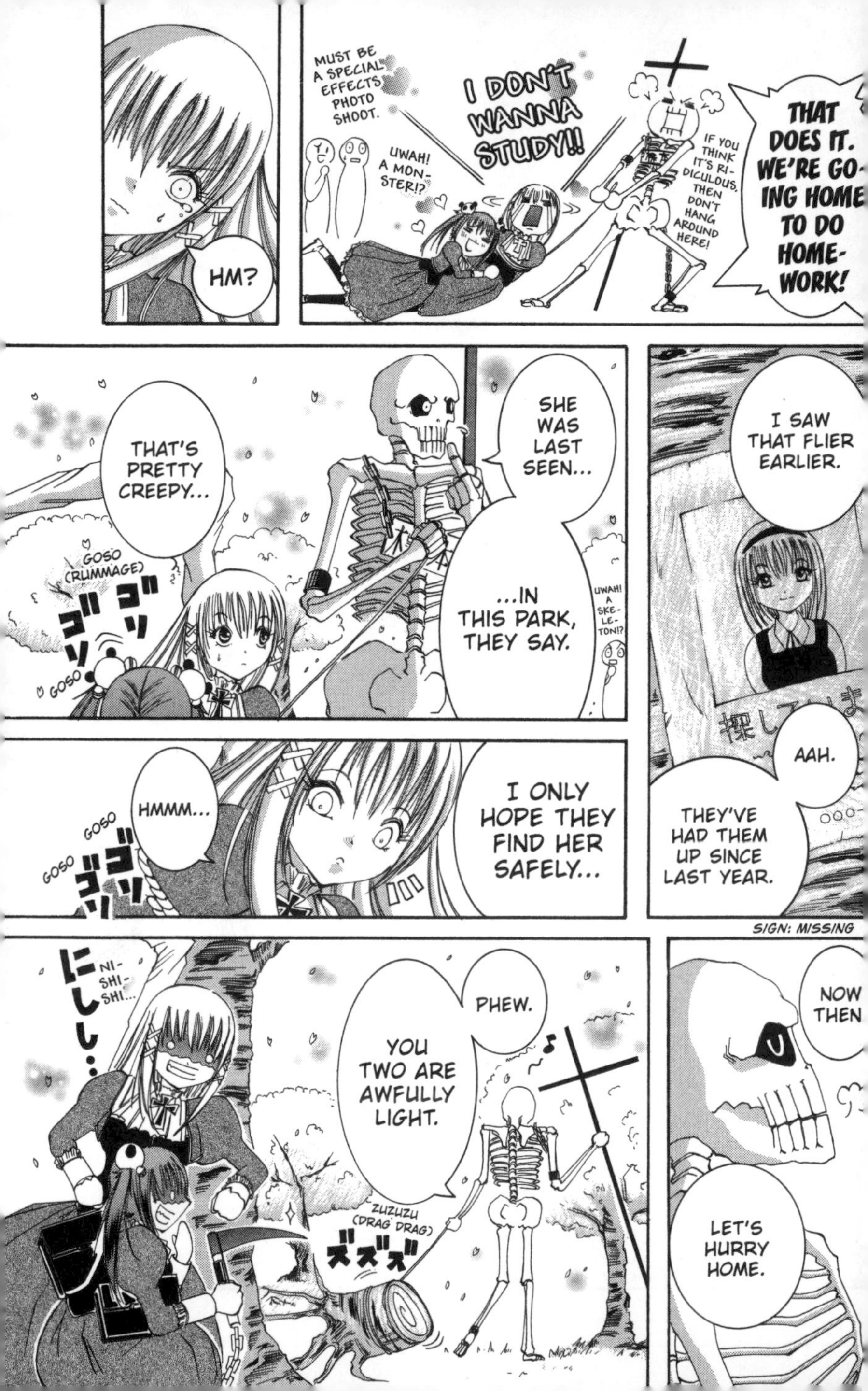
THAT DOES IT. WE'RE GOING HOME TO DO HOMEWORK!
IF YOU THINK IT'S RIDICULOUS, THEN DON'T HANG AROUND HERE!
I DON'T WANNA STUDY!!
MUST BE A SPECIAL EFFECTS PHOTO SHOOT.
UWAH! A MONSTER!?
HM?
I SAW THAT FLIER EARLIER.
AAH.
THEY'VE HAD THEM UP SINCE LAST YEAR.
SIGN: MISSING
SHE WAS LAST SEEN...
...IN THIS PARK, THEY SAY.
UWAH! A SKELETON!?
THAT'S PRETTY CREEPY...
GOSO (RUMMAGE)
GOSO
I ONLY HOPE THEY FIND HER SAFELY...
HMMM...
GOSO GOSO
NOW THEN
LET'S HURRY HOME.
PHEW.
YOU TWO ARE AWFULLY LIGHT.
ZUZUZU (DRAG DRAG)
NI-SHI-SHI...

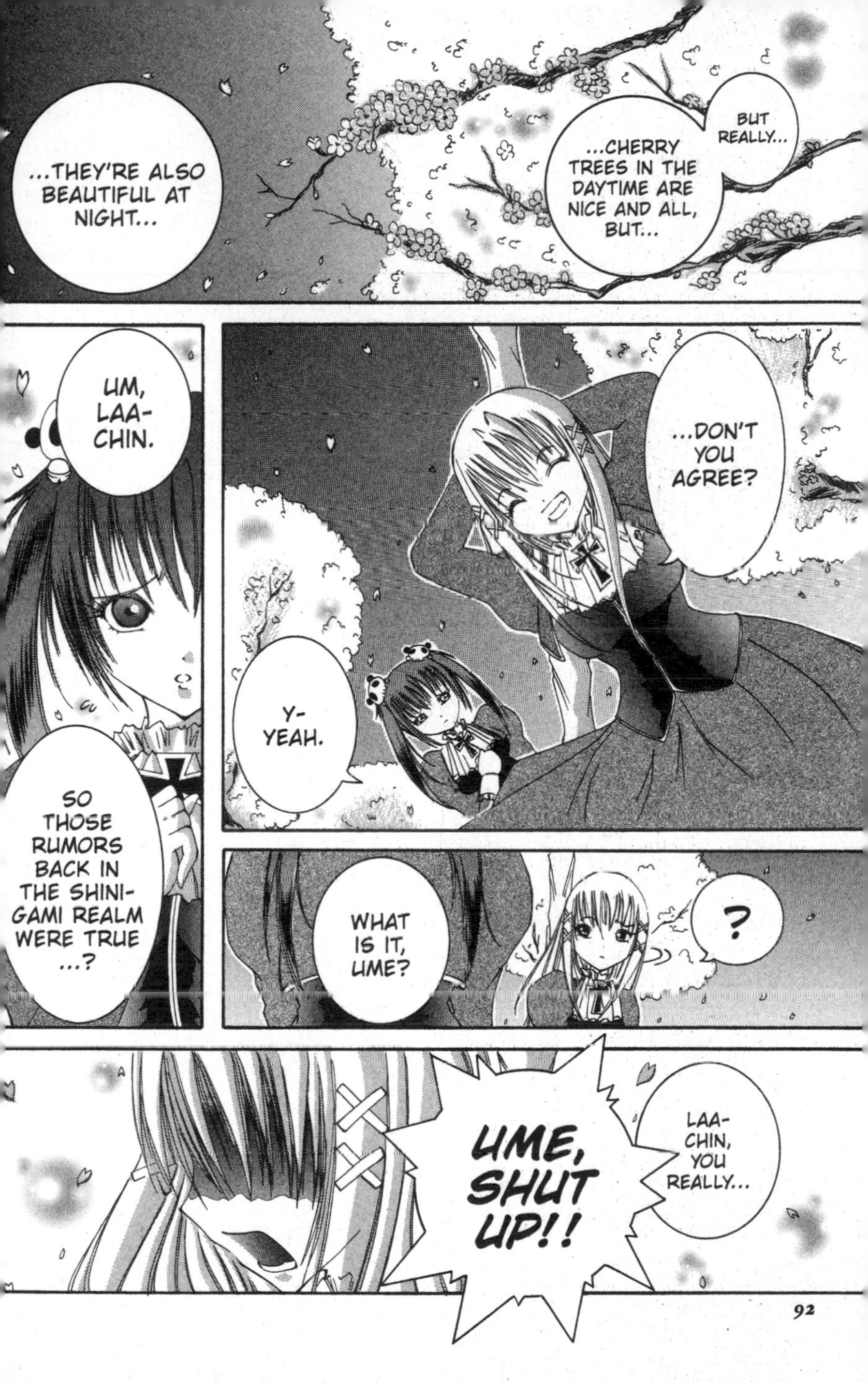
BUT REALLY...
...CHERRY TREES IN THE DAYTIME ARE NICE AND ALL, BUT...
...THEY'RE ALSO BEAUTIFUL AT NIGHT...
...DON'T YOU AGREE?
Y-YEAH.
?
WHAT IS IT, UME?
UM, LAA-CHIN.
SO THOSE RUMORS BACK IN THE SHINIGAMI REALM WERE TRUE ...?
LAA-CHIN, YOU REALLY...
UME, SHUT UP!!

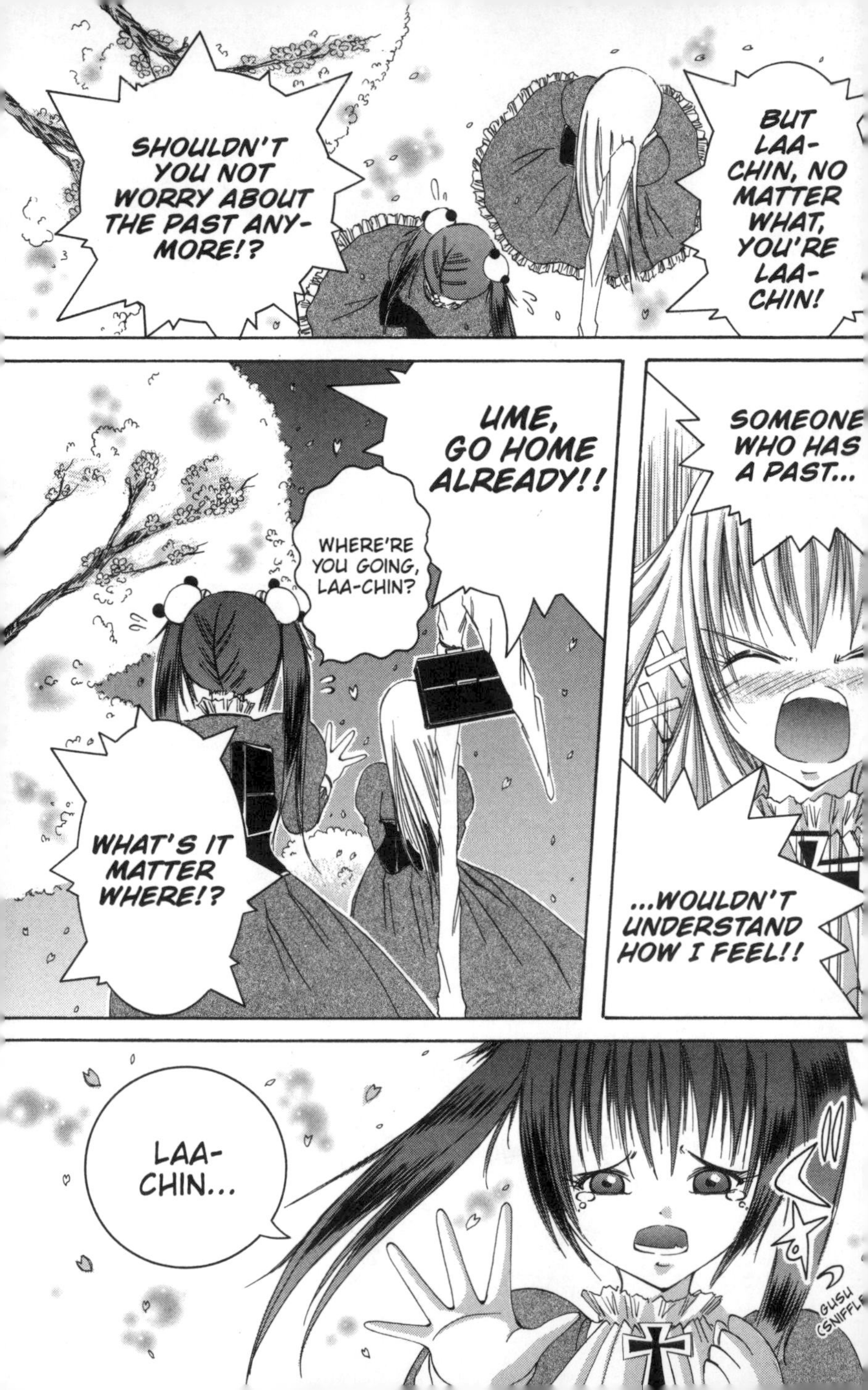
BUT LAA-CHIN, NO MATTER WHAT, YOU'RE LAA-CHIN!
SHOULDN'T YOU NOT WORRY ABOUT THE PAST ANYMORE!?
SOMEONE WHO HAS A PAST...
...WOULDN'T UNDERSTAND HOW I FEEL!!
UME, GO HOME ALREADY!!
WHERE'RE YOU GOING, LAA-CHIN?
WHAT'S IT MATTER WHERE!?
GUSU (SNIFFLE)
LAA-CHIN...

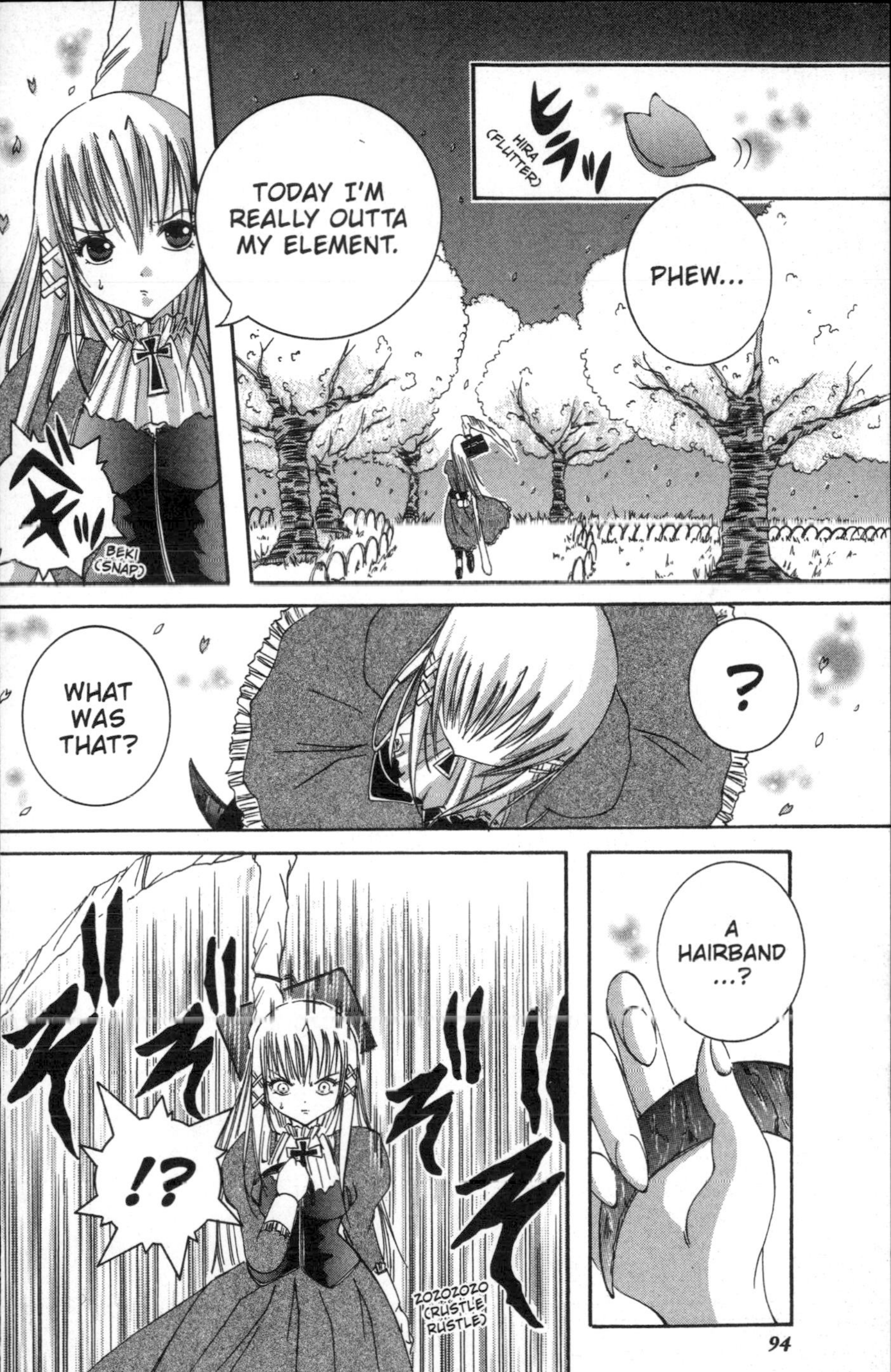
HIRA (FLUTTER)
PHEW...
TODAY I'M REALLY OUTTA MY ELEMENT.
BEKI (SNAP)
?
WHAT WAS THAT?
A HAIRBAND ...?
!?
ZOZOZOZO (RUSTLE RUSTLE)

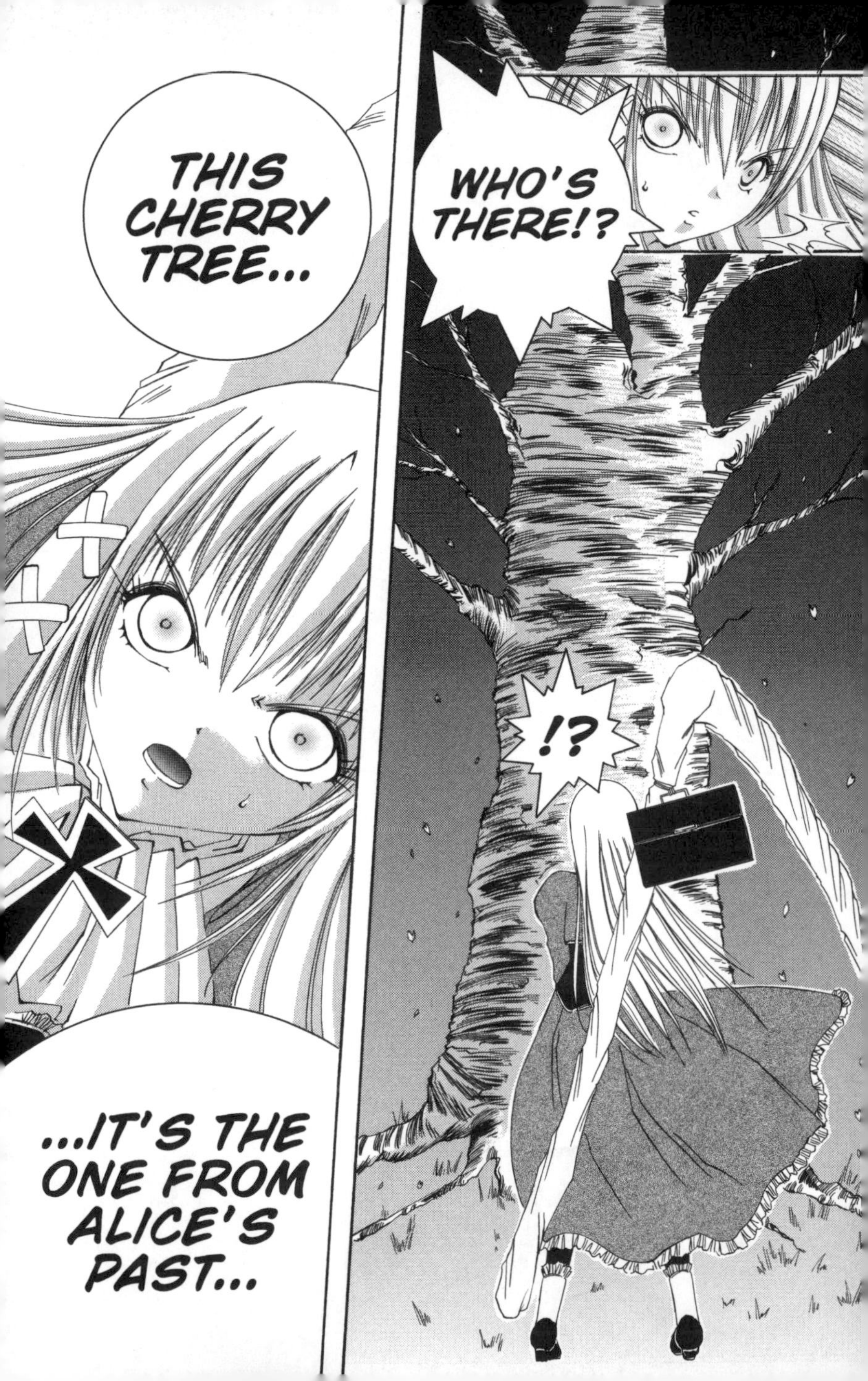
WHO'S THERE!?
!?
THIS CHERRY TREE...
...IT'S THE ONE FROM ALICE'S PAST...

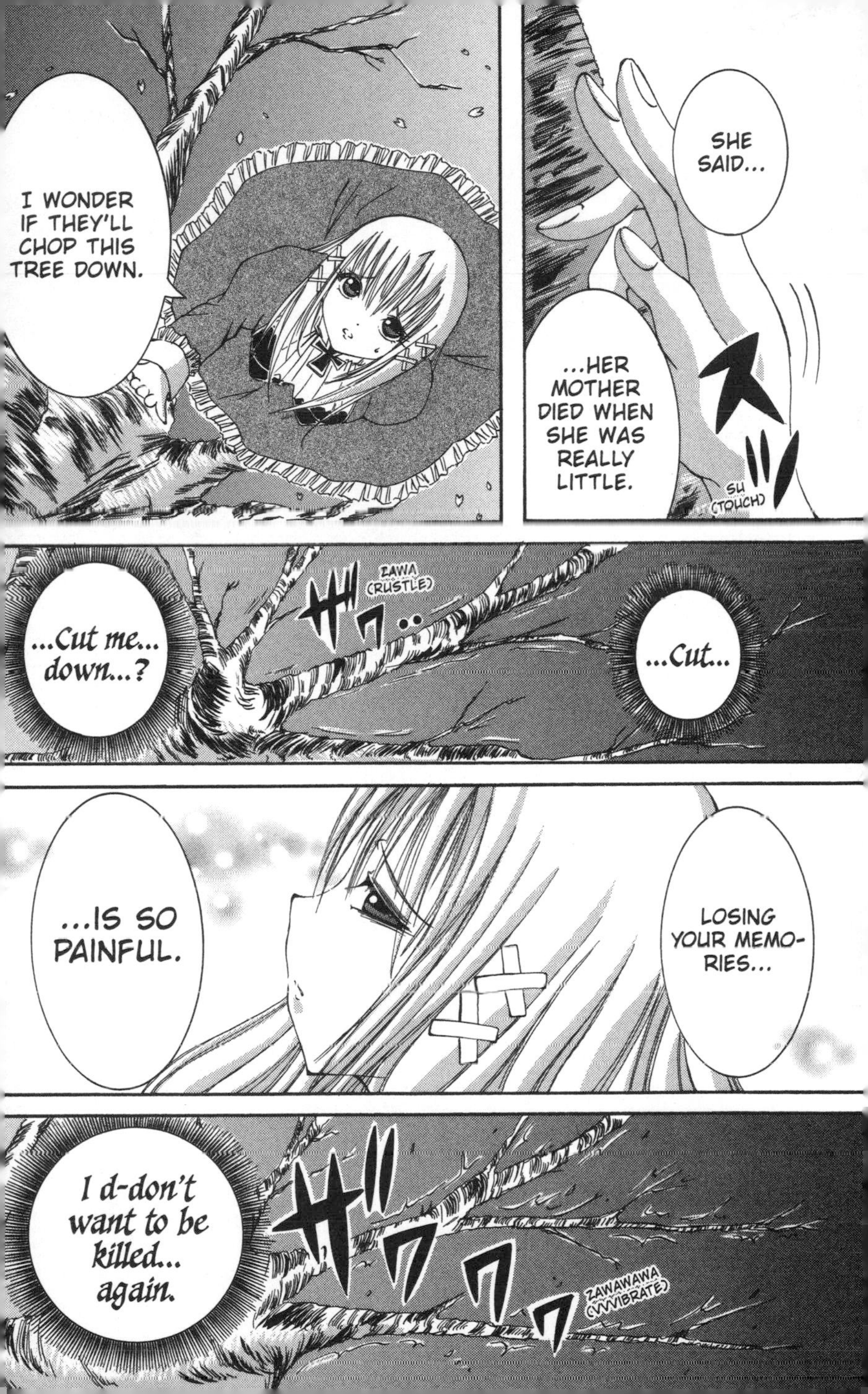
SHE SAID...
...HER MOTHER DIED WHEN SHE WAS REALLY LITTLE.
SU (TOUCH)
I WONDER IF THEY'LL CHOP THIS TREE DOWN.
...Cut...
ZAWA (RUSTLE)
...Cut me... down...?
LOSING YOUR MEMO-RIES...
...IS SO PAINFUL.
ZAWAWAWA (VVVIBRATE)
I d-don't want to be killed... again.

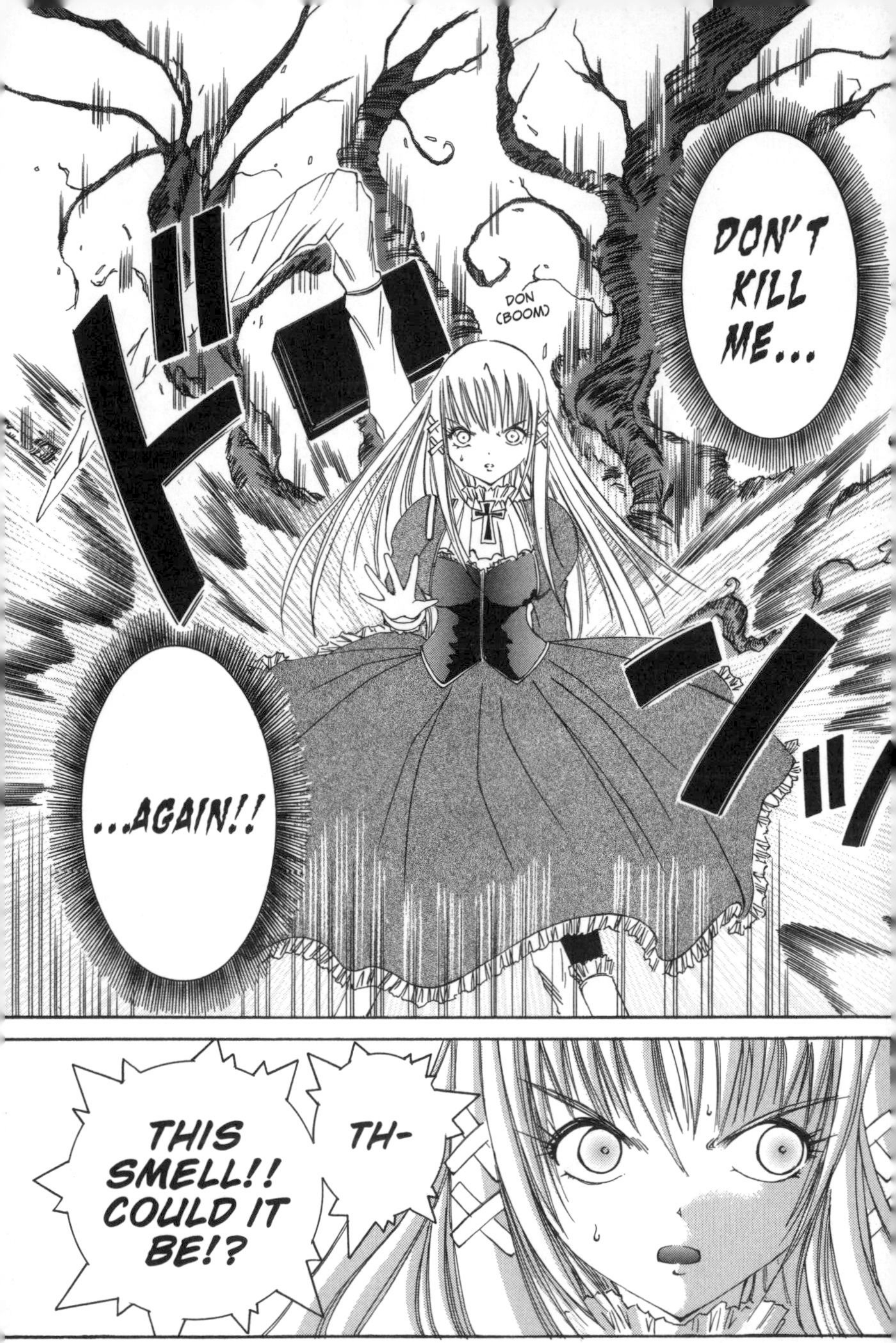
DON'T KILL ME...
DON (BOOM)
...AGAIN!!
TH-
THIS SMELL!! COULD IT BE!?

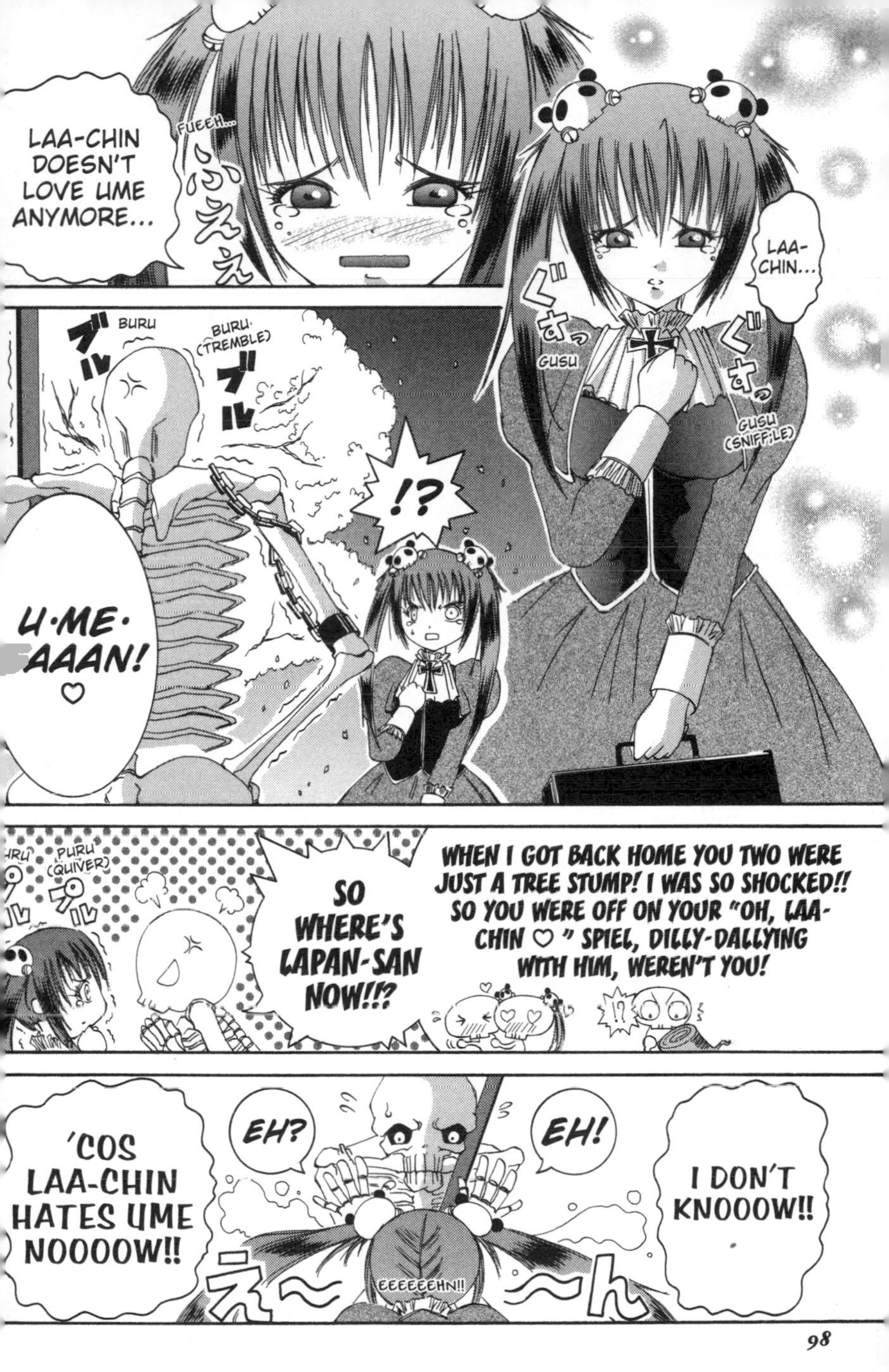
LAA-CHIN...
GUSU
GUSU (SNIFFLE)
FUEEH...
LAA-CHIN DOESN'T LOVE UME ANYMORE...
!?
BURU
BURU (TREMBLE)
U·ME·AAAN! ♡
WHEN I GOT BACK HOME YOU TWO WERE JUST A TREE STUMP! I WAS SO SHOCKED!! SO YOU WERE OFF ON YOUR "OH, LAA-CHIN ♡" SPIEL, DILLY-DALLYING WITH HIM, WEREN'T YOU!
SO WHERE'S LAPAN-SAN NOW!!?
PURU (QUIVER)
I DON'T KNOOOW!!
EH!
EH?
'COS LAA-CHIN HATES UME NOOOOW!!
EEEEEEEHN!!

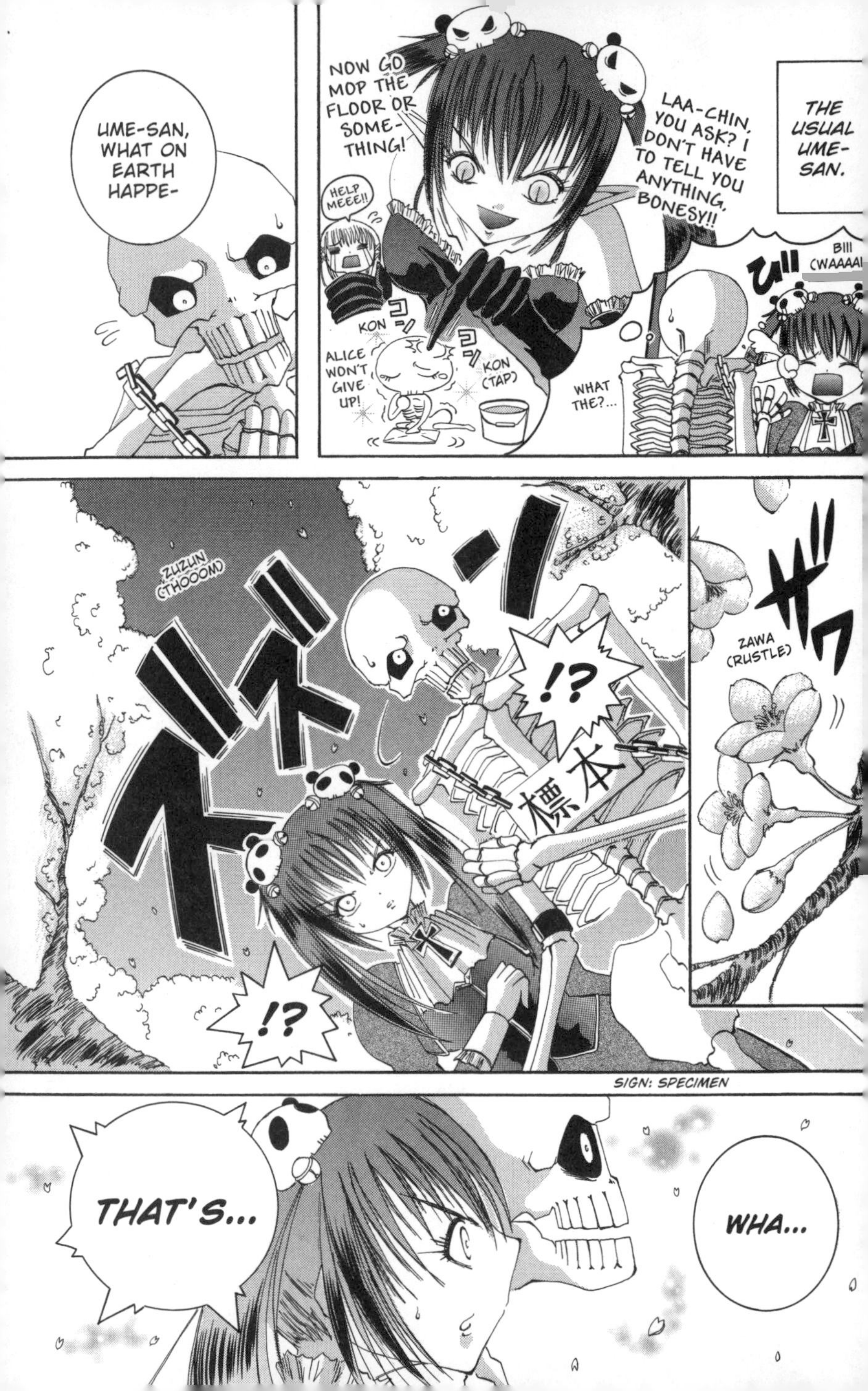
THE USUAL UME-SAN.
LAA-CHIN, YOU ASK? I DON'T HAVE TO TELL YOU ANYTHING, BONESY!!
BIII (WAAAA
NOW GO MOP THE FLOOR OR SOME-THING!
HELP MEEE!!
KON (TAP)
KON
ALICE WON'T GIVE UP!
WHAT THE?...
UME-SAN, WHAT ON EARTH HAPPE-
ZAWA (RUSTLE)
!?
ZUZUN (THOOOM)
標本
!?
SIGN: SPECIMEN
WHA...
THAT'S...

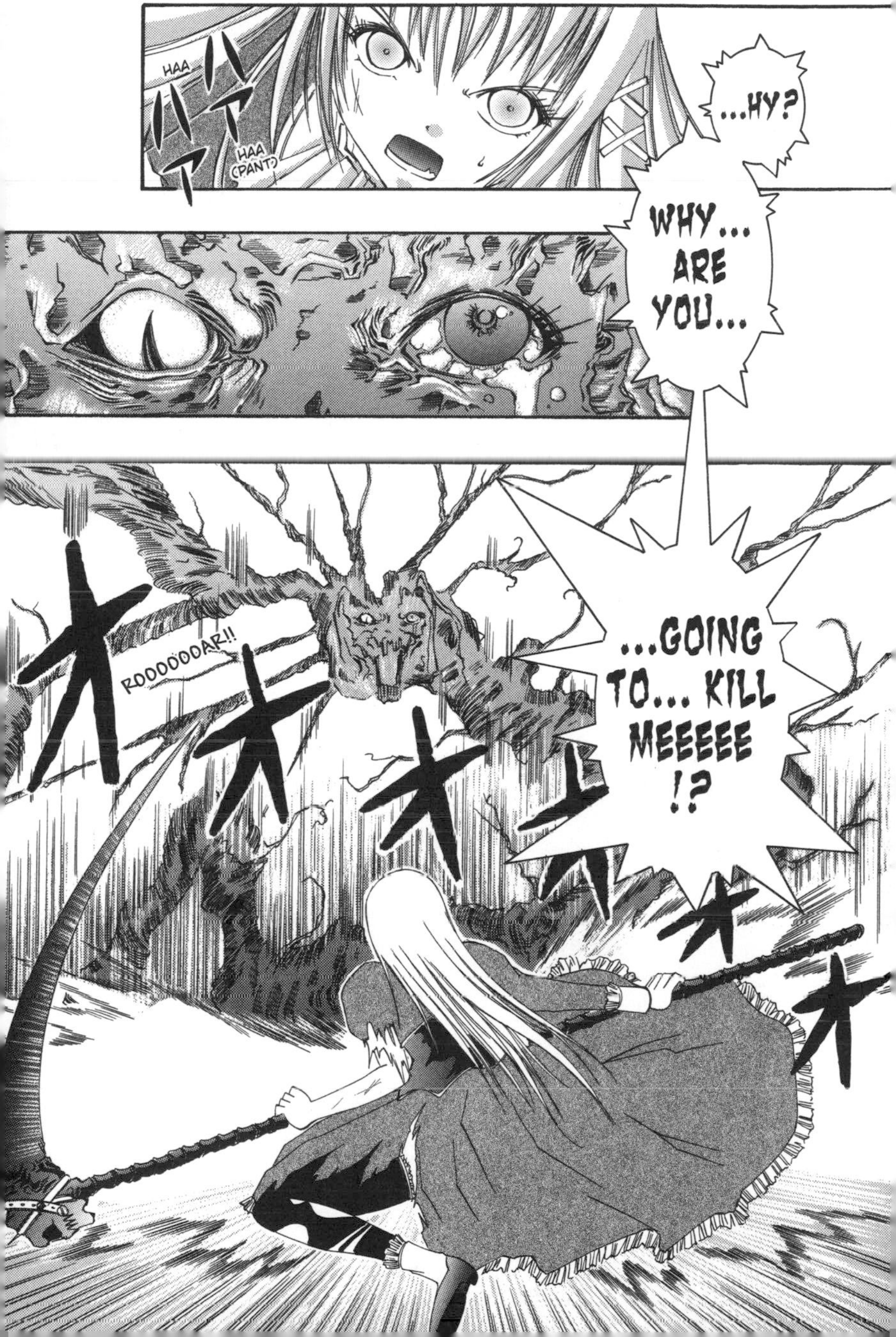
...HY?
HAA
HAA (PANT)
WHY... ARE YOU...
...GOING TO... KILL MEEEEE !?
ROOOOOOAR!!

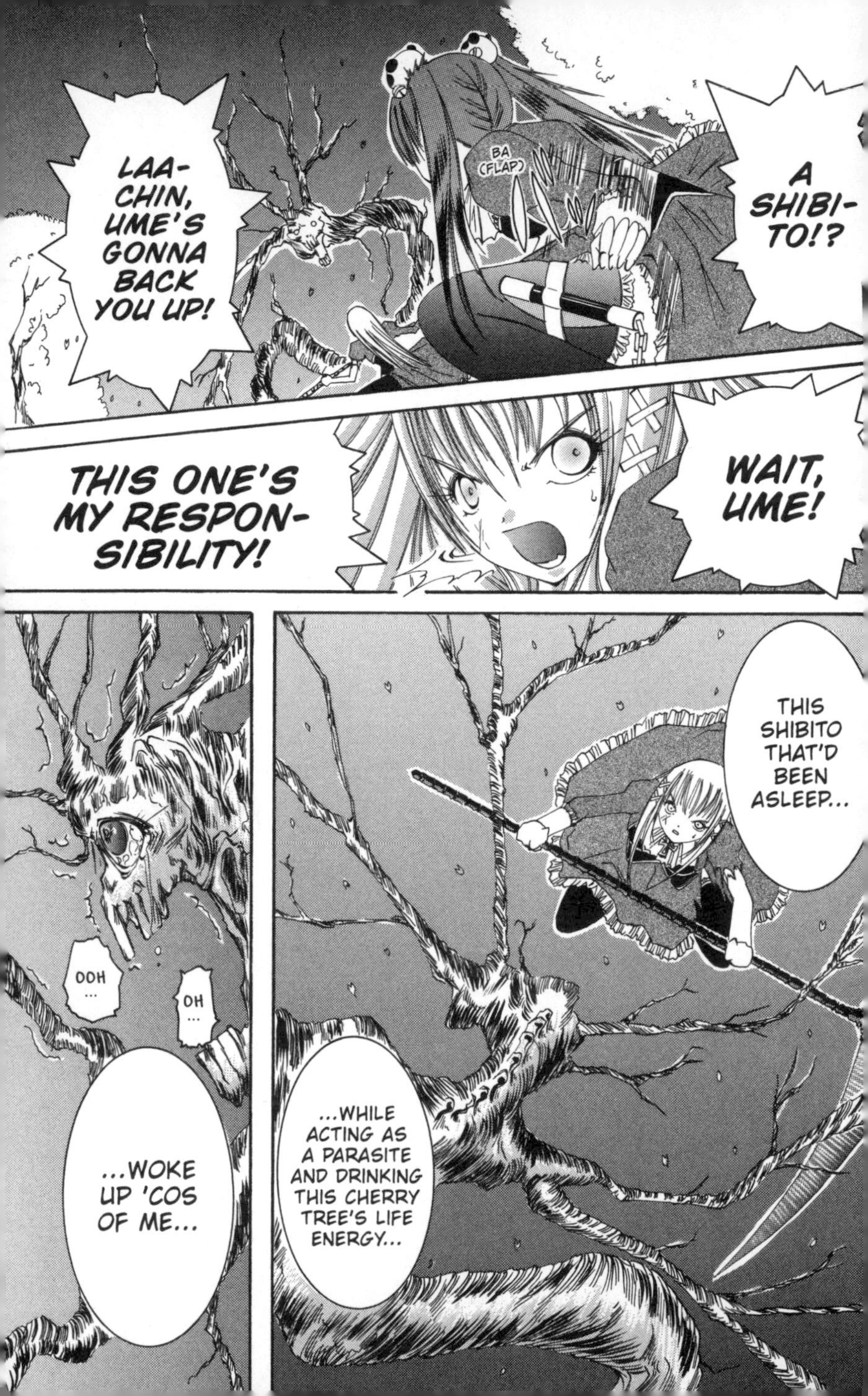

A SHIBI-TO!?
BA (FLAP)
LAA-CHIN, UME'S GONNA BACK YOU UP!
WAIT, UME!
THIS ONE'S MY RESPON-SIBILITY!
THIS SHIBITO THAT'D BEEN ASLEEP...
...WHILE ACTING AS A PARASITE AND DRINKING THIS CHERRY TREE'S LIFE ENERGY...
OH ...
OOH ...
...WOKE UP 'COS OF ME...

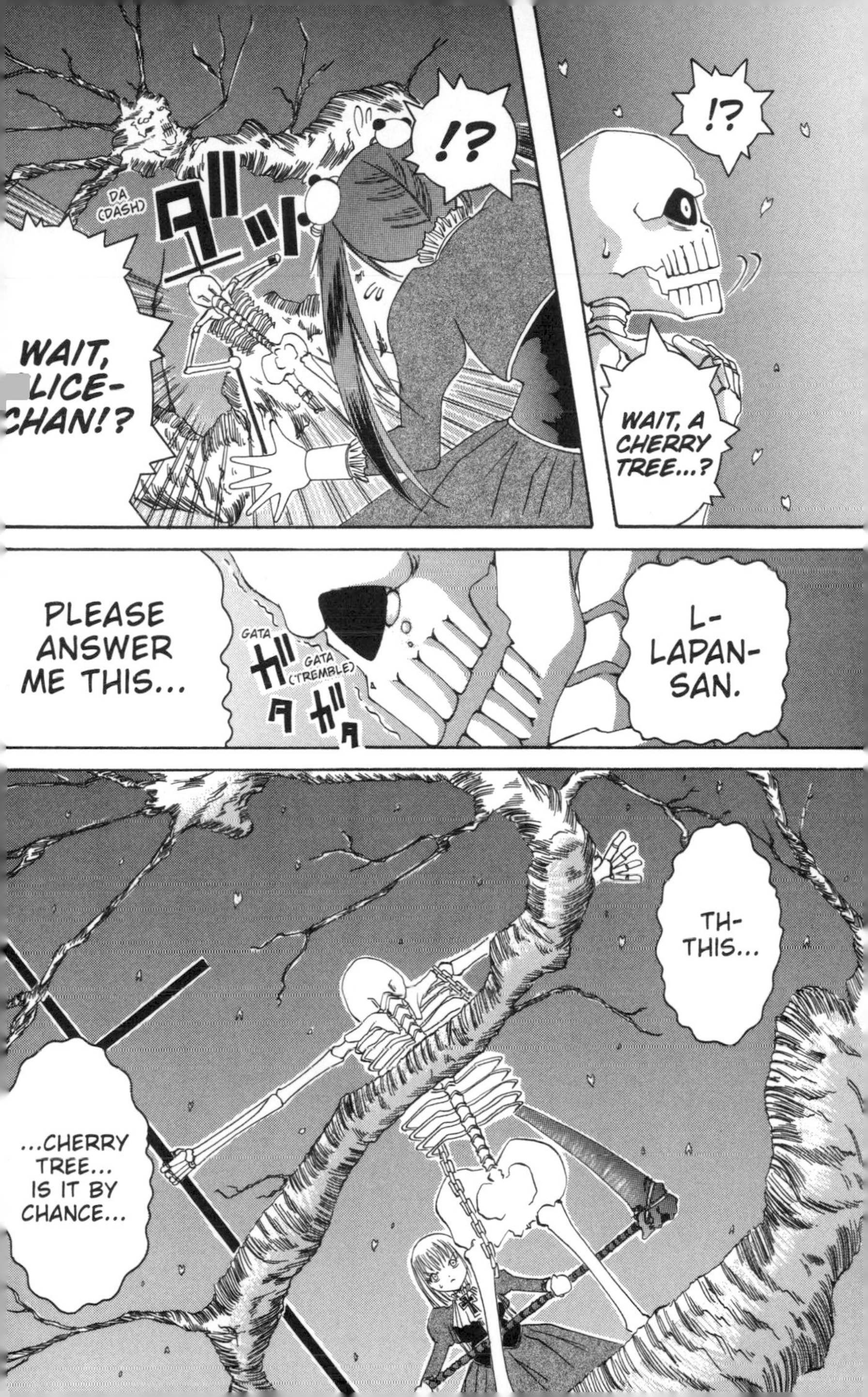
!?
WAIT, A CHERRY TREE...?
!?
DA (DASH)
WAIT, LICE-CHAN!?
L-LAPAN-SAN.
GATA GATA (TREMBLE)
PLEASE ANSWER ME THIS...
TH-THIS...
...CHERRY TREE... IS IT BY CHANCE...

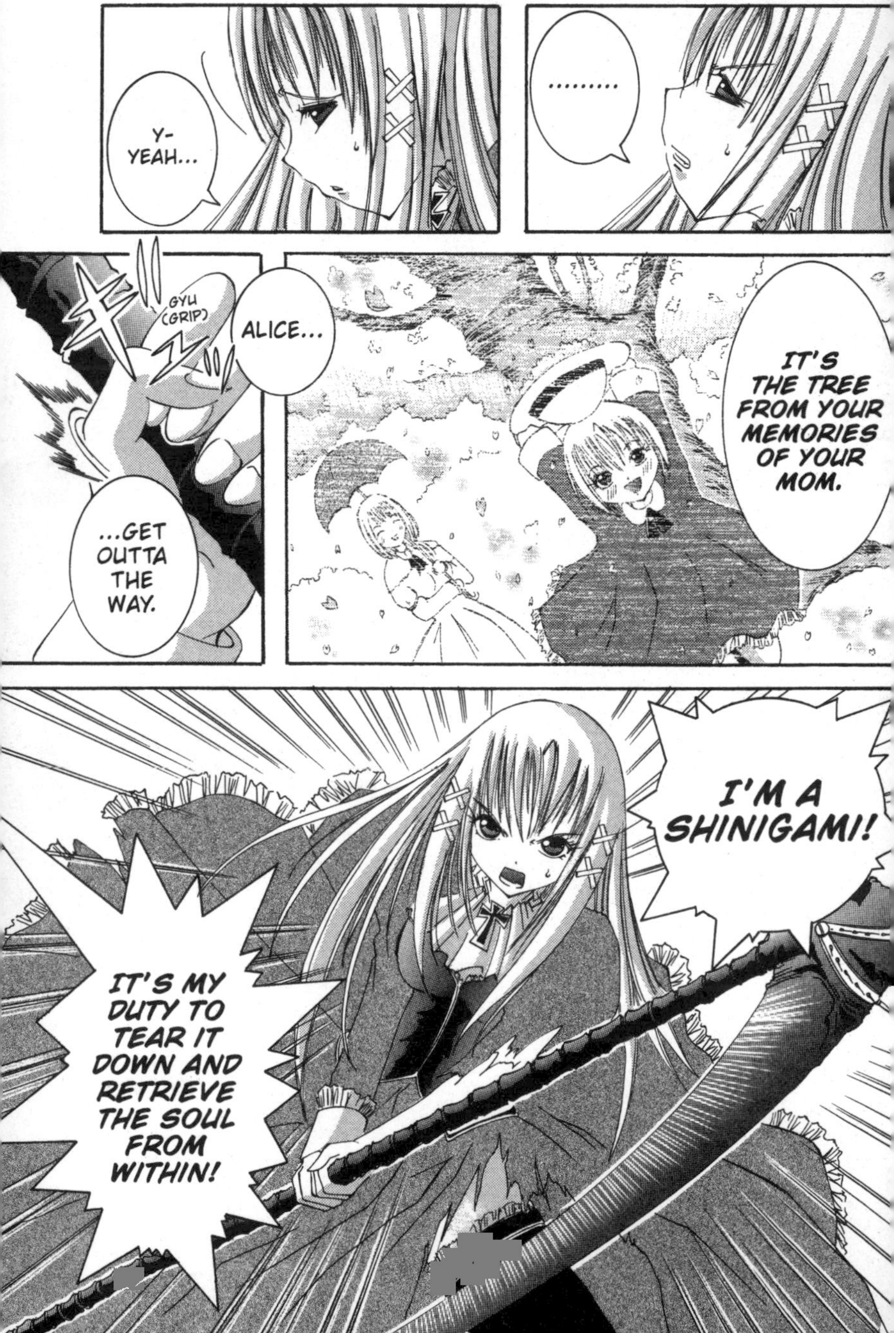
....
Y- YEAH...
IT'S THE TREE FROM YOUR MEMORIES OF YOUR MOM.
ALICE...
GYU (GRIP)
...GET OUTTA THE WAY.
I'M A SHINIGAMI!
IT'S MY DUTY TO TEAR IT DOWN AND RETRIEVE THE SOUL FROM WITHIN!

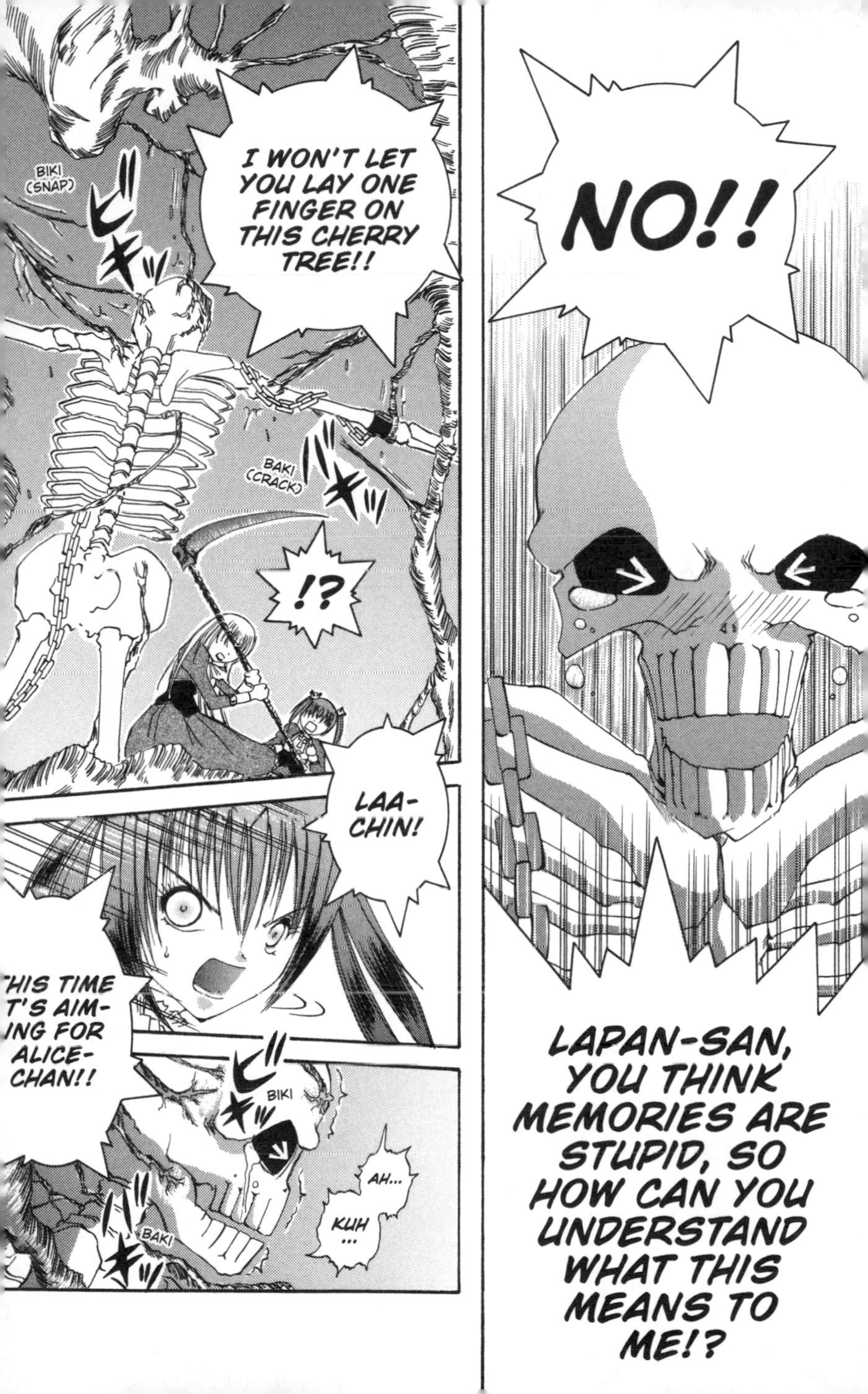
NO!!
LAPAN-SAN, YOU THINK MEMORIES ARE STUPID, SO HOW CAN YOU UNDERSTAND WHAT THIS MEANS TO ME!?
I WON'T LET YOU LAY ONE FINGER ON THIS CHERRY TREE!!
BIKI (SNAP)
BAKI (CRACK)
!?
LAA-CHIN!
HIS TIME T'S AIM- ING FOR ALICE- CHAN!!
BIKI
AH...
KUH...
BAKI

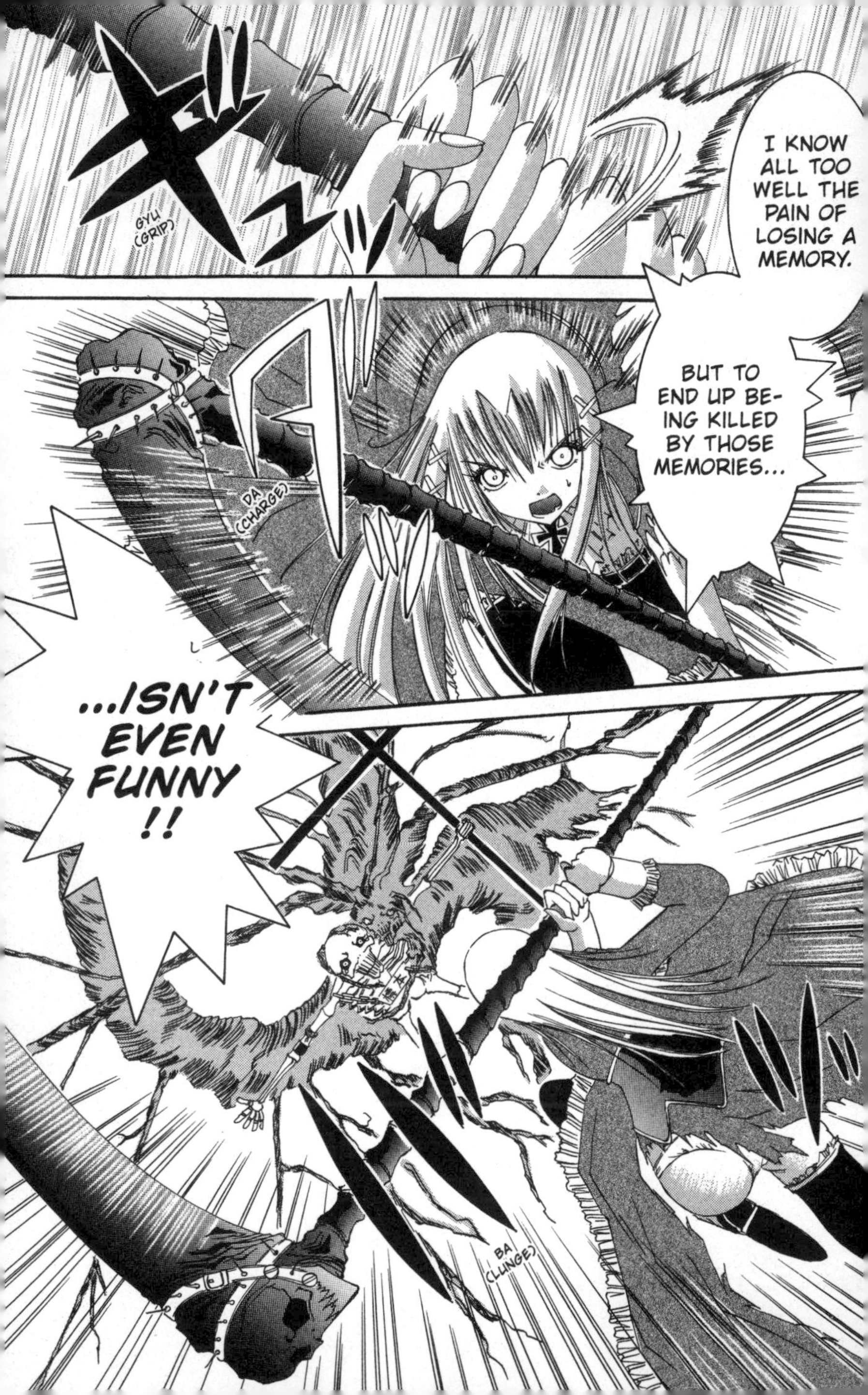
I KNOW ALL TOO WELL THE PAIN OF LOSING A MEMORY.
GYU (GRIP)
BUT TO END UP BE-ING KILLED BY THOSE MEMORIES...
DA (CHARGE)
...ISN'T EVEN FUNNY!!
BA (LUNGE)

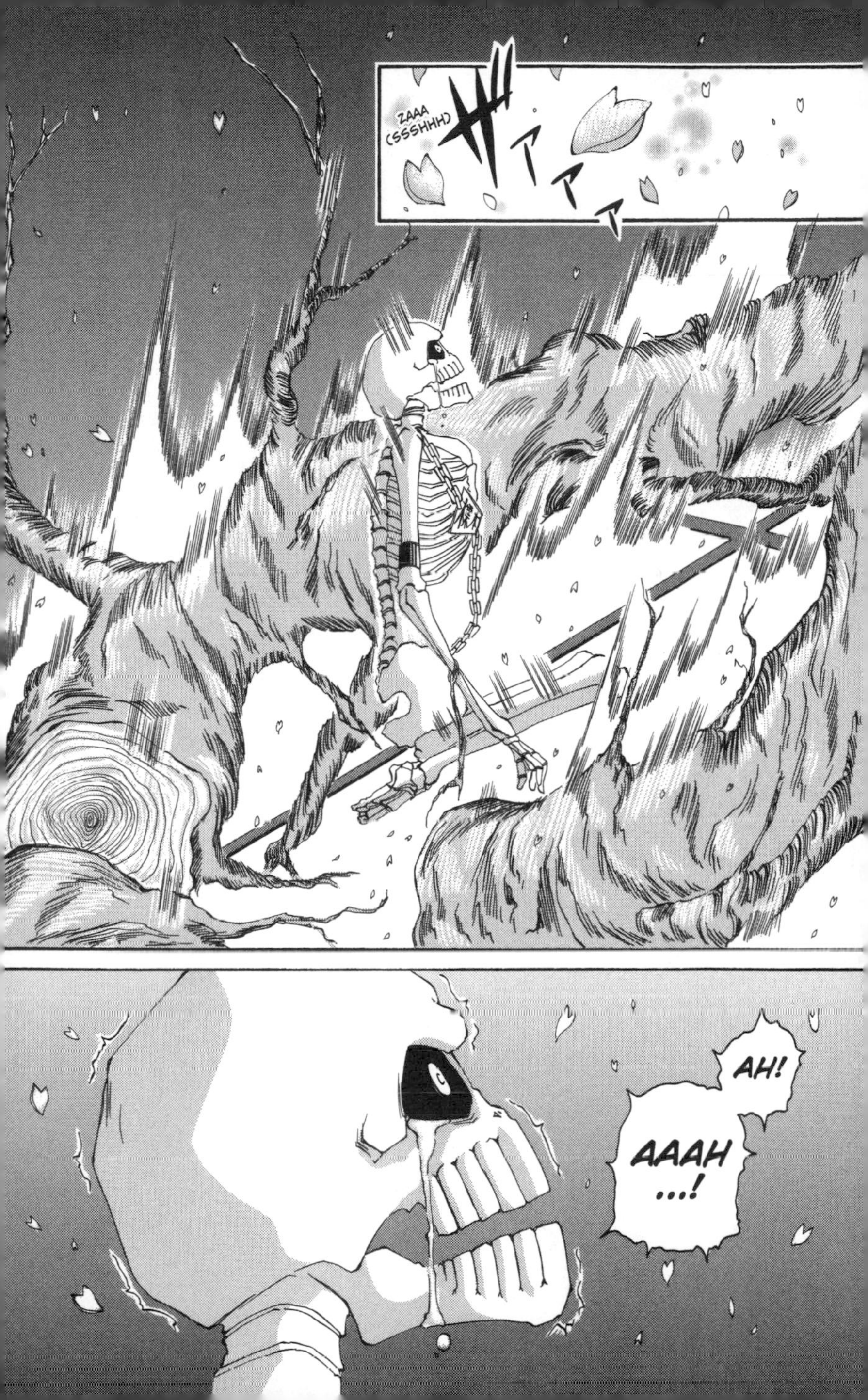
ZAAA (SSSHHH)
AH!
AAAH ...!

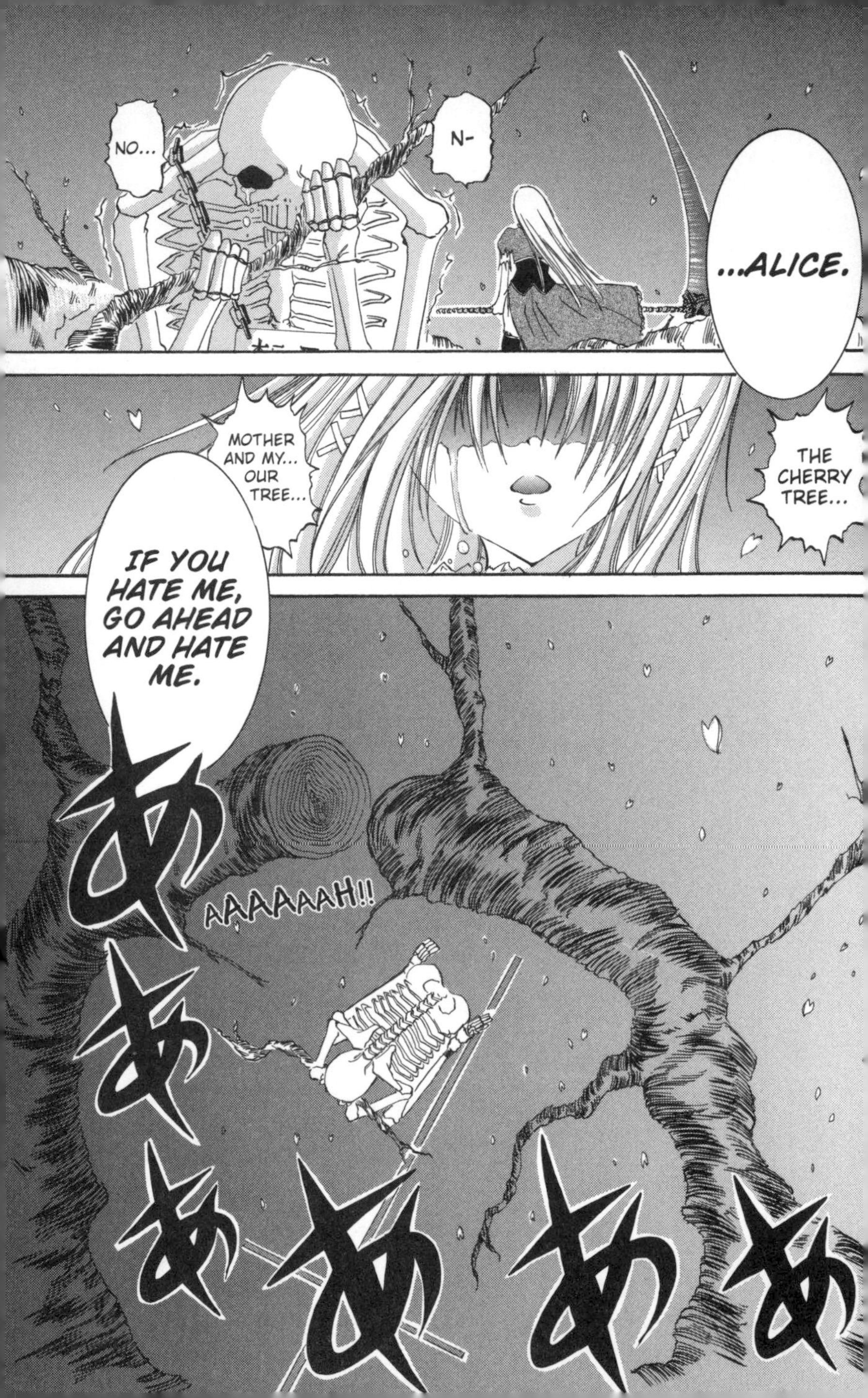
...ALICE.
N-
NO...
THE CHERRY TREE...
MOTHER AND MY... OUR TREE...
IF YOU HATE ME, GO AHEAD AND HATE ME.
AAAAAAH!!

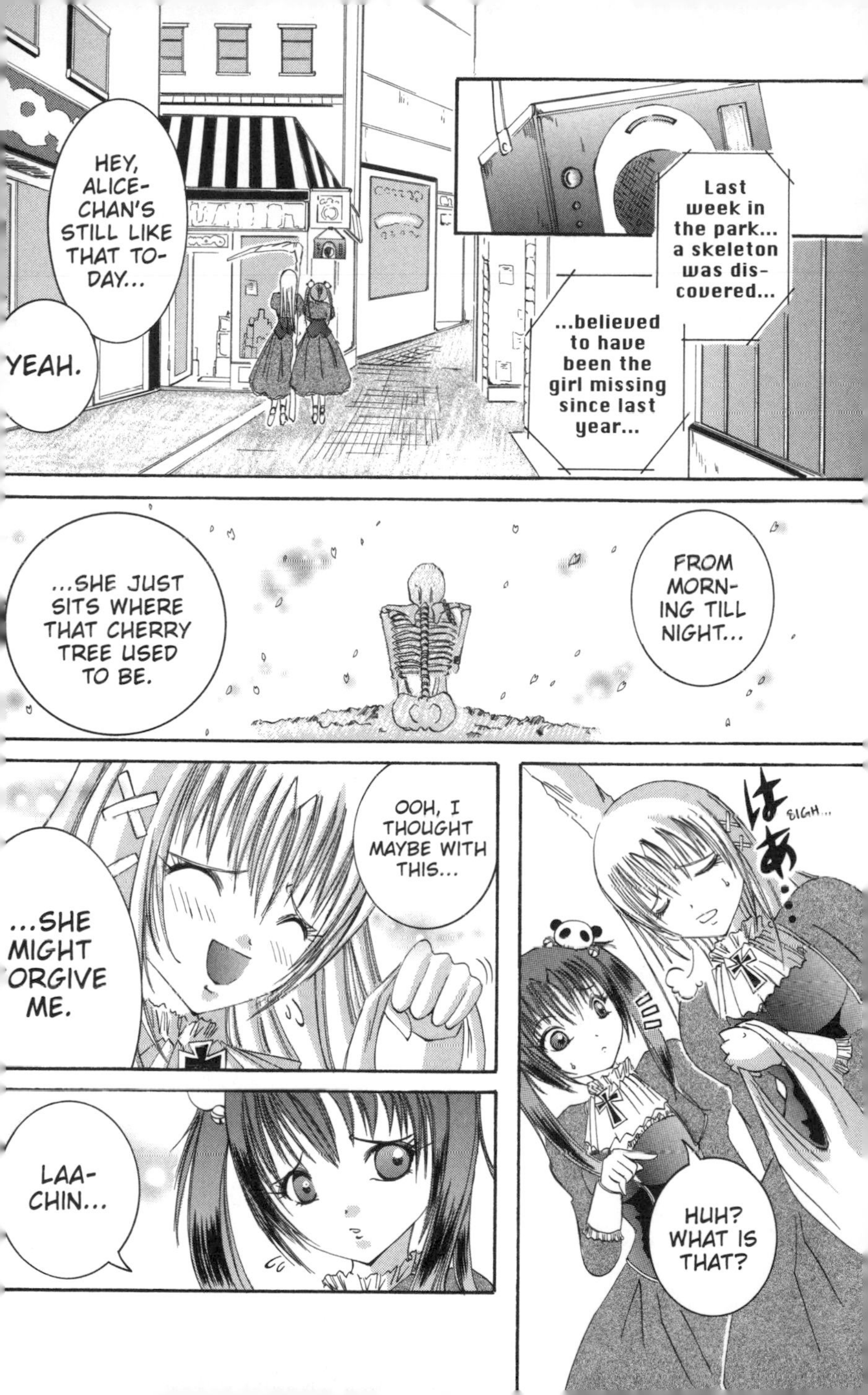
Last week in the park... a skeleton was discovered...
...believed to have been the girl missing since last year...
HEY, ALICE-CHAN'S STILL LIKE THAT TODAY...
YEAH.
FROM MORNING TILL NIGHT...
...SHE JUST SITS WHERE THAT CHERRY TREE USED TO BE.
はあ
SIGH...
HUH? WHAT IS THAT?
OOH, I THOUGHT MAYBE WITH THIS...
...SHE MIGHT ORGIVE ME.
LAA-CHIN...

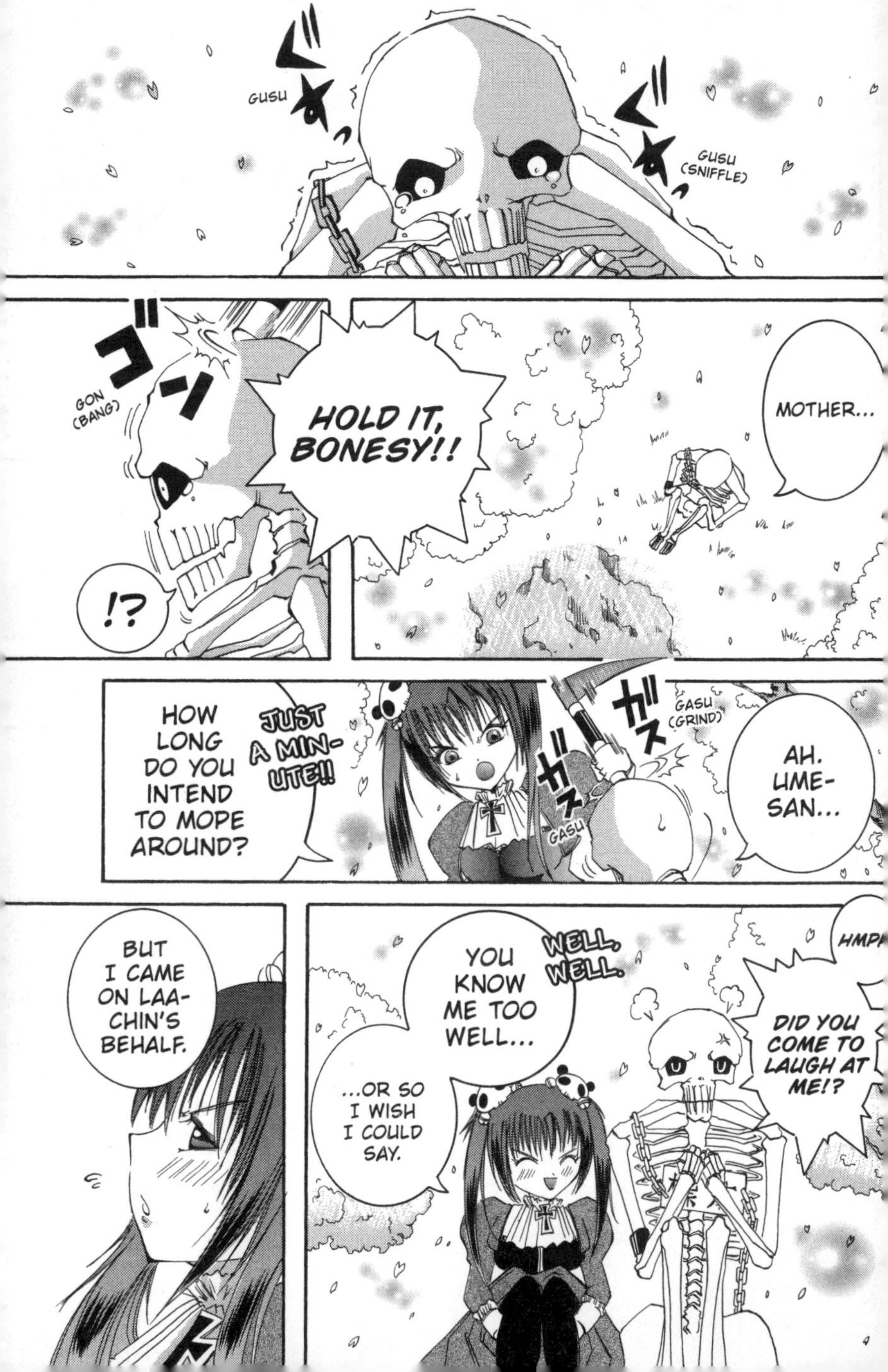
GUSU (SNIFFLE)
GUSU
MOTHER...
HOLD IT, BONESY!!
GON (BANG)
!?
AH. UME-SAN...
GASU (GRIND)
GASU
JUST A MIN-UTE!!
HOW LONG DO YOU INTEND TO MOPE AROUND?
HMP
DID YOU COME TO LAUGH AT ME!?
WELL, WELL.
YOU KNOW ME TOO WELL...
...OR SO I WISH I COULD SAY.
BUT I CAME ON LAA-CHIN'S BEHALF.

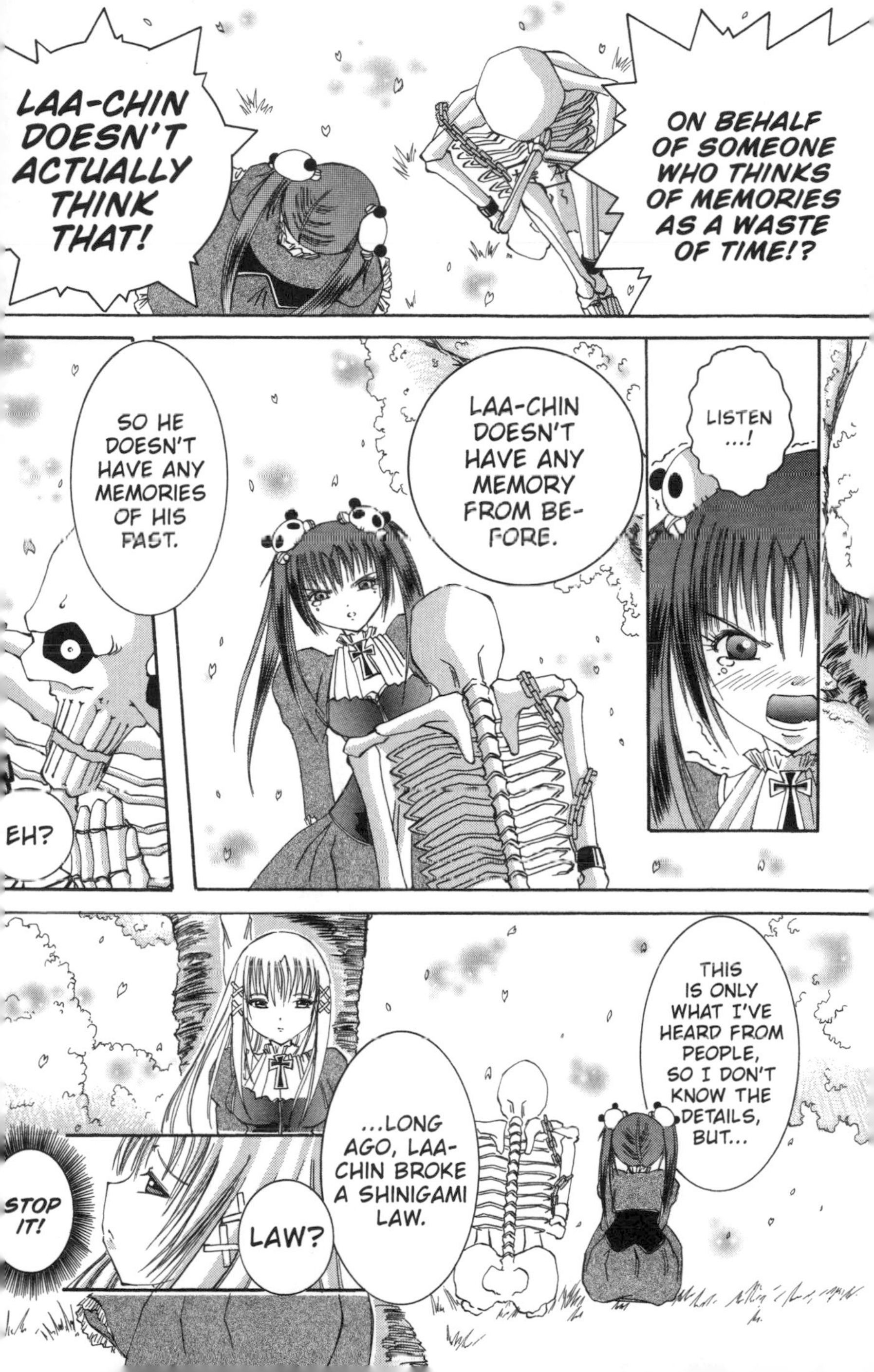
ON BEHALF OF SOMEONE WHO THINKS OF MEMORIES AS A WASTE OF TIME!?
LAA-CHIN DOESN'T ACTUALLY THINK THAT!
LISTEN ...!
LAA-CHIN DOESN'T HAVE ANY MEMORY FROM BE-FORE.
SO HE DOESN'T HAVE ANY MEMORIES OF HIS PAST.
EH?
THIS IS ONLY WHAT I'VE HEARD FROM PEOPLE, SO I DON'T KNOW THE DETAILS, BUT...
...LONG AGO, LAA-CHIN BROKE A SHINIGAMI LAW.
LAW?
STOP IT!

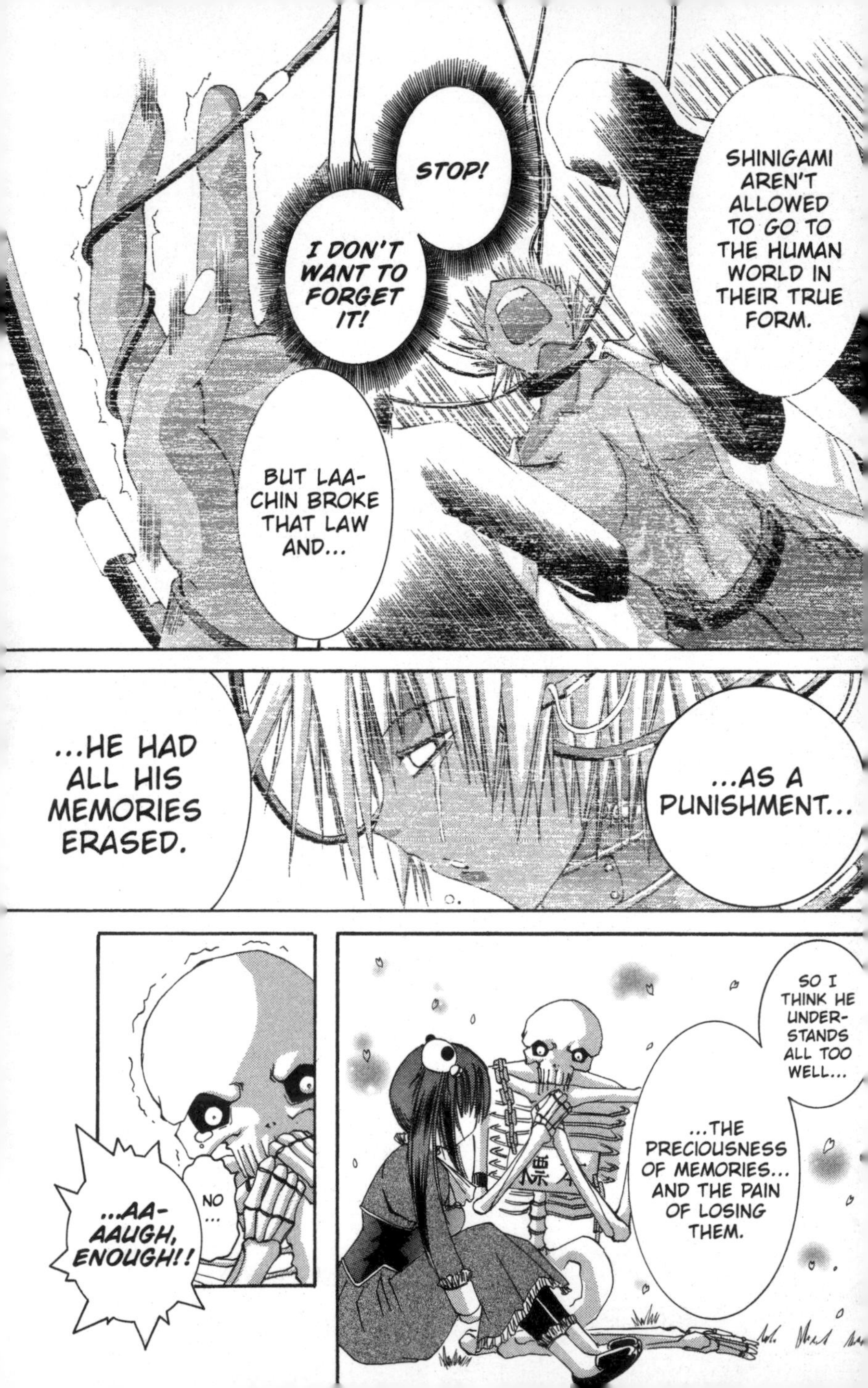
SHINIGAMI AREN'T ALLOWED TO GO TO THE HUMAN WORLD IN THEIR TRUE FORM.
STOP!
I DON'T WANT TO FORGET IT!
BUT LAA-CHIN BROKE THAT LAW AND...
...AS A PUNISHMENT...
...HE HAD ALL HIS MEMORIES ERASED.
SO I THINK HE UNDERSTANDS ALL TOO WELL...
...THE PRECIOUSNESS OF MEMORIES... AND THE PAIN OF LOSING THEM.
NO ...
...AA-AAUGH, ENOUGH!!

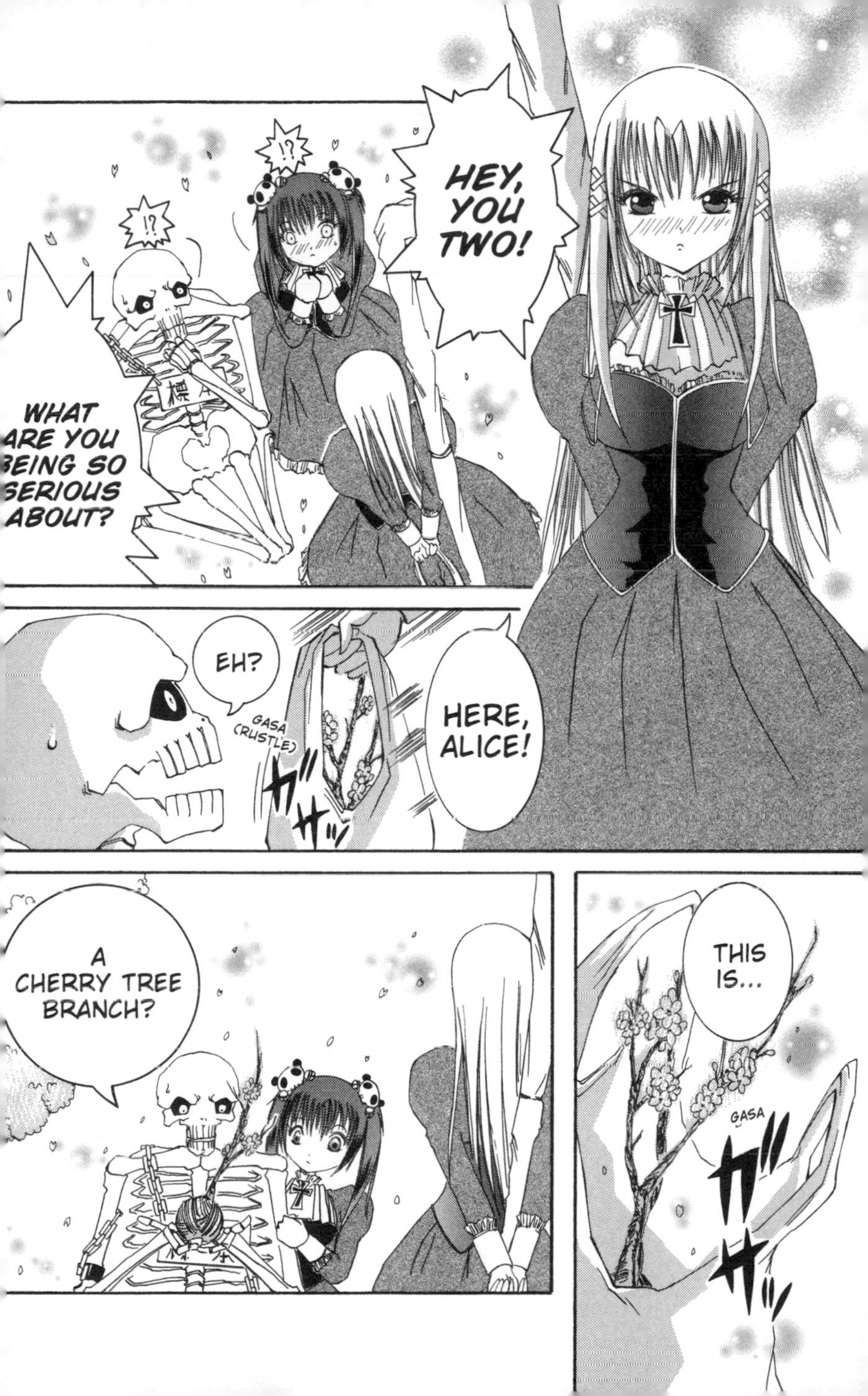
HEY, YOU TWO!
!?
!?
WHAT ARE YOU BEING SO SERIOUS ABOUT?
HERE, ALICE!
GASA (RUSTLE)
EH?
THIS IS...
GASA
A CHERRY TREE BRANCH?

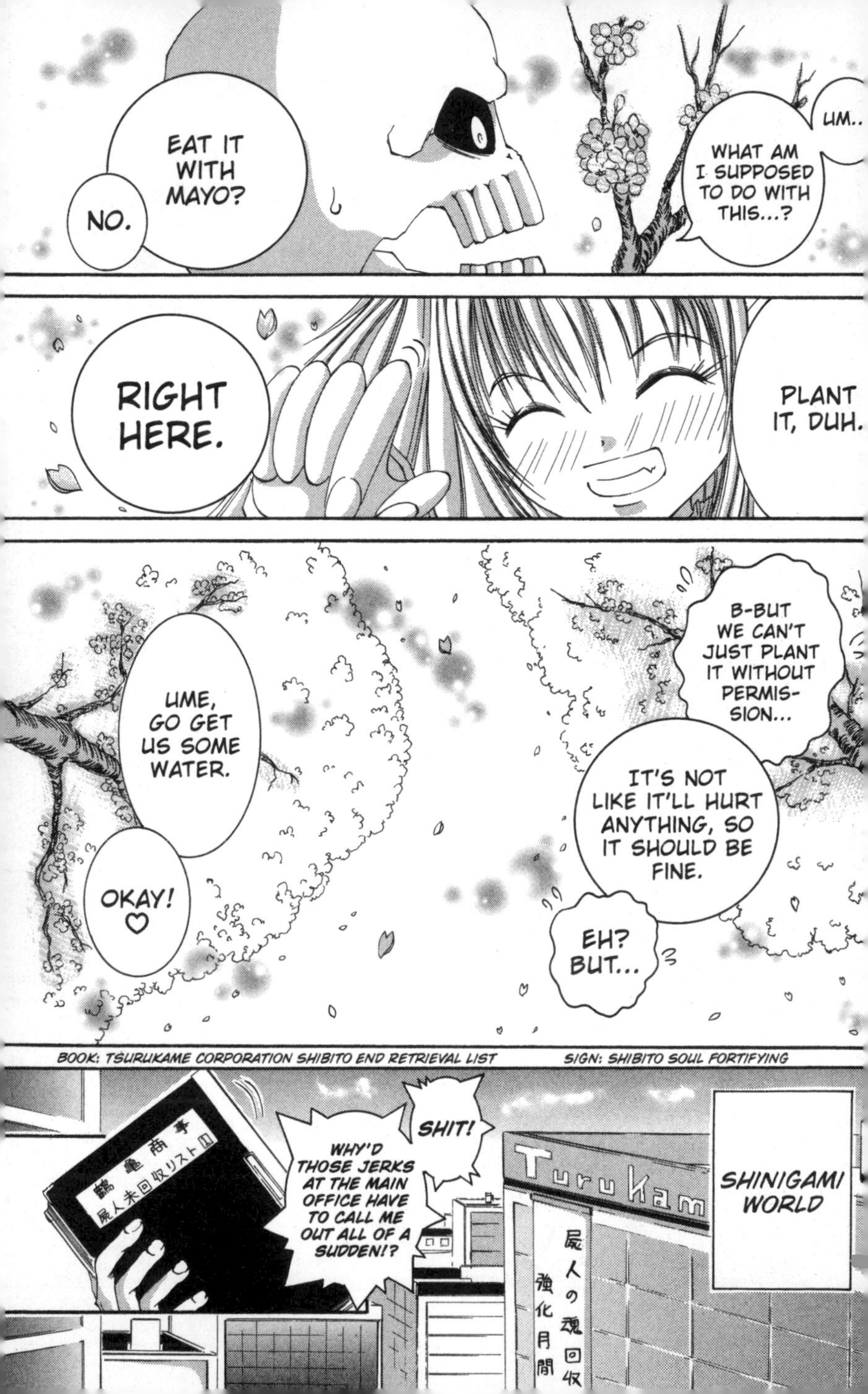
UM..
WHAT AM I SUPPOSED TO DO WITH THIS...?
EAT IT WITH MAYO?
NO.
PLANT IT, DUH.
RIGHT HERE.
B-BUT WE CAN'T JUST PLANT IT WITHOUT PERMIS-SION...
IT'S NOT LIKE IT'LL HURT ANYTHING, SO IT SHOULD BE FINE.
EH? BUT...
UME, GO GET US SOME WATER.
OKAY! ♡
BOOK: TSURUKAME CORPORATION SHIBITO END RETRIEVAL LIST
SIGN: SHIBITO SOUL FORTIFYING
SHINIGAMI WORLD
屍人の魂回収強化月間
Turukam
SHIT!
WHY'D THOSE JERKS AT THE MAIN OFFICE HAVE TO CALL ME OUT ALL OF A SUDDEN!?
鶴亀商事
屍人未回収リスト

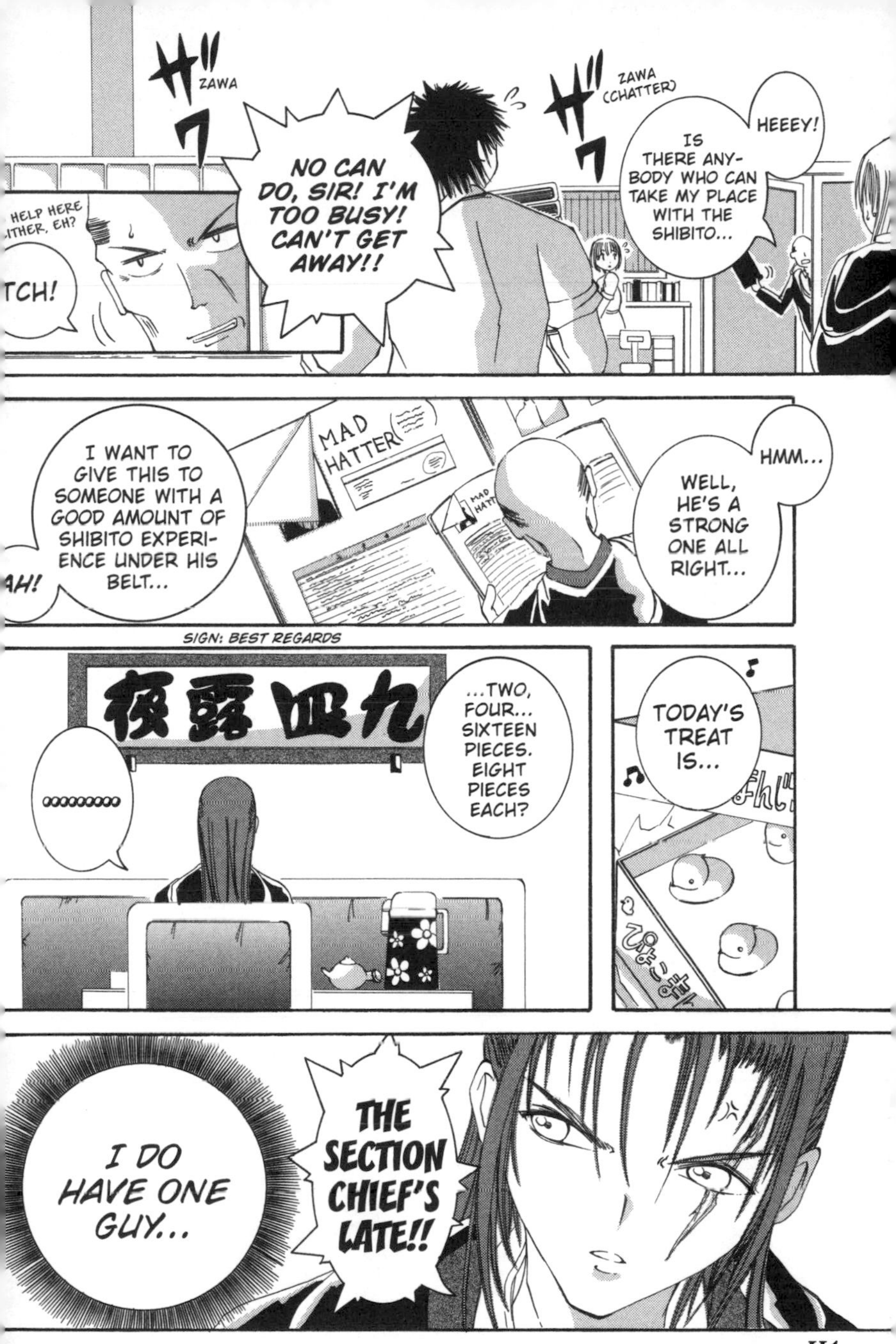
HEEEY!
IS THERE ANYBODY WHO CAN TAKE MY PLACE WITH THE SHIBITO...
ZAWA (CHATTER)
NO CAN DO, SIR! I'M TOO BUSY! CAN'T GET AWAY!!
ZAWA
HELP HERE ITHER, EH?
TCH!
HMM...
WELL, HE'S A STRONG ONE ALL RIGHT...
MAD HATTER
I WANT TO GIVE THIS TO SOMEONE WITH A GOOD AMOUNT OF SHIBITO EXPERIENCE UNDER HIS BELT...
AH!
TODAY'S TREAT IS...
...TWO, FOUR... SIXTEEN PIECES. EIGHT PIECES EACH?
SIGN: BEST REGARDS
夜露四九
....
THE SECTION CHIEF'S LATE!!
I DO HAVE ONE GUY...

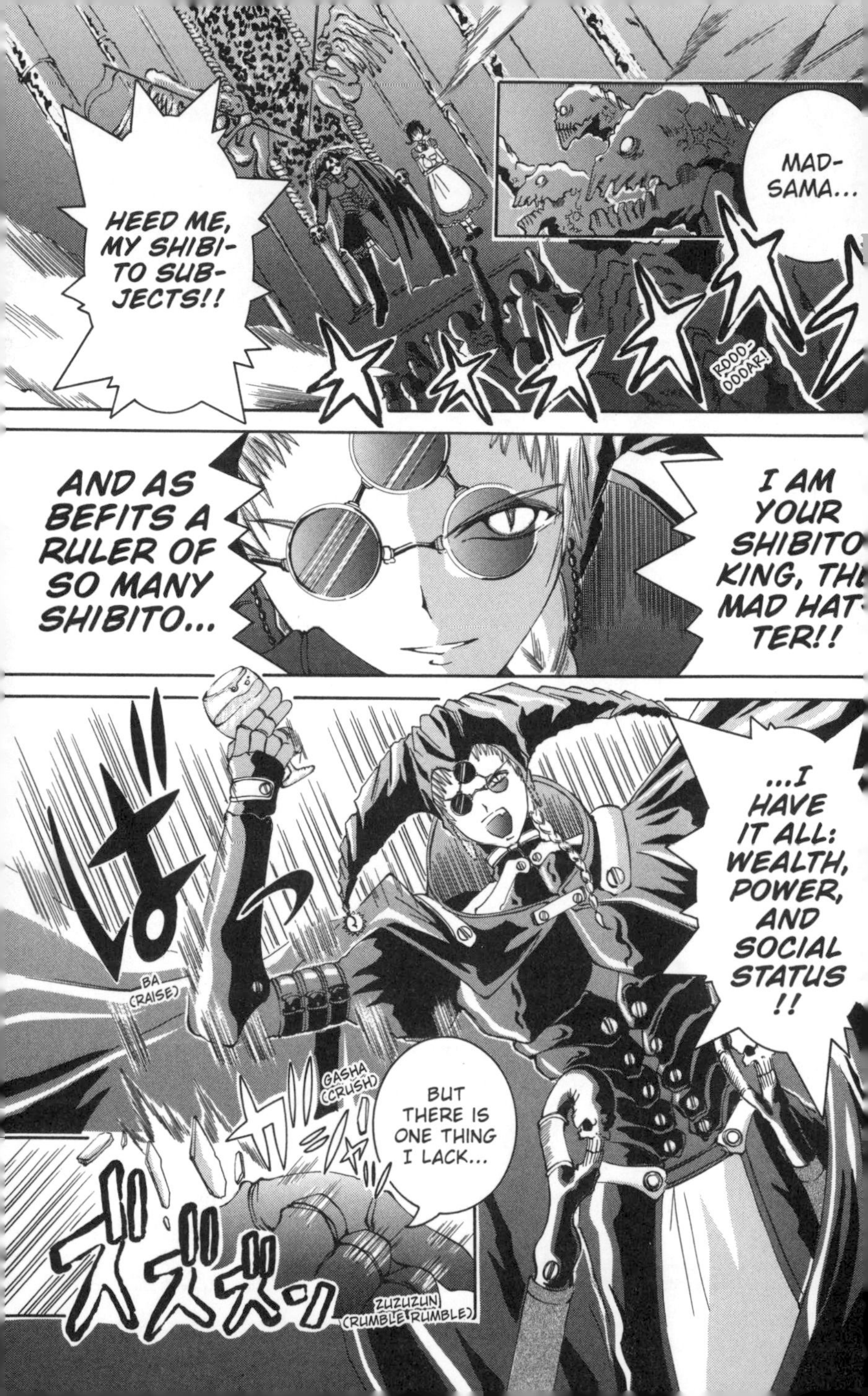
MAD-SAMA...
HEED ME, MY SHIBI-TO SUB-JECTS!!
ROOO-OOOAR!
I AM YOUR SHIBITO KING, THE MAD HAT-TER!!
AND AS BEFITS A RULER OF SO MANY SHIBITO...
...I HAVE IT ALL: WEALTH, POWER, AND SOCIAL STATUS !!
BA (RAISE)
GASHA (CRUSH)
BUT THERE IS ONE THING I LACK...
ZUZUZUN (RUMBLE RUMBLE)

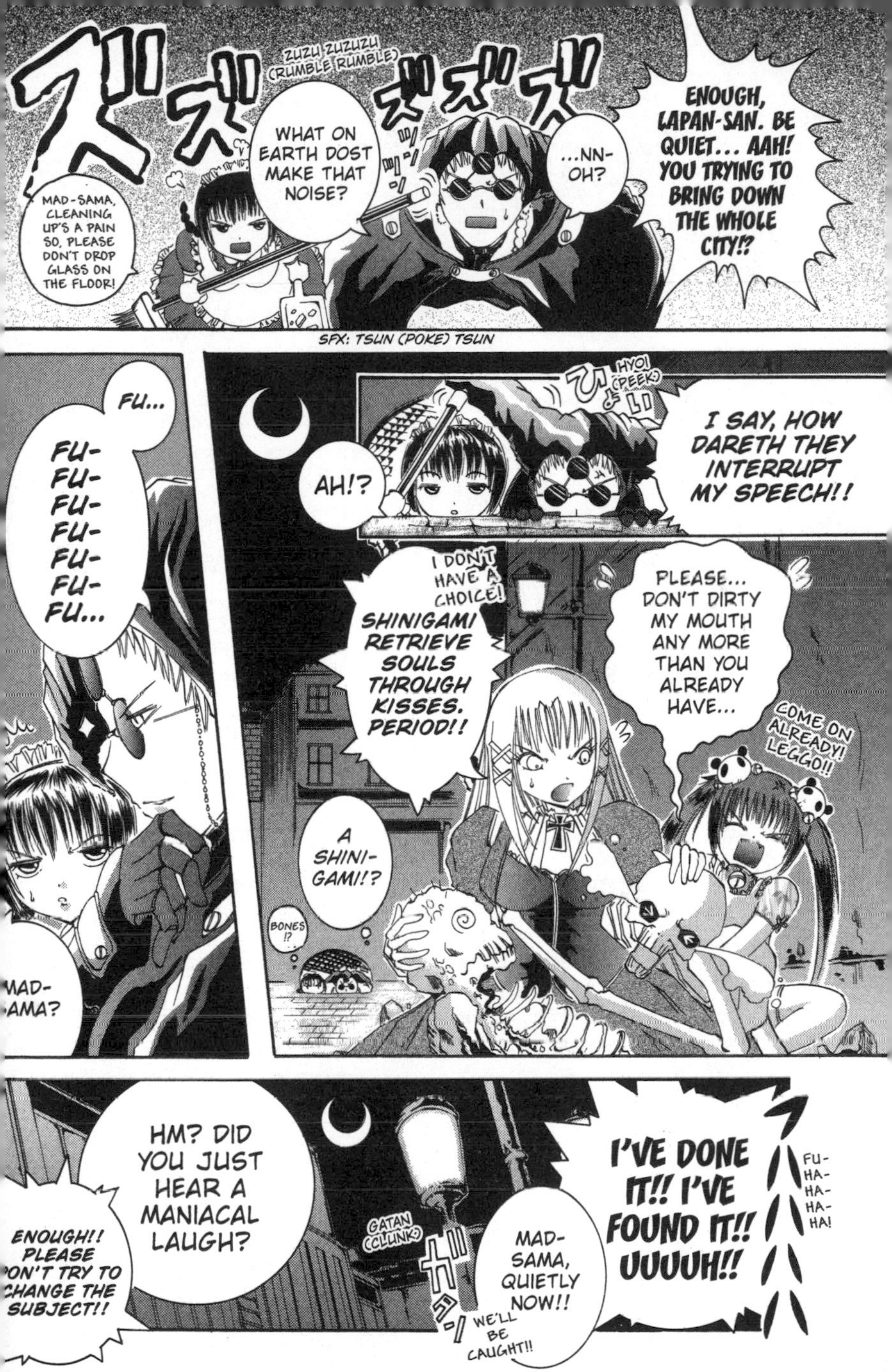
ZUZU ZUZUZU (RUMBLE RUMBLE)
ENOUGH, LAPAN-SAN. BE QUIET... AAH! YOU TRYING TO BRING DOWN THE WHOLE CITY!?
...NN-OH?
WHAT ON EARTH DOST MAKE THAT NOISE?
MAD-SAMA, CLEANING UP'S A PAIN SO, PLEASE DON'T DROP GLASS ON THE FLOOR!
SFX: TSUN (POKE) TSUN
HYOI (PEEK)
I SAY, HOW DARETH THEY INTERRUPT MY SPEECH!!
AH!?
COME ON ALREADY! LEGGO!!
PLEASE... DON'T DIRTY MY MOUTH ANY MORE THAN YOU ALREADY HAVE...
I DON'T HAVE A CHOICE!
SHINIGAMI RETRIEVE SOULS THROUGH KISSES. PERIOD!!
A SHINIGAMI!?
BONES !?
FU...
FU-FU-FU-FU-FU-FU-FU...
MAD-AMA?
FU-HA-HA-HA-HA!
I'VE DONE IT!! I'VE FOUND IT!! UUUUH!!
MAD-SAMA, QUIETLY NOW!!
WE'LL BE CAUGHT!!
GATAN (CLUNK)
HM? DID YOU JUST HEAR A MANIACAL LAUGH?
ENOUGH!! PLEASE DON'T TRY TO CHANGE THE SUBJECT!!

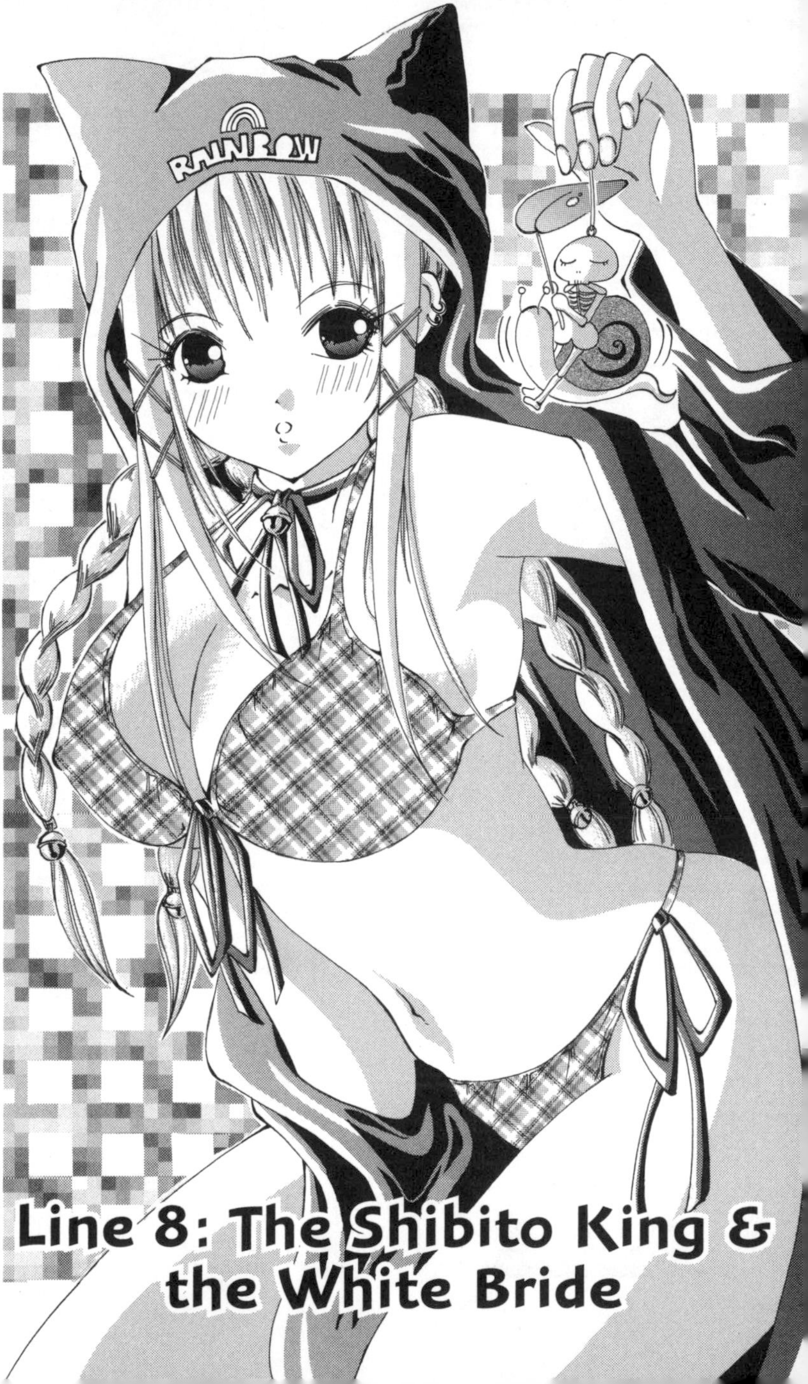
RAINBOW

Line 8: The Shibito King & the White Bride

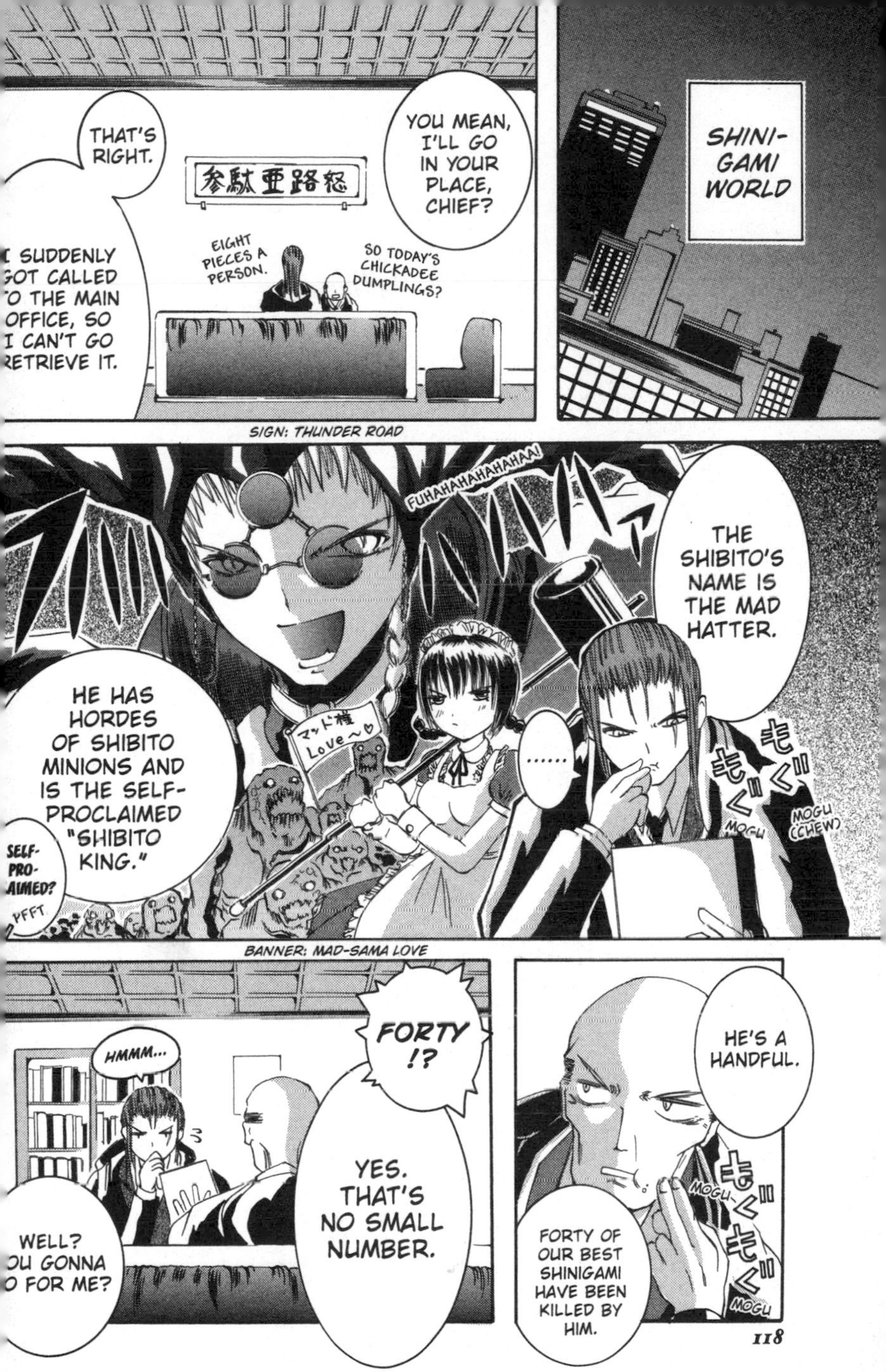
SHINI-GAMI WORLD
YOU MEAN, I'LL GO IN YOUR PLACE, CHIEF?
THAT'S RIGHT.
SO TODAY'S CHICKADEE DUMPLINGS?
EIGHT PIECES A PERSON.
I SUDDENLY GOT CALLED TO THE MAIN OFFICE, SO I CAN'T GO RETRIEVE IT.
SIGN: THUNDER ROAD
FUHAHAHAHAHAHAA!
THE SHIBITO'S NAME IS THE MAD HATTER.
もぐ もぐ
MOGU MOGU (CHEW)
......
マッド様 Love～♡
HE HAS HORDES OF SHIBITO MINIONS AND IS THE SELF-PROCLAIMED "SHIBITO KING."
SELF-PROCLAIMED?
PFFT
BANNER: MAD-SAMA LOVE
HE'S A HANDFUL.
もぐ もぐ
MOGU MOGU
FORTY OF OUR BEST SHINIGAMI HAVE BEEN KILLED BY HIM.
FORTY !?
YES. THAT'S NO SMALL NUMBER.
HMMM...
WELL? YOU GONNA GO FOR ME?

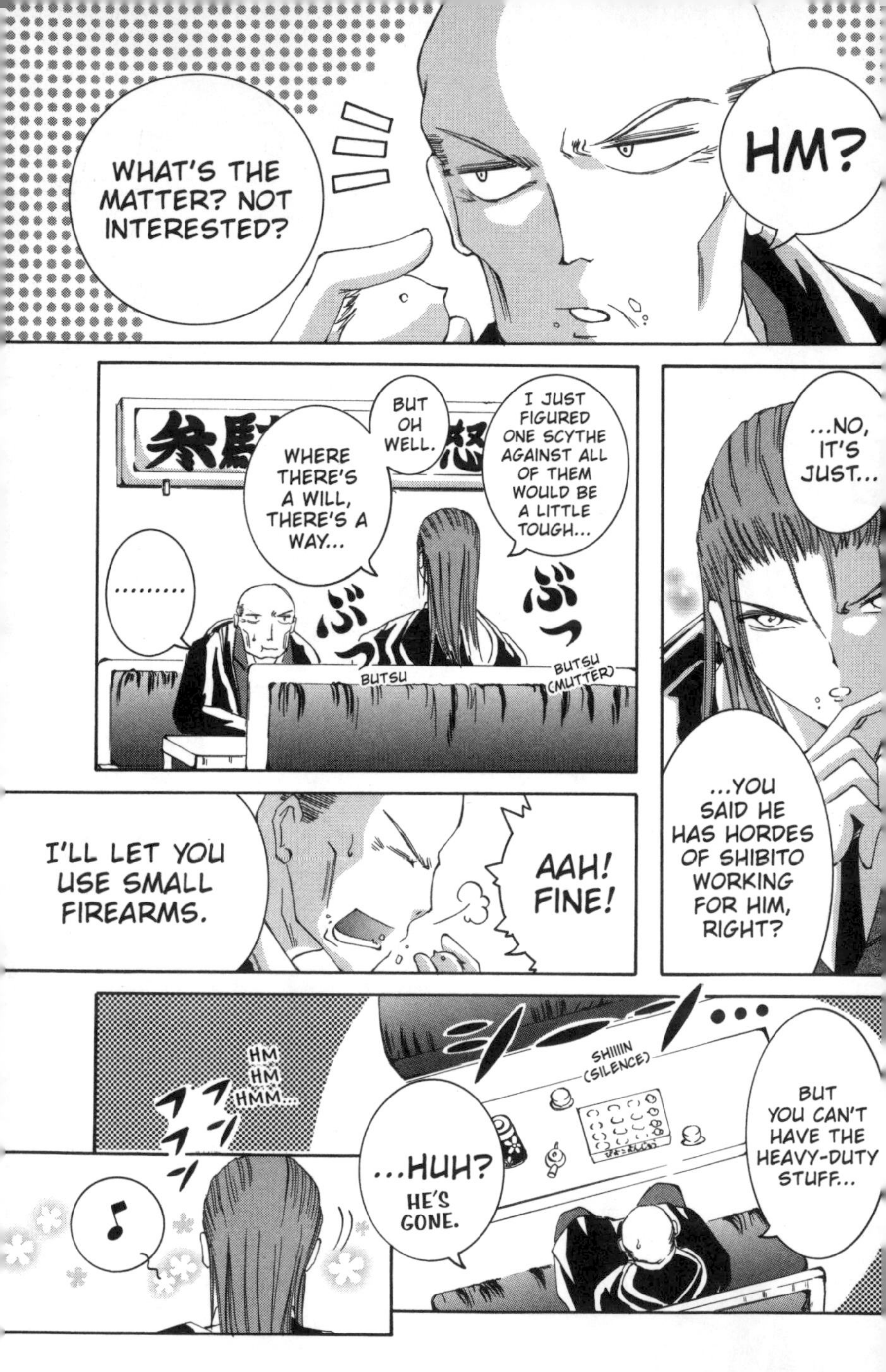
HM?
WHAT'S THE MATTER? NOT INTERESTED?
...NO, IT'S JUST...
...YOU SAID HE HAS HORDES OF SHIBITO WORKING FOR HIM, RIGHT?
I JUST FIGURED ONE SCYTHE AGAINST ALL OF THEM WOULD BE A LITTLE TOUGH...
BUT OH WELL.
WHERE THERE'S A WILL, THERE'S A WAY...
BUTSU (MUTTER)
BUTSU
....
AAH! FINE!
I'LL LET YOU USE SMALL FIREARMS.
...
BUT YOU CAN'T HAVE THE HEAVY-DUTY STUFF...
SHIIIIN (SILENCE)
...HUH? HE'S GONE.
HM HM HMM...
♪

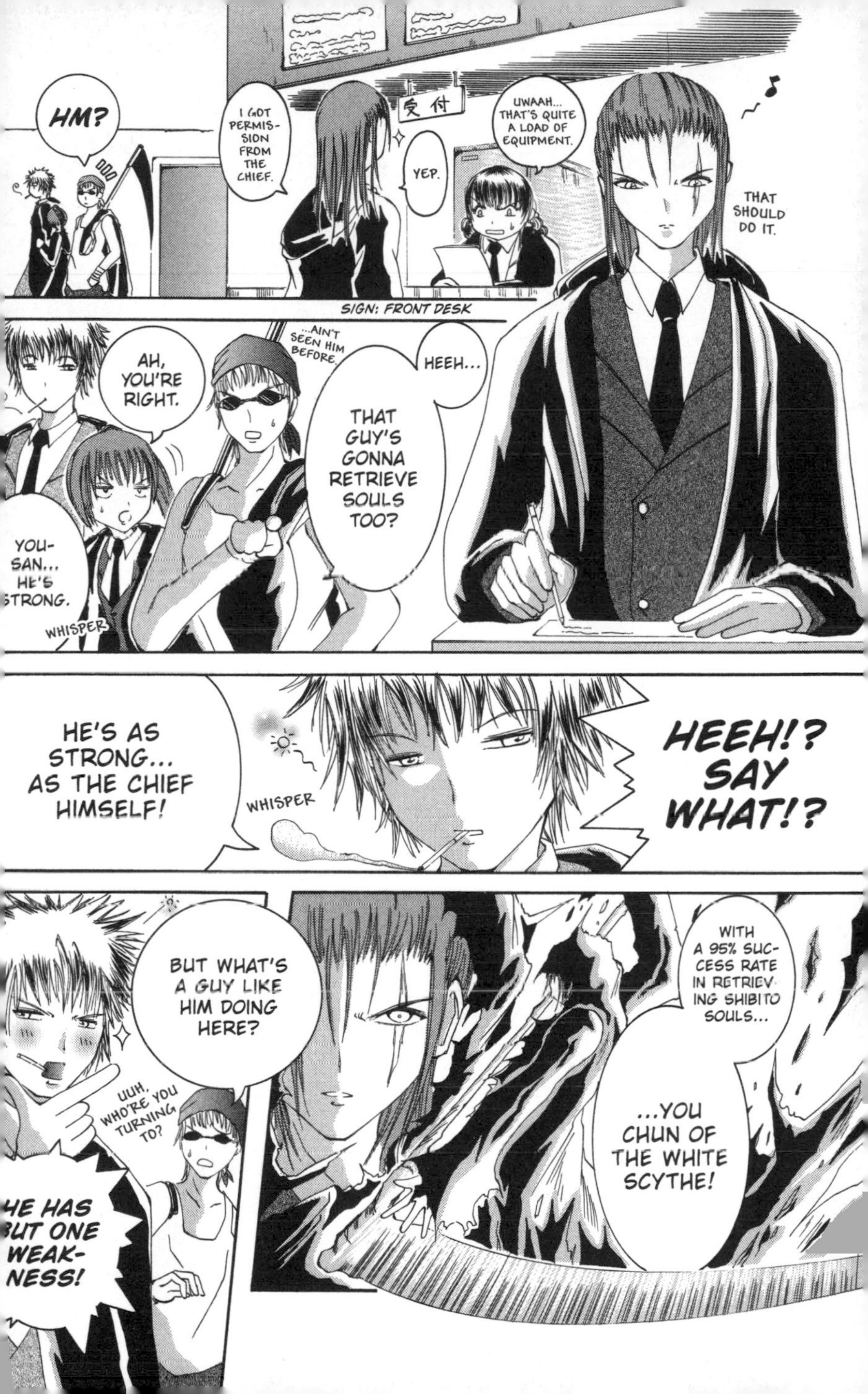
UWAAH... THAT'S QUITE A LOAD OF EQUIPMENT.
YEP.
I GOT PERMISSION FROM THE CHIEF.
HM?
SIGN: FRONT DESK
THAT SHOULD DO IT.
HEEH...
...AIN'T SEEN HIM BEFORE.
THAT GUY'S GONNA RETRIEVE SOULS TOO?
AH, YOU'RE RIGHT.
YOU-SAN... HE'S STRONG.
WHISPER
HEEH!? SAY WHAT!?
WHISPER
HE'S AS STRONG... AS THE CHIEF HIMSELF!
WITH A 95% SUCCESS RATE IN RETRIEVING SHIBITO SOULS...
...YOU CHUN OF THE WHITE SCYTHE!
BUT WHAT'S A GUY LIKE HIM DOING HERE?
UUH, WHO'RE YOU TURNING TO?
HE HAS BUT ONE WEAKNESS!

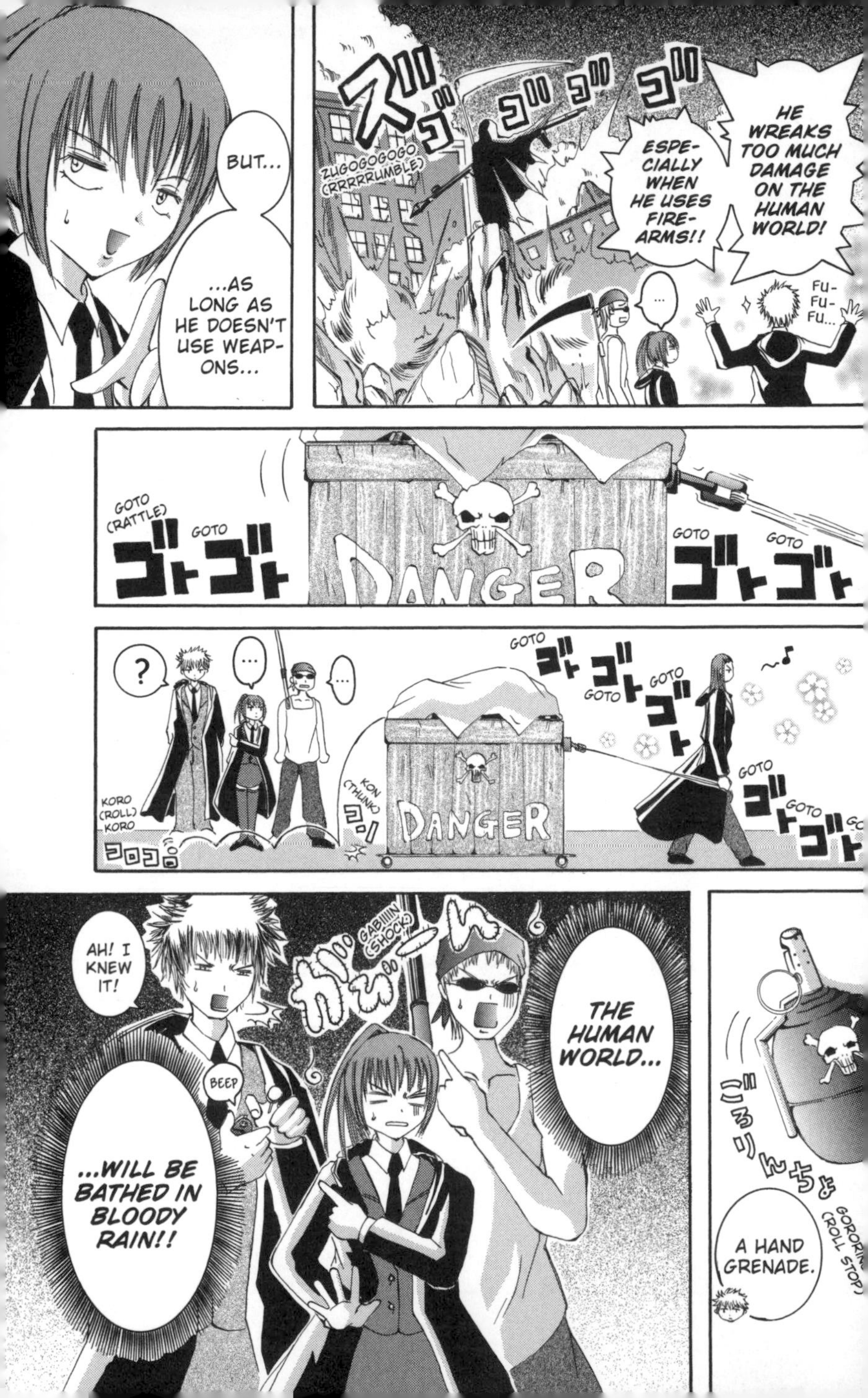
ZUGOGOGOGO (RRRRRUMBLE)
HE WREAKS TOO MUCH DAMAGE ON THE HUMAN WORLD!
ESPECIALLY WHEN HE USES FIREARMS!!
FU-FU-FU...
...
BUT...
...AS LONG AS HE DOESN'T USE WEAPONS...
GOTO GOTO
GOTO (RATTLE) GOTO
DANGER
GOTO GOTO GOTO GOTO GOTO
~♪
DANGER
KON (THUNK)
...
...
?
KORO (ROLL) KORO
GORORIN (ROLL STOP)
A HAND GRENADE.
GABIIIN (SHOCK)
THE HUMAN WORLD...
AH! I KNEW IT!
BEEP
...WILL BE BATHED IN BLOODY RAIN!!

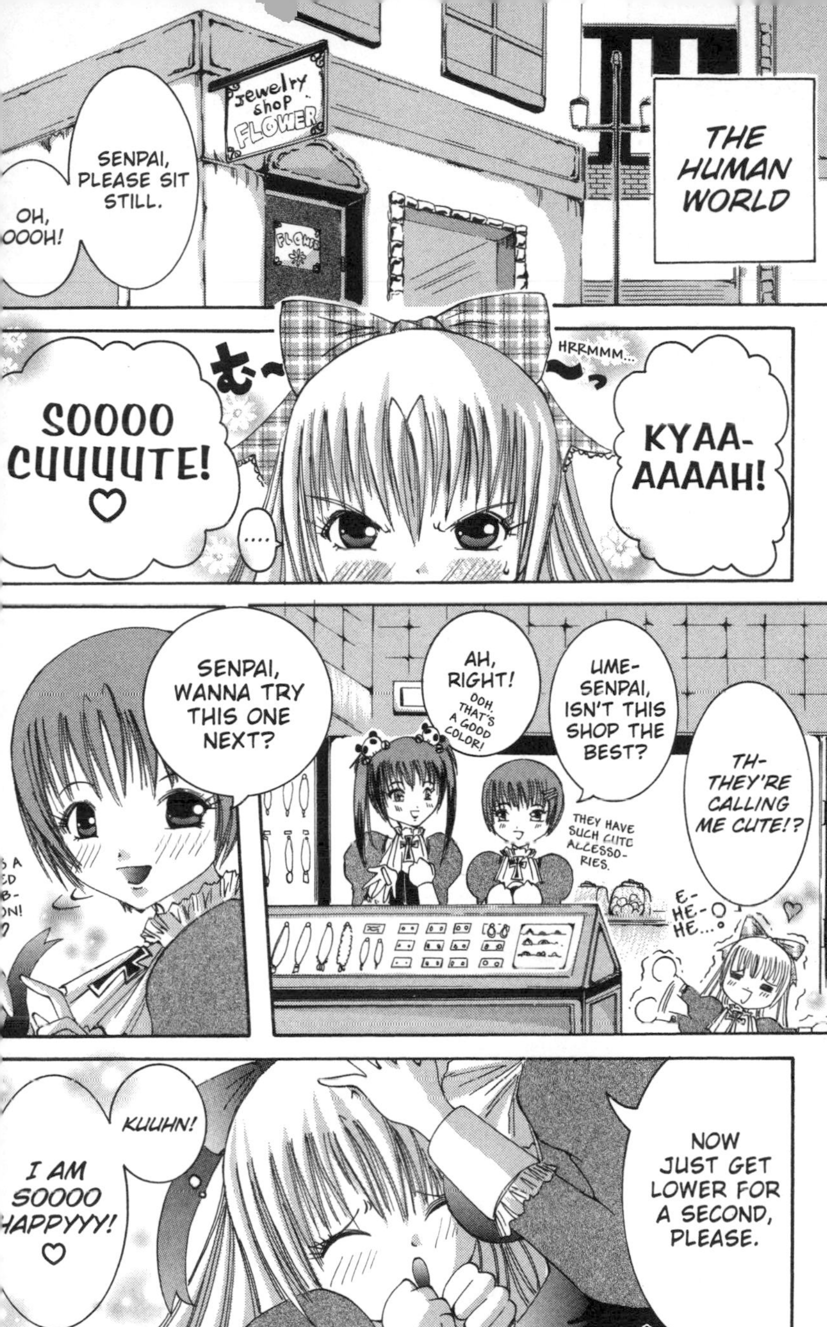
THE HUMAN WORLD
Jewelry shop FLOWER
SENPAI, PLEASE SIT STILL.
OH, OOOH!
HRRMMM...
KYAA-AAAAH!
SOOOO CUUUUTE! ♡
....
TH-THEY'RE CALLING ME CUTE!?
E-HE-HE...
UME-SENPAI, ISN'T THIS SHOP THE BEST?
THEY HAVE SUCH CUTE ACCESSORIES.
AH, RIGHT!
OOH, THAT'S A GOOD COLOR!
SENPAI, WANNA TRY THIS ONE NEXT?
NOW JUST GET LOWER FOR A SECOND, PLEASE.
KUUHN!
I AM SOOOO APPYYY! ♡

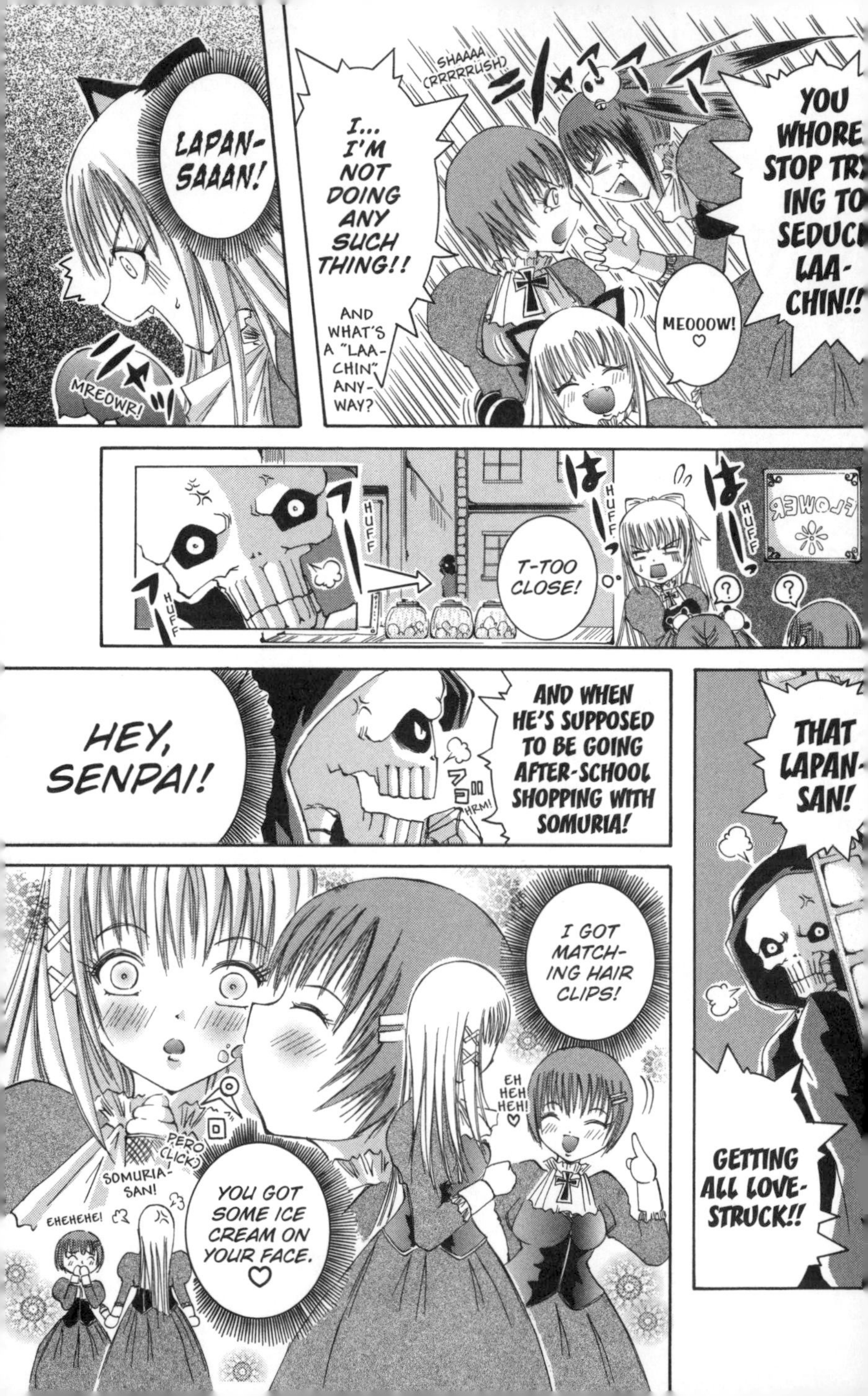
SHAAAA (RRRRRUSH)
YOU WHORE STOP TRYING TO SEDUCE LAA-CHIN!!
MEOOOW! ♡
I... I'M NOT DOING ANY SUCH THING!!
AND WHAT'S A "LAA-CHIN" ANYWAY?
LAPAN-SAAAN!
MREOWR!
HUFF
HUFF
T-TOO CLOSE!
HUFF
HUFF
THAT LAPAN-SAN!
GETTING ALL LOVE-STRUCK!!
AND WHEN HE'S SUPPOSED TO BE GOING AFTER-SCHOOL SHOPPING WITH SOMURIA!
HRM!
HEY, SENPAI!
I GOT MATCHING HAIR CLIPS!
EH HEH HEH! ♡
PERO (LICK)
YOU GOT SOME ICE CREAM ON YOUR FACE. ♡
SOMURIA-SAN!
EHEHEHE!

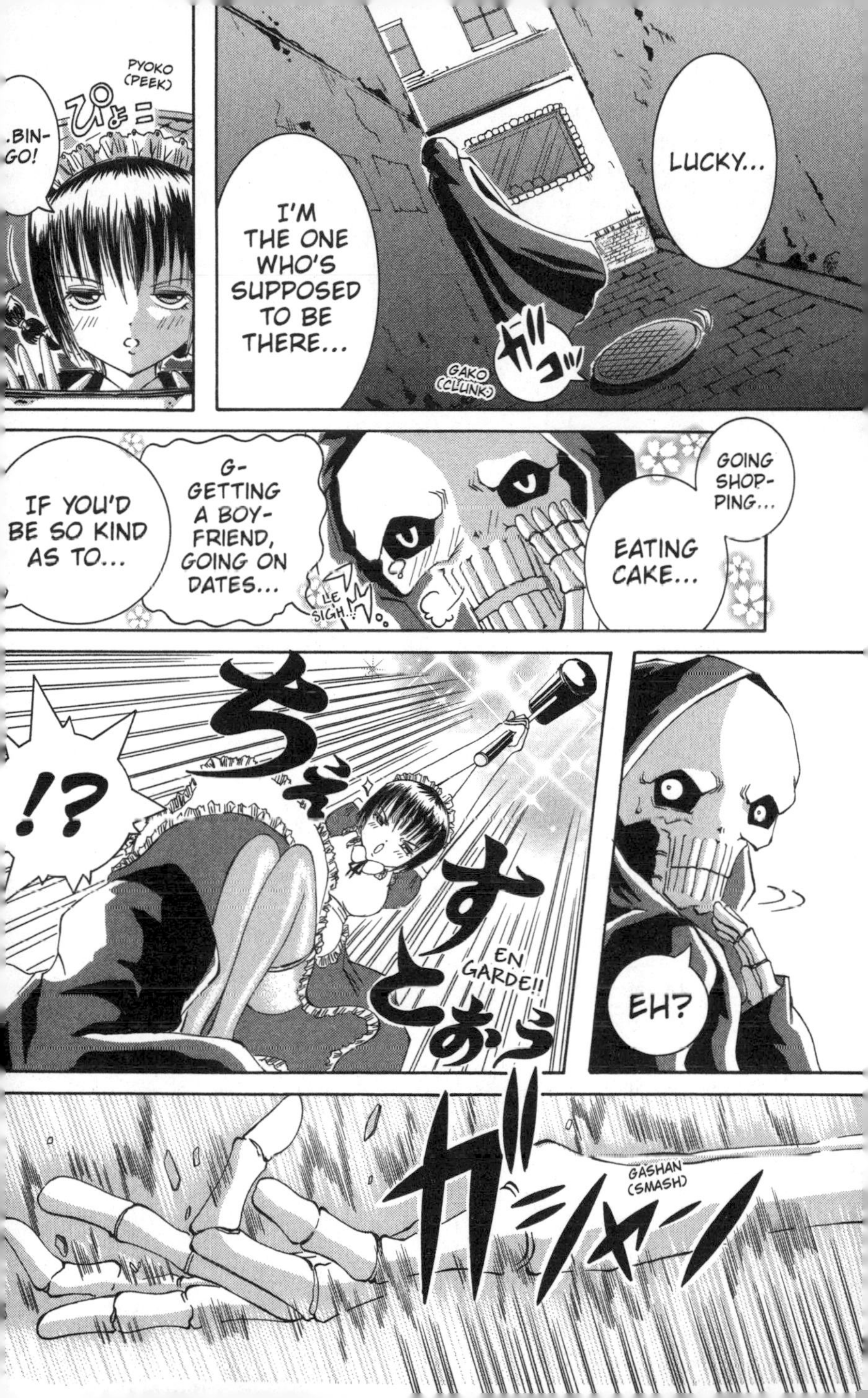
LUCKY...
I'M THE ONE WHO'S SUPPOSED TO BE THERE...
GAKO (CLUNK)
PYOKO (PEEK)
.BIN-GO!
GOING SHOP-PING...
EATING CAKE...
LE SIGH...
G-GETTING A BOY-FRIEND, GOING ON DATES...
IF YOU'D BE SO KIND AS TO...
EH?
!?
EN GARDE!!
GASHAN (SMASH)

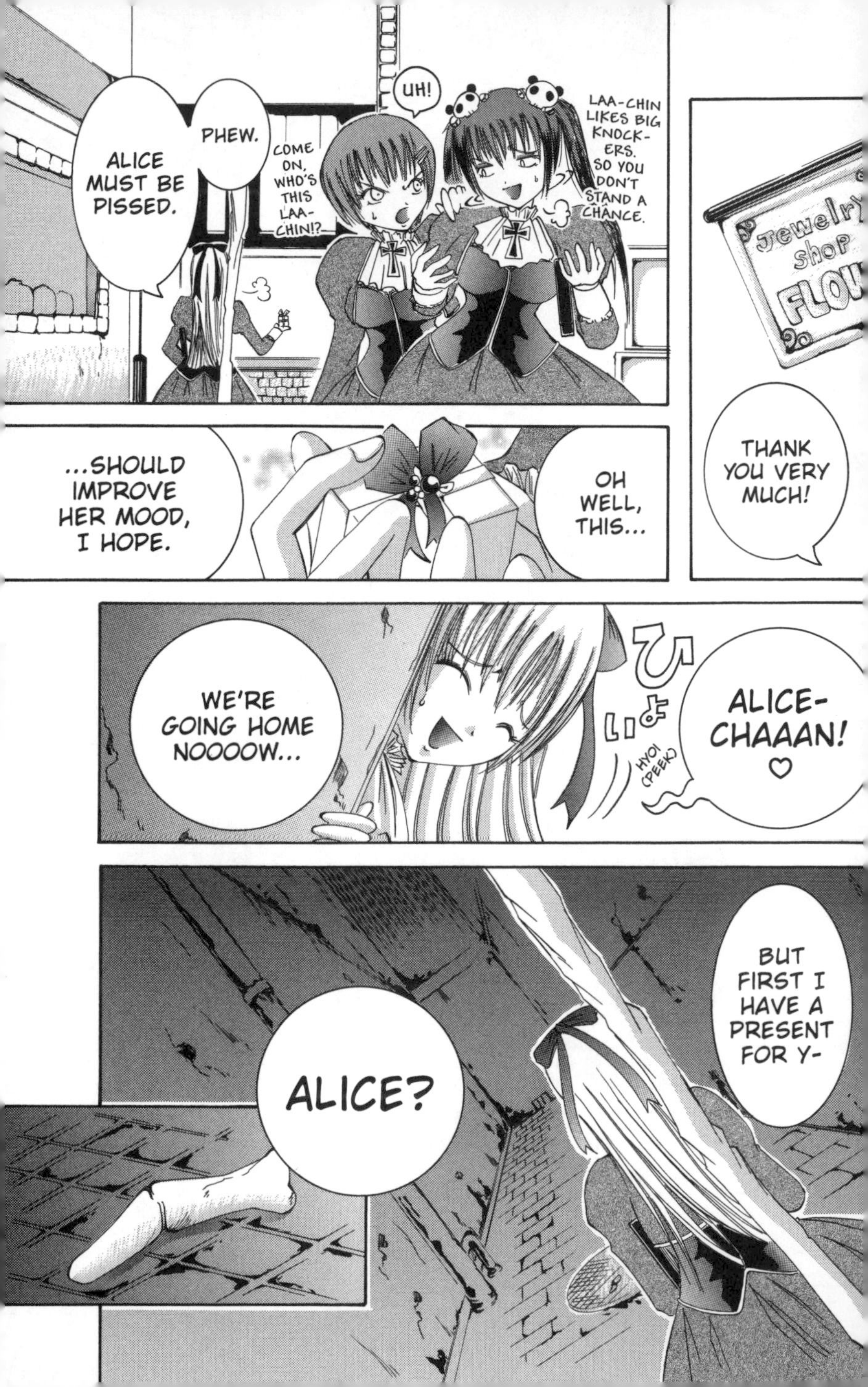
Jewelry shop
FLOU
THANK YOU VERY MUCH!
LAA-CHIN LIKES BIG KNOCKERS. SO YOU DON'T STAND A CHANCE.
UH!
COME ON, WHO'S THIS LAA-CHIN!?
PHEW.
ALICE MUST BE PISSED.
OH WELL, THIS...
...SHOULD IMPROVE HER MOOD, I HOPE.
ALICE-CHAAAN! ♡
ひょい
HYOI (PEEK)
WE'RE GOING HOME NOOOOW...
BUT FIRST I HAVE A PRESENT FOR Y-
ALICE?

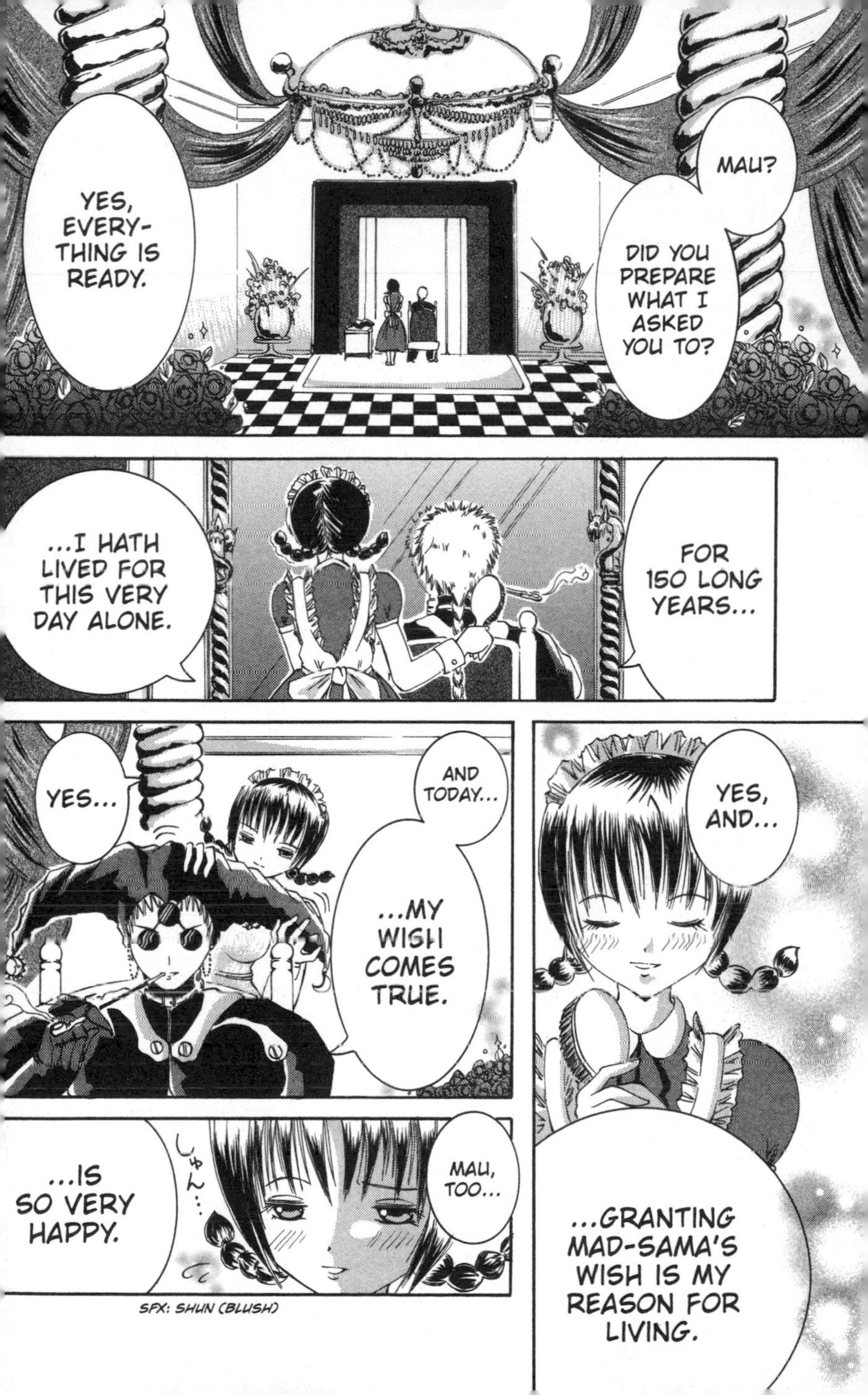
MAU?
DID YOU PREPARE WHAT I ASKED YOU TO?
YES, EVERY-THING IS READY.
FOR 150 LONG YEARS...
...I HATH LIVED FOR THIS VERY DAY ALONE.
YES, AND...
...GRANTING MAD-SAMA'S WISH IS MY REASON FOR LIVING.
AND TODAY...
...MY WISH COMES TRUE.
YES...
MAU, TOO...
しゅん…
...IS SO VERY HAPPY.

SFX: SHUN (BLUSH)

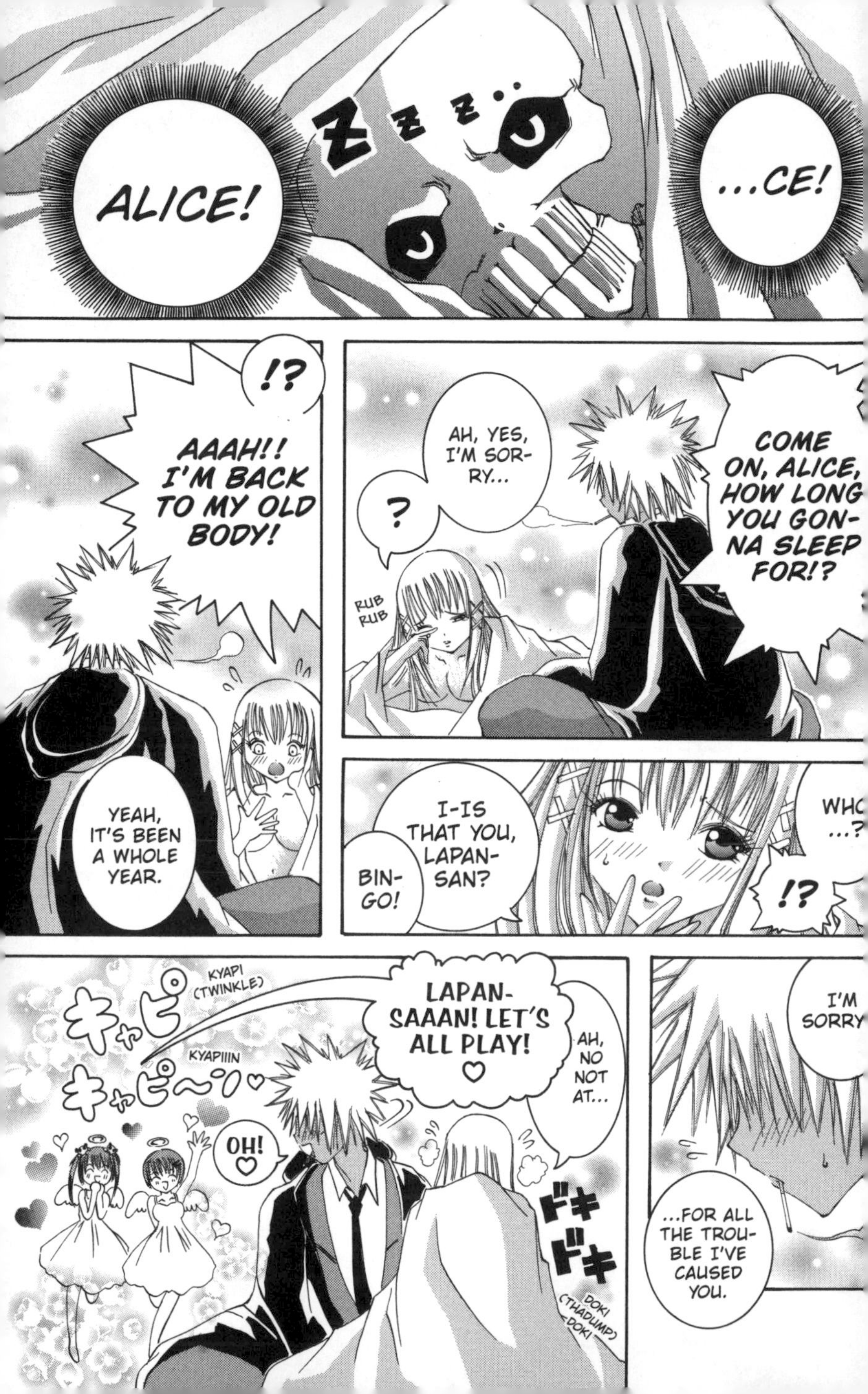
...CE!
Z z z..
ALICE!
COME ON, ALICE, HOW LONG YOU GONNA SLEEP FOR!?
AH, YES, I'M SORRY...
?
RUB RUB
WH ...?
!?
I-IS THAT YOU, LAPAN-SAN?
BINGO!
!?
AAAH!! I'M BACK TO MY OLD BODY!
YEAH, IT'S BEEN A WHOLE YEAR.
I'M SORRY
...FOR ALL THE TROUBLE I'VE CAUSED YOU.
AH, NO NOT AT...
LAPAN-SAAAN! LET'S ALL PLAY! ♡
キャピ
KYAPI (TWINKLE)
キャピ〜♡
KYAPIIIN
OH! ♡
ドキドキ
DOKI (THADUMP) DOKI

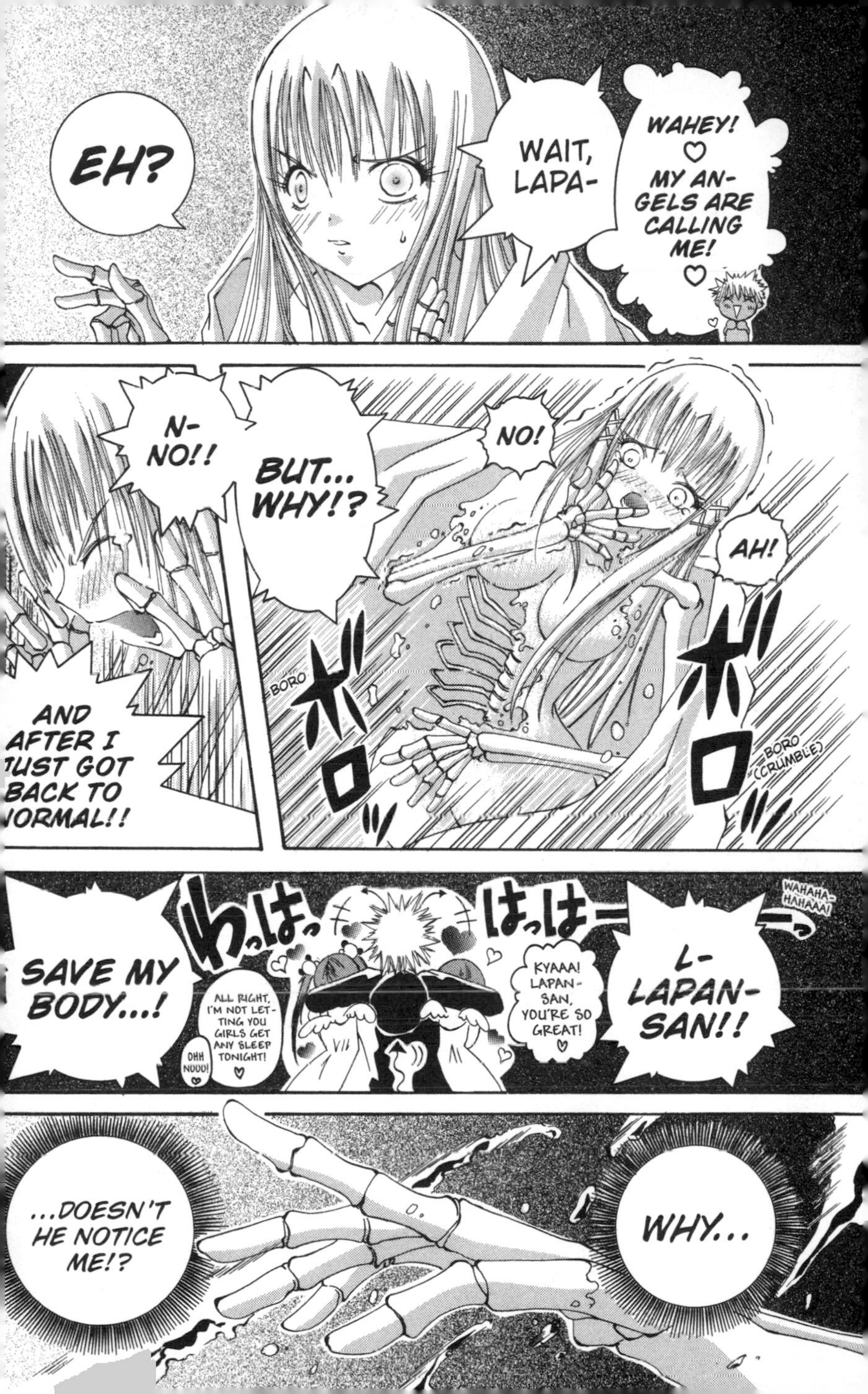
WAHEY! ♡ MY AN-GELS ARE CALLING ME! ♡
WAIT, LAPA-
EH?
AH!
NO!
BORO (CRUMBLE)
BORO
BUT... WHY!?
N-NO!!
AND AFTER I JUST GOT BACK TO NORMAL!!
WAHAHA-HAHAAA!
わっはっはっはー
L-LAPAN-SAN!!
KYAAA! LAPAN-SAN, YOU'RE SO GREAT! ♡
ALL RIGHT, I'M NOT LET-TING YOU GIRLS GET ANY SLEEP TONIGHT! ♡
OHH NOOO!
SAVE MY BODY...!
WHY...
...DOESN'T HE NOTICE ME!?

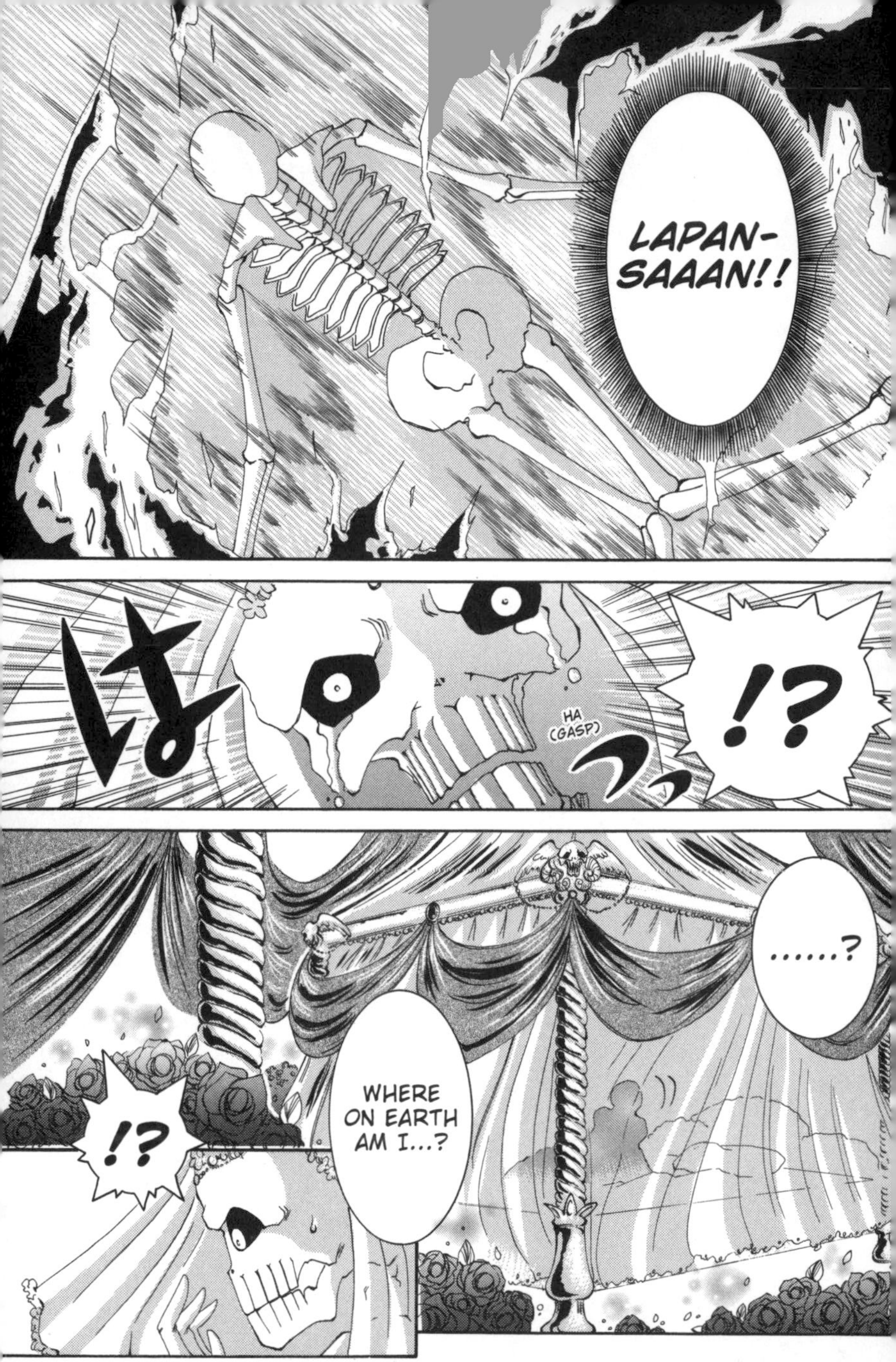
LAPAN-SAAAN!!
!?
HA (GASP)
......?
WHERE ON EARTH AM I...?
!?

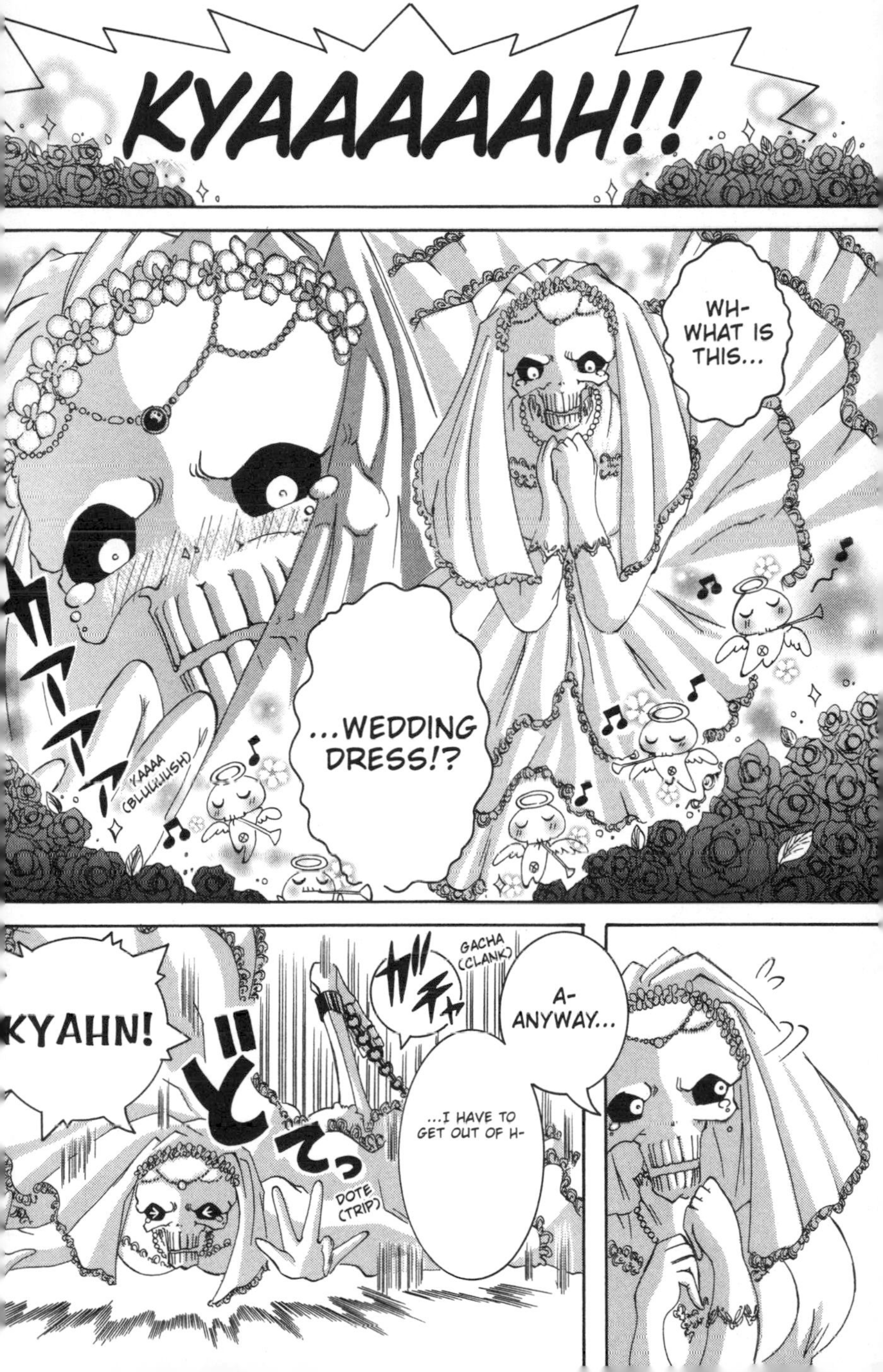
KYAAAAAAH!!
WH- WHAT IS THIS...
...WEDDING DRESS!?
YAAAA (BLUUUUSH)
A- ANYWAY...
...I HAVE TO GET OUT OF H-
GACHA (CLANK)
KYAHN!
DOTE (TRIP)

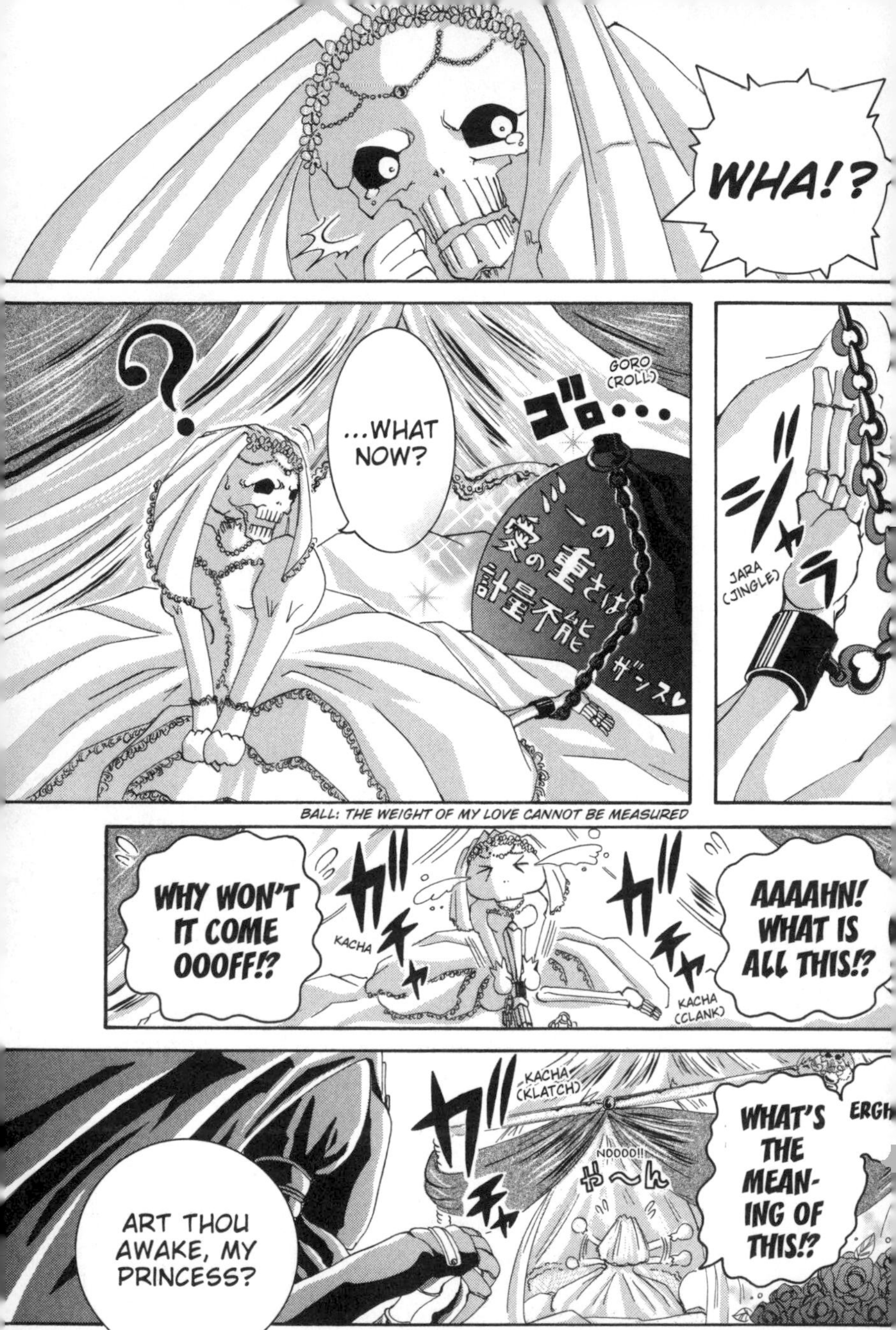
WHA!?
JARA (JINGLE)
ジャラ
GORO (ROLL)
ゴロ…
...WHAT NOW?
愛の重さは計量不能ザンス♥
BALL: THE WEIGHT OF MY LOVE CANNOT BE MEASURED
AAAAHN! WHAT IS ALL THIS!?
KACHA (CLANK)
ガチャ
ガチャ
KACHA
WHY WON'T IT COME OOOFF!?
ERGH
WHAT'S THE MEAN-ING OF THIS!?
KACHA (KLATCH)
ガチャ
NOOOO!!
やーん
ART THOU AWAKE, MY PRINCESS?

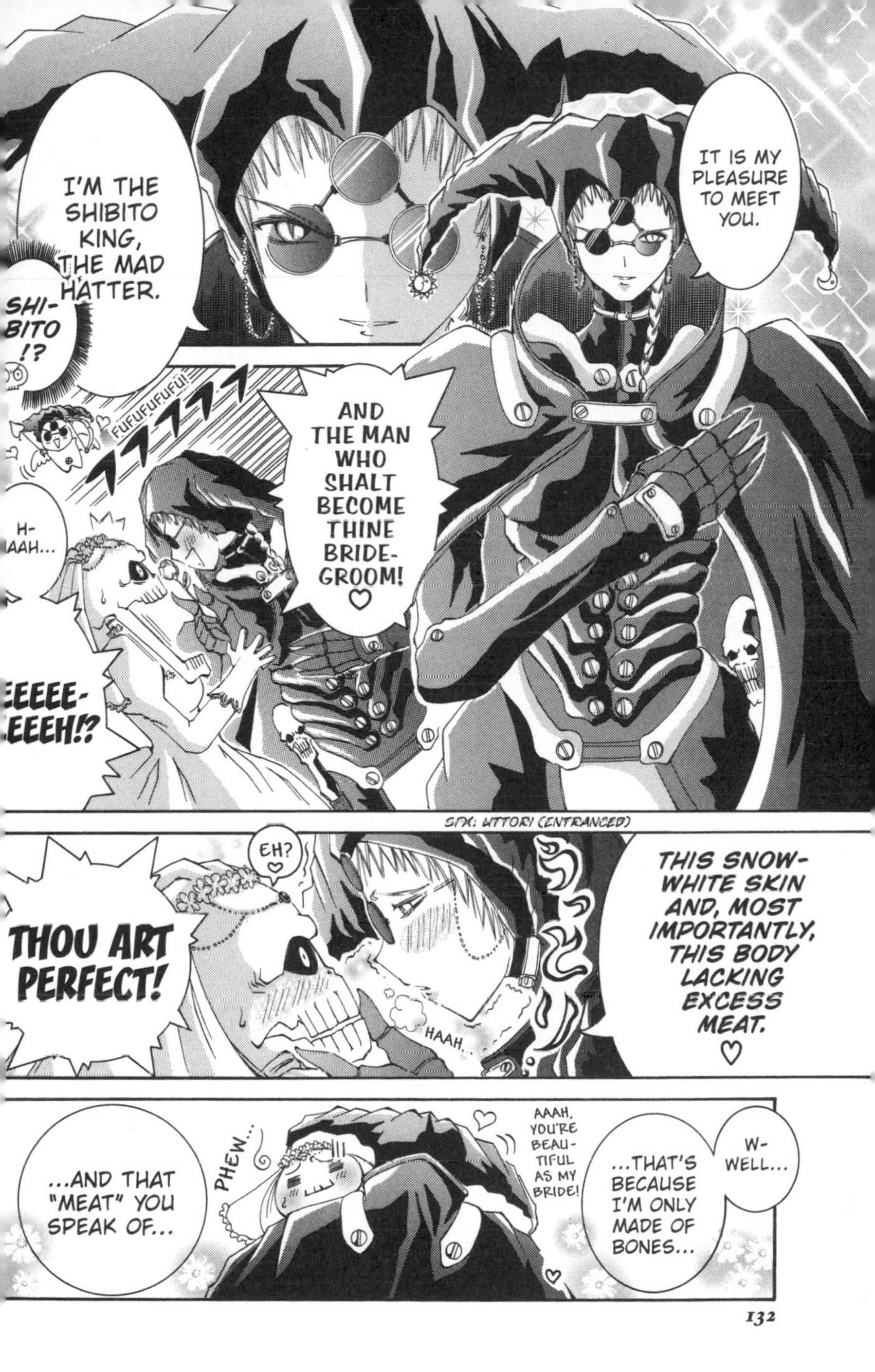
IT IS MY PLEASURE TO MEET YOU.
I'M THE SHIBITO KING, THE MAD HATTER.
SHI-BITO !?
AND THE MAN WHO SHALT BECOME THINE BRIDE-GROOM! ♡
FUFUFUFUFU!
H-AAH...
EEEEE-EEEH!?
SFX: UTTORI (ENTRANCED)
THIS SNOW-WHITE SKIN AND, MOST IMPORTANTLY, THIS BODY LACKING EXCESS MEAT. ♡
HAAH...
EH? ♡
THOU ART PERFECT!
W-WELL...
...THAT'S BECAUSE I'M ONLY MADE OF BONES...
AAAH, YOU'RE BEAUTIFUL AS MY BRIDE!
PHEW...
...AND THAT "MEAT" YOU SPEAK OF...

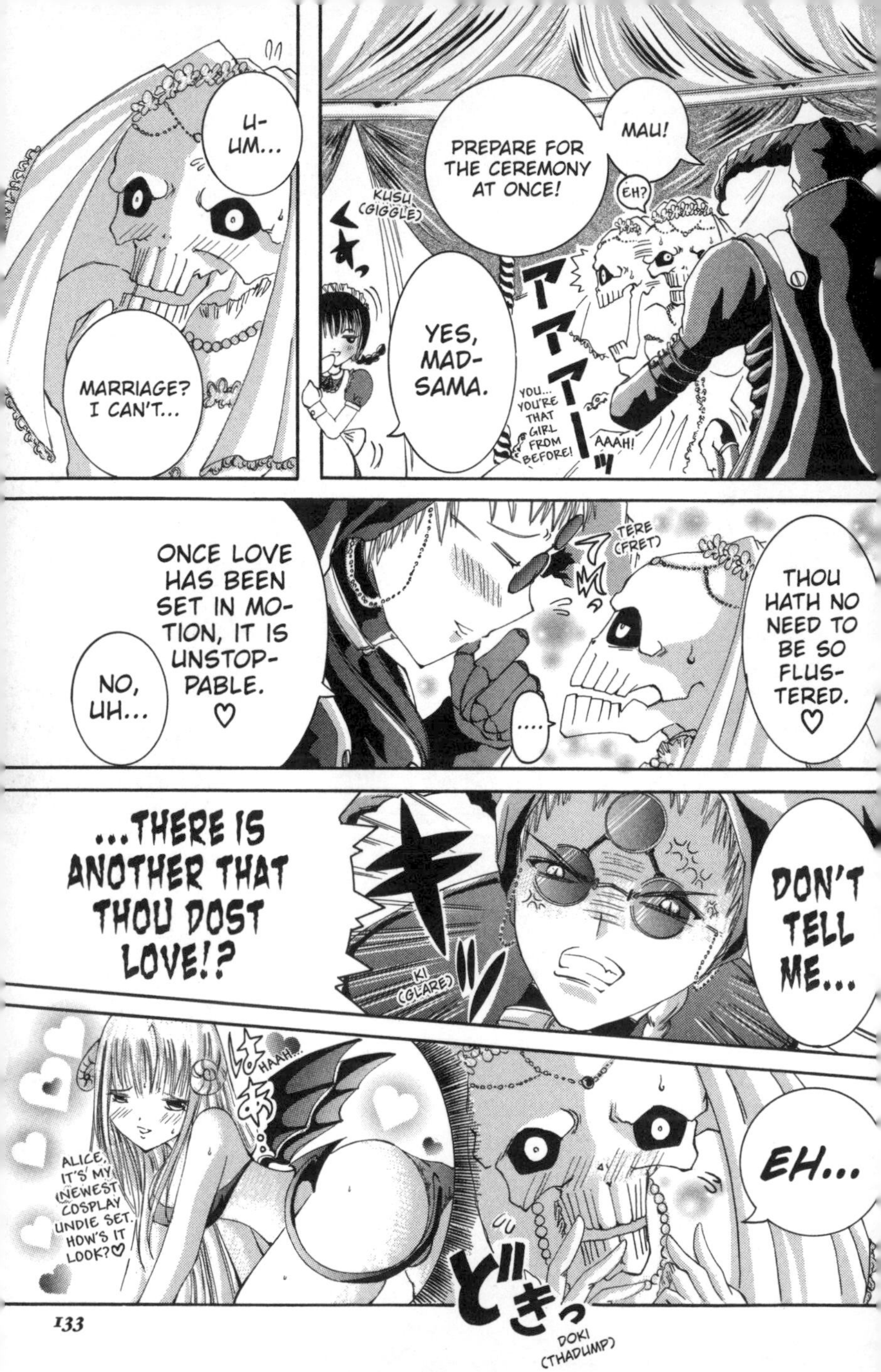
MAU!
PREPARE FOR THE CEREMONY AT ONCE!
EH?
くすっ
KUSU (GIGGLE)
YES, MAD-SAMA.
アアアーッ
AAAH!
YOU... YOU'RE THAT GIRL FROM BEFORE!
U-UM...
MARRIAGE? I CAN'T...
THOU HATH NO NEED TO BE SO FLUSTERED. ♡
TERE (FRET)
....
ONCE LOVE HAS BEEN SET IN MOTION, IT IS UNSTOPPABLE. ♡
NO, UH...
DON'T TELL ME...
キッ
KI (GLARE)
...THERE IS ANOTHER THAT THOU DOST LOVE!?
EH...
どきっ
DOKI (THADUMP)
はぁ
HAAH...
ALICE, IT'S MY NEWEST COSPLAY UNDIE SET. HOW'S IT LOOK?♡

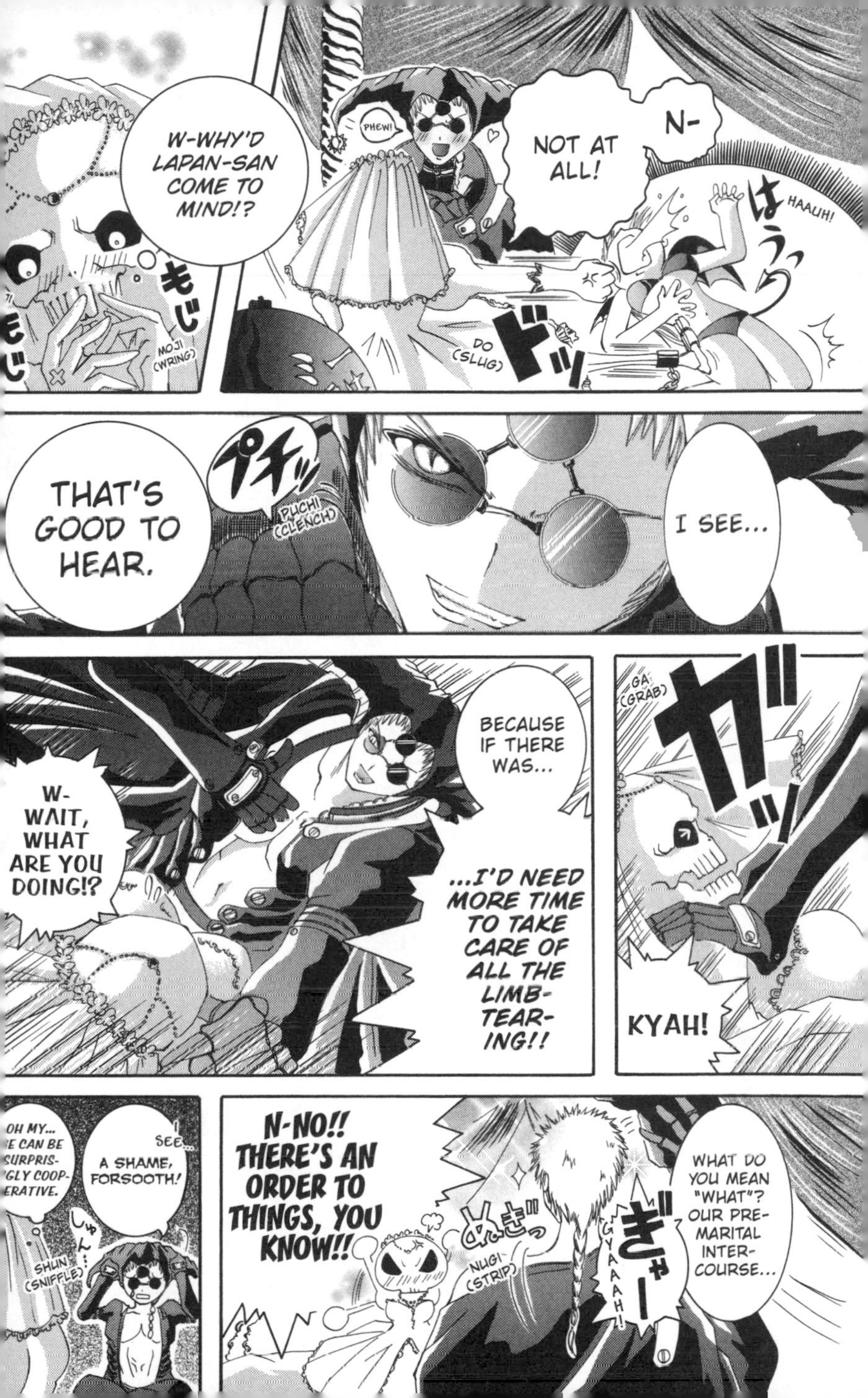
N-
NOT AT ALL!
PHEW!
はぅっ
HAAUH!
ドッ
DO (SLUG)
W-WHY'D LAPAN-SAN COME TO MIND!?
もじもじ
MOJI (WRING)
I SEE...
プチッ
PUCHI (CLENCH)
THAT'S GOOD TO HEAR.
ガッ
GA (GRAB)
KYAH!
BECAUSE IF THERE WAS...
...I'D NEED MORE TIME TO TAKE CARE OF ALL THE LIMB-TEARING!!
W-WAIT, WHAT ARE YOU DOING!?
WHAT DO YOU MEAN "WHAT"? OUR PRE-MARITAL INTER-COURSE...
ぎゃー
GYAAAH!
ぬぎっ
NUGI (STRIP)
N-NO!! THERE'S AN ORDER TO THINGS, YOU KNOW!!
I SEE...
A SHAME, FORSOOTH!
OH MY... E CAN BE SURPRIS- GLY COOP- ERATIVE.
しゅん...
SHUN (SNIFFLE)

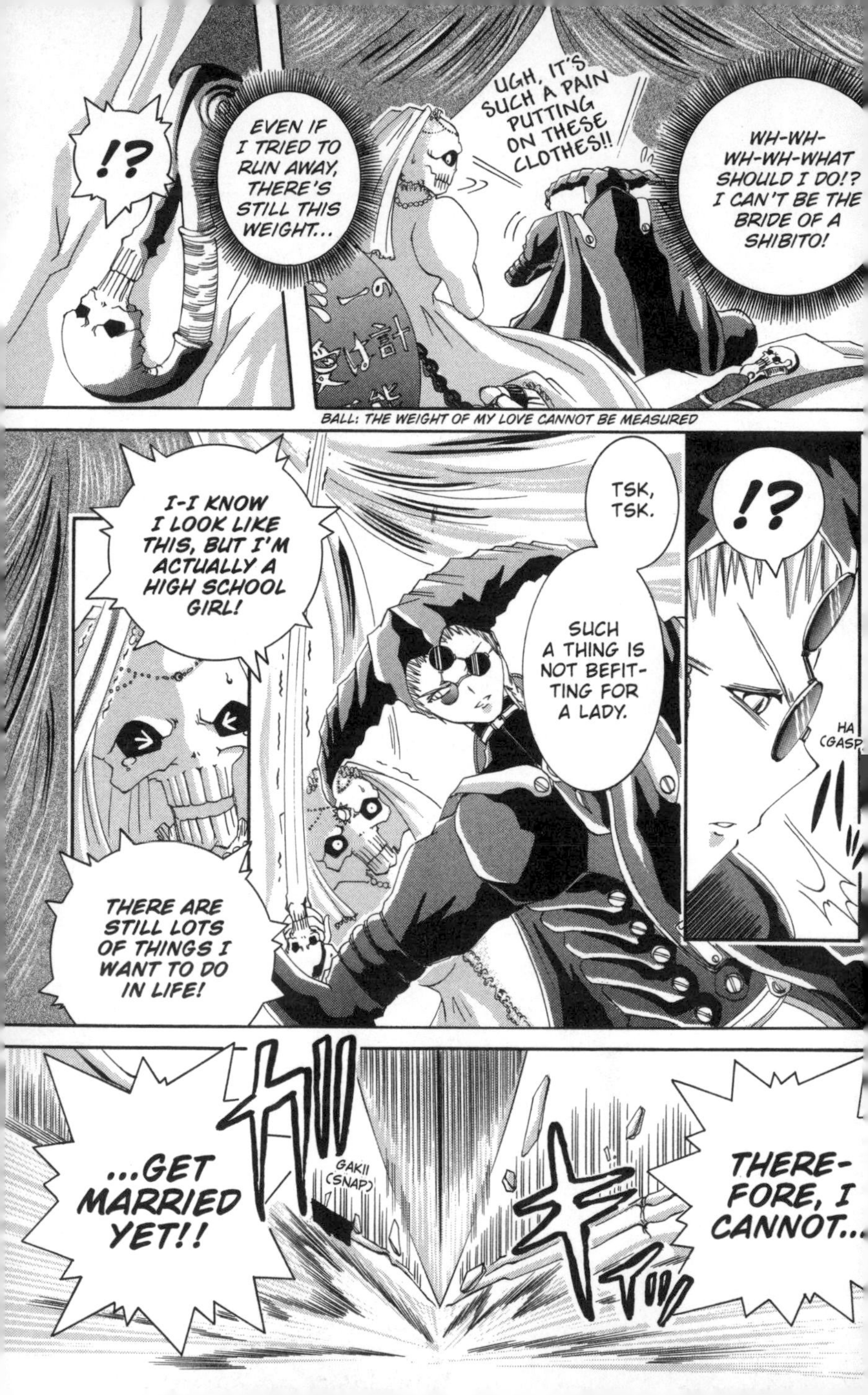
WH-WH-WH-WH-WHAT SHOULD I DO!? I CAN'T BE THE BRIDE OF A SHIBITO!
UGH, IT'S SUCH A PAIN PUTTING ON THESE CLOTHES!!
EVEN IF I TRIED TO RUN AWAY, THERE'S STILL THIS WEIGHT...
!?
BALL: THE WEIGHT OF MY LOVE CANNOT BE MEASURED
!?
HA (GASP)
TSK, TSK.
SUCH A THING IS NOT BEFIT-TING FOR A LADY.
I-I KNOW I LOOK LIKE THIS, BUT I'M ACTUALLY A HIGH SCHOOL GIRL!
THERE ARE STILL LOTS OF THINGS I WANT TO DO IN LIFE!
THERE-FORE, I CANNOT...
GAKII (SNAP)
...GET MARRIED YET!!

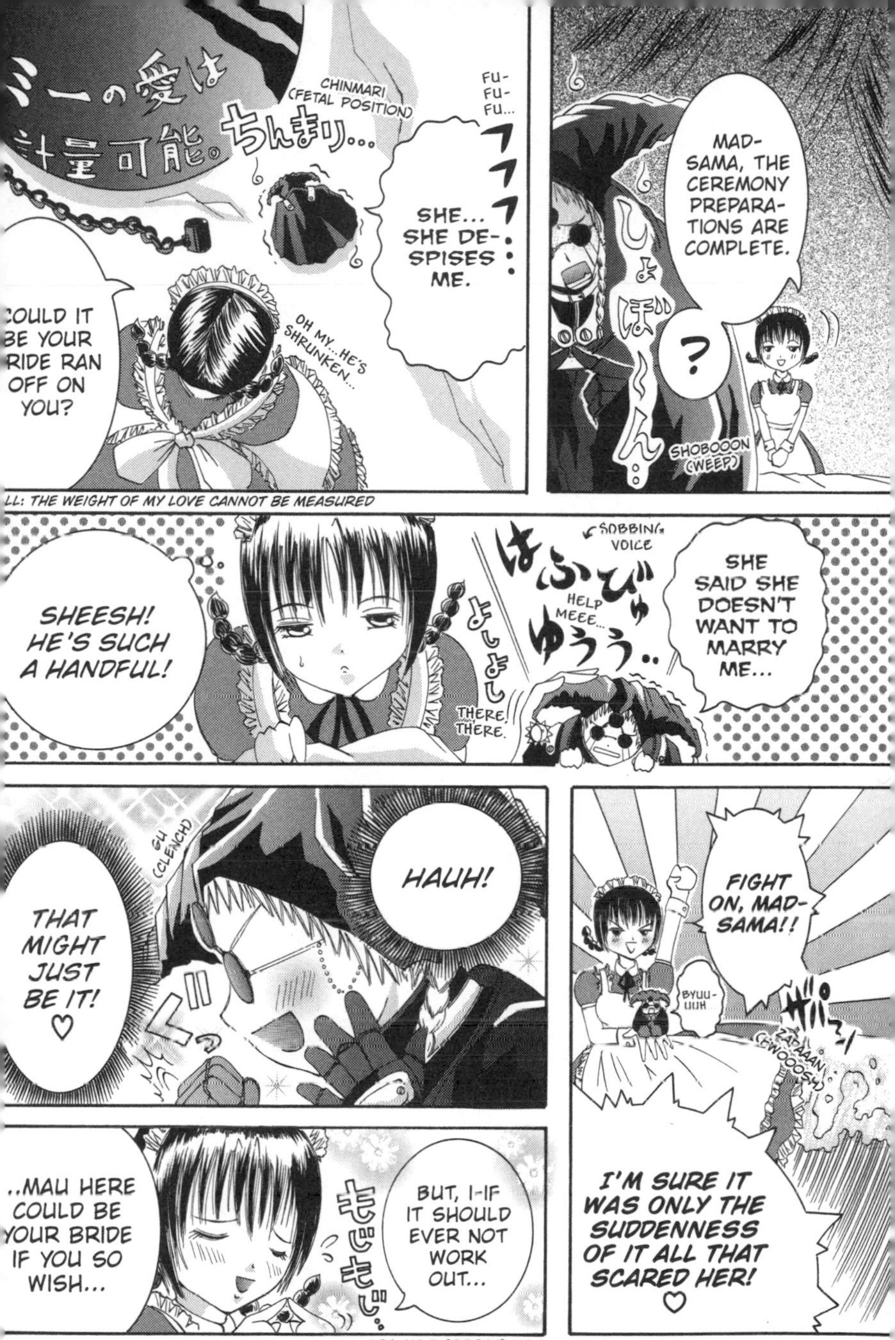
MAD-SAMA, THE CEREMONY PREPARATIONS ARE COMPLETE.
?
しょぼ〜ん。
SHOBOOON (WEEP)
ミーの愛は計量可能。
FU-FU-FU...
フフフ・・・
SHE... SHE DESPISES ME.
ちんまり…
CHINMARI (FETAL POSITION)
OH MY...HE'S SHRUNKEN...
COULD IT BE YOUR BRIDE RAN OFF ON YOU?
LL: THE WEIGHT OF MY LOVE CANNOT BE MEASURED
SHE SAID SHE DOESN'T WANT TO MARRY ME...
はふびゅゆううう..
SOBBING VOICE
HELP MEEE...
よしよし
THERE THERE.
SHEESH! HE'S SUCH A HANDFUL!
FIGHT ON, MAD-SAMA!!
BYUU-UUH...
ザパーン
ZAPAAAN (WHOOOSH)
I'M SURE IT WAS ONLY THE SUDDENNESS OF IT ALL THAT SCARED HER! ♡
HAUH!
GU (CLENCH)
THAT MIGHT JUST BE IT! ♡
BUT, I-IF IT SHOULD EVER NOT WORK OUT...
もじもじ。
..MAU HERE COULD BE YOUR BRIDE IF YOU SO WISH...
SFX: MOJI (FIDGET) MOJI

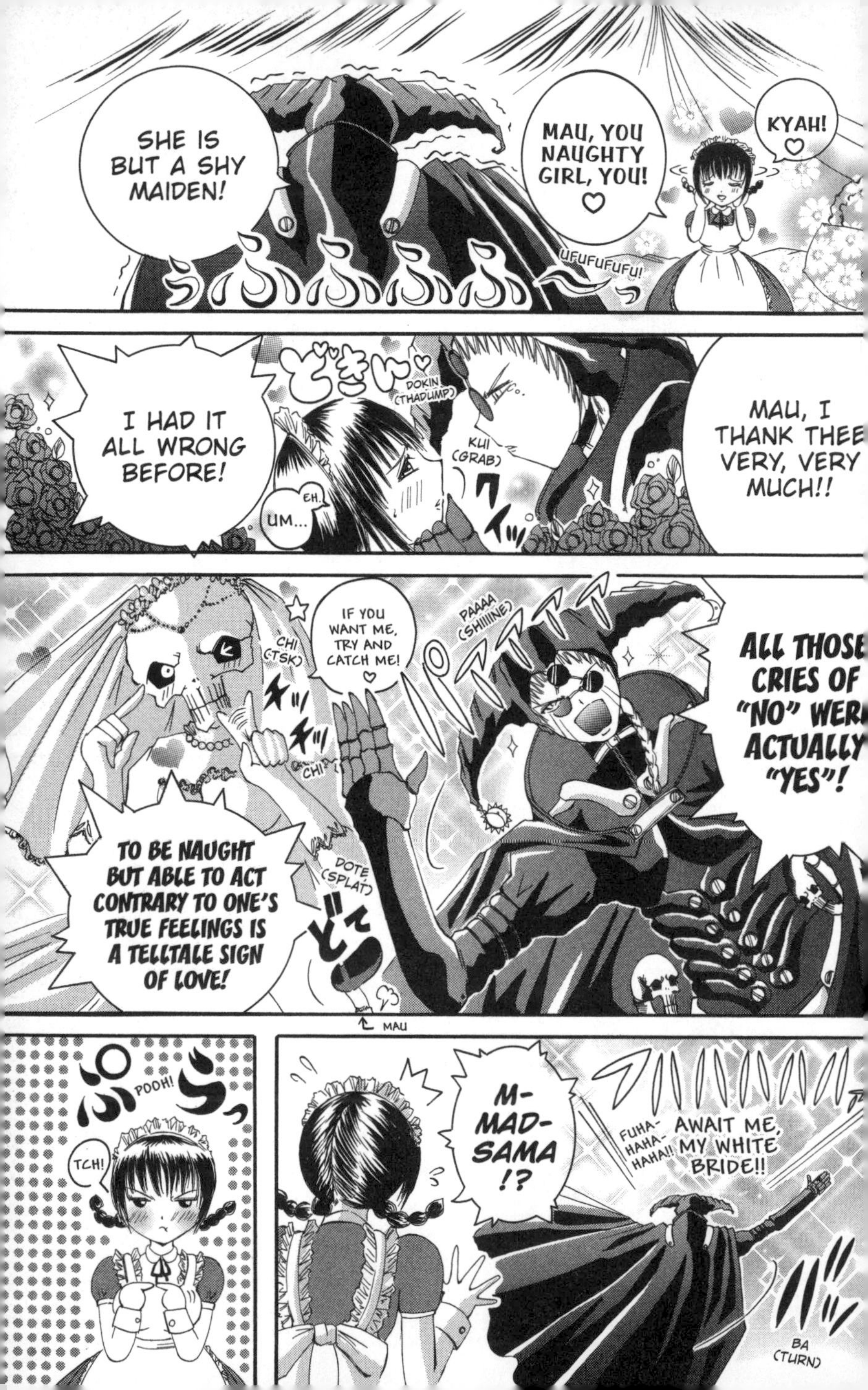
KYAH! ♡
MAU, YOU NAUGHTY GIRL, YOU! ♡
UFUFUFUFU!
SHE IS BUT A SHY MAIDEN!
MAU, I THANK THEE VERY, VERY MUCH!!
DOKIN (THADUMP)
KUI (GRAB)
EH.
UM...
I HAD IT ALL WRONG BEFORE!
ALL THOSE CRIES OF "NO" WER ACTUALLY "YES"!
PAAAA (SHIIIINE)
IF YOU WANT ME, TRY AND CATCH ME! ♡
CHI (TSK)
CHI
DOTE (SPLAT)
TO BE NAUGHT BUT ABLE TO ACT CONTRARY TO ONE'S TRUE FEELINGS IS A TELLTALE SIGN OF LOVE!
MAU
AWAIT ME, MY WHITE BRIDE!!
FUHA-HAHA-HAHA!!
M-MAD-SAMA!?
BA (TURN)
POOH!
TCH!

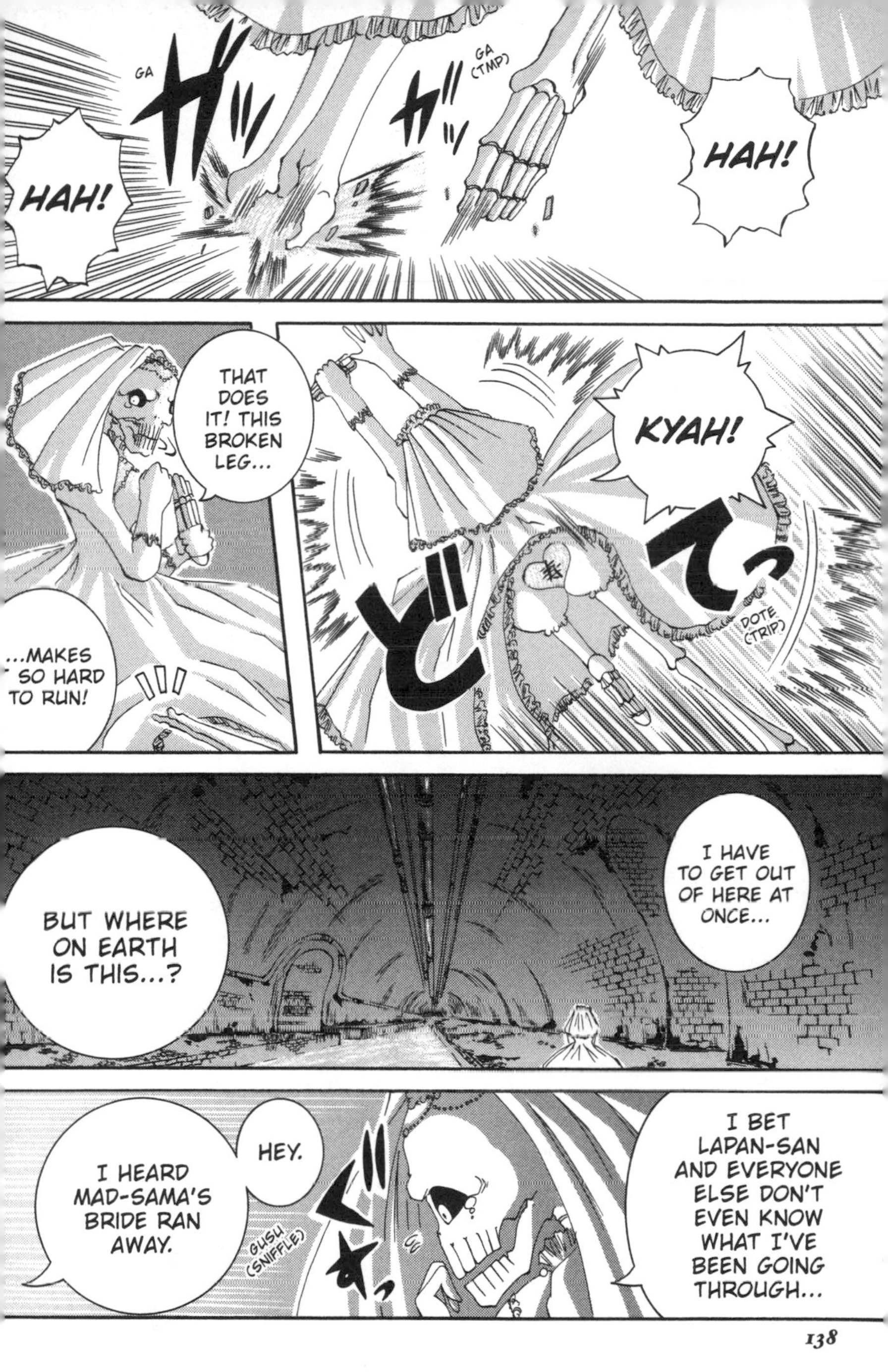

GA (TMP)
HAH!
GA
HAH!
KYAH!
DOTE (TRIP)
THAT DOES IT! THIS BROKEN LEG...
...MAKES SO HARD TO RUN!
I HAVE TO GET OUT OF HERE AT ONCE...
BUT WHERE ON EARTH IS THIS...?
I BET LAPAN-SAN AND EVERYONE ELSE DON'T EVEN KNOW WHAT I'VE BEEN GOING THROUGH...
GUSU (SNIFFLE)
HEY.
I HEARD MAD-SAMA'S BRIDE RAN AWAY.

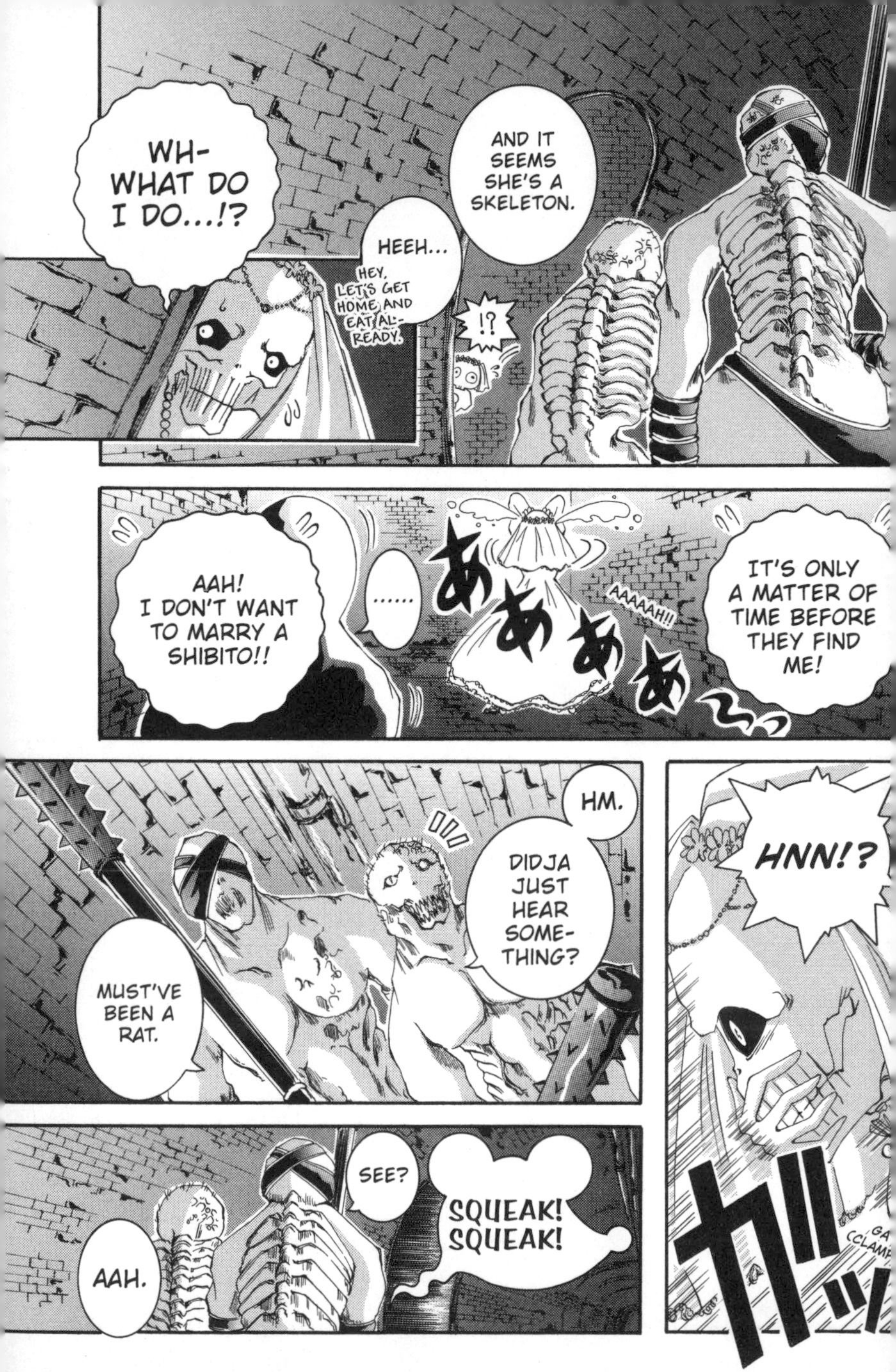
AND IT SEEMS SHE'S A SKELETON.
HEEH...
HEY, LET'S GET HOME AND EAT AL-READY.
!?
WH- WHAT DO I DO...!?
IT'S ONLY A MATTER OF TIME BEFORE THEY FIND ME!
あああああ
AAAAAH!!
......
AAH! I DON'T WANT TO MARRY A SHIBITO!!
HNN!?
ガッ
GA
HM.
DIDJA JUST HEAR SOME-THING?
MUST'VE BEEN A RAT.
SQUEAK! SQUEAK!
SEE?
AAH.

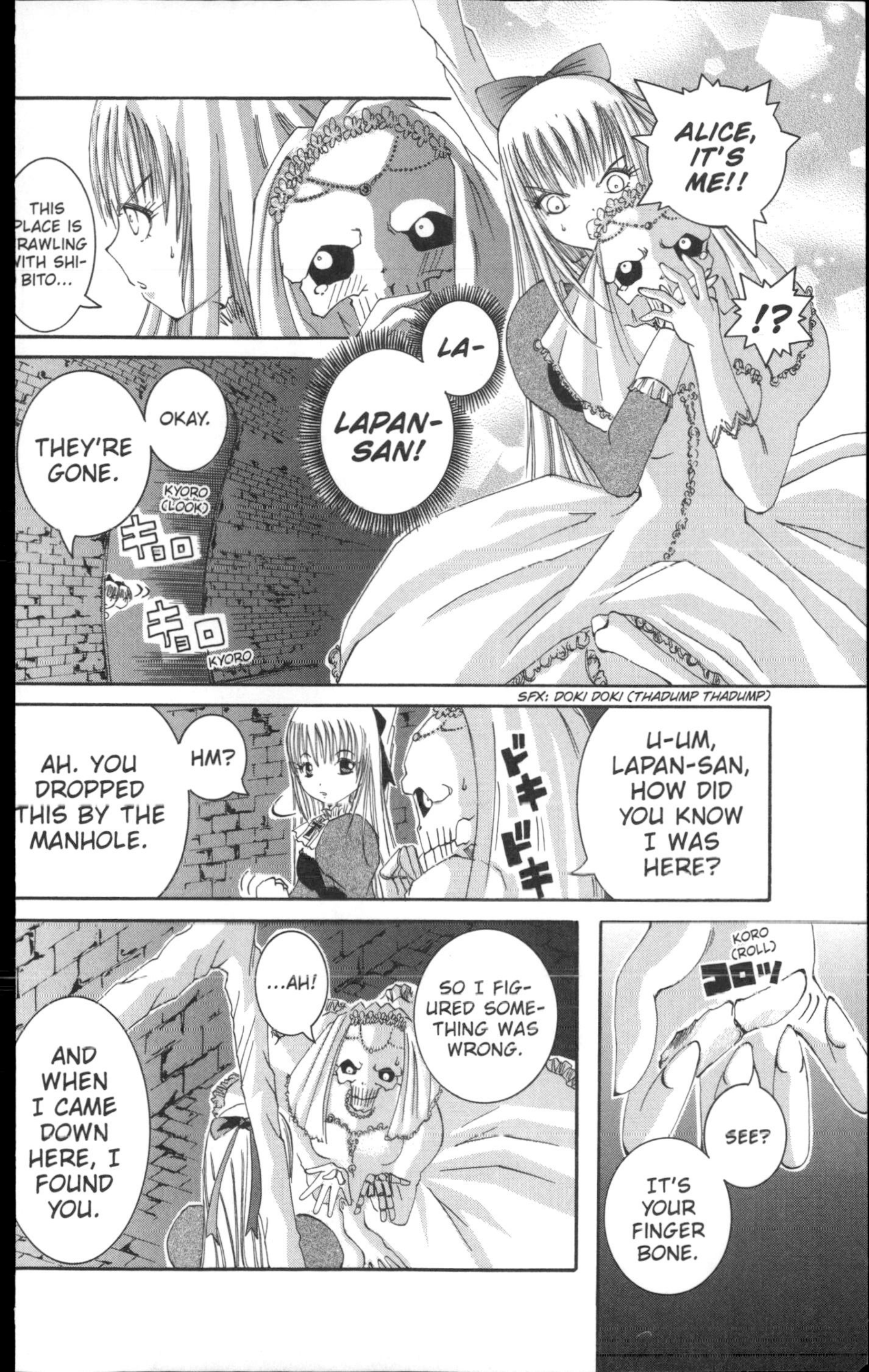
ALICE, IT'S ME!!
!?
LA-
LAPAN-SAN!
THIS PLACE IS RAWLING WITH SHI-BITO...
OKAY.
THEY'RE GONE.
KYORO (LOOK)
キョロ
キョロ
KYORO
SFX: DOKI DOKI (THADUMP THADUMP)
ドキドキ
U-UM, LAPAN-SAN, HOW DID YOU KNOW I WAS HERE?
HM?
AH. YOU DROPPED THIS BY THE MANHOLE.
KORO (ROLL)
コロッ
SEE?
IT'S YOUR FINGER BONE.
SO I FIG-URED SOME-THING WAS WRONG.
...AH!
AND WHEN I CAME DOWN HERE, I FOUND YOU.

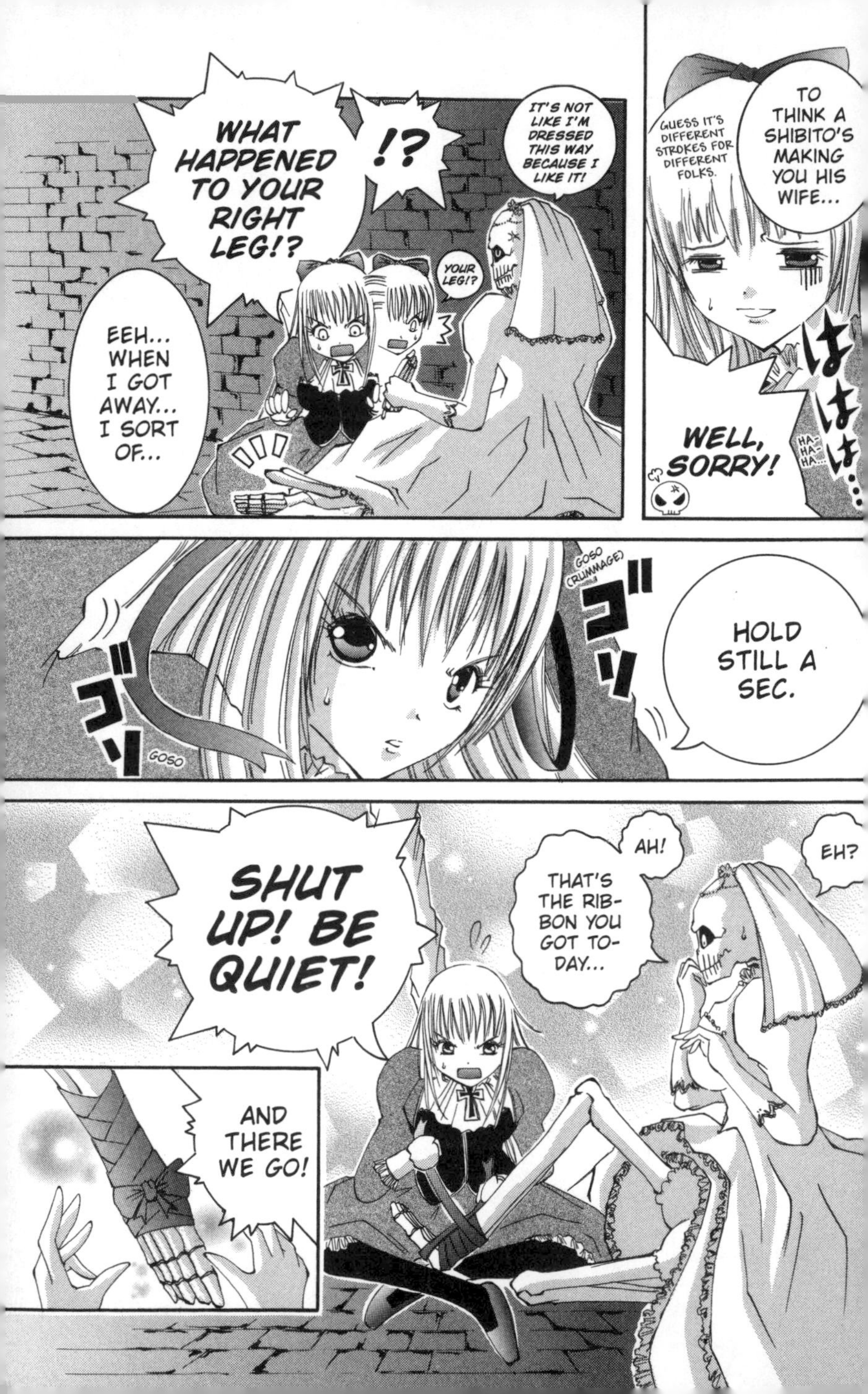
TO THINK A SHIBITO'S MAKING YOU HIS WIFE...
GUESS IT'S DIFFERENT STROKES FOR DIFFERENT FOLKS.
ははは…
HA-HA-HA...
WELL, SORRY!
IT'S NOT LIKE I'M DRESSED THIS WAY BECAUSE I LIKE IT!
!?
WHAT HAPPENED TO YOUR RIGHT LEG!?
YOUR LEG!?
EEH... WHEN I GOT AWAY... I SORT OF...
ゴソ
GOSO (RUMMAGE)
HOLD STILL A SEC.
ゴソ
GOSO
EH?
AH!
THAT'S THE RIB-BON YOU GOT TO-DAY...
SHUT UP! BE QUIET!
AND THERE WE GO!

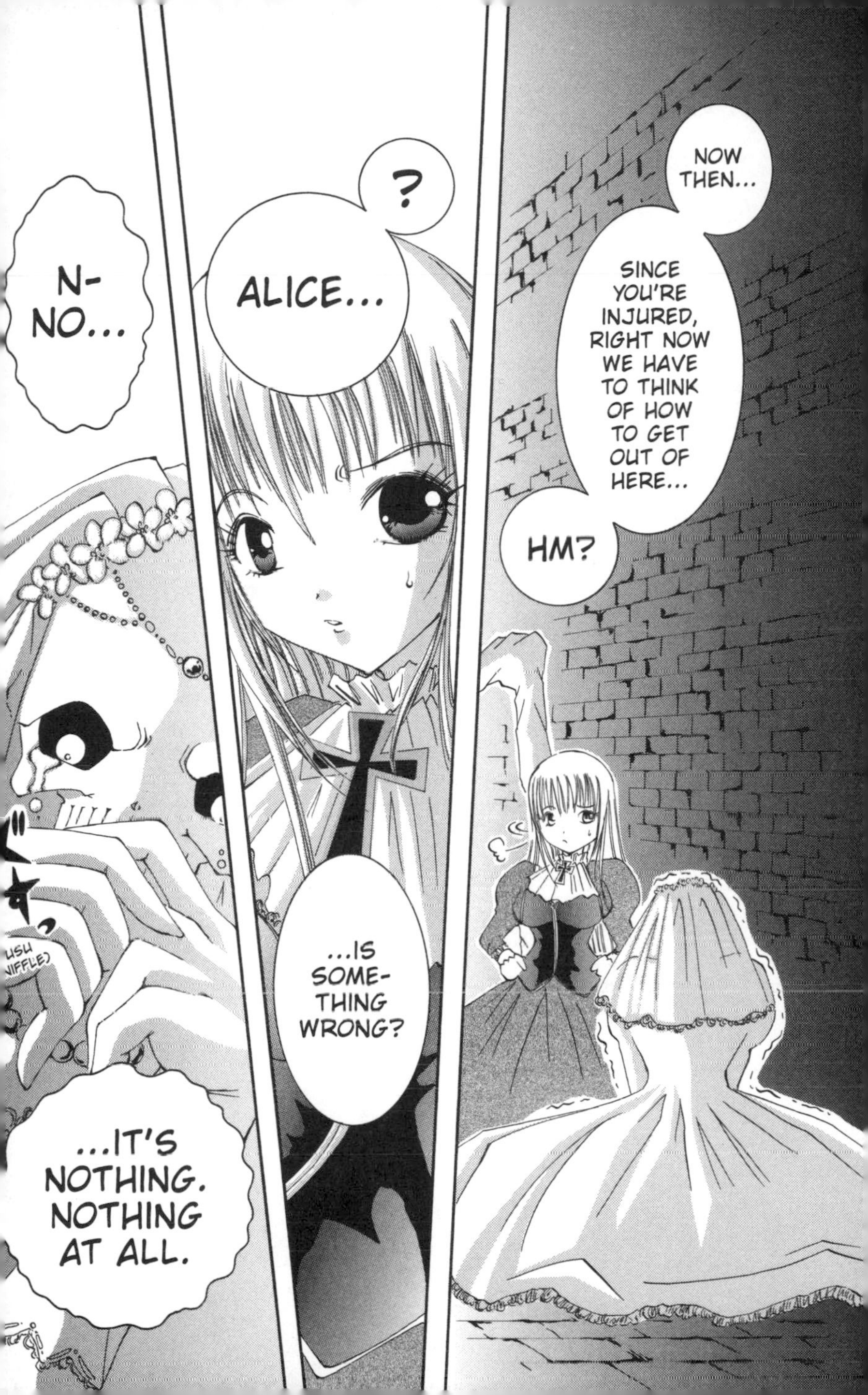
NOW THEN...
SINCE YOU'RE INJURED, RIGHT NOW WE HAVE TO THINK OF HOW TO GET OUT OF HERE...
HM?
?
ALICE...
...IS SOME-THING WRONG?
N-NO...
...IT'S NOTHING. NOTHING AT ALL.

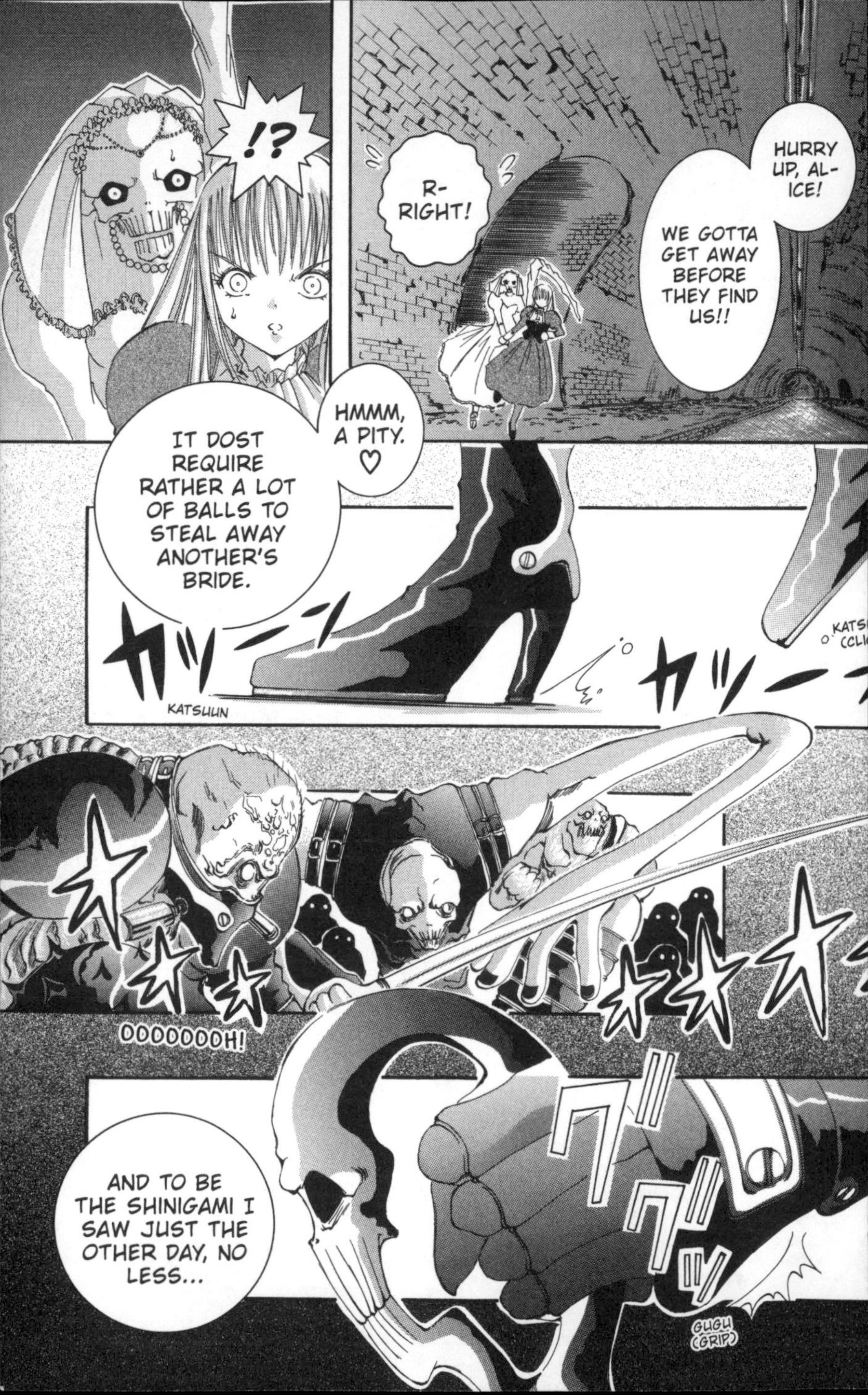
HURRY UP, AL-ICE!
WE GOTTA GET AWAY BEFORE THEY FIND US!!
R-RIGHT!
!?
HMMM, A PITY. ♡
IT DOST REQUIRE RATHER A LOT OF BALLS TO STEAL AWAY ANOTHER'S BRIDE.
KATSUUN
OOOOOOOOH!
AND TO BE THE SHINIGAMI I SAW JUST THE OTHER DAY, NO LESS...
GUGU (GRIP)

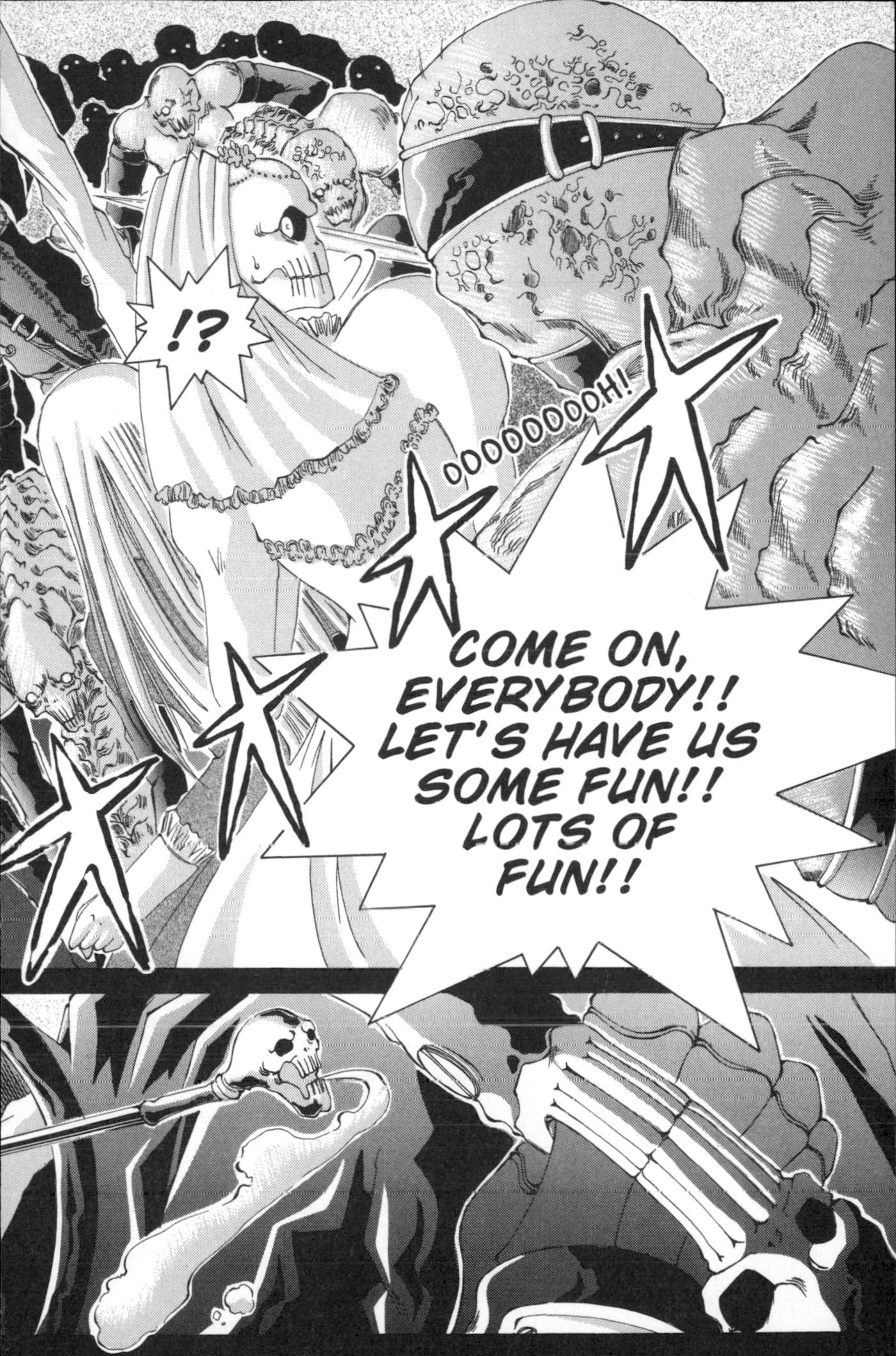
COME ON, EVERYBODY!! LET'S HAVE US SOME FUN!! LOTS OF FUN!!
OOOOOOOOOOOOH!
!?

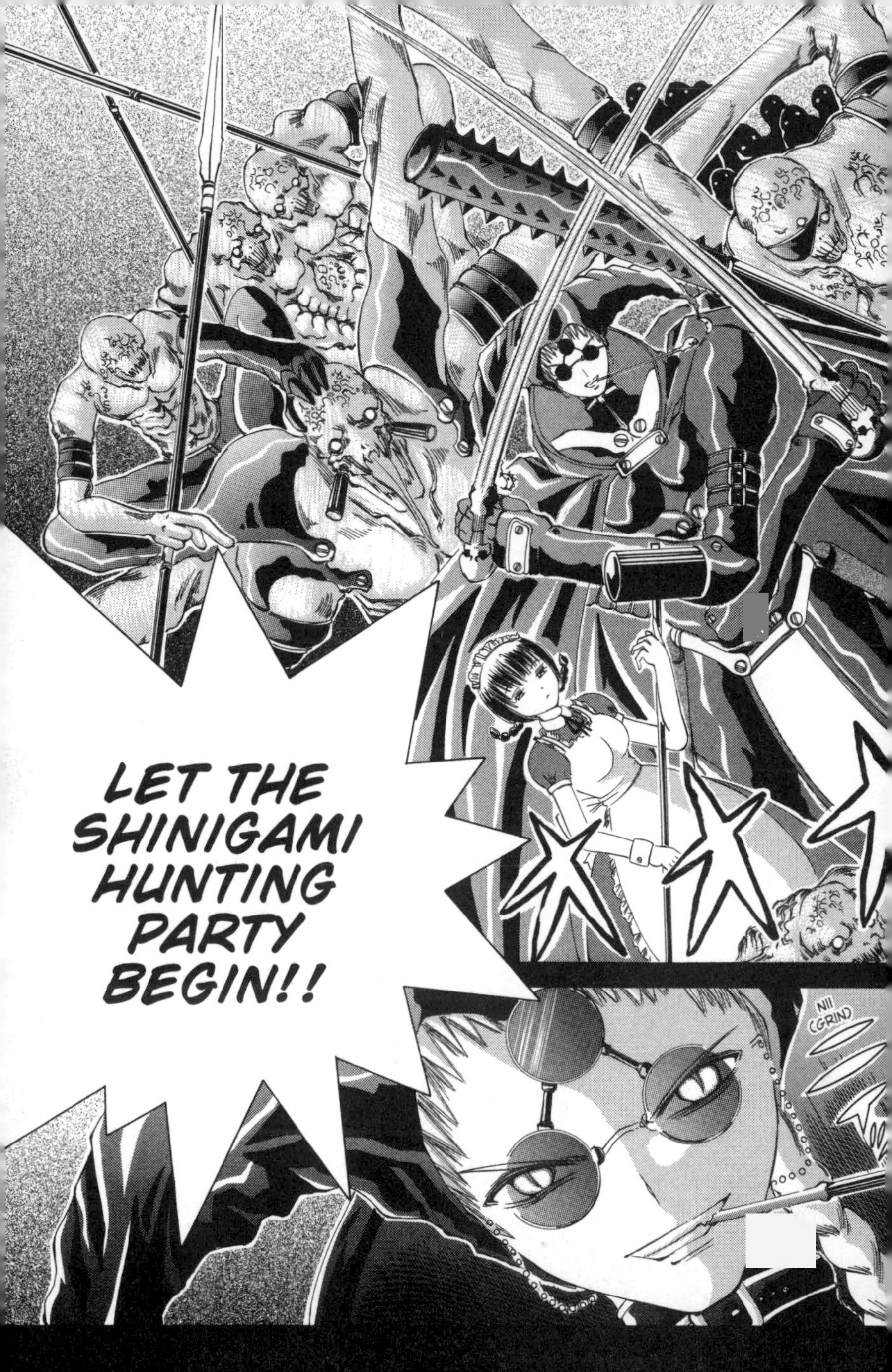
LET THE SHINIGAMI HUNTING PARTY BEGIN!!
NII (GRIN)

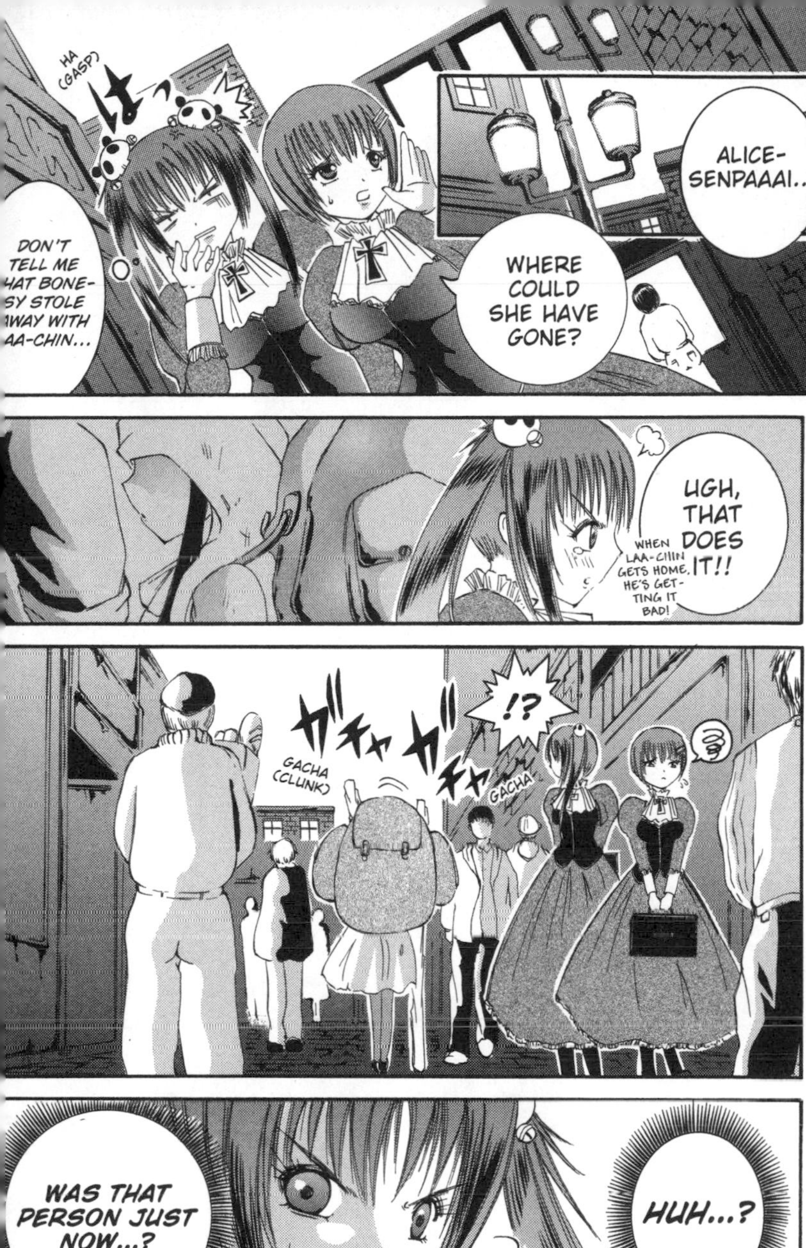
ALICE-SENPAAAI...
WHERE COULD SHE HAVE GONE?
HA (GASP)
DON'T TELL ME HAT BONE-SY STOLE WAY WITH AA-CHIN...
UGH, THAT DOES IT!!
WHEN LAA-CHIIN GETS HOME, HE'S GETTING IT BAD!
!?
GACHA (CLUNK)
GACHA
HUH...?
WAS THAT PERSON JUST NOW...?

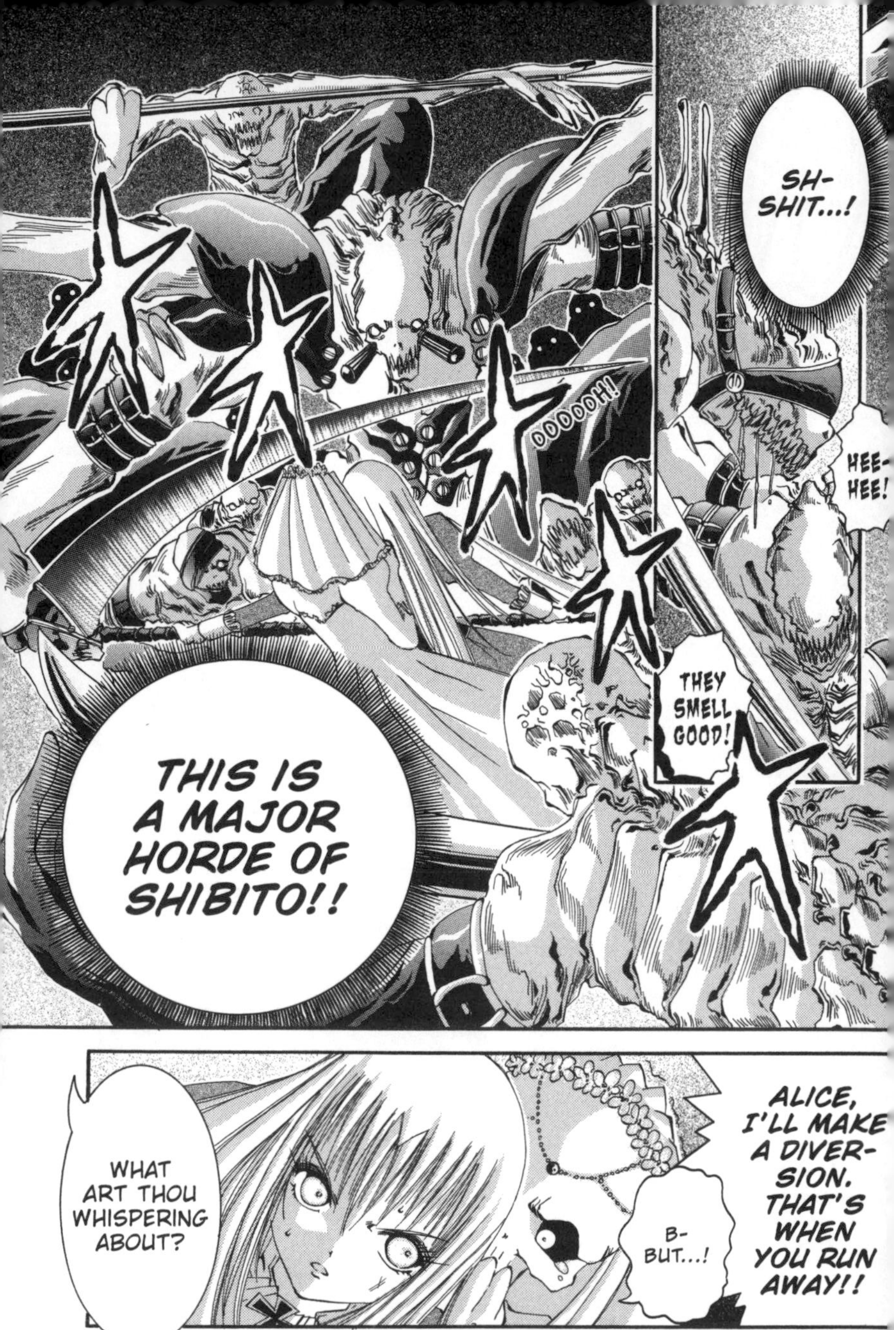
SH-SHIT...!
HEE-HEE!
THEY SMELL GOOD!
OOOOOOH!
THIS IS A MAJOR HORDE OF SHIBITO!!
ALICE, I'LL MAKE A DIVERSION. THAT'S WHEN YOU RUN AWAY!!
B-BUT...!
WHAT ART THOU WHISPERING ABOUT?

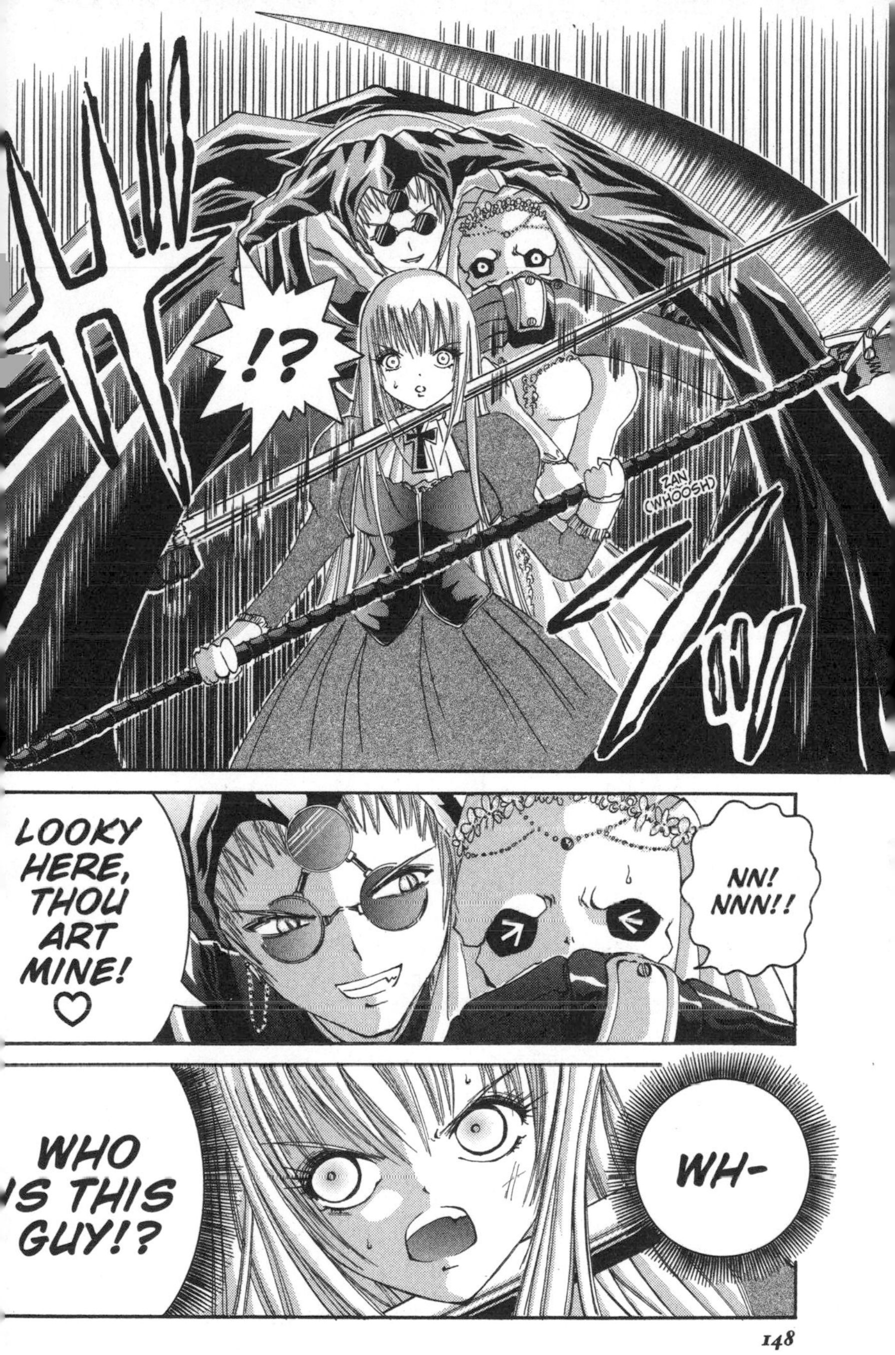
!?
ZAN (WHOOSH)
NN! NNN!!
LOOKY HERE, THOU ART MINE! ♡
WH-
WHO IS THIS GUY!?

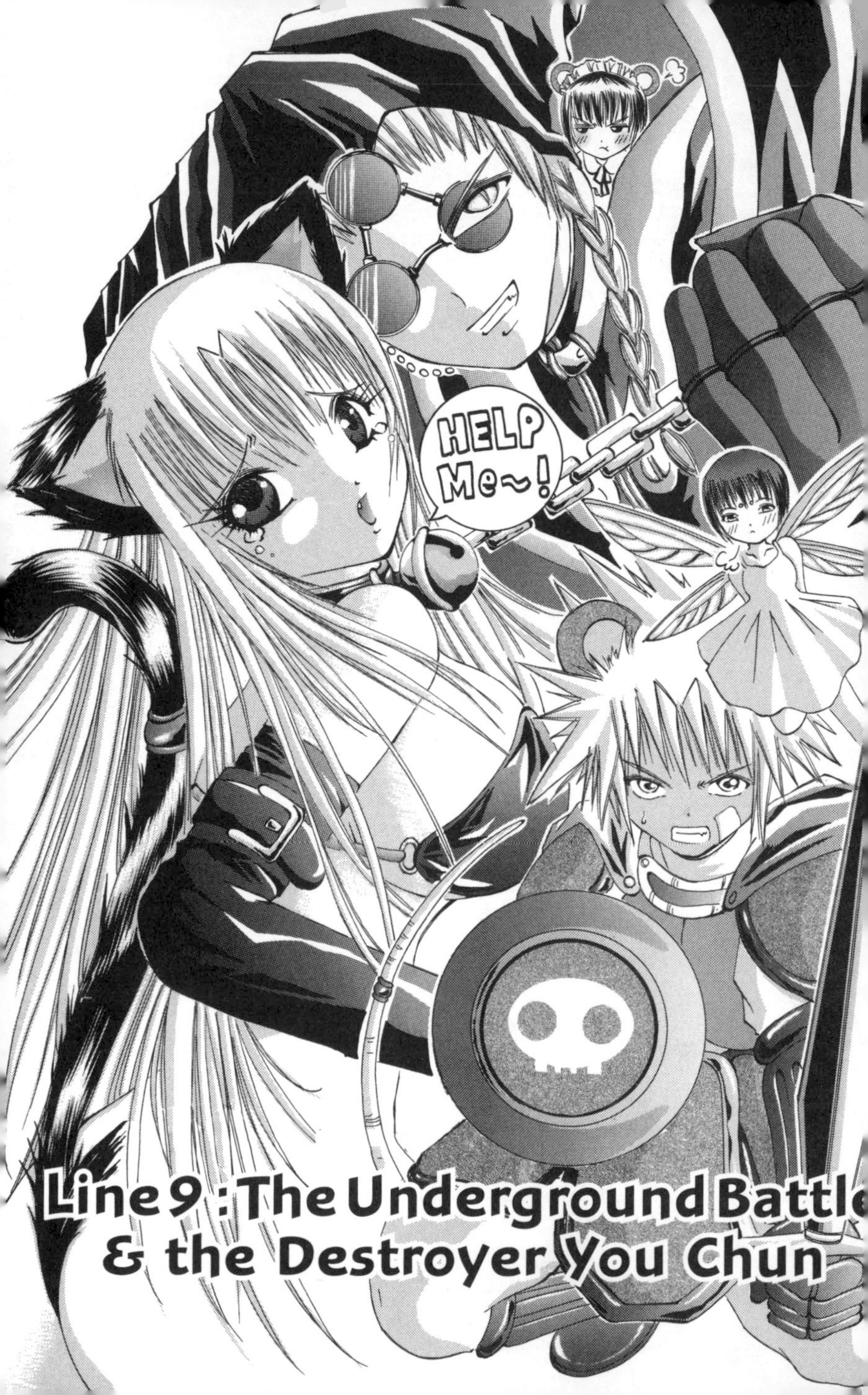
HELP Me~!
Line 9 : The Underground Battl
& the Destroyer You Chun

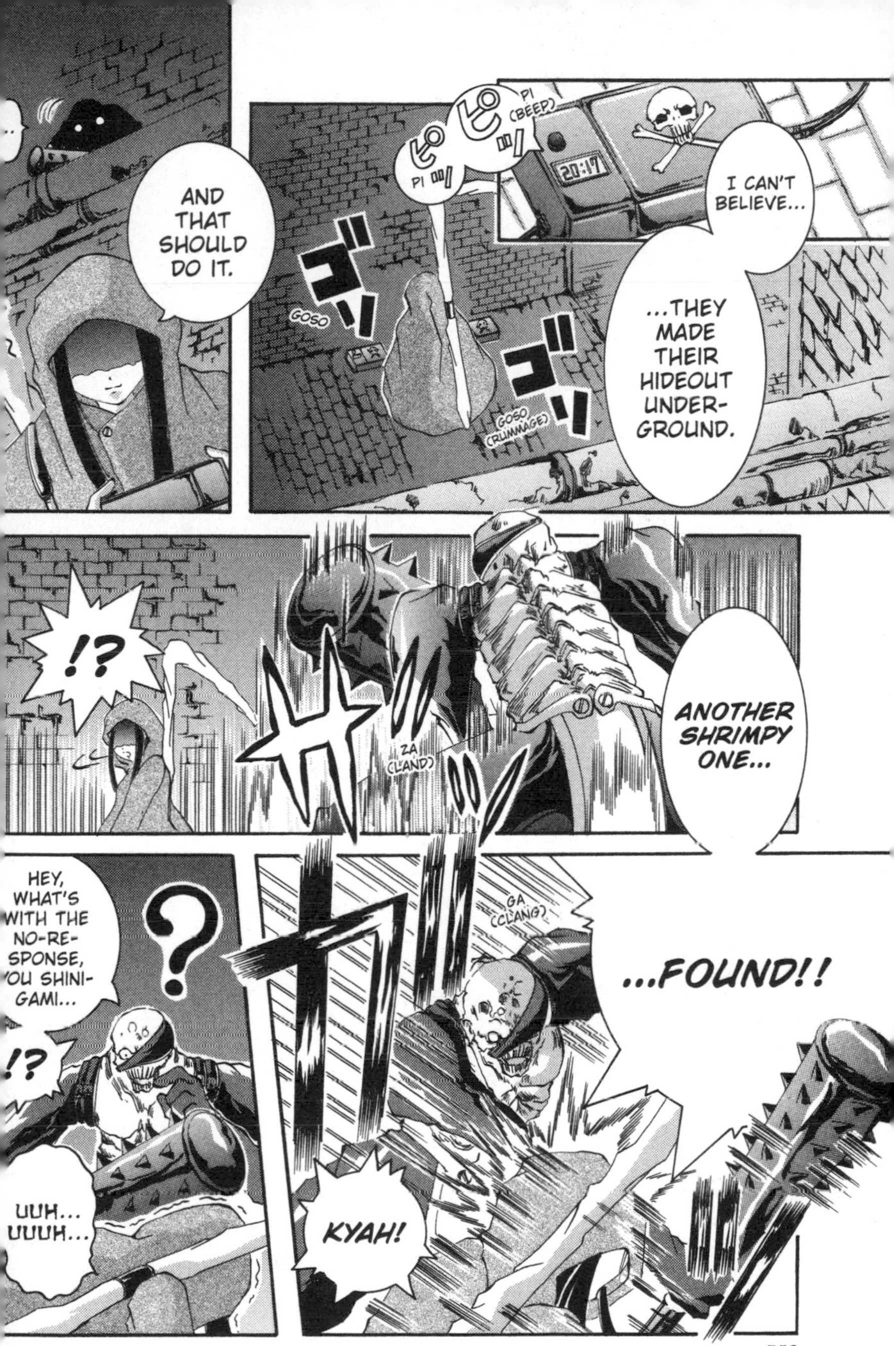
I CAN'T BELIEVE...
...THEY MADE THEIR HIDEOUT UNDER-GROUND.
PI (BEEP)
PI
GOSO (RUMMAGE)
GOSO
AND THAT SHOULD DO IT.
ANOTHER SHRIMPY ONE...
ZA (LAND)
!?
...FOUND!!
GA (CLANG)
KYAH!
HEY, WHAT'S WITH THE NO-RE-SPONSE, YOU SHINI-GAMI...
!?
UUH... UUUH...

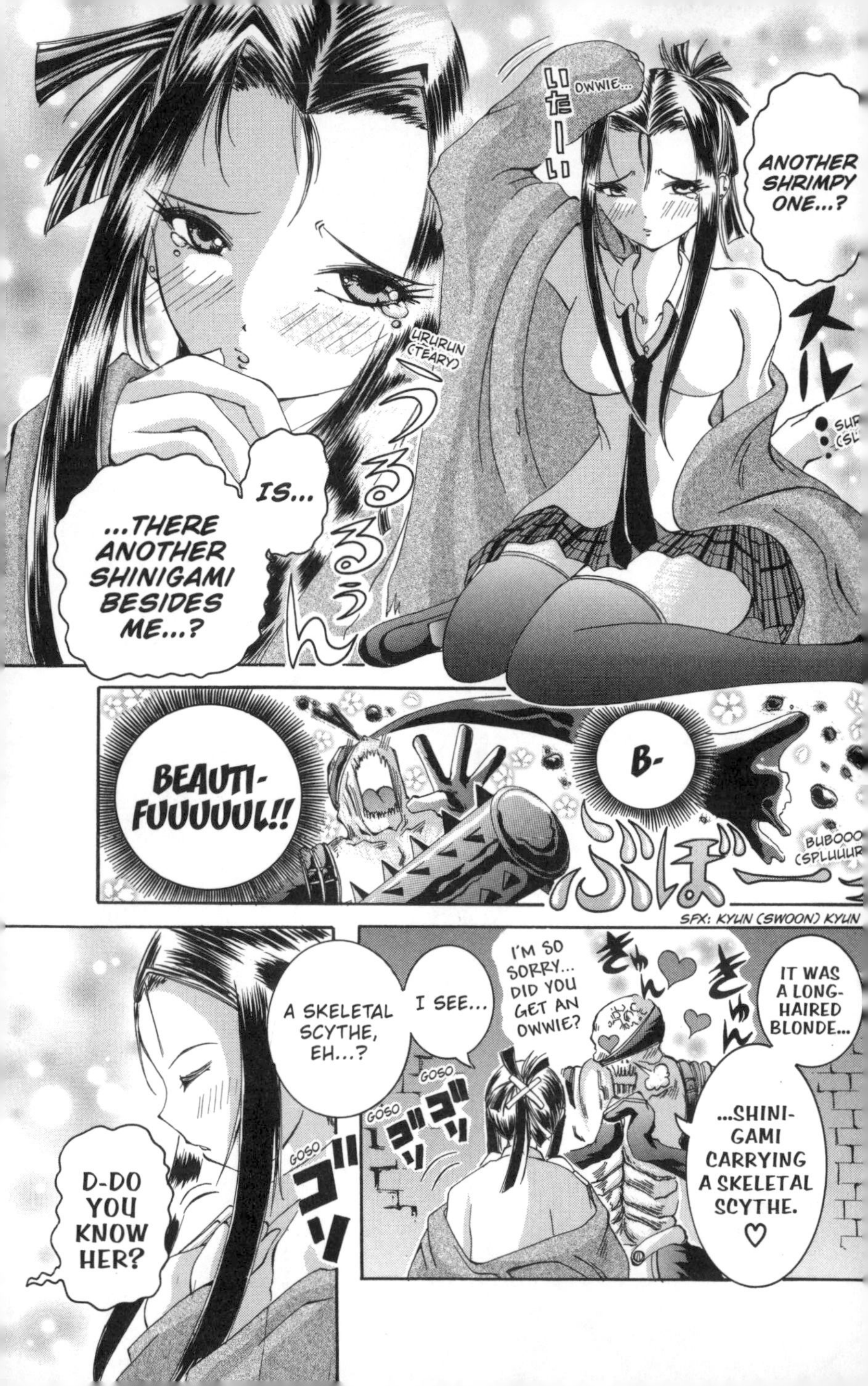

OWWIE...
ANOTHER SHRIMPY ONE...?
URURUN (TEARY)
IS...
...THERE ANOTHER SHINIGAMI BESIDES ME...?
B-
BEAUTI-FUUUUUL!!
SFX: KYUN (SWOON) KYUN
IT WAS A LONG-HAIRED BLONDE...
...SHINI-GAMI CARRYING A SKELETAL SCYTHE. ♡
I'M SO SORRY... DID YOU GET AN OWWIE?
GOSO
GOSO
GOSO
I SEE...
A SKELETAL SCYTHE, EH...?
D-DO YOU KNOW HER?

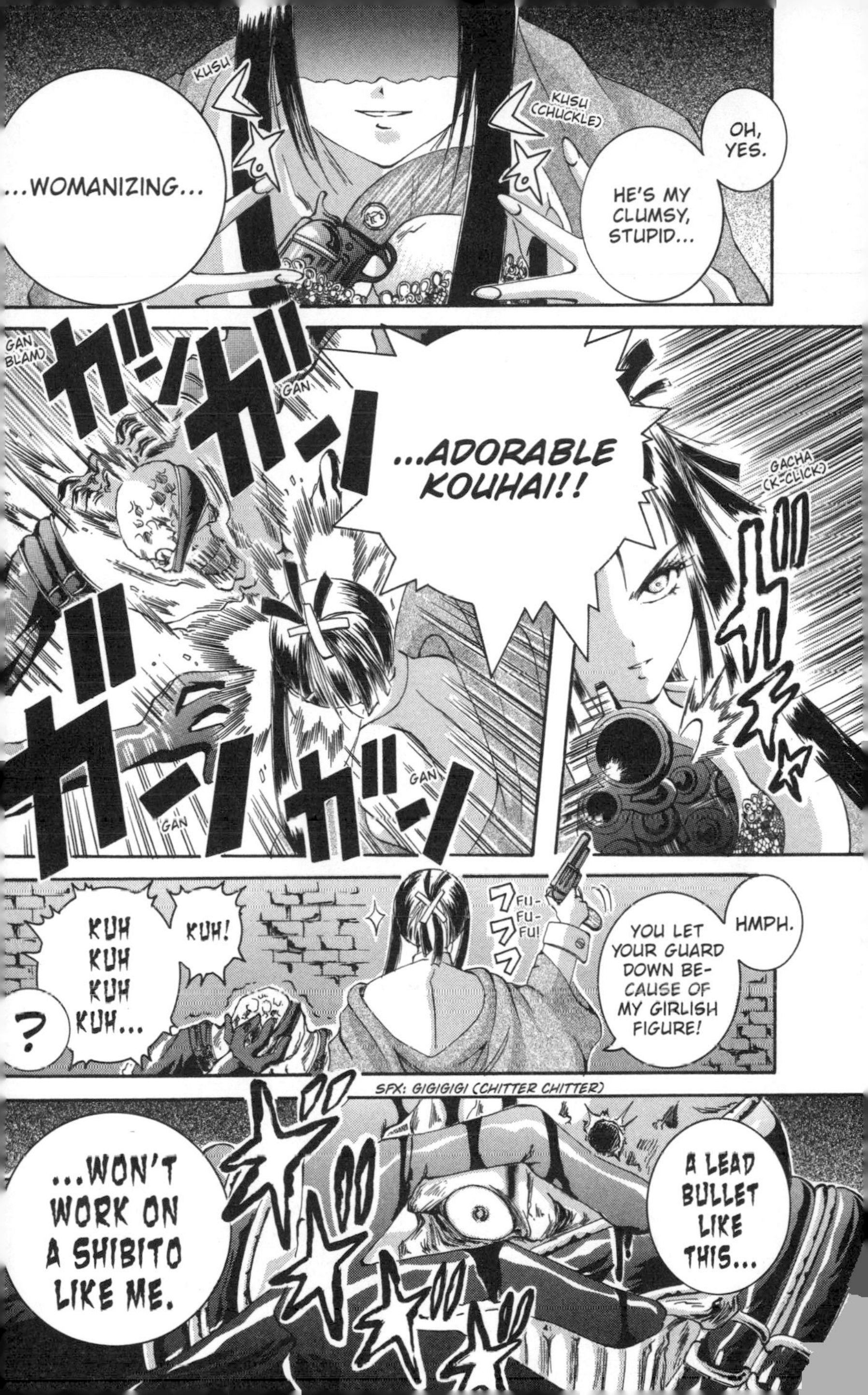
OH, YES.
HE'S MY CLUMSY, STUPID...
KUSU (CHUCKLE)
KUSU
...WOMANIZING...
GACHA (K-CLICK)
...ADORABLE KOUHAI!!
GAN BLAM
GAN
GAN
GAN
HMPH.
YOU LET YOUR GUARD DOWN BE-CAUSE OF MY GIRLISH FIGURE!
FU-FU-FU!
KUH!
KUH KUH KUH KUH...
?
SFX: GIGIGIGI (CHITTER CHITTER)
A LEAD BULLET LIKE THIS...
...WON'T WORK ON A SHIBITO LIKE ME.

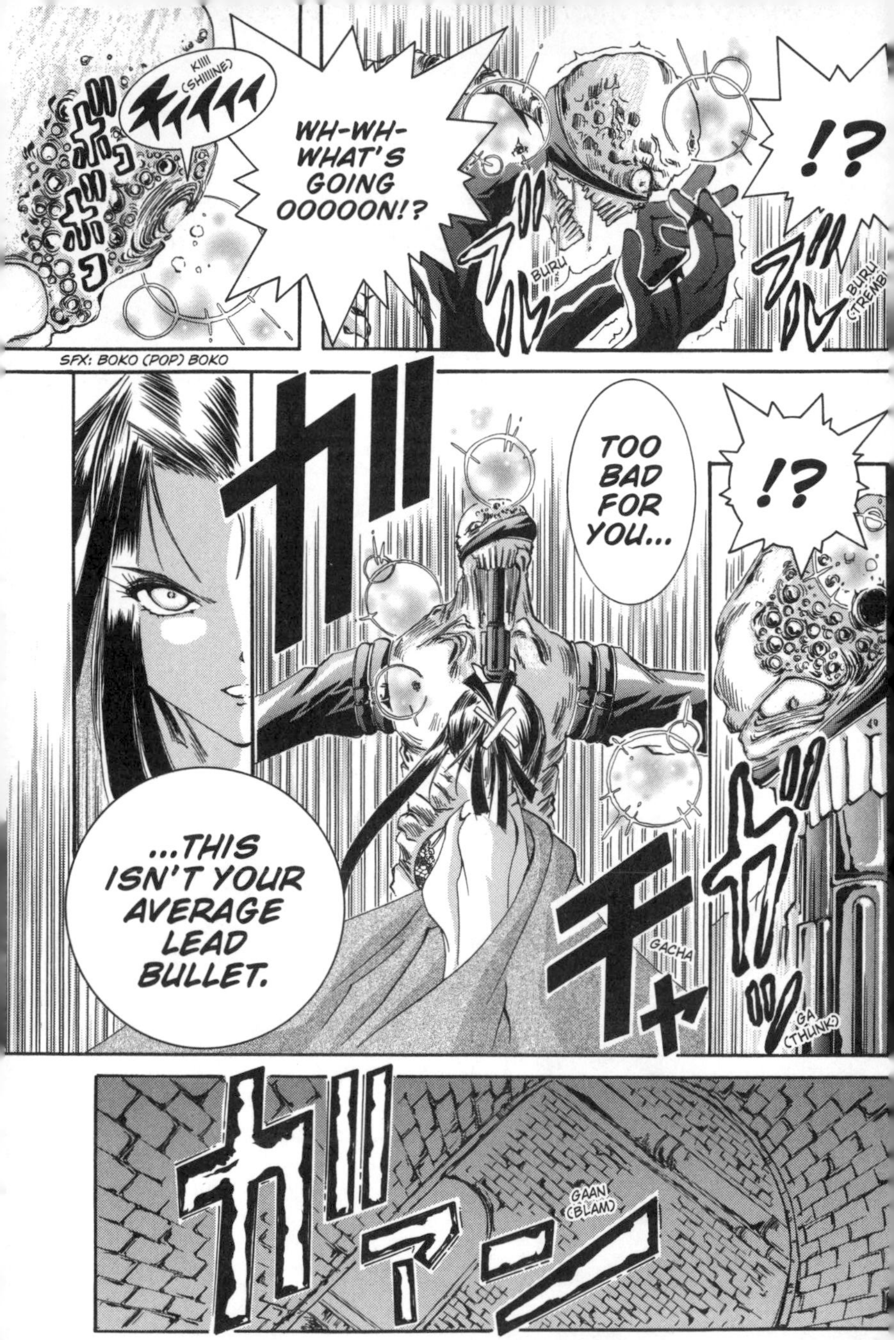
!?
BURU (TREMBLE)
BURU
WH-WH-WHAT'S GOING OOOOON!?
KIIII (SHIIIINE)
SFX: BOKO (POP) BOKO
!?
TOO BAD FOR YOU...
GA (THUNK)
GACHA
...THIS ISN'T YOUR AVERAGE LEAD BULLET.
GAAN (BLAM)

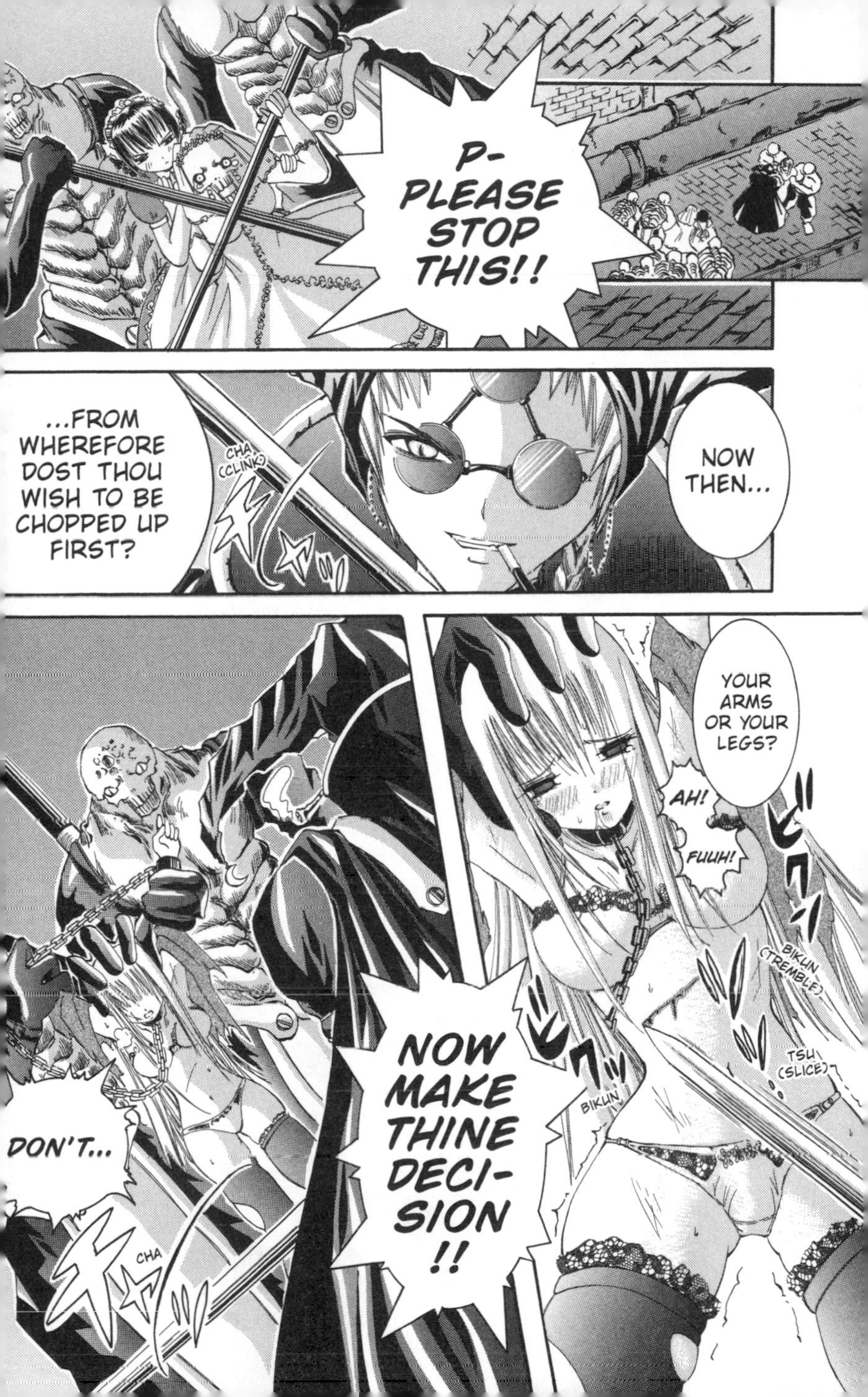
P-PLEASE STOP THIS!!
NOW THEN...
CHA (CLINK)
...FROM WHEREFORE DOST THOU WISH TO BE CHOPPED UP FIRST?
YOUR ARMS OR YOUR LEGS?
AH!
FUUH!
BIKUN (TREMBLE)
TSU (SLICE)
BIKUN
NOW MAKE THINE DECISION!!
DON'T...
CHA

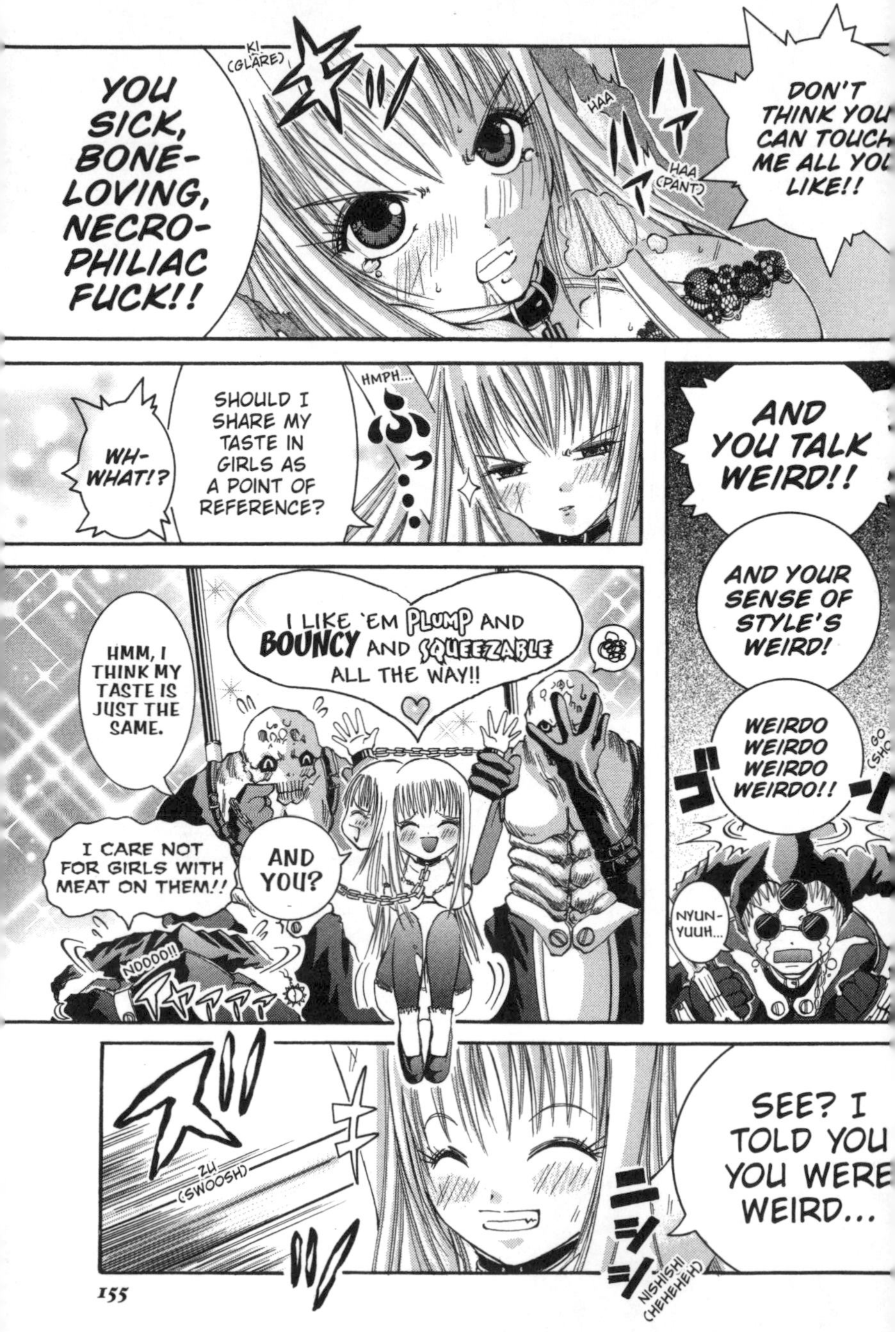
DON'T THINK YOU CAN TOUCH ME ALL YOU LIKE!!
HAA
HAA (PANT)
KI (GLARE)
YOU SICK, BONE-LOVING, NECRO-PHILIAC FUCK!!
AND YOU TALK WEIRD!!
AND YOUR SENSE OF STYLE'S WEIRD!
GO
WEIRDO WEIRDO WEIRDO WEIRDO!!
NYUN-YUUH...
HMPH...
SHOULD I SHARE MY TASTE IN GIRLS AS A POINT OF REFERENCE?
WH-WHAT!?
I LIKE 'EM PLUMP AND BOUNCY AND SQUEEZABLE ALL THE WAY!!
HMM, I THINK MY TASTE IS JUST THE SAME.
AND YOU?
I CARE NOT FOR GIRLS WITH MEAT ON THEM!!
NOOOO!!
SEE? I TOLD YOU YOU WERE WEIRD...
NISHISHI (CHEHEHEH)
ZU (SWOOSH)

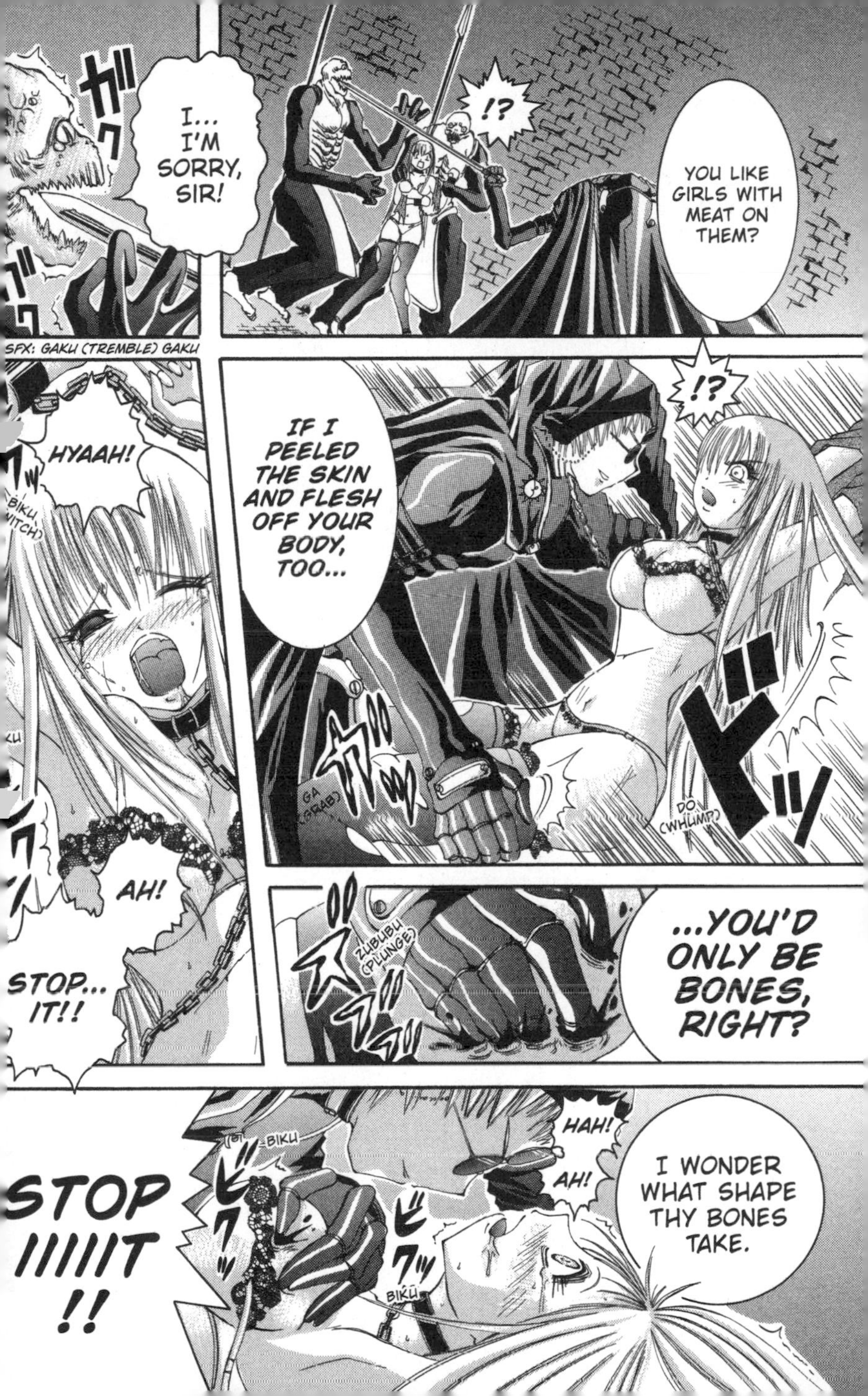
!?
YOU LIKE GIRLS WITH MEAT ON THEM?
I... I'M SORRY, SIR!
SFX: GAKU (TREMBLE) GAKU
!?
IF I PEELED THE SKIN AND FLESH OFF YOUR BODY, TOO...
DO (WHUMP)
GA (GRAB)
...YOU'D ONLY BE BONES, RIGHT?
ZUBUBU (PLUNGE)
HYAAH!
BIKU (TWITCH)
AH!
STOP... IT!!
I WONDER WHAT SHAPE THY BONES TAKE.
HAH!
AH!
BIKU
BIKU
STOP IIIIIT !!

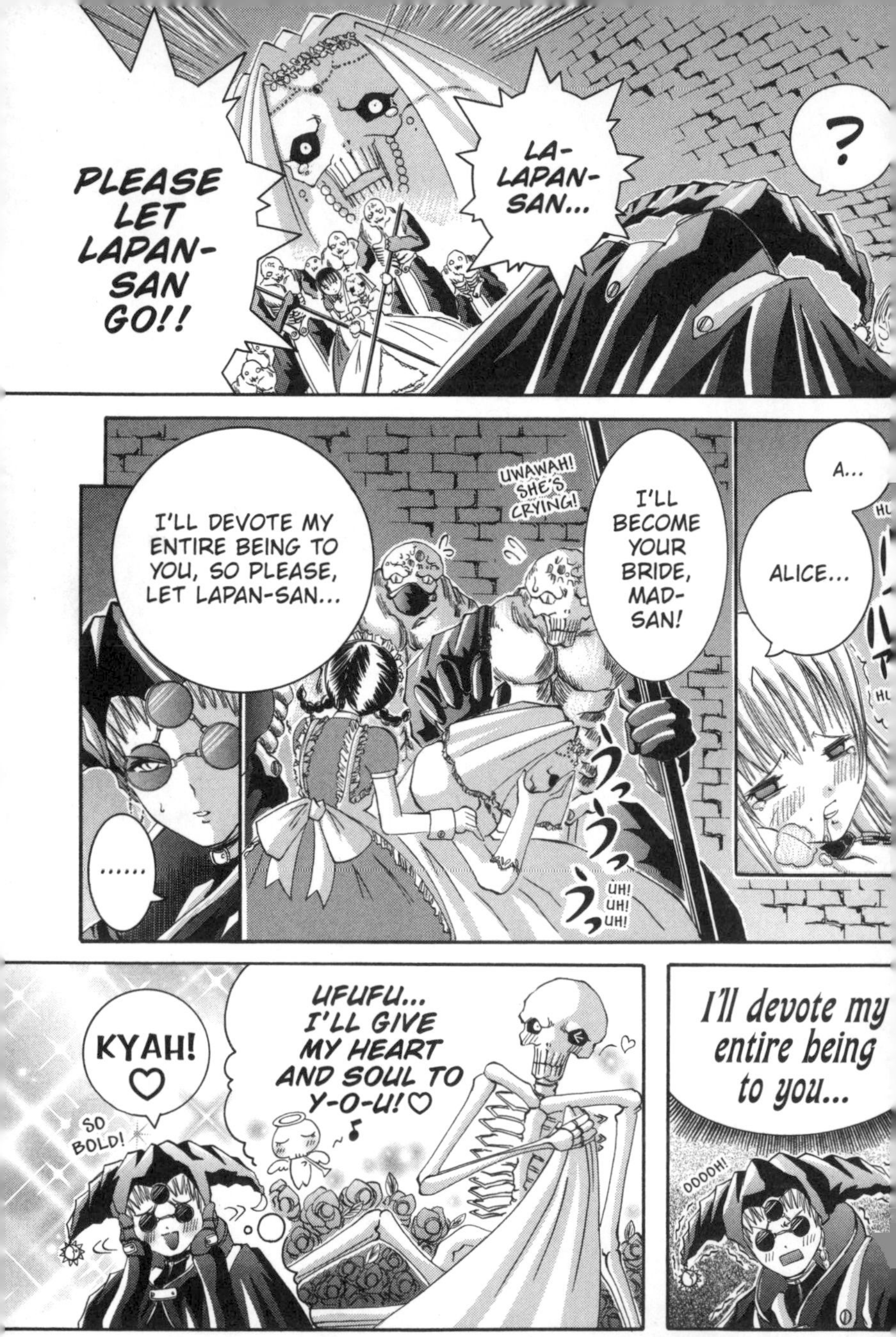
?
LA- LAPAN- SAN...
PLEASE LET LAPAN- SAN GO!!
A...
ALICE...
I'LL BECOME YOUR BRIDE, MAD- SAN!
UWAWAH! SHE'S CRYING!
I'LL DEVOTE MY ENTIRE BEING TO YOU, SO PLEASE, LET LAPAN-SAN...
UH! UH! UH!
......
I'll devote my entire being to you...
OOOOH!
UFUFU... I'LL GIVE MY HEART AND SOUL TO Y-O-U!♡
KYAH! ♡
SO BOLD!

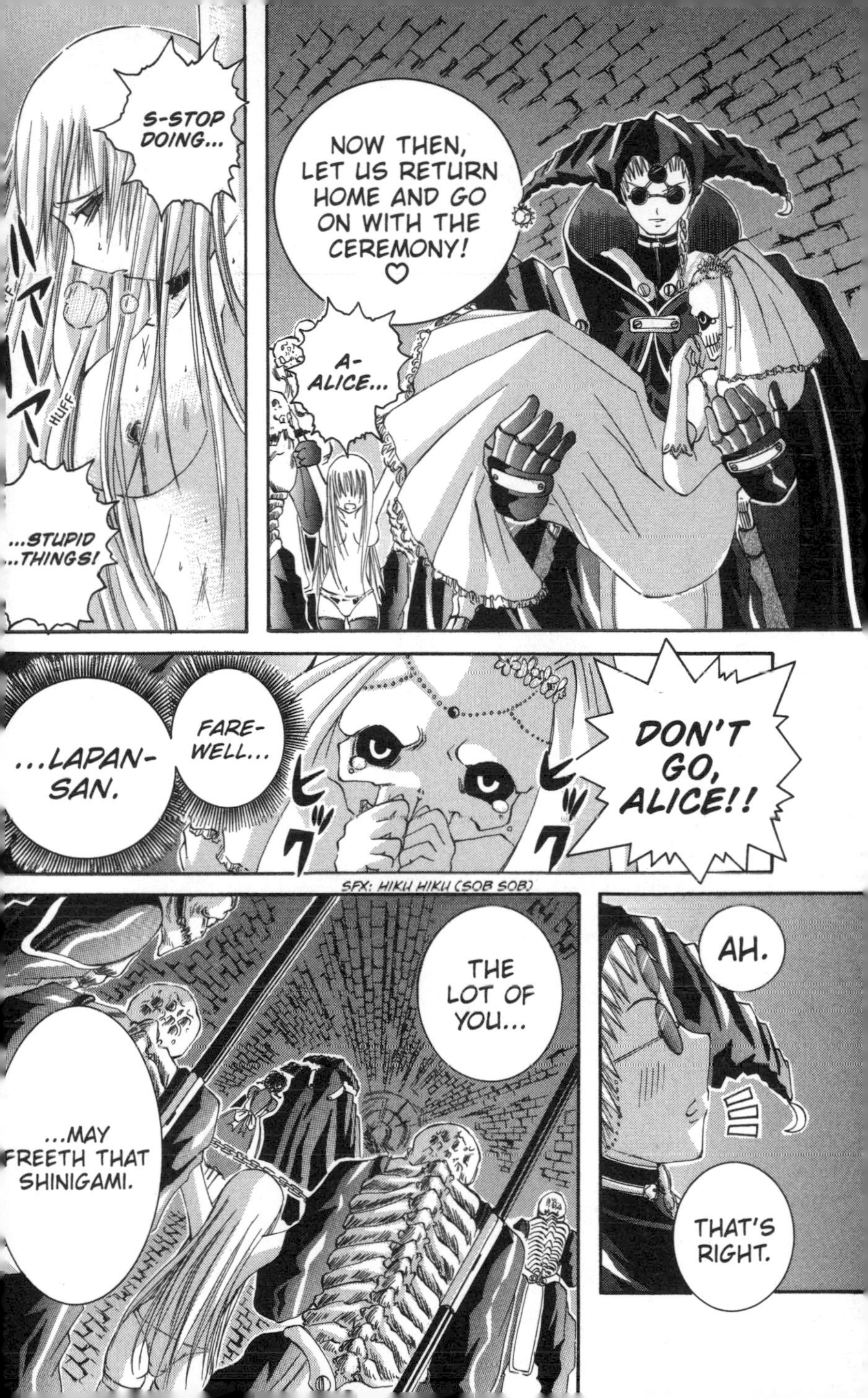
NOW THEN, LET US RETURN HOME AND GO ON WITH THE CEREMONY! ♡
A- ALICE...
S-STOP DOING...
HUFF
...STUPID ...THINGS!
DON'T GO, ALICE!!
FARE- WELL...
...LAPAN- SAN.
SFX: HIKU HIKU (SOB SOB)
AH.
THAT'S RIGHT.
THE LOT OF YOU...
...MAY FREETH THAT SHINIGAMI.

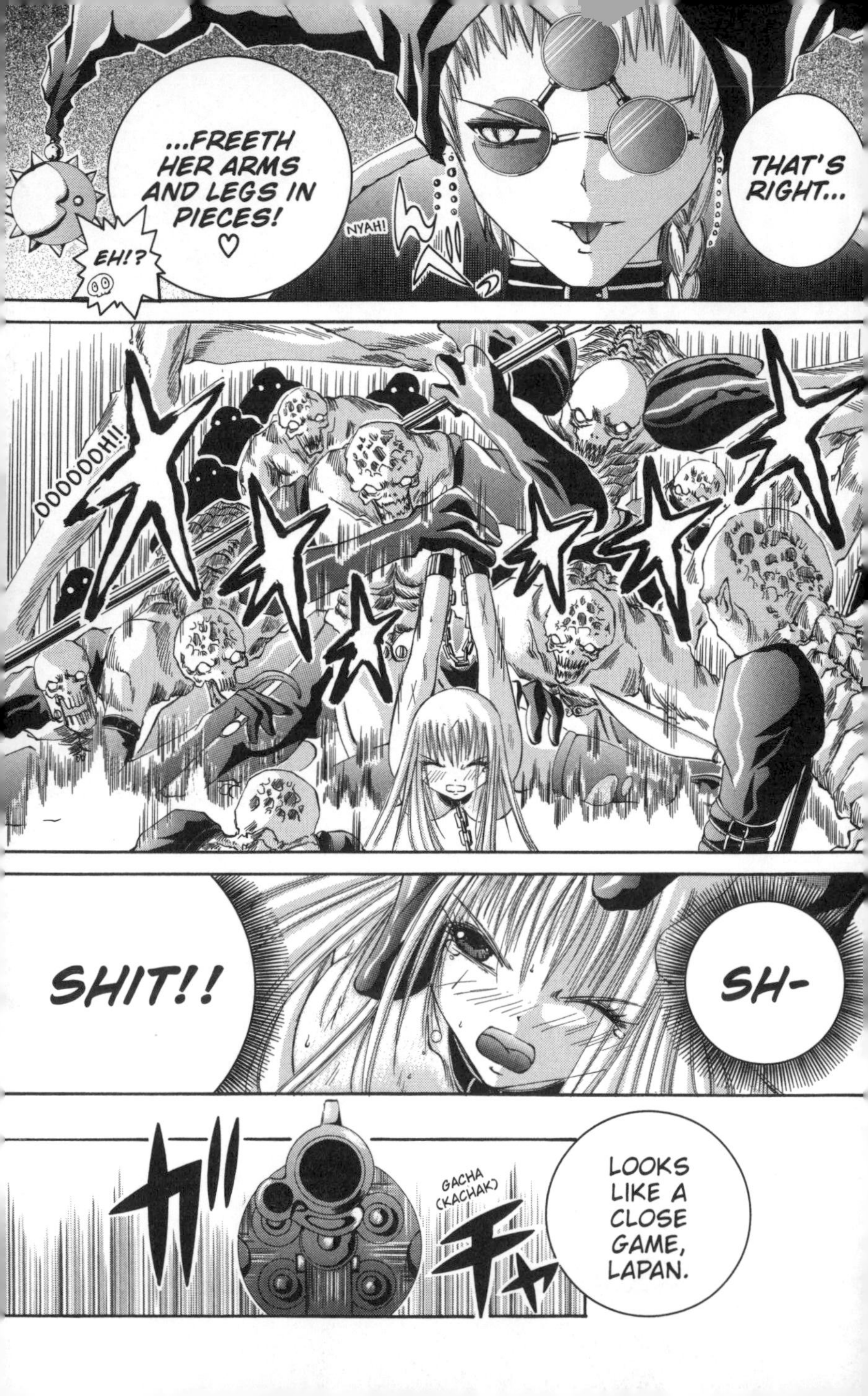

THAT'S RIGHT...
NYAH!
...FREETH HER ARMS AND LEGS IN PIECES! ♡
EH!?
OOOOOOH!!
SH-
SHIT!!
LOOKS LIKE A CLOSE GAME, LAPAN.
GACHA (KACHAK)

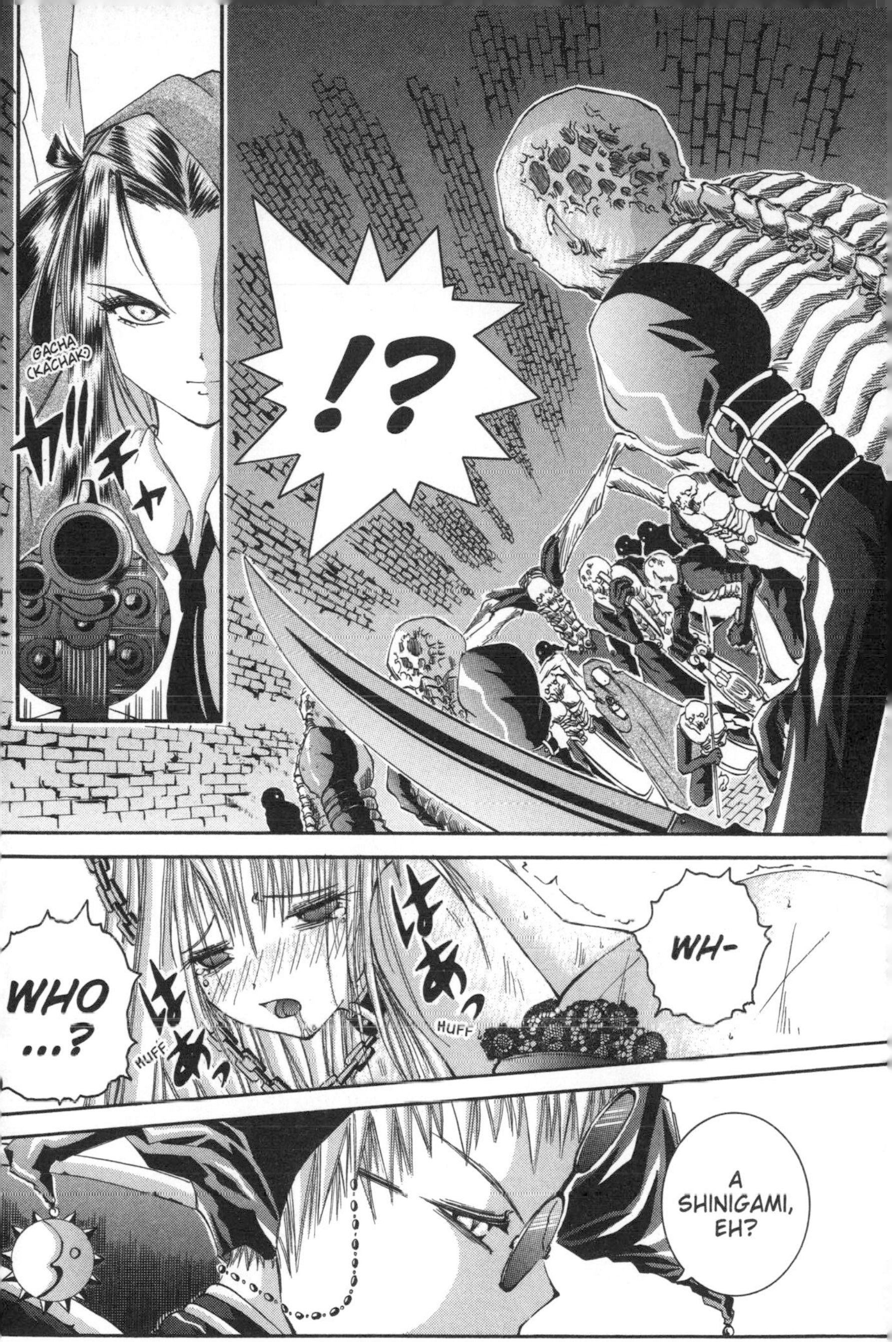
!?
GACHA (KACHAK)
ガッチャ
WH-
HUFF
はあっ
WHO ...?
HUFF
はあっ
A SHINIGAMI, EH?

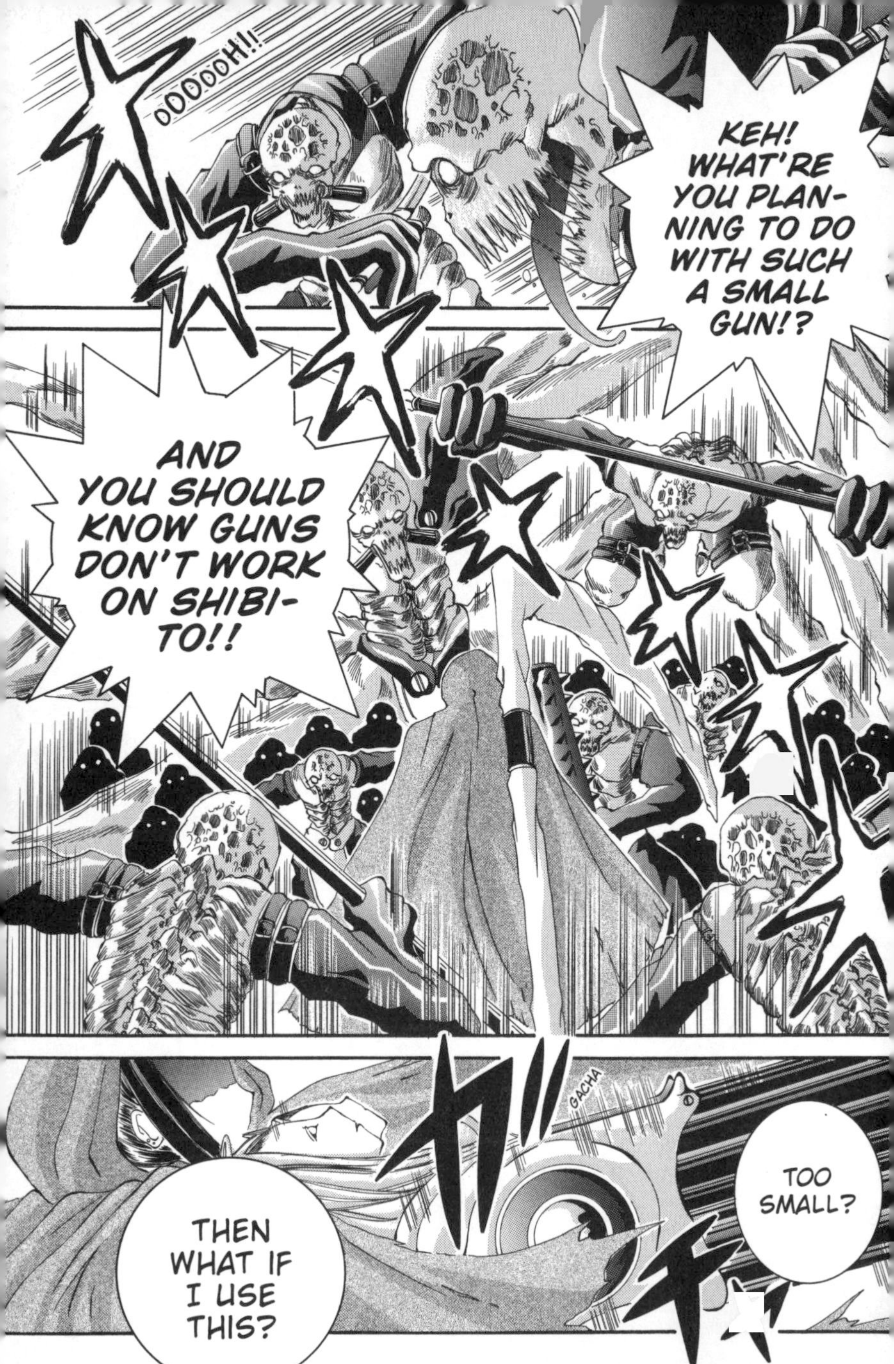
KEH! WHAT'RE YOU PLAN-NING TO DO WITH SUCH A SMALL GUN!?
OOOOOH!!
AND YOU SHOULD KNOW GUNS DON'T WORK ON SHIBI-TO!!
GACHA
TOO SMALL?
THEN WHAT IF I USE THIS?

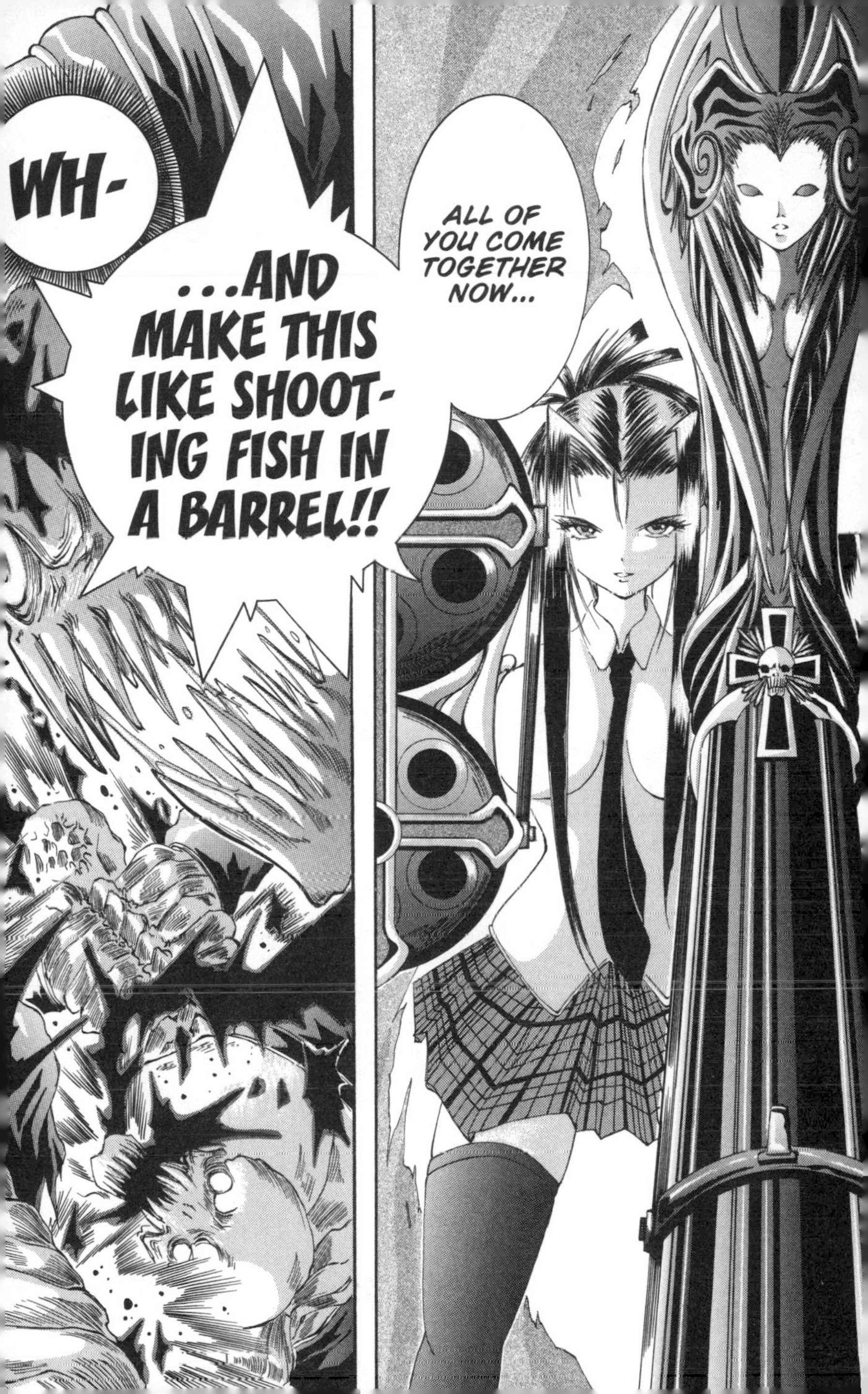
ALL OF YOU COME TOGETHER NOW...
...AND MAKE THIS LIKE SHOOT-ING FISH IN A BARREL!!
WH-

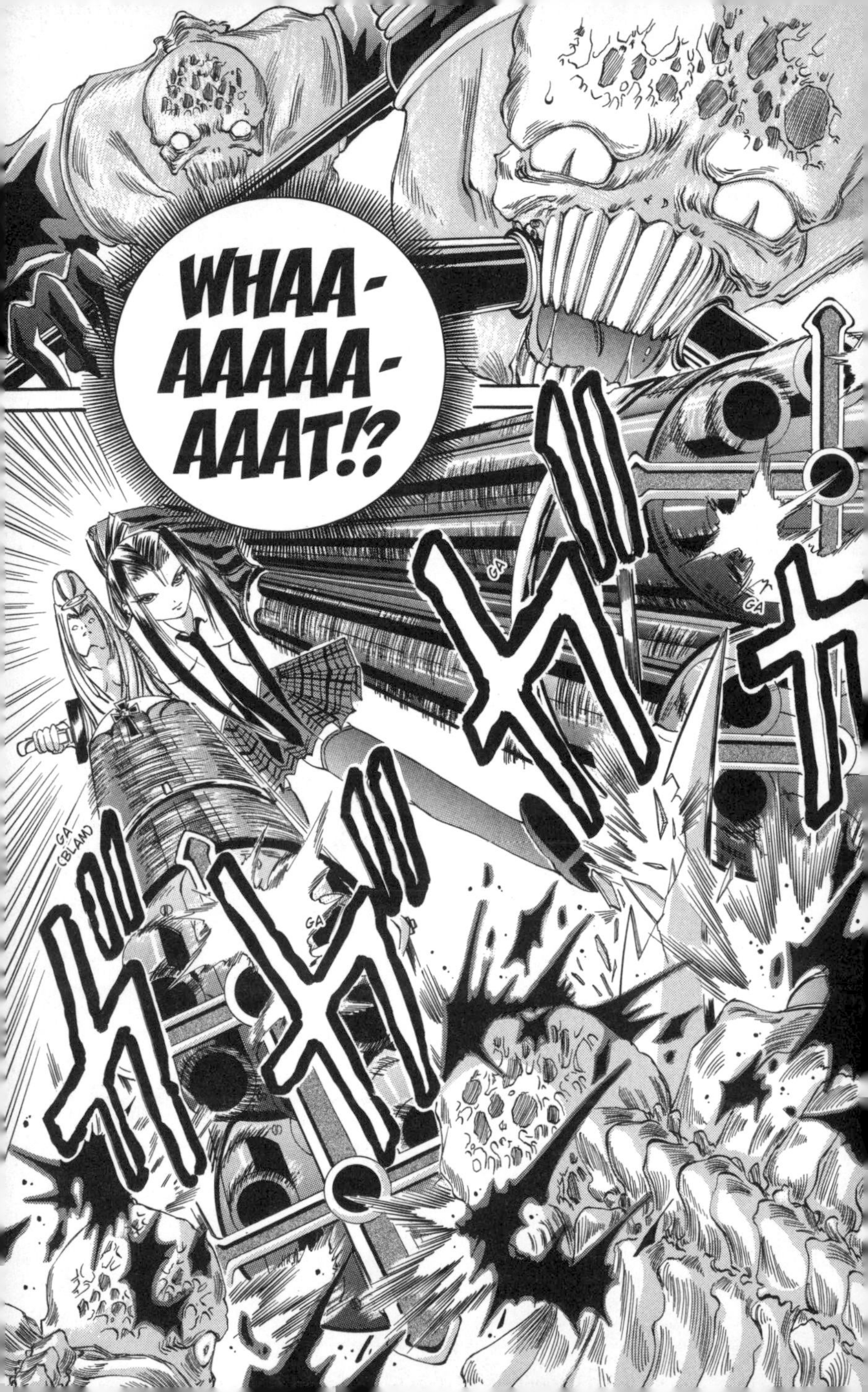
WHAA-AAAAA-AAAT!?
GA
GA
GA
GA (BLAM)

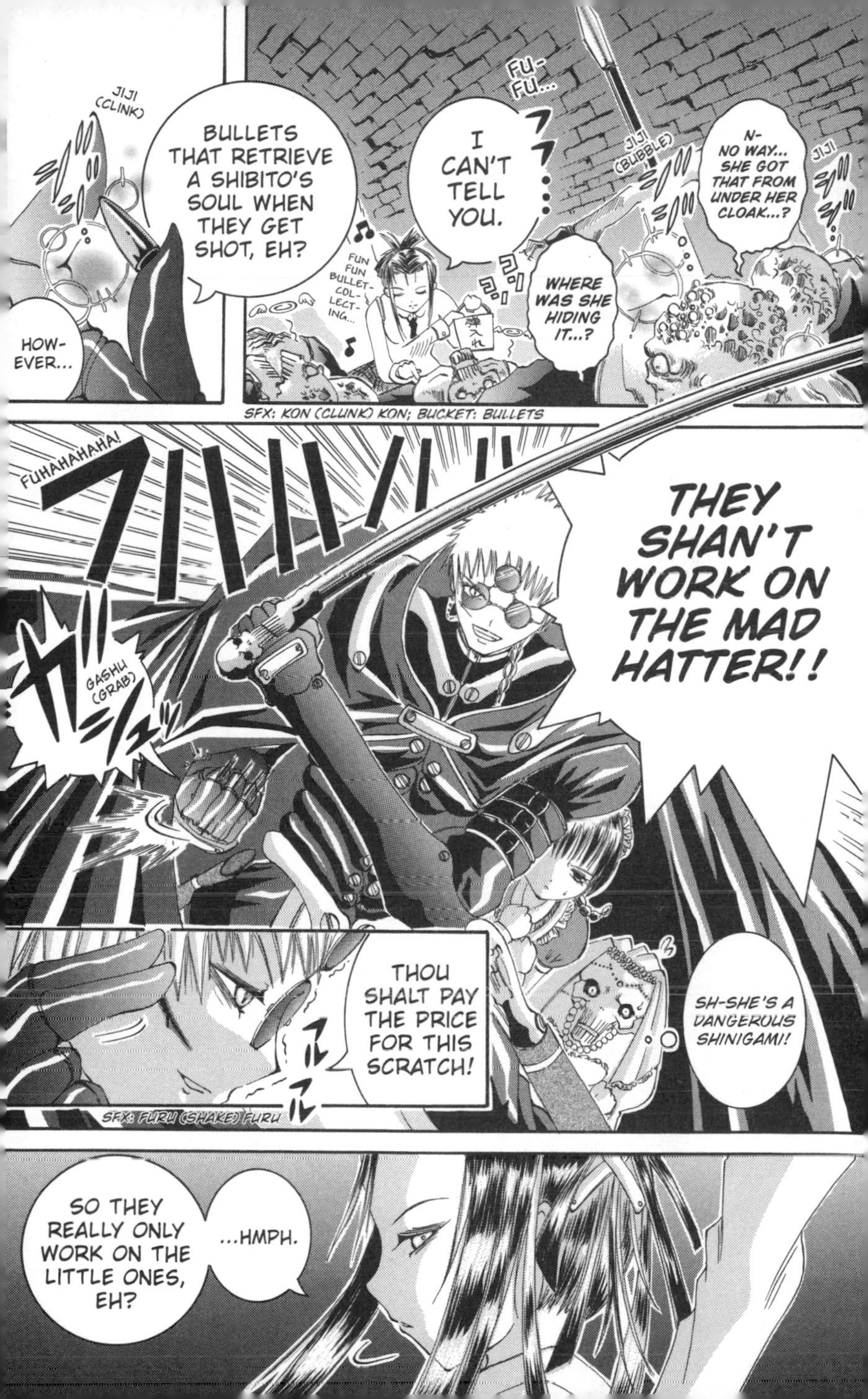
JIJI
N-NO WAY... SHE GOT THAT FROM UNDER HER CLOAK...?
JIJI (BUBBLE)
FU-FU...
I CAN'T TELL YOU.
WHERE WAS SHE HIDING IT...?
FUN FUN BULLET-COLLECTING...
SFX: KON (CLUNK) KON; BUCKET: BULLETS
JIJI (CLINK)
BULLETS THAT RETRIEVE A SHIBITO'S SOUL WHEN THEY GET SHOT, EH?
HOW-EVER...
THEY SHAN'T WORK ON THE MAD HATTER!!
FUHAHAHAHA!
GASHU (GRAB)
SH-SHE'S A DANGEROUS SHINIGAMI!
THOU SHALT PAY THE PRICE FOR THIS SCRATCH!
SFX: FURU (SHAKE) FURU
...HMPH.
SO THEY REALLY ONLY WORK ON THE LITTLE ONES, EH?

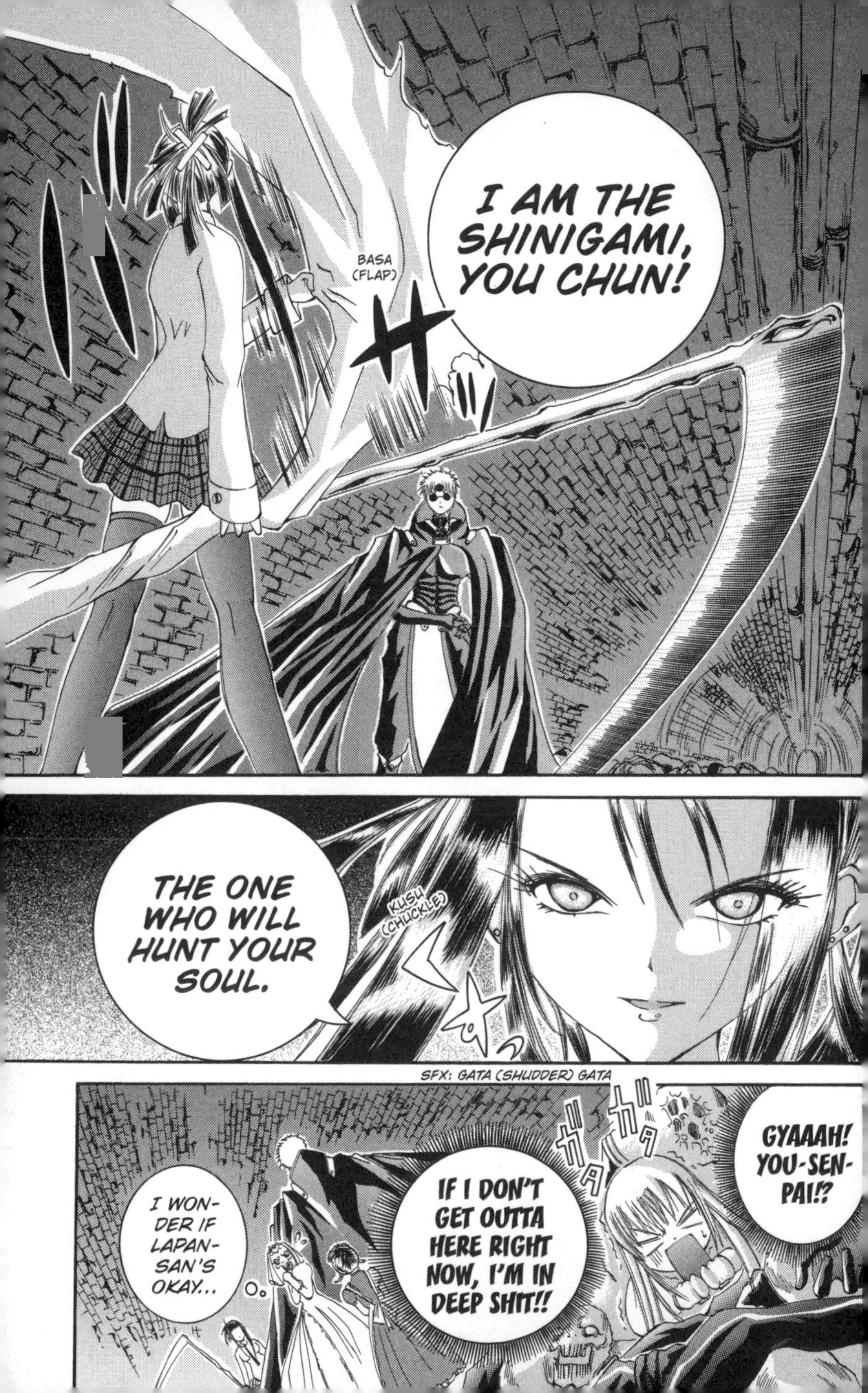
I AM THE SHINIGAMI, YOU CHUN!
BASA (FLAP)
KUSU (CHUCKLE)
THE ONE WHO WILL HUNT YOUR SOUL.
SFX: GATA (SHUDDER) GATA
GYAAAH! YOU-SEN-PAI!?
IF I DON'T GET OUTTA HERE RIGHT NOW, I'M IN DEEP SHIT!!
I WONDER IF LAPAN-SAN'S OKAY...

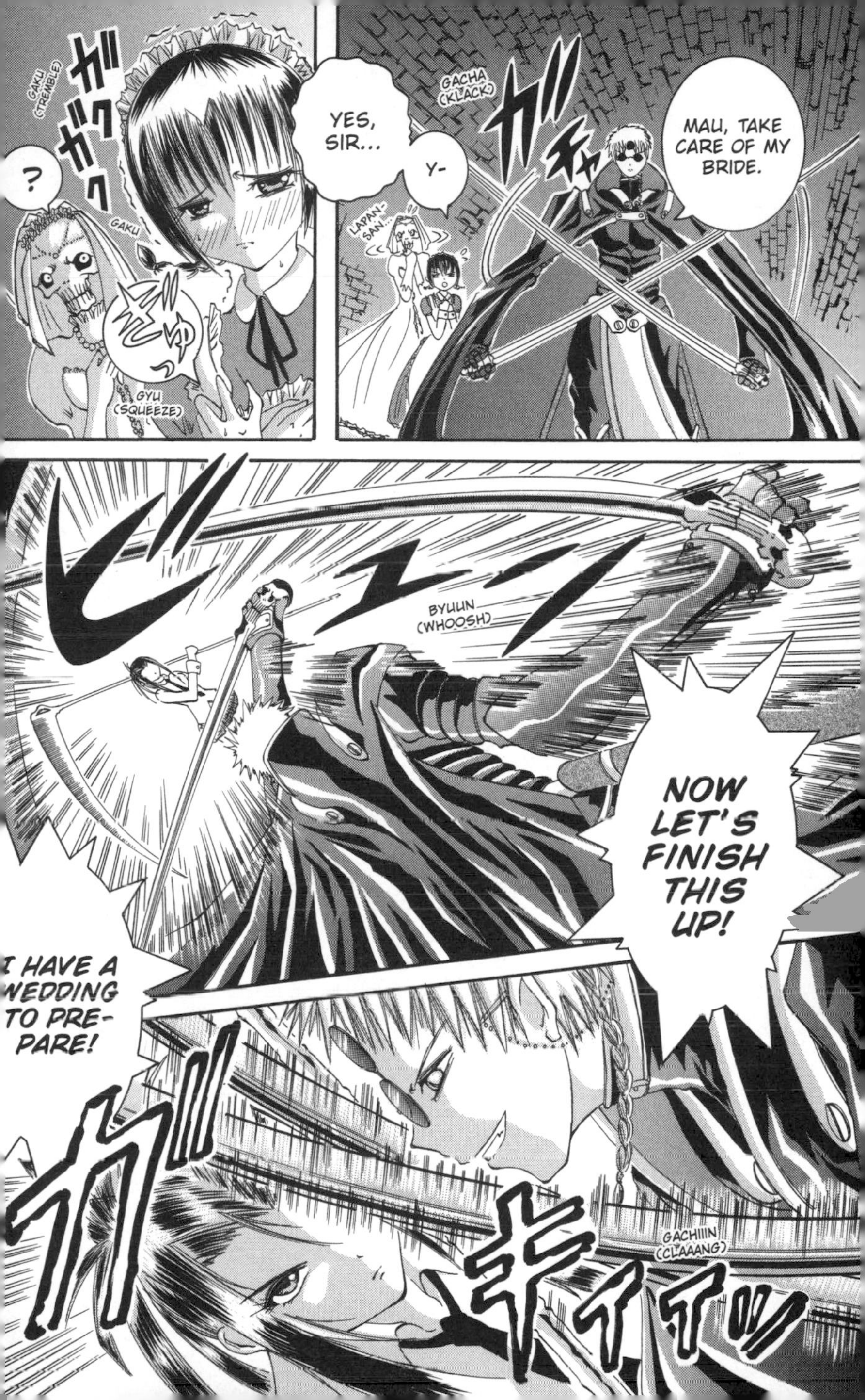
GACHA (KLACK)
MAU, TAKE CARE OF MY BRIDE.
LAPAN-SAN...
Y-
YES, SIR...
GAKU (TREMBLE)
?
GAKU
GYU (SQUEEZE)
BYUUN (WHOOSH)
NOW LET'S FINISH THIS UP!
I HAVE A WEDDING TO PRE-PARE!
GACHIIIN (CLAAANG)

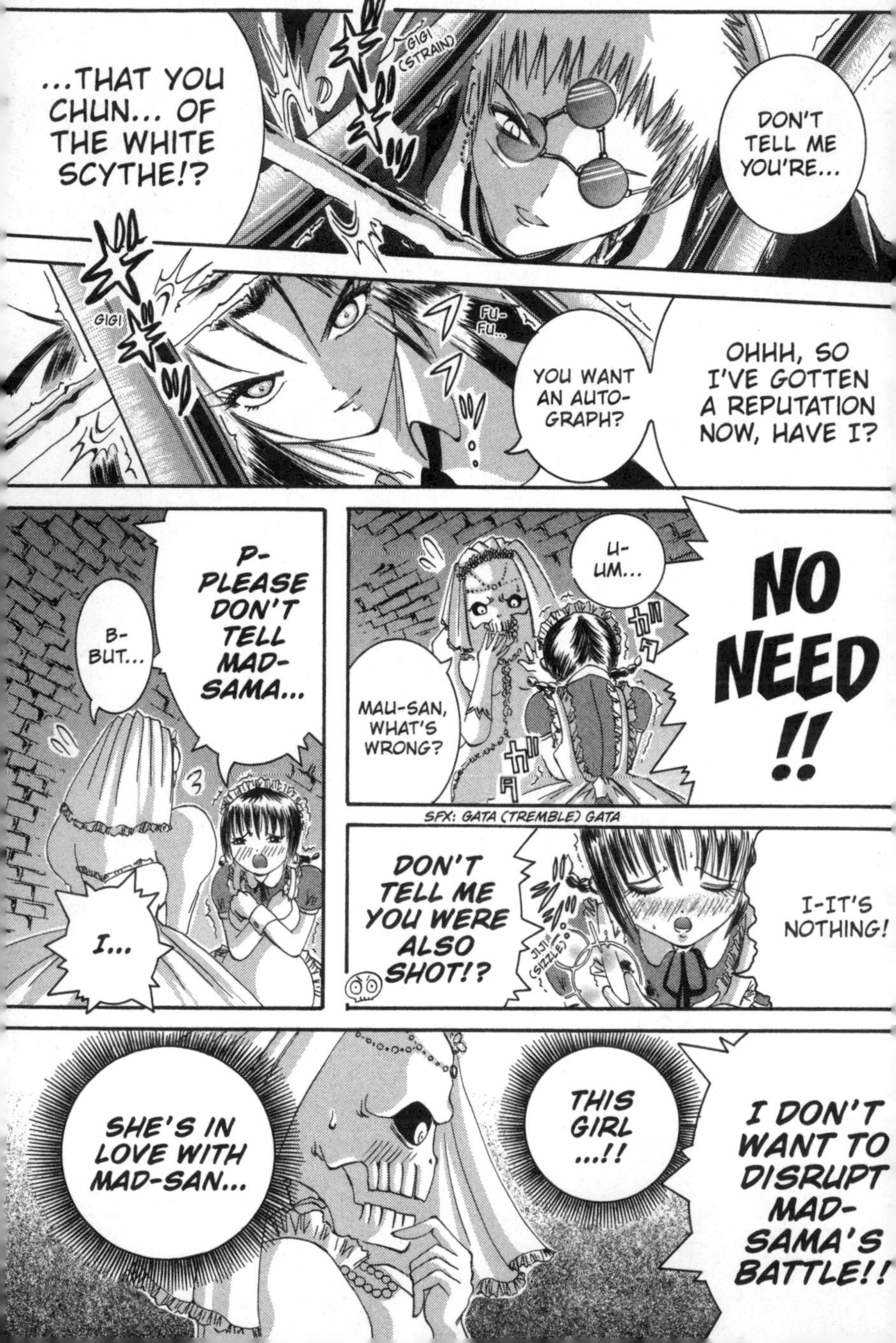
DON'T TELL ME YOU'RE...
GIGI (STRAIN)
...THAT YOU CHUN... OF THE WHITE SCYTHE!?
OHHH, SO I'VE GOTTEN A REPUTATION NOW, HAVE I?
FU-FU...
YOU WANT AN AUTO-GRAPH?
GIGI
NO NEED!!
U-UM...
MAU-SAN, WHAT'S WRONG?
SFX: GATA (TREMBLE) GATA
I-IT'S NOTHING!
JIJI (SIZZLE)
DON'T TELL ME YOU WERE ALSO SHOT!?
P-PLEASE DON'T TELL MAD-SAMA...
B-BUT...
I...
I DON'T WANT TO DISRUPT MAD-SAMA'S BATTLE!!
THIS GIRL ...!!
SHE'S IN LOVE WITH MAD-SAN...

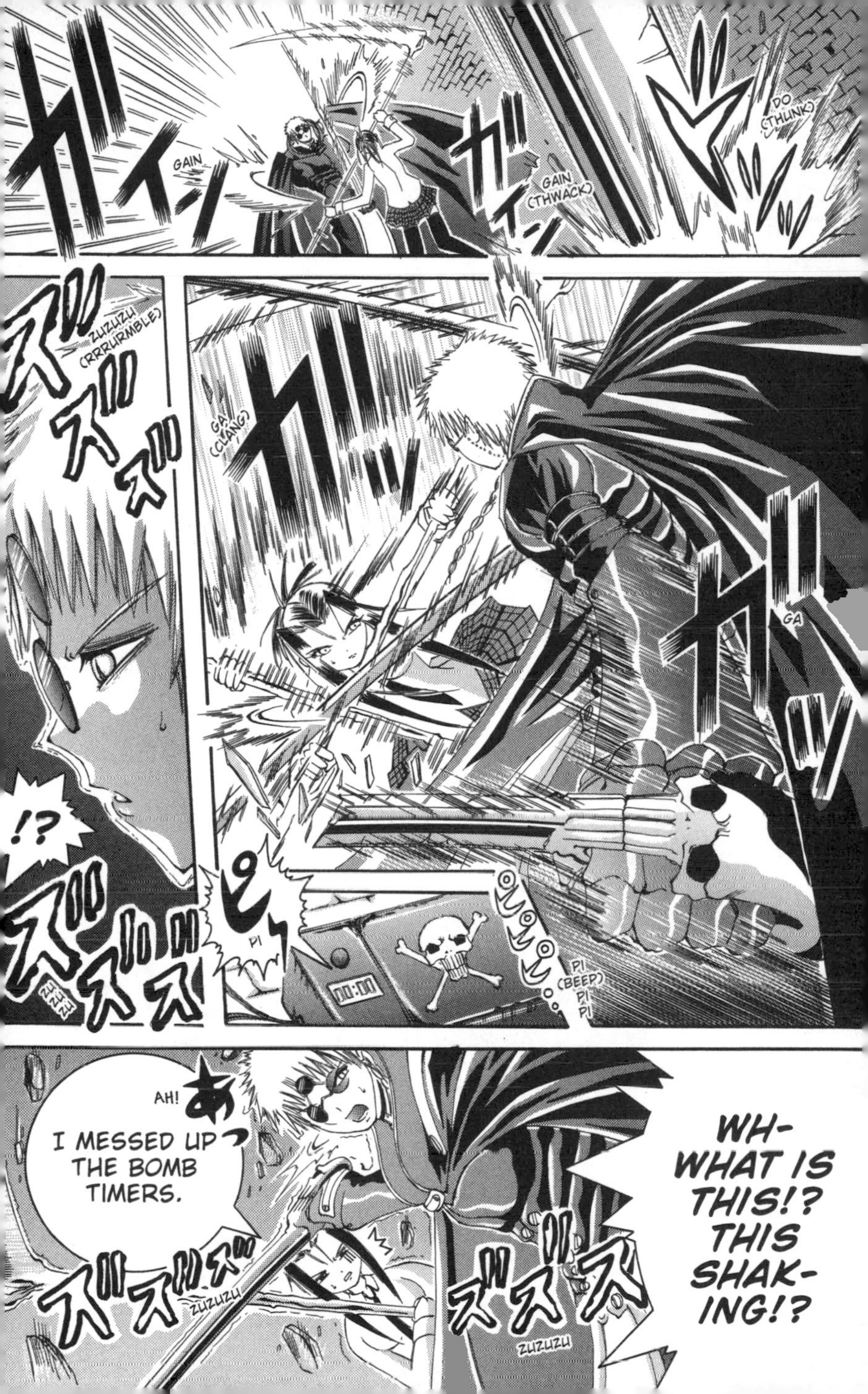
DO (THUNK)
GAIN (THWACK)
GAIN
GA
GA (CLANG)
PI (BEEP) PI PI
PI
ZUZUZU (RRRURMBLE)
!?
ZUZUZU
WH- WHAT IS THIS!? THIS SHAK- ING!?
ZUZUZU
AH!
I MESSED UP THE BOMB TIMERS.
ZUZUZU

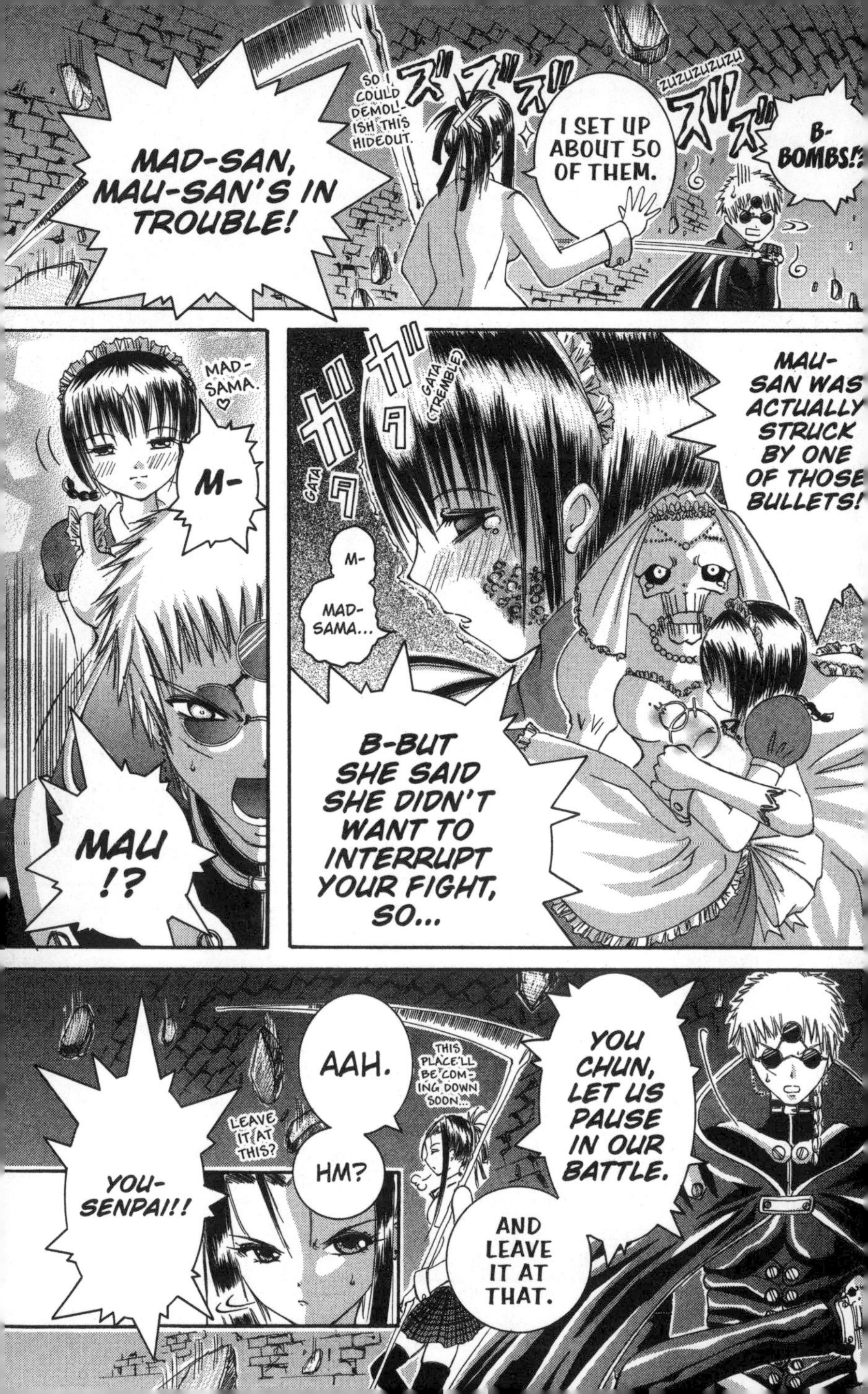
B-BOMBS!?
ZUZUZUZUZU
I SET UP ABOUT 50 OF THEM.
SO I COULD DEMOL-ISH THIS HIDEOUT.
MAD-SAN, MAU-SAN'S IN TROUBLE!
MAU-SAN WAS ACTUALLY STRUCK BY ONE OF THOSE BULLETS!
GATA (TREMBLE)
GATA
M- MAD-SAMA...
B-BUT SHE SAID SHE DIDN'T WANT TO INTERRUPT YOUR FIGHT, SO...
MAD-SAMA. ♡
M-
MAU !?
YOU CHUN, LET US PAUSE IN OUR BATTLE.
AND LEAVE IT AT THAT.
THIS PLACE'LL BE COM-ING DOWN SOON...
AAH.
HM?
LEAVE IT AT THIS?
YOU-SENPAI!!

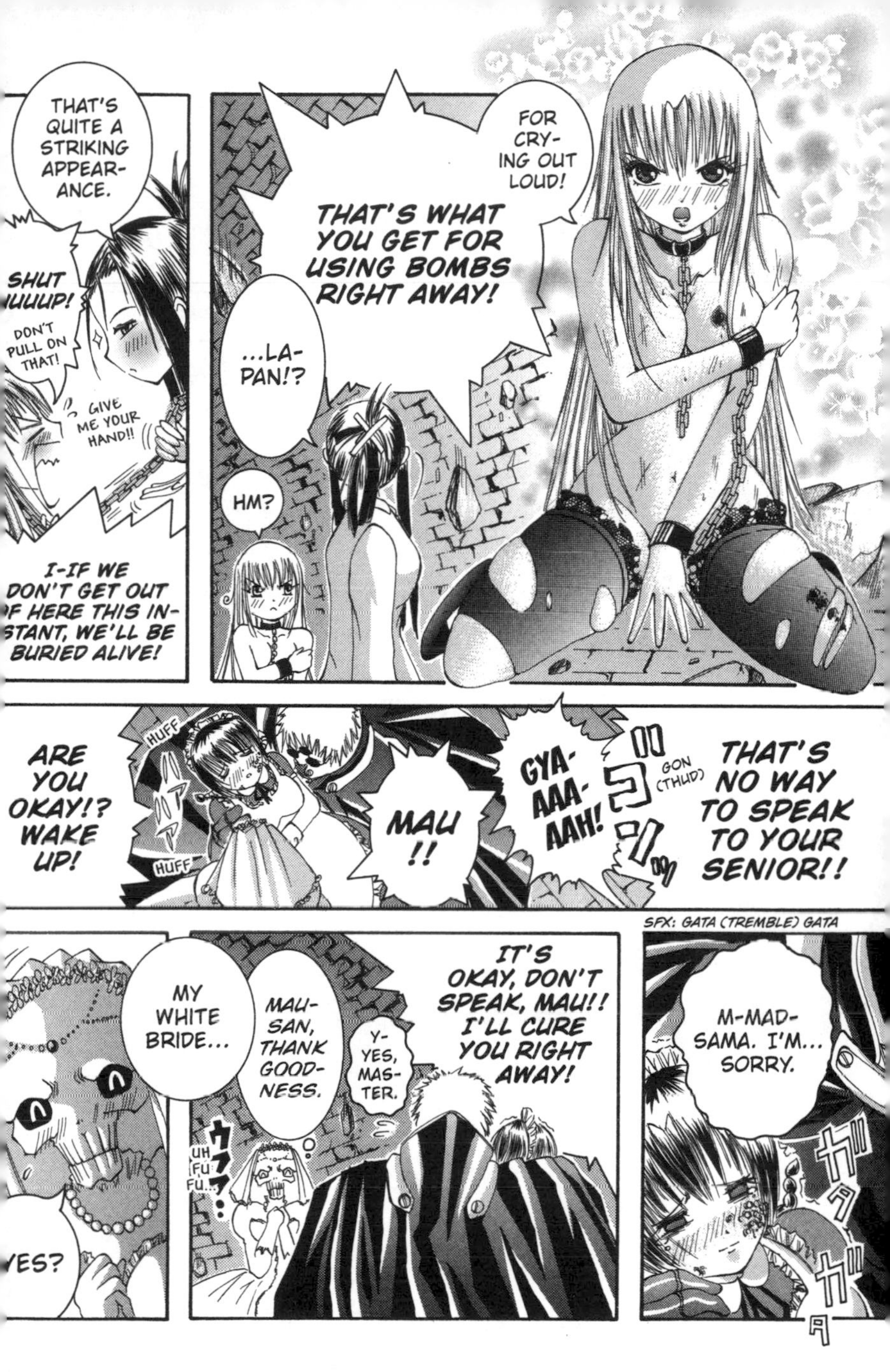
FOR CRY-ING OUT LOUD!
THAT'S WHAT YOU GET FOR USING BOMBS RIGHT AWAY!
...LA-PAN!?
HM?
THAT'S QUITE A STRIKING APPEAR-ANCE.
SHUT UUUUP!
DON'T PULL ON THAT!
GIVE ME YOUR HAND!!
I-IF WE DON'T GET OUT F HERE THIS IN- STANT, WE'LL BE BURIED ALIVE!
THAT'S NO WAY TO SPEAK TO YOUR SENIOR!!
GON (THUD)
GYA-AAA-AAH!
MAU!!
HUFF
HUFF
ARE YOU OKAY!? WAKE UP!
SFX: GATA (TREMBLE) GATA
M-MAD-SAMA. I'M... SORRY.
IT'S OKAY, DON'T SPEAK, MAU!! I'LL CURE YOU RIGHT AWAY!
Y-YES, MAS-TER.
MAU-SAN, THANK GOOD-NESS.
MY WHITE BRIDE...
UH FU FU...
ES?

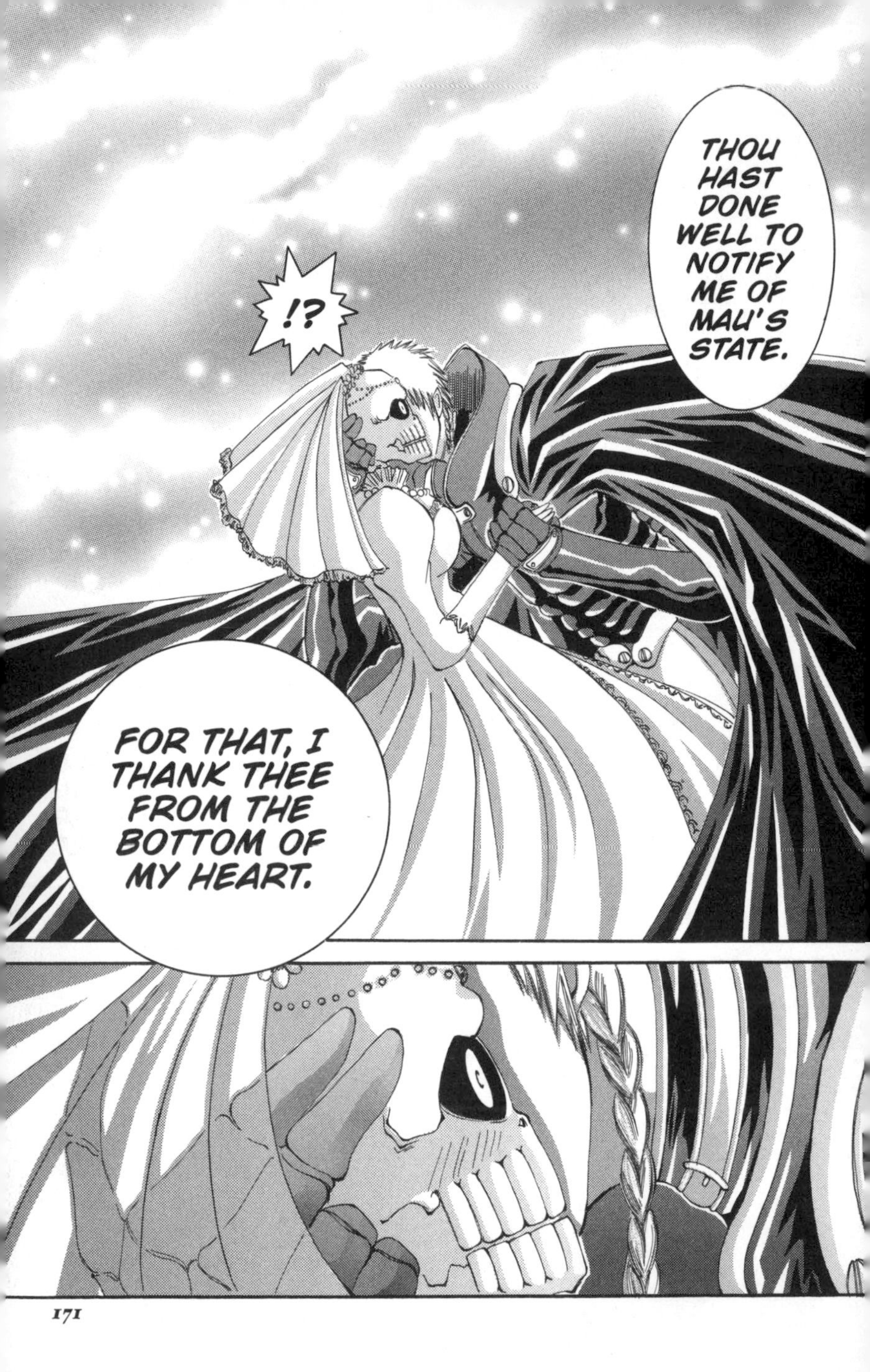
THOU HAST DONE WELL TO NOTIFY ME OF MAU'S STATE.
!?
FOR THAT, I THANK THEE FROM THE BOTTOM OF MY HEART.

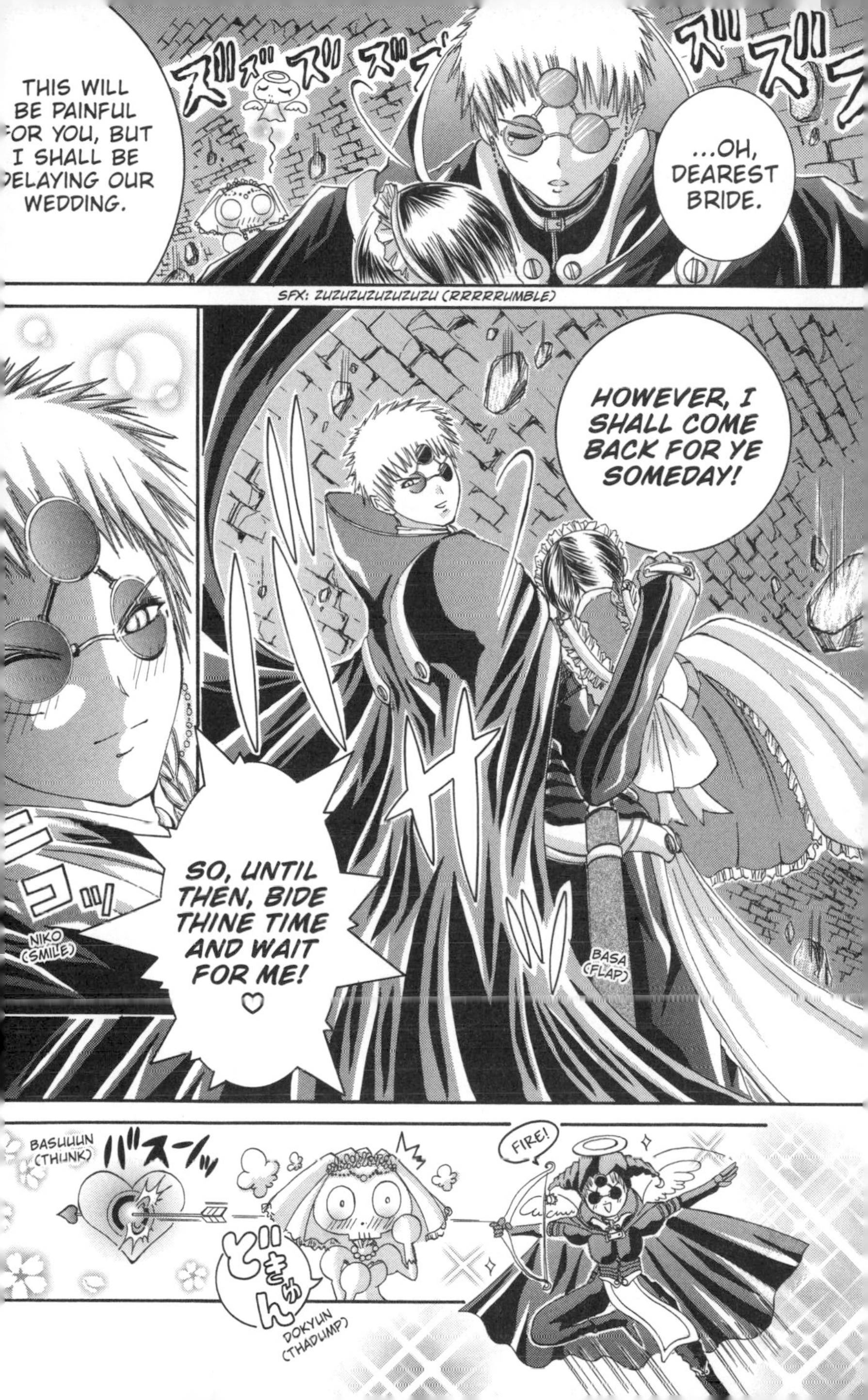
THIS WILL BE PAINFUL FOR YOU, BUT I SHALL BE DELAYING OUR WEDDING.
...OH, DEAREST BRIDE.
SFX: ZUZUZUZUZUZUZU (RRRRRUMBLE)
HOWEVER, I SHALL COME BACK FOR YE SOMEDAY!
SO, UNTIL THEN, BIDE THINE TIME AND WAIT FOR ME! ♡
BASA (FLAP)
NIKO (SMILE)
FIRE!
どきゅん
DOKYUN (THADUMP)
BASUUUN (THUNK)

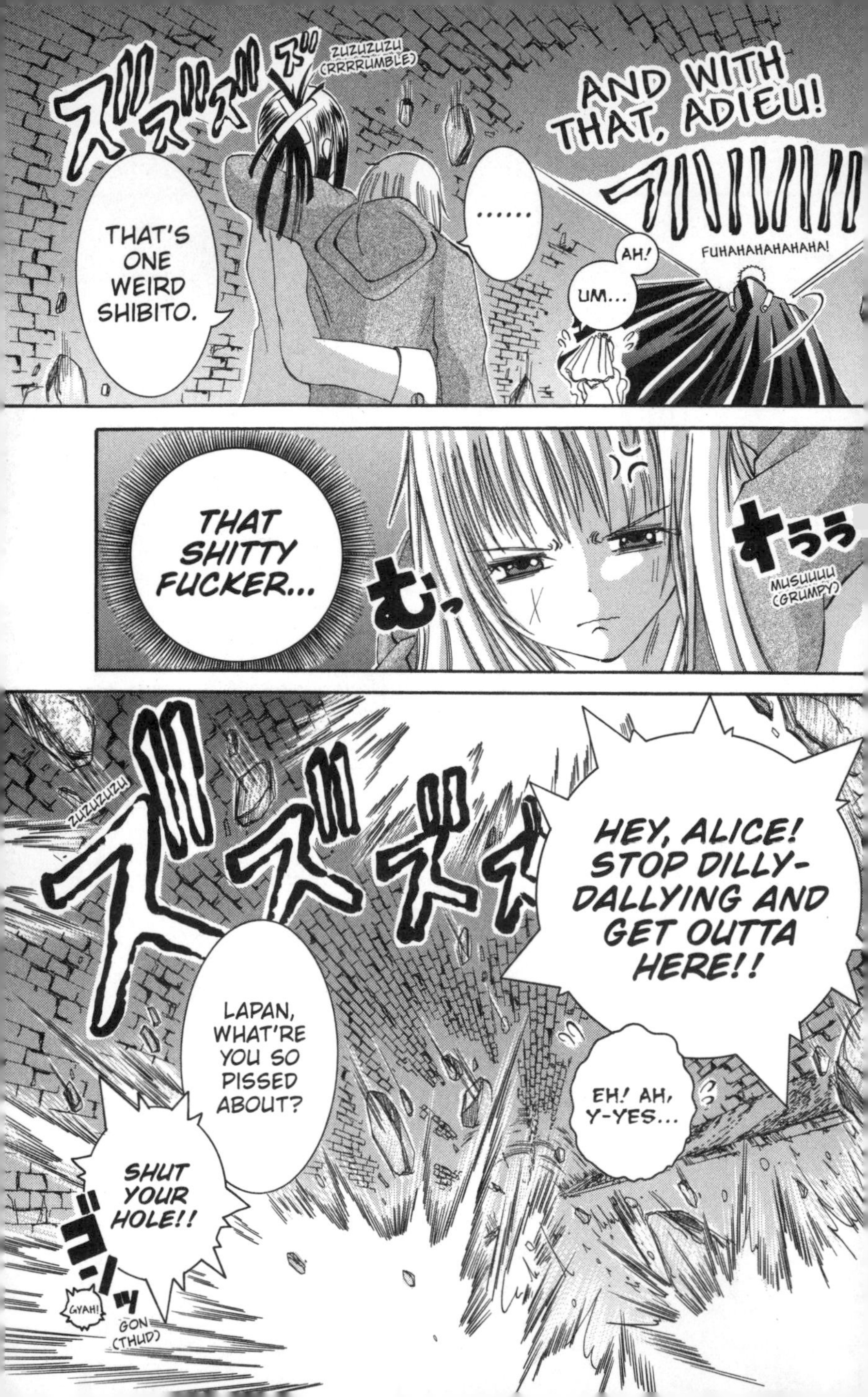
AND WITH THAT, ADIEU!
FUHAHAHAHAHAHA!
AH!
UM...
......
ZUZUZUZU (RRRRUMBLE)
THAT'S ONE WEIRD SHIBITO.
MUSUUUU (GRUMPY)
THAT SHITTY FUCKER...
HEY, ALICE! STOP DILLY-DALLYING AND GET OUTTA HERE!!
EH! AH, Y-YES...
LAPAN, WHAT'RE YOU SO PISSED ABOUT?
ZUZUZUZU
SHUT YOUR HOLE!!
GON (THUD)
GYAH!

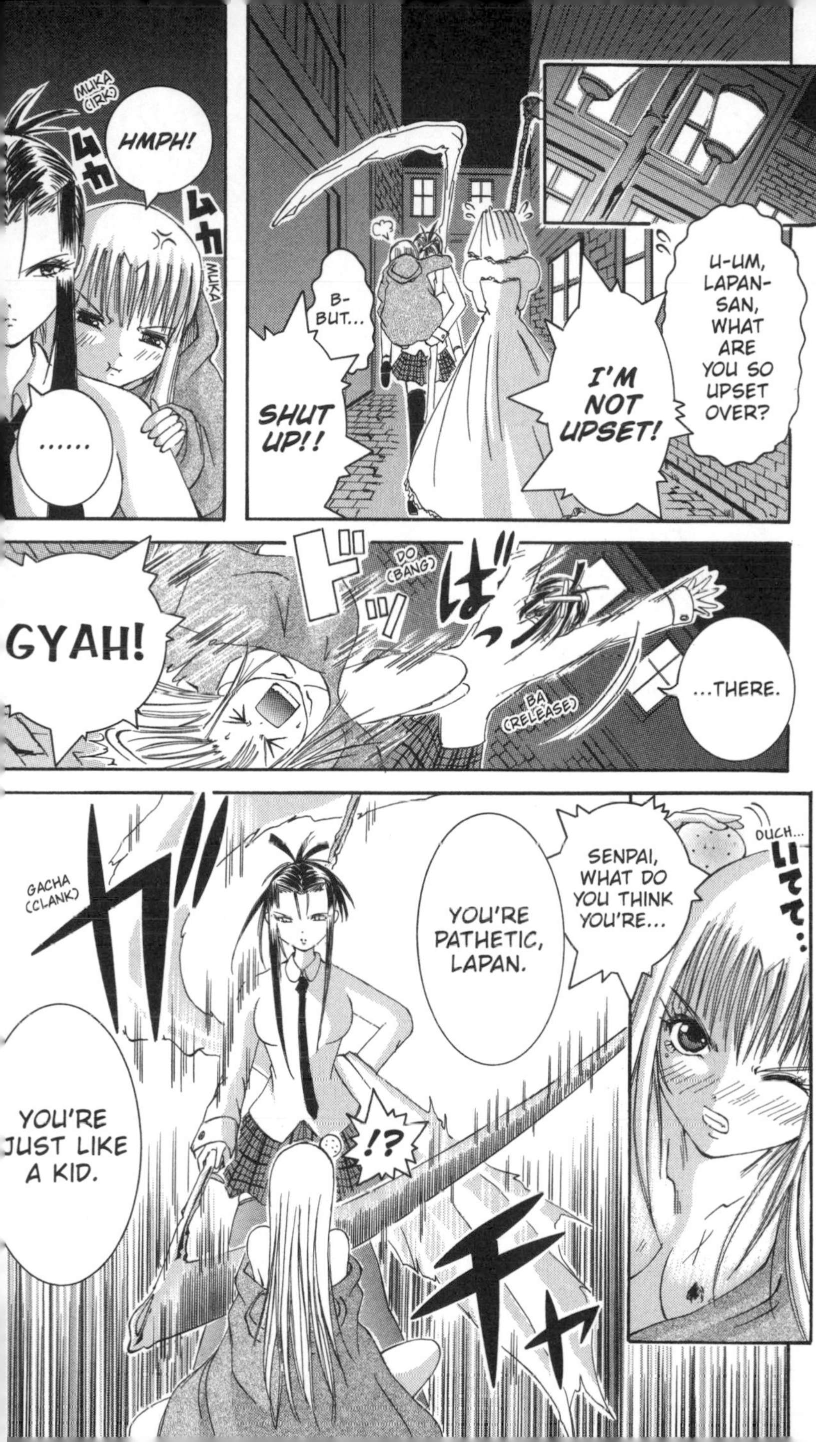
U-UM, LAPAN-SAN, WHAT ARE YOU SO UPSET OVER?
I'M NOT UPSET!
B-BUT...
SHUT UP!!
HMPH!
MUKA (IRK)
MUKA
......
...THERE.
BA (RELEASE)
DO (BANG)
GYAH!
OUCH...
SENPAI, WHAT DO YOU THINK YOU'RE...
YOU'RE PATHETIC, LAPAN.
GACHA (CLANK)
!?
YOU'RE JUST LIKE A KID.

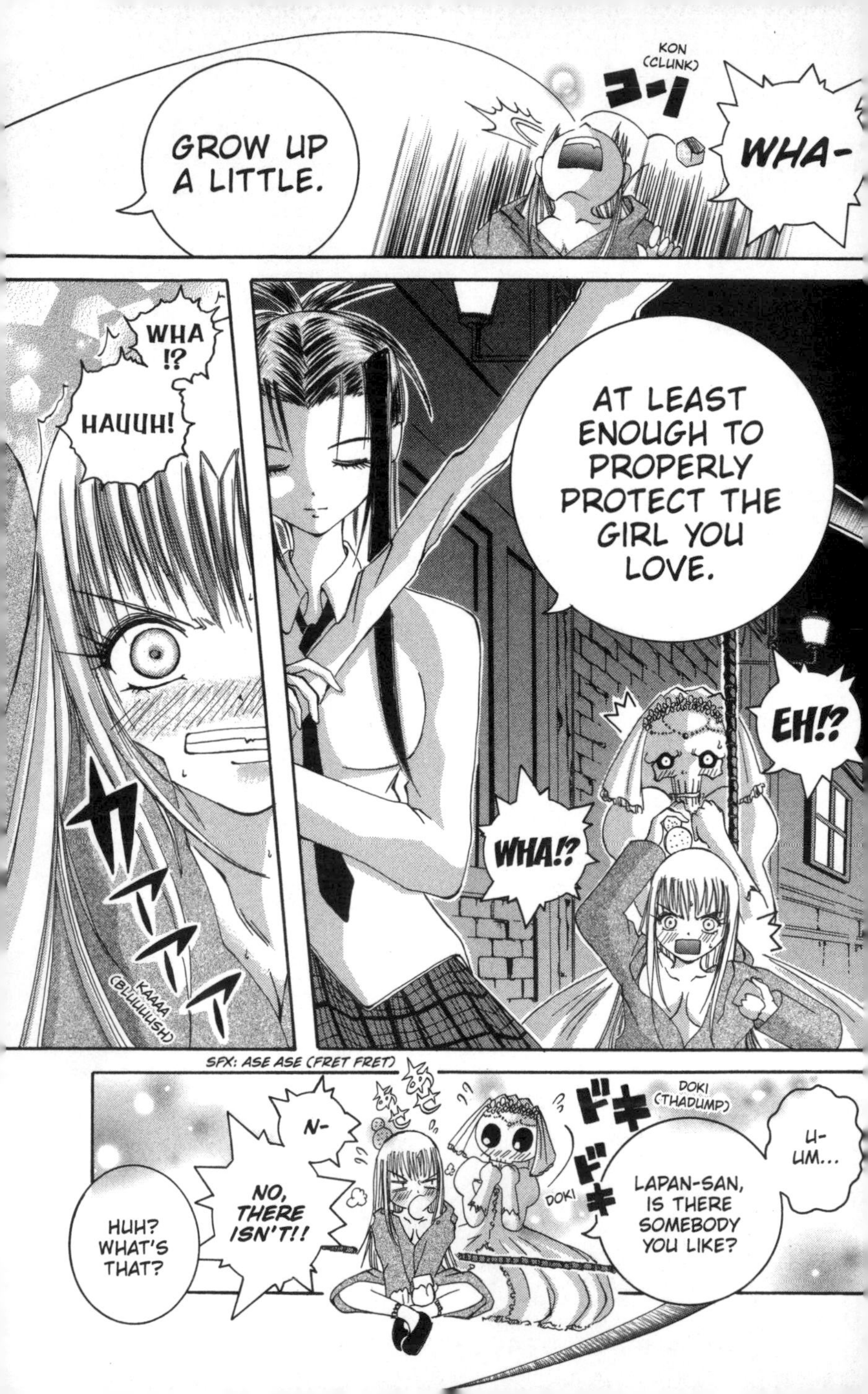
KON (CLUNK)
WHA-
GROW UP A LITTLE.
AT LEAST ENOUGH TO PROPERLY PROTECT THE GIRL YOU LOVE.
EH!?
WHA!?
WHA !?
HAUUH!
KAAAA (BLUUUSH)
SFX: ASE ASE (FRET FRET)
U-UM...
DOKI (THADUMP)
LAPAN-SAN, IS THERE SOMEBODY YOU LIKE?
DOKI
N-
NO, THERE ISN'T!!
HUH? WHAT'S THAT?

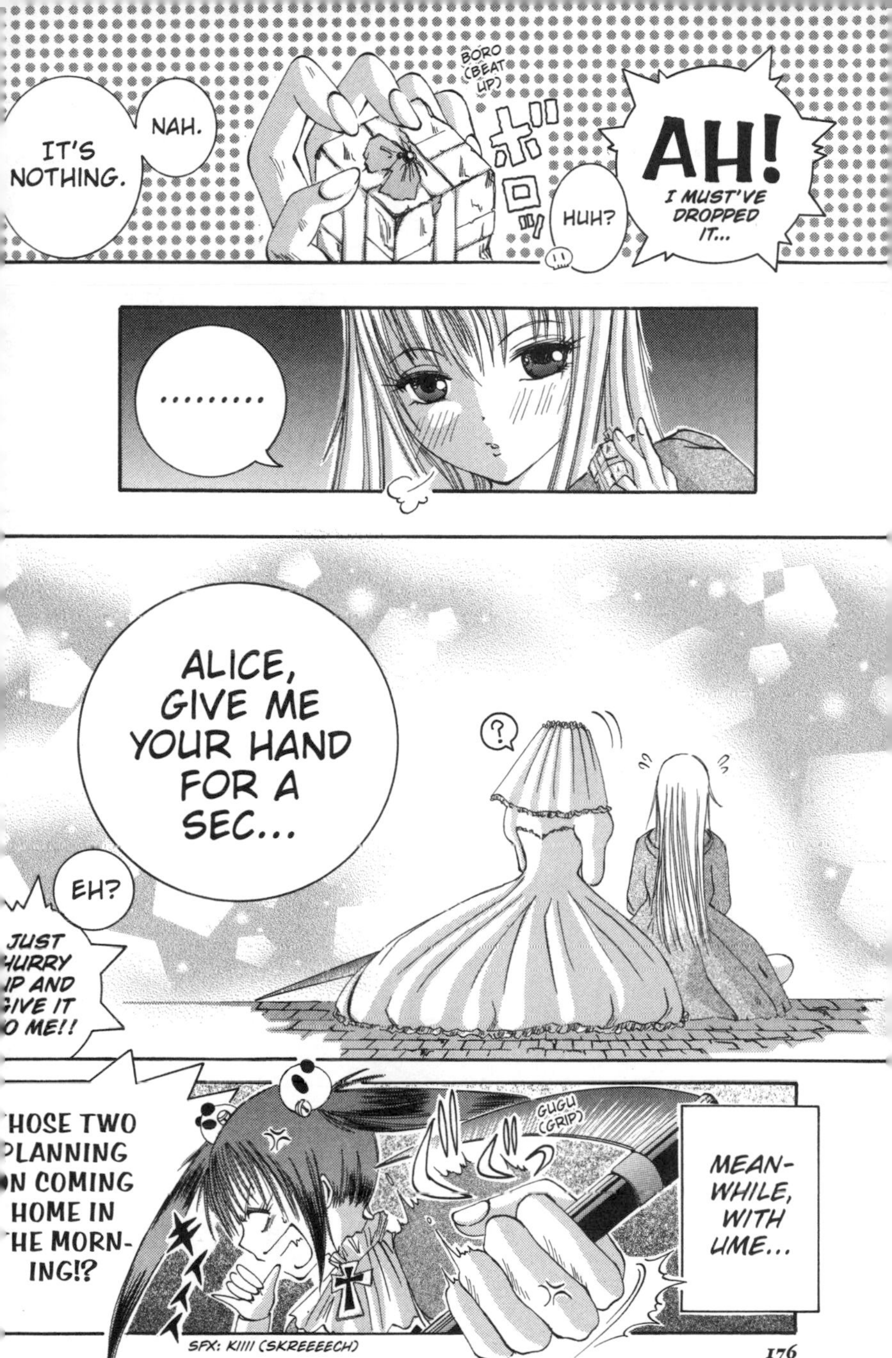
AH! I MUST'VE DROPPED IT...
HUH?
BORO (BEAT UP)
NAH.
IT'S NOTHING.
....
ALICE, GIVE ME YOUR HAND FOR A SEC...
EH?
JUST URRY P AND IVE IT O ME!!
MEAN-WHILE, WITH UME...
GUGU (GRIP)
HOSE TWO LANNING N COMING HOME IN HE MORN-ING!?
SFX: KIIII (SKREEEECH)

ALICE ON DEADLINES [2] THE END

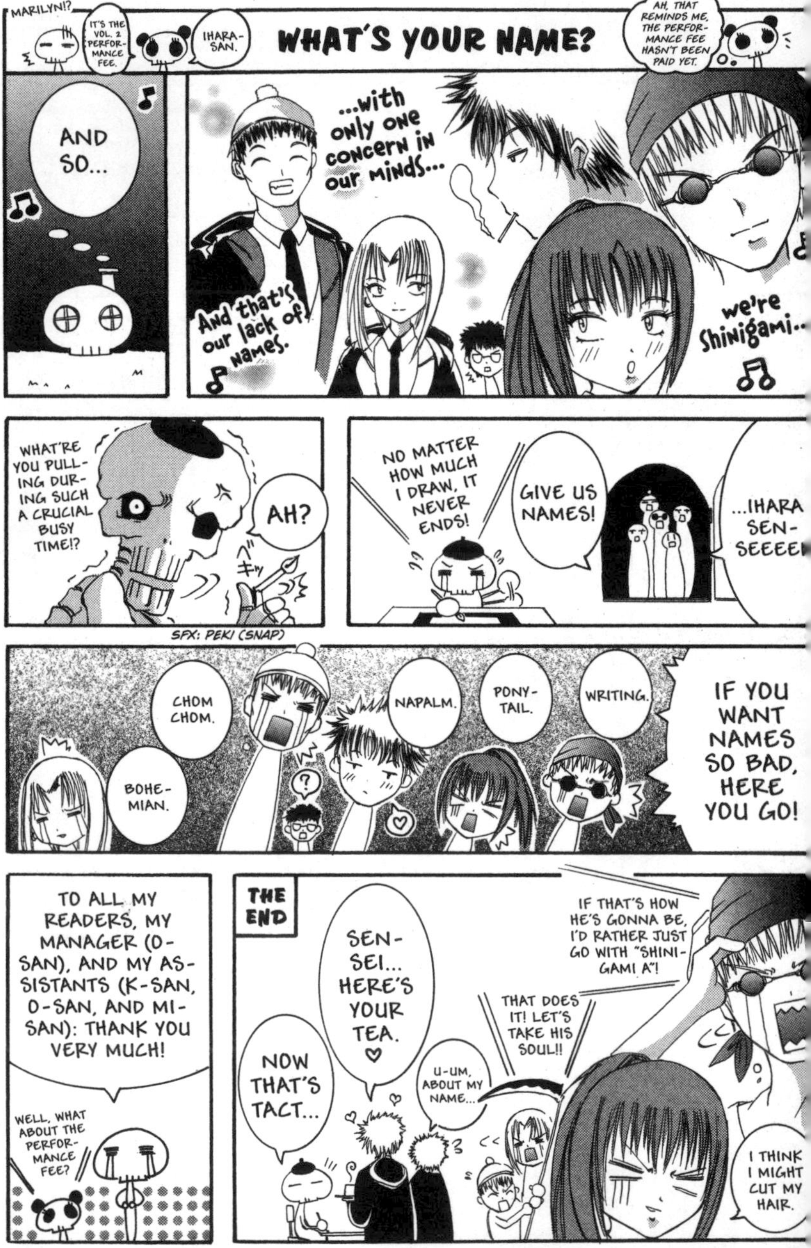
WHAT'S YOUR NAME?
AH, THAT REMINDS ME, THE PERFORMANCE FEE HASN'T BEEN PAID YET.
IHARA-SAN.
IT'S THE VOL. 2 PERFORMANCE FEE.
MARILYN!?
we're Shinigami...
...with only one concern in our minds...
And that's our lack of names.
AND SO...
...IHARA SEN-SEEEEE
GIVE US NAMES!
NO MATTER HOW MUCH I DRAW, IT NEVER ENDS!
AH?
WHAT'RE YOU PULLING DURING SUCH A CRUCIAL BUSY TIME!?
SFX: PEKI (SNAP)
IF YOU WANT NAMES SO BAD, HERE YOU GO!
WRITING.
PONY-TAIL.
NAPALM.
CHOM CHOM.
BOHEMIAN.
I THINK I MIGHT CUT MY HAIR.
IF THAT'S HOW HE'S GONNA BE, I'D RATHER JUST GO WITH "SHINIGAMI A"!
THAT DOES IT! LET'S TAKE HIS SOUL!!
U-UM, ABOUT MY NAME...
SENSEI... HERE'S YOUR TEA. ♡
NOW THAT'S TACT...
THE END
TO ALL MY READERS, MY MANAGER (O-SAN), AND MY ASSISTANTS (K-SAN, O-SAN, AND MI-SAN): THANK YOU VERY MUCH!
WELL, WHAT ABOUT THE PERFORMANCE FEE?

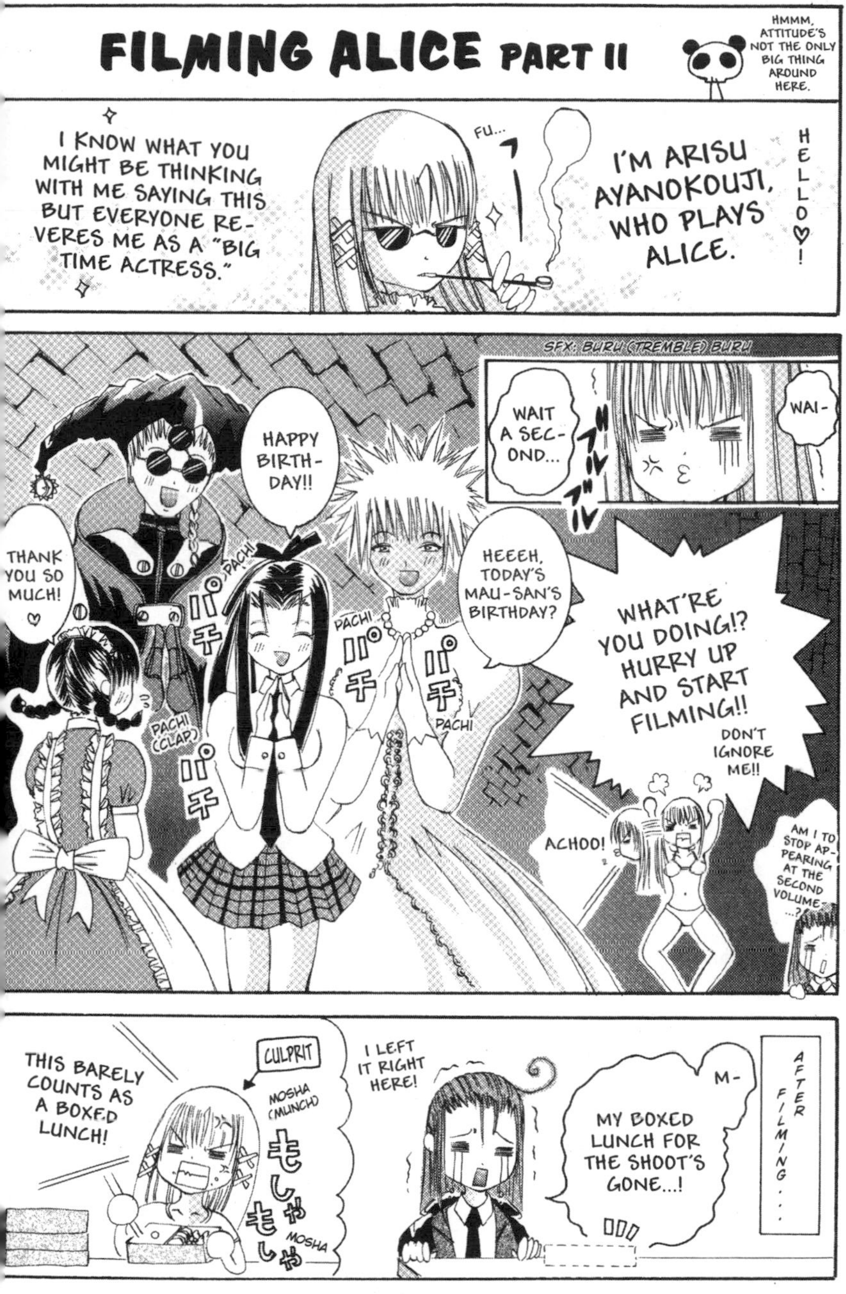
FILMING ALICE PART II
HMMM, ATTITUDE'S NOT THE ONLY BIG THING AROUND HERE.
HELLO♡!
FU...
I'M ARISU AYANOKOUJI, WHO PLAYS ALICE.
I KNOW WHAT YOU MIGHT BE THINKING WITH ME SAYING THIS BUT EVERYONE RE-VERES ME AS A "BIG TIME ACTRESS."
SFX: BURU (TREMBLE) BURU
WAI-
WAIT A SEC-OND...
WHAT'RE YOU DOING!? HURRY UP AND START FILMING!!
DON'T IGNORE ME!!
AM I TO STOP AP-PEARING AT THE SECOND VOLUME-...?
ACHOO!
HEEEH, TODAY'S MAU-SAN'S BIRTHDAY?
HAPPY BIRTH-DAY!!
PACHI
PACHI
PACHI
THANK YOU SO MUCH! ♡
PACHI (CLAP)
AFTER FILMING...
M-
MY BOXED LUNCH FOR THE SHOOT'S GONE...!
I LEFT IT RIGHT HERE!
MOSHA (MUNCH)
MOSHA
CULPRIT
THIS BARELY COUNTS AS A BOXED LUNCH!

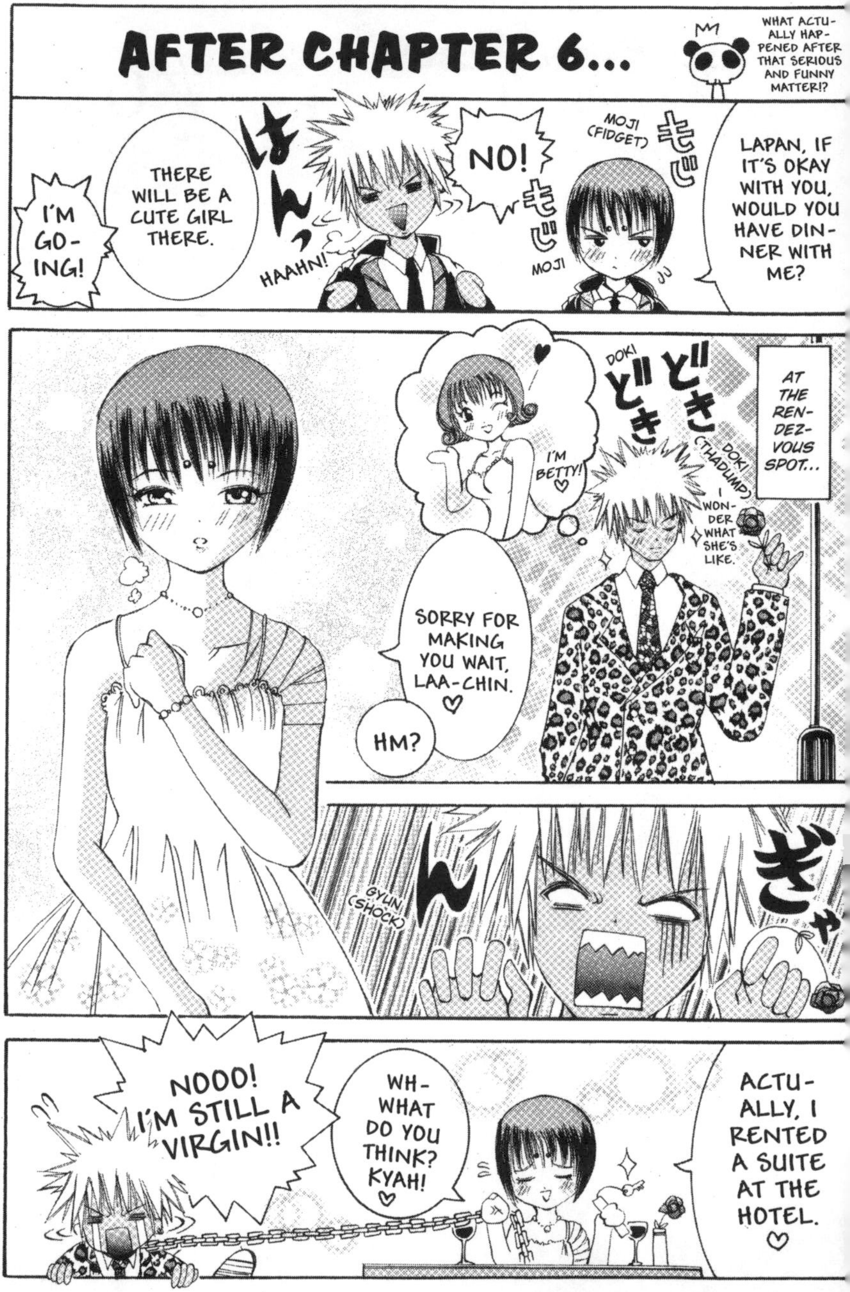
AFTER CHAPTER 6...
WHAT ACTUALLY HAPPENED AFTER THAT SERIOUS AND FUNNY MATTER!?
LAPAN, IF IT'S OKAY WITH YOU, WOULD YOU HAVE DINNER WITH ME?
MOJI (FIDGET) もじ
もじ MOJI
JU
NO!
はん, HAAHN!
THERE WILL BE A CUTE GIRL THERE.
I'M GOING!
AT THE RENDEZVOUS SPOT...
DOKI どき
どき DOKI (THADUMP)
I WONDER WHAT SHE'S LIKE.
I'M BETTY! ♡
SORRY FOR MAKING YOU WAIT, LAA-CHIN. ♡
HM?
ぎゃ
ん
GYUN (SHOCK)
ACTUALLY, I RENTED A SUITE AT THE HOTEL. ♡
WH-WHAT DO YOU THINK? KYAH! ♡
NOOO! I'M STILL A VIRGIN!!

D線上のアリス

ALICE ON DEADLINES

#03

SNEAK PEEK

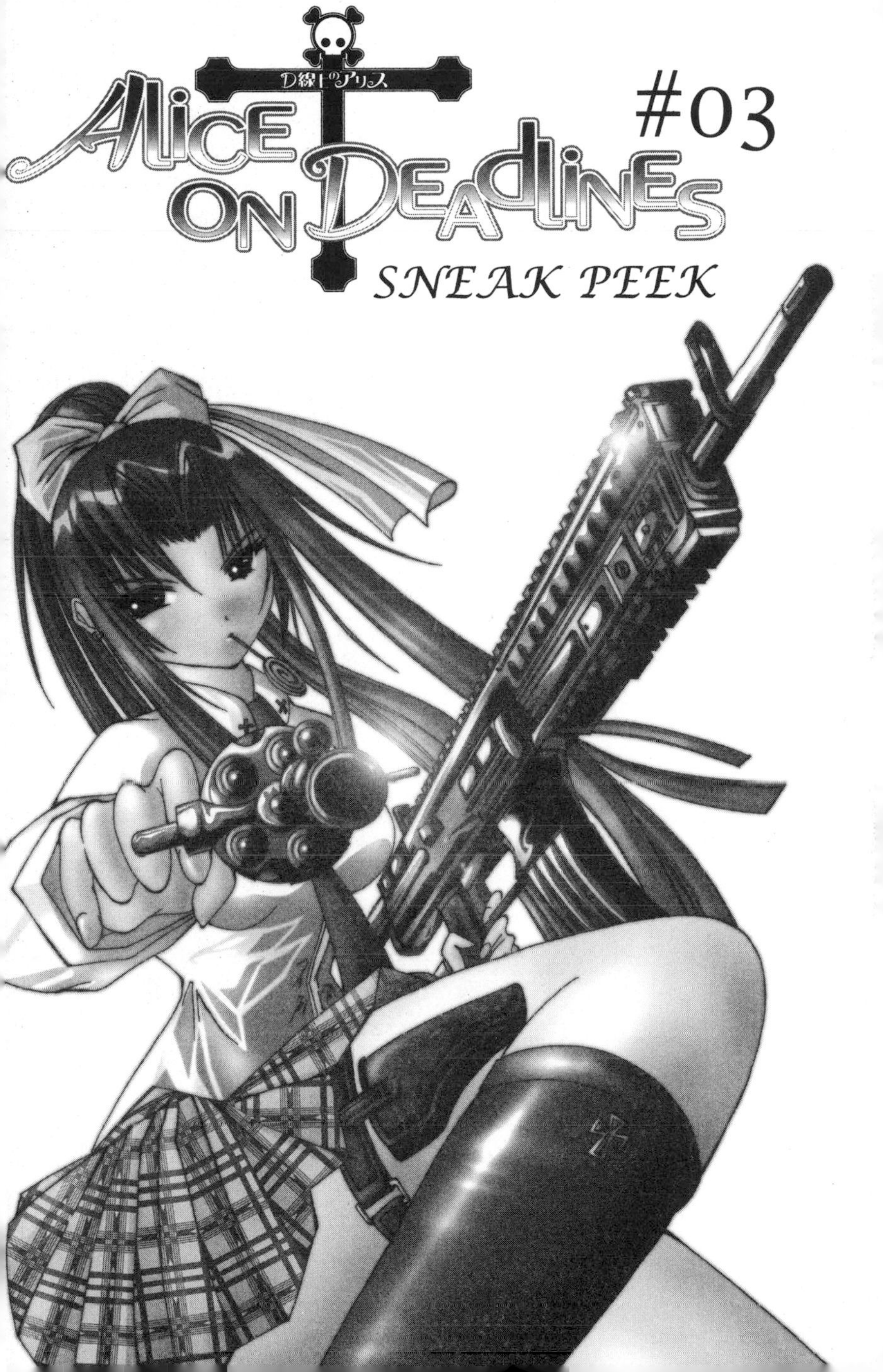

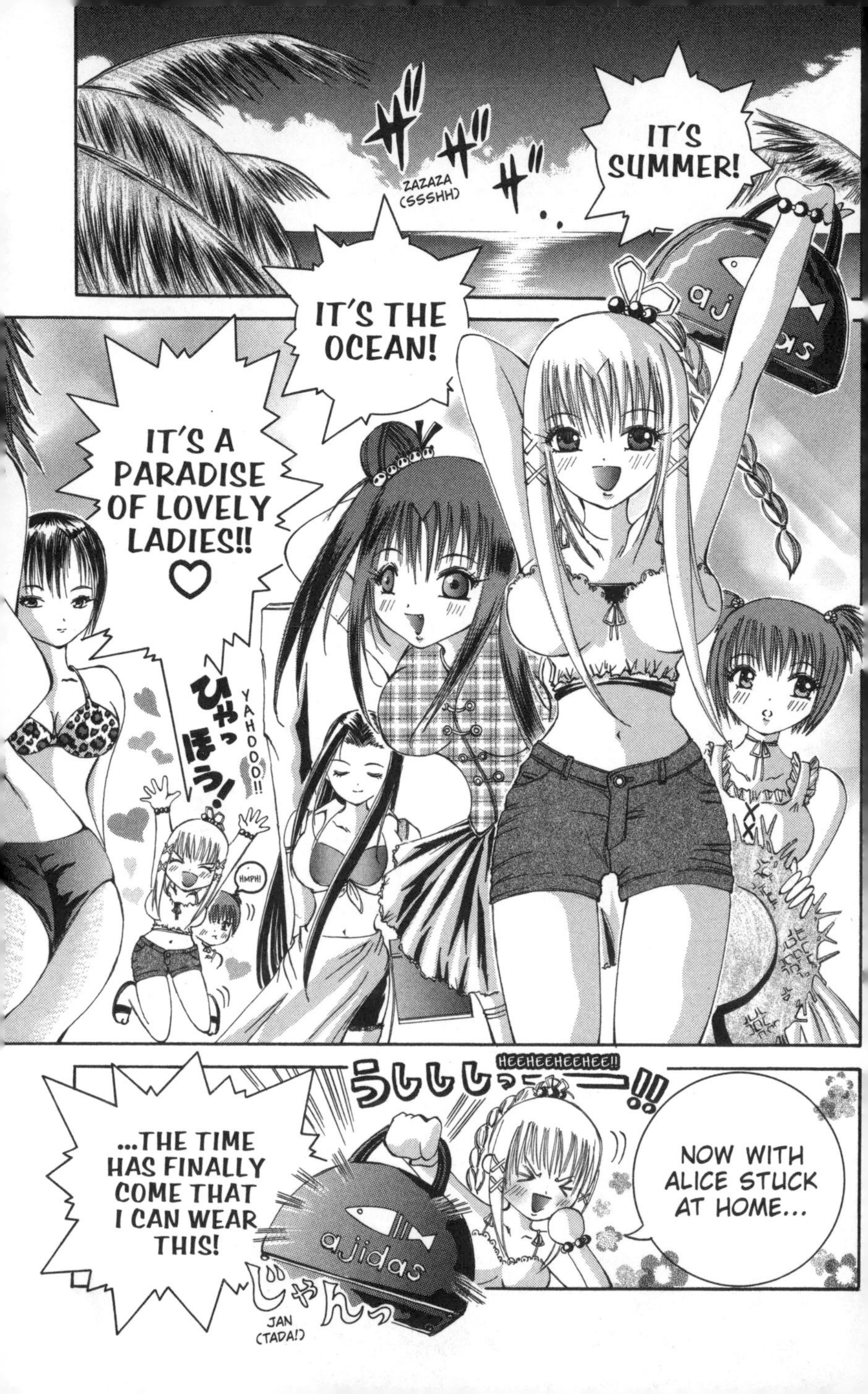
IT'S SUMMER!
ザザザ
ZAZAZA (SSSHH)
IT'S THE OCEAN!
IT'S A PARADISE OF LOVELY LADIES!! ♡
ひゃっほう!
YAHOOOO!!
HMPH!
NOW WITH ALICE STUCK AT HOME...
うしししっーー!!
HEEHEEHEEHEE!!
...THE TIME HAS FINALLY COME THAT I CAN WEAR THIS!
ajidas
じゃんっ
JAN (TADA!)

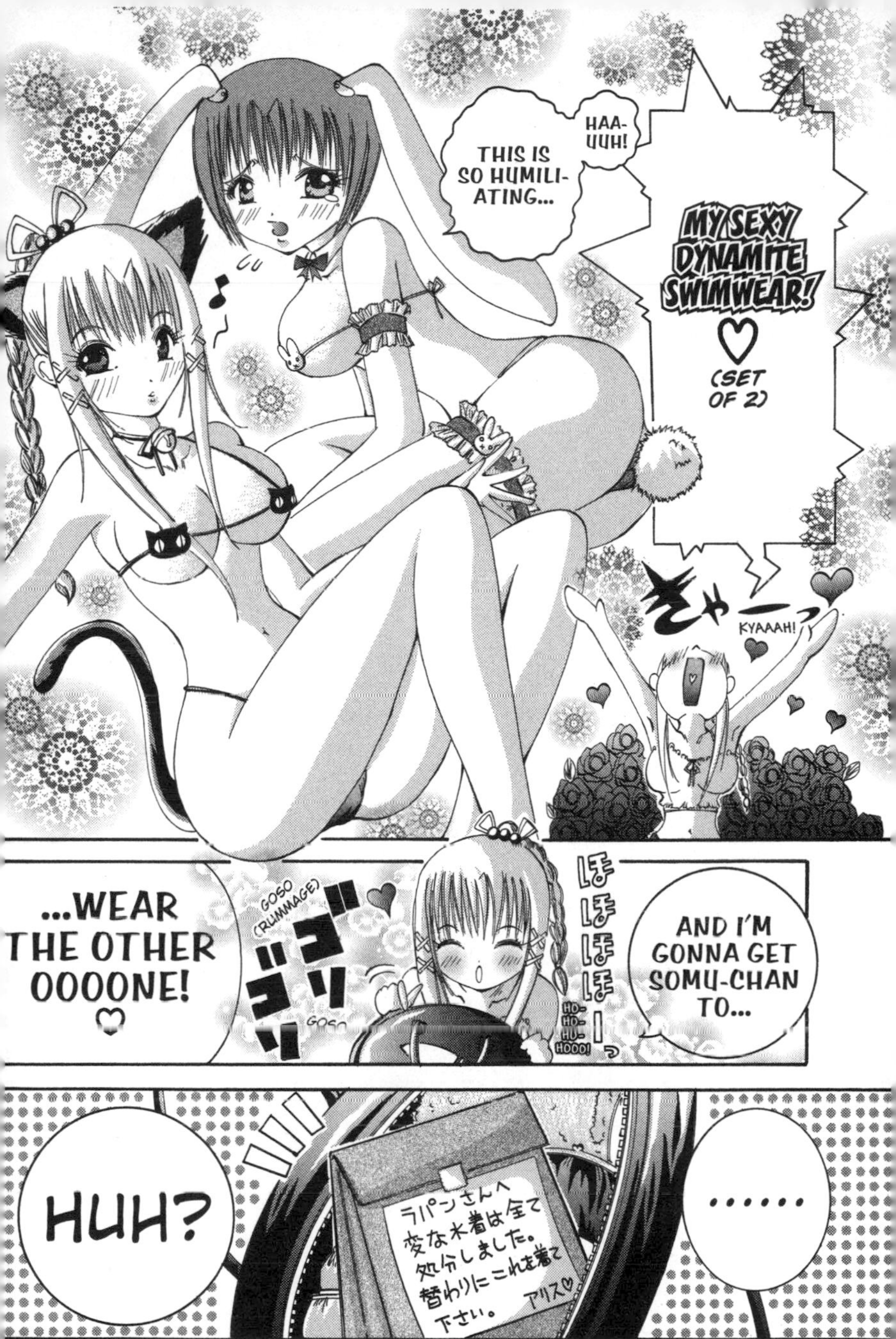
MY SEXY DYNAMITE SWIMWEAR! ♡
(SET OF 2)
HAA-UUH!
THIS IS SO HUMILI-ATING...
きゃーっ
KYAAAH!
AND I'M GONNA GET SOMU-CHAN TO...
ほほほほー
HO-HO-HU-HOOO!
ゴソゴソ
GOSO (RUMMAGE)
GOSO
...WEAR THE OTHER OOOONE! ♡
......
ラパンさんへ
変な水着は全て
処分しました。
替わりにこれを着て
下さい。 アリス♡
HUH?

OTE: DEAR LAPAN-SAN, I DISPOSED OF ALL YOUR STRANGE BATHING SUITS. PLEASE WEAR THIS INSTEAD. ALICE ♡

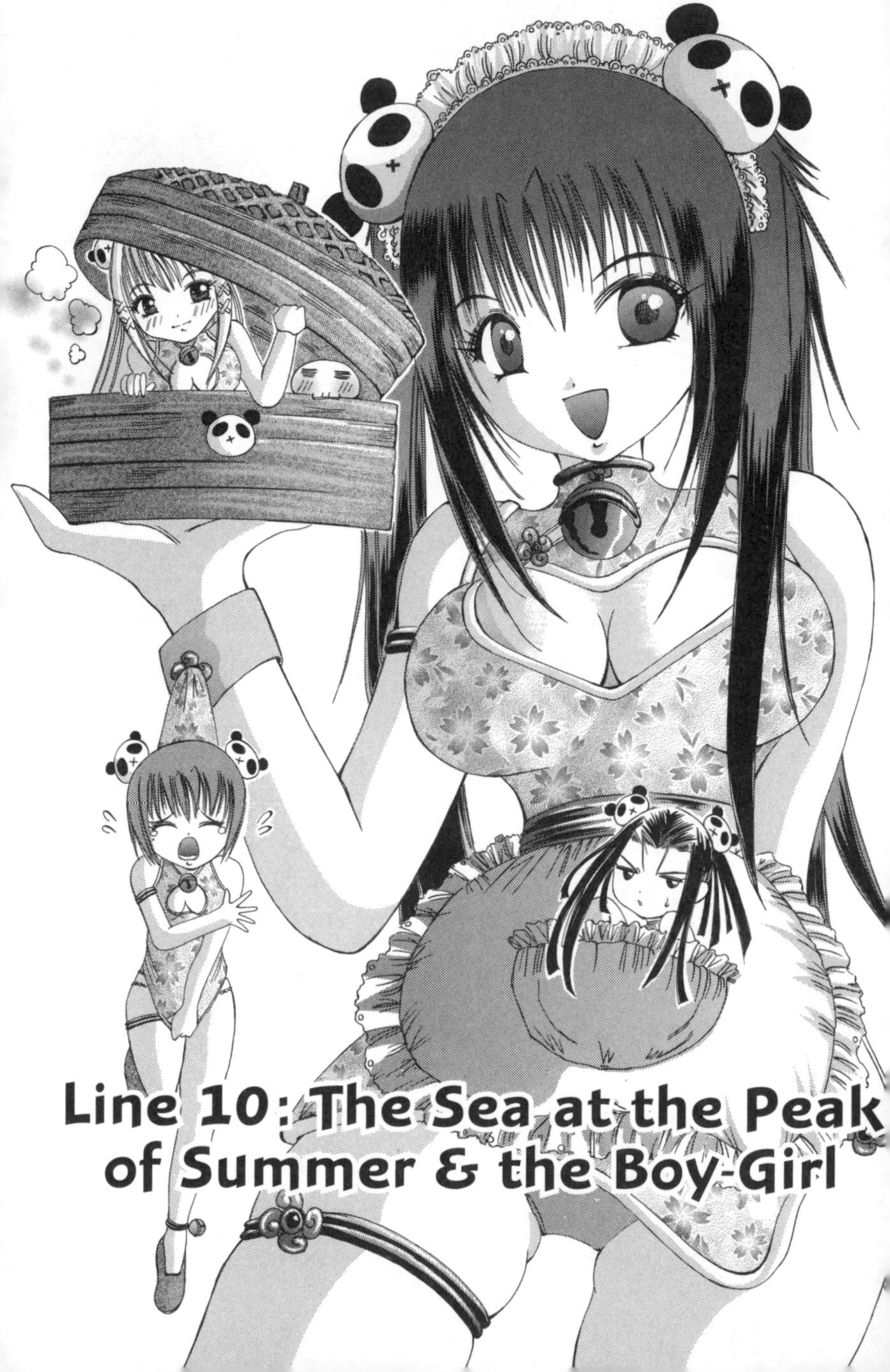
Line 10: The Sea at the Peak of Summer & the Boy-Girl

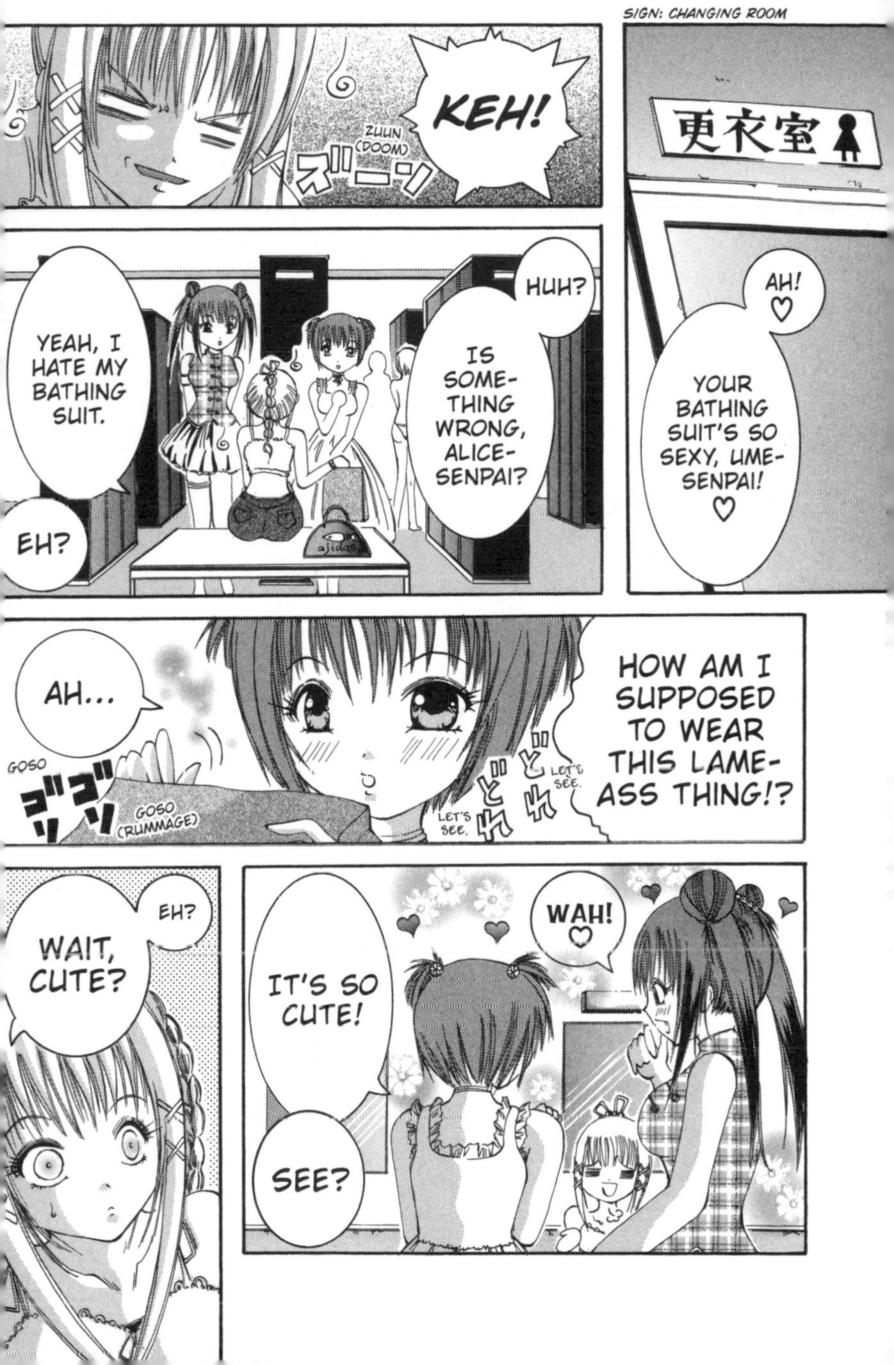
SIGN: CHANGING ROOM
更衣室
AH! ♡
YOUR BATHING SUIT'S SO SEXY, UME-SENPAI! ♡
KEH!
ZUUN (DOOM)
ズーン
HUH?
IS SOMETHING WRONG, ALICE-SENPAI?
EH?
YEAH, I HATE MY BATHING SUIT.
HOW AM I SUPPOSED TO WEAR THIS LAME-ASS THING!?
どれ LET'S SEE.
どれ LET'S SEE.
AH...
GOSO
ゴソゴソ
GOSO (RUMMAGE)
WAH! ♡
IT'S SO CUTE!
SEE?
EH?
WAIT, CUTE?

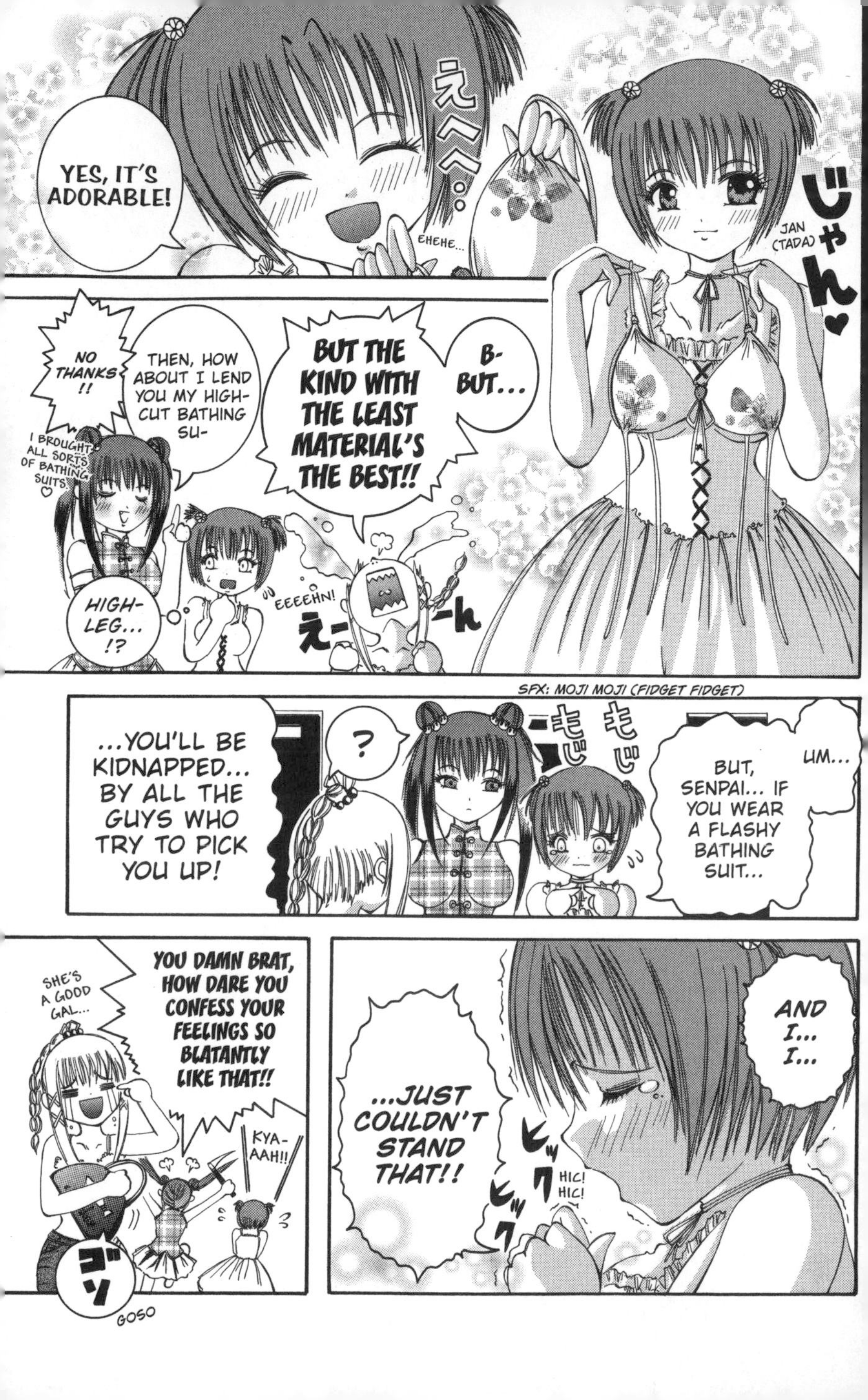
じゃん♥
JAN (TADA)
えへへ。。
EHEHE...
YES, IT'S ADORABLE!
B-BUT...
BUT THE KIND WITH THE LEAST MATERIAL'S THE BEST!!
えーーん
EEEEHN!
THEN, HOW ABOUT I LEND YOU MY HIGH-CUT BATHING SU-
NO THANKS!!
I BROUGHT ALL SORTS OF BATHING SUITS ♡
HIGH-LEG...!?
SFX: MOJI MOJI (FIDGET FIDGET)
もじもじ
UM...
BUT, SENPAI... IF YOU WEAR A FLASHY BATHING SUIT...
?
...YOU'LL BE KIDNAPPED... BY ALL THE GUYS WHO TRY TO PICK YOU UP!
AND I... I...
ヒックヒック
HIC! HIC!
...JUST COULDN'T STAND THAT!!
YOU DAMN BRAT, HOW DARE YOU CONFESS YOUR FEELINGS SO BLATANTLY LIKE THAT!!
SHE'S A GOOD GAL...
KYA-AAH!!
ゴソ
GOSO

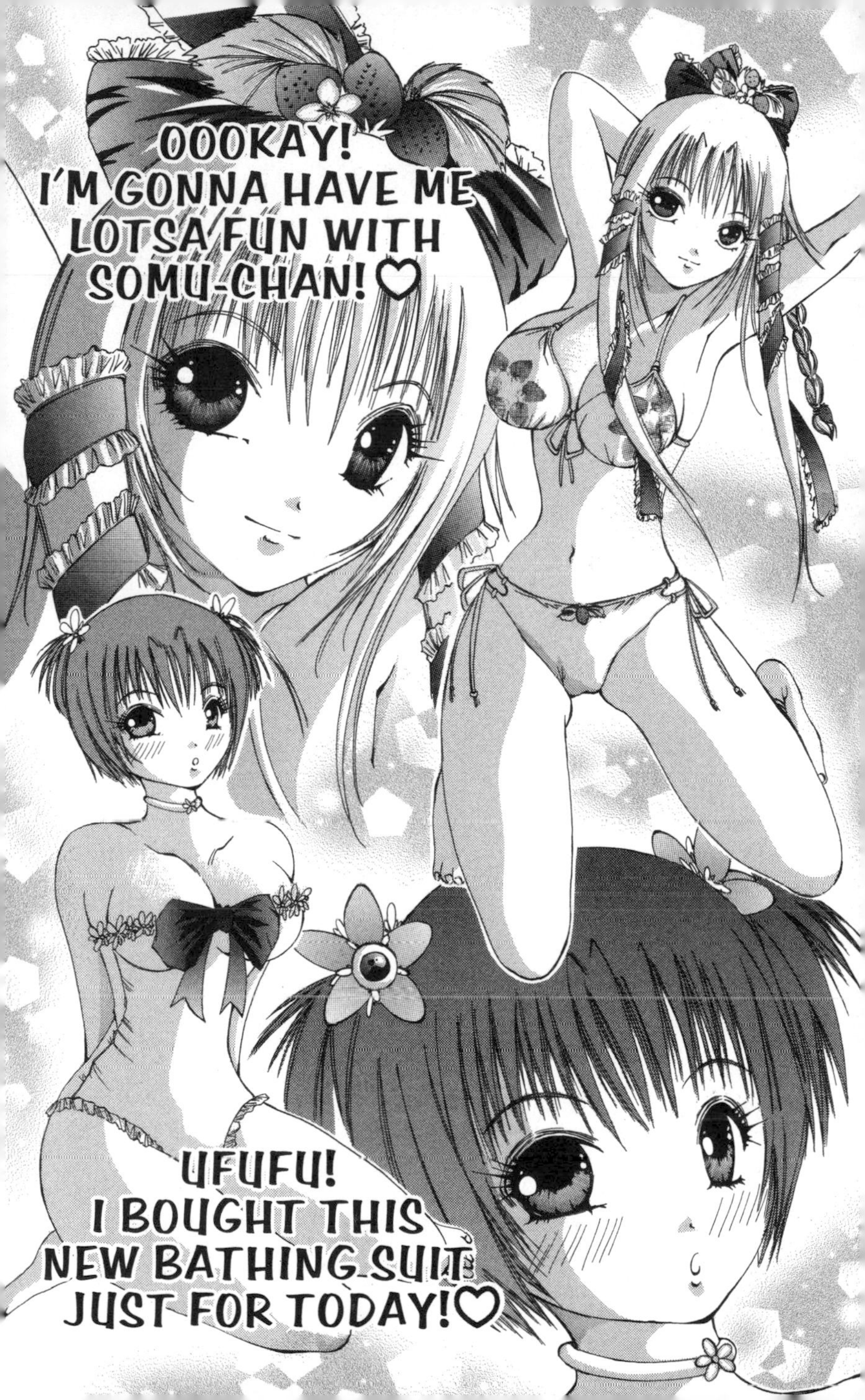
OOOKAY! I'M GONNA HAVE ME LOTSA FUN WITH SOMU-CHAN! ♡
UFUFU! I BOUGHT THIS NEW BATHING SUIT JUST FOR TODAY! ♡

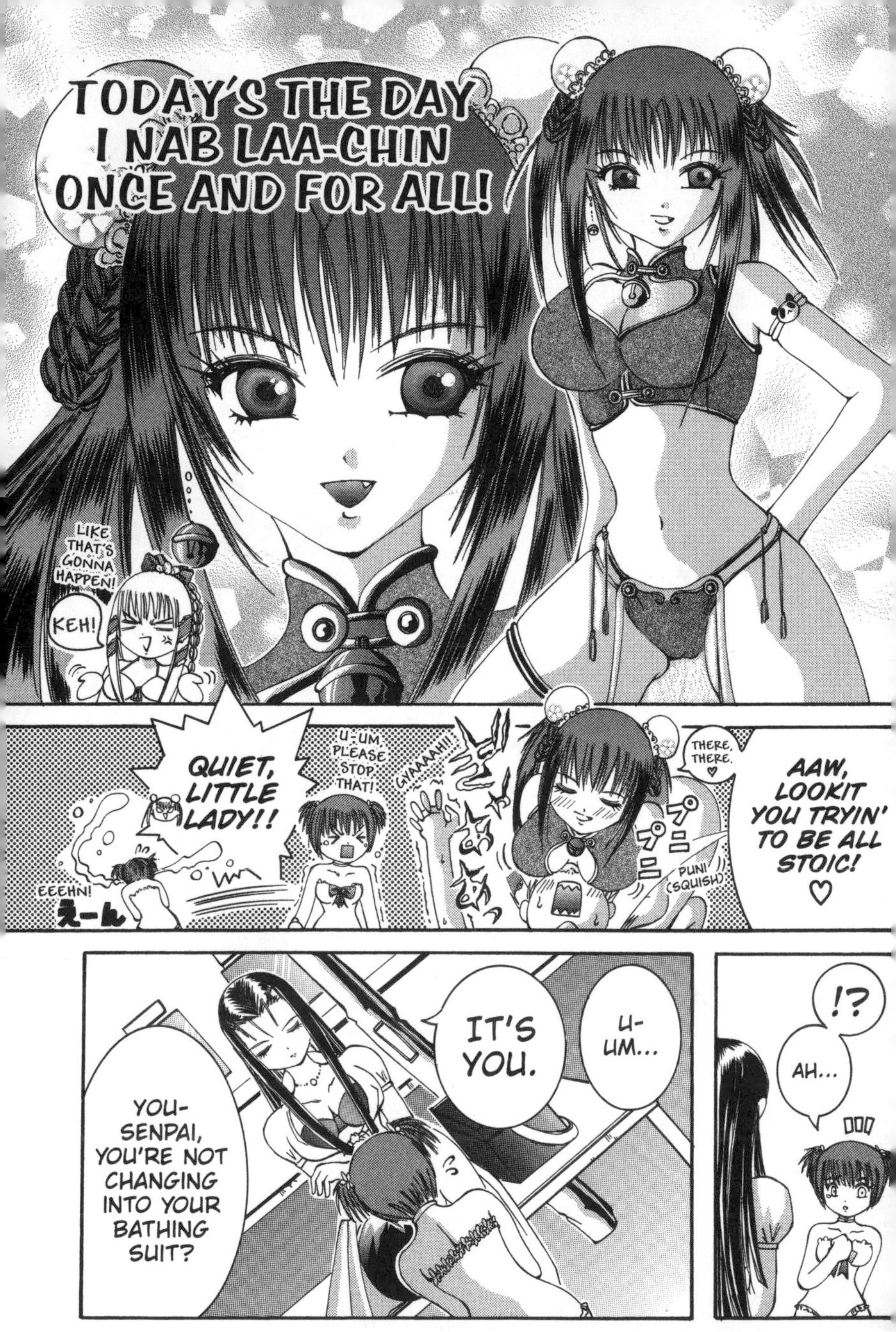
TODAY'S THE DAY I NAB LAA-CHIN ONCE AND FOR ALL!
LIKE THAT'S GONNA HAPPEN!
KEH!
AAW, LOOKIT YOU TRYIN' TO BE ALL STOIC! ♡
THERE, THERE. ♡
PUNI (SQUISH)
GYAAAAH!!
U-UM, PLEASE STOP THAT!
QUIET, LITTLE LADY!!
EEEHN!
えーん
!?
AH...
U-UM...
IT'S YOU.
YOU-SENPAI, YOU'RE NOT CHANGING INTO YOUR BATHING SUIT?

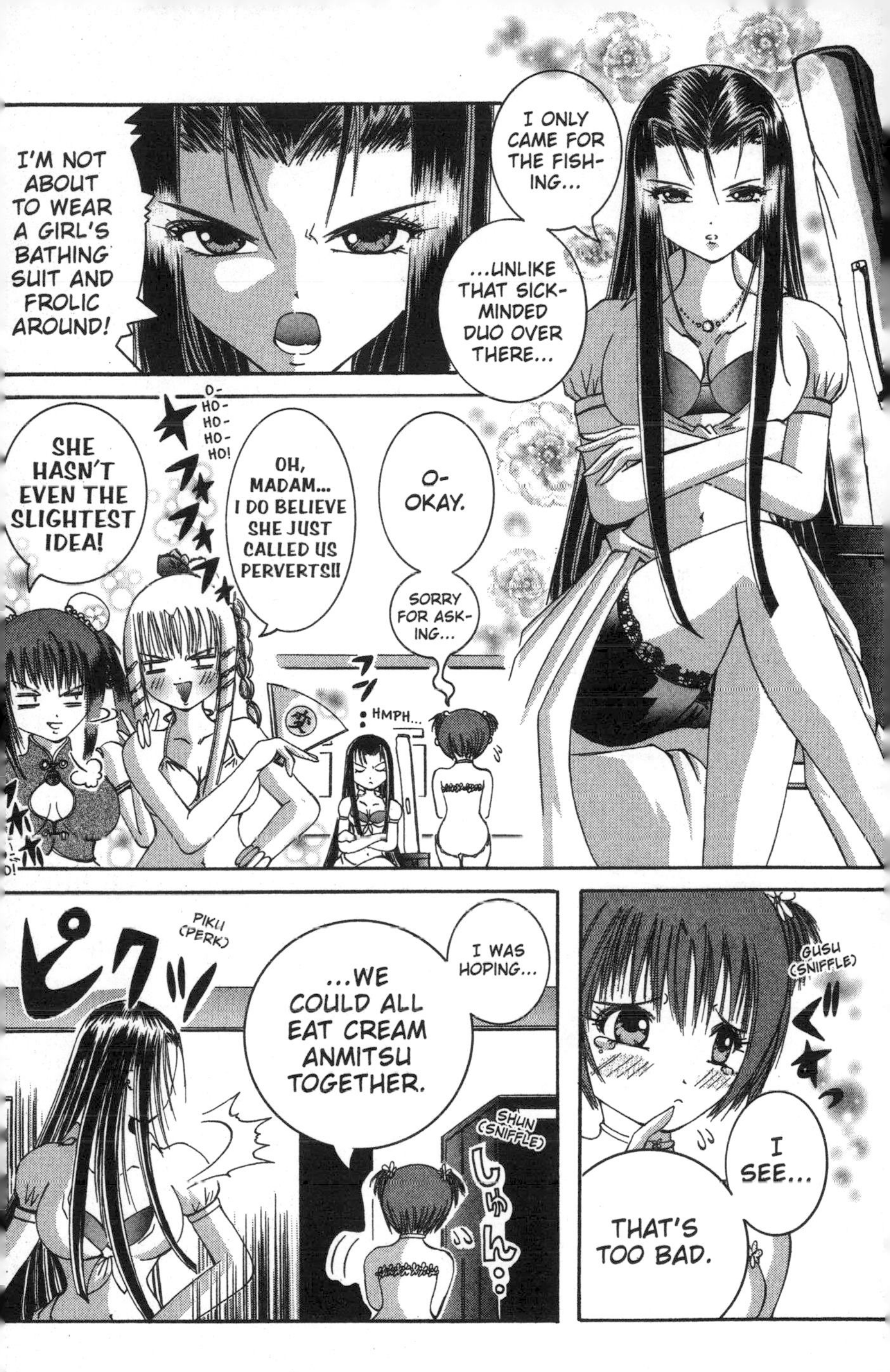
I ONLY CAME FOR THE FISHING...
...UNLIKE THAT SICK-MINDED DUO OVER THERE...
I'M NOT ABOUT TO WEAR A GIRL'S BATHING SUIT AND FROLIC AROUND!
O-OKAY.
SORRY FOR ASKING...
HMPH...
OH, MADAM... I DO BELIEVE SHE JUST CALLED US PERVERTS!!
O-HO-HO-HO-HO!
SHE HASN'T EVEN THE SLIGHTEST IDEA!
GUSU (SNIFFLE)
I SEE...
THAT'S TOO BAD.
I WAS HOPING...
...WE COULD ALL EAT CREAM ANMITSU TOGETHER.
SHUN (SNIFFLE)
しゅん。
PIKU (PERK)
ピクッ

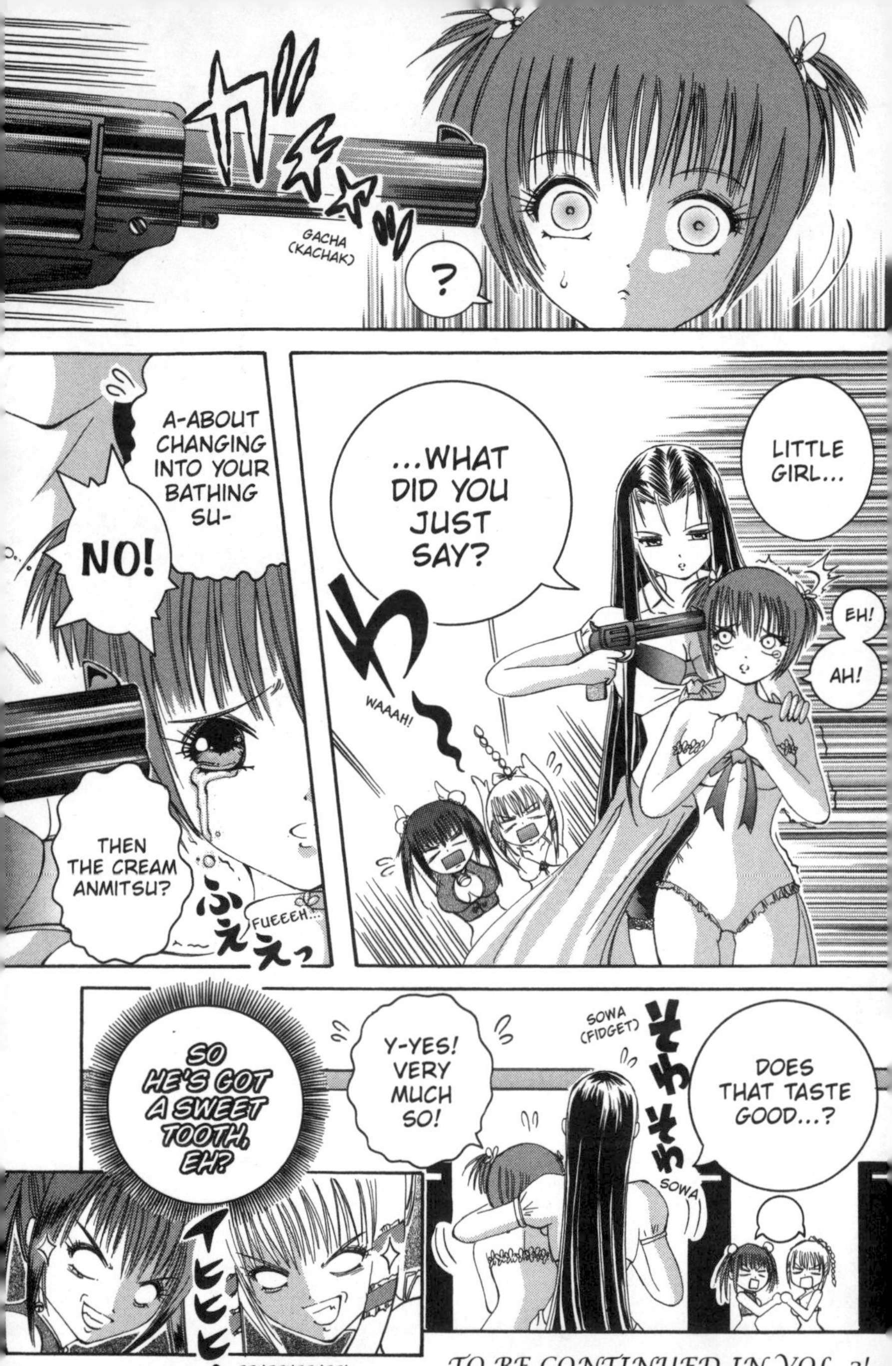
GACHA (KACHAK)
?
LITTLE GIRL...
EH!
AH!
...WHAT DID YOU JUST SAY?
WAAAH!
A-ABOUT CHANGING INTO YOUR BATHING SU-
NO!
THEN THE CREAM ANMITSU?
FUEEEH...
DOES THAT TASTE GOOD...?
SOWA (FIDGET)
SOWA
Y-YES! VERY MUCH SO!
SO HE'S GOT A SWEET TOOTH, EH?
EEHEEHEEHEE!

TO BE CONTINUED IN VOL. 3!

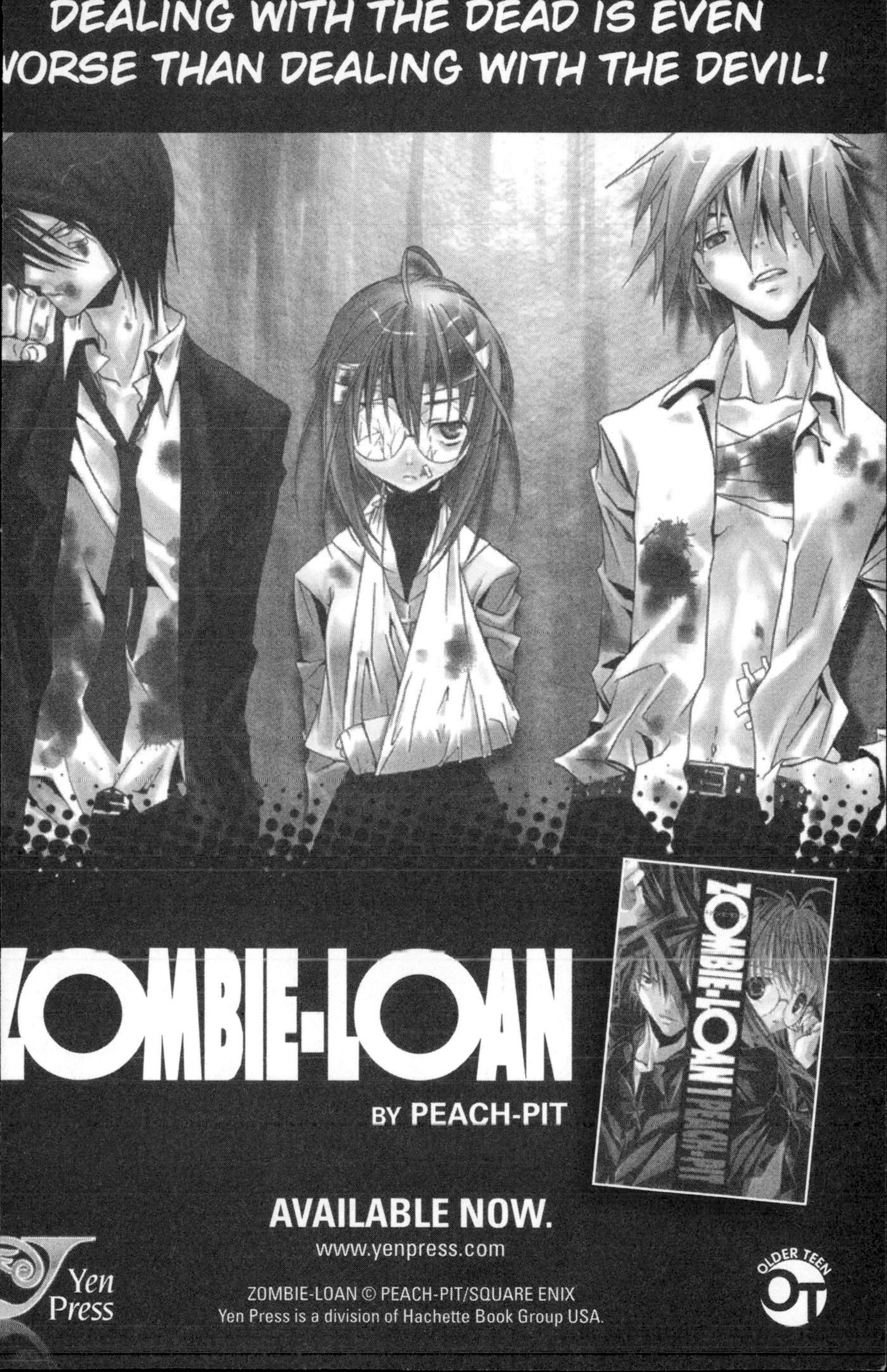

DEALING WITH THE DEAD IS EVEN
WORSE THAN DEALING WITH THE DEVIL!
ZOMBIE-LOAN
BY PEACH-PIT
AVAILABLE NOW.
www.yenpress.com
Yen Press
ZOMBIE-LOAN © PEACH-PIT/SQUARE ENIX
Yen Press is a division of Hachette Book Group USA.
OLDER TEEN
OT

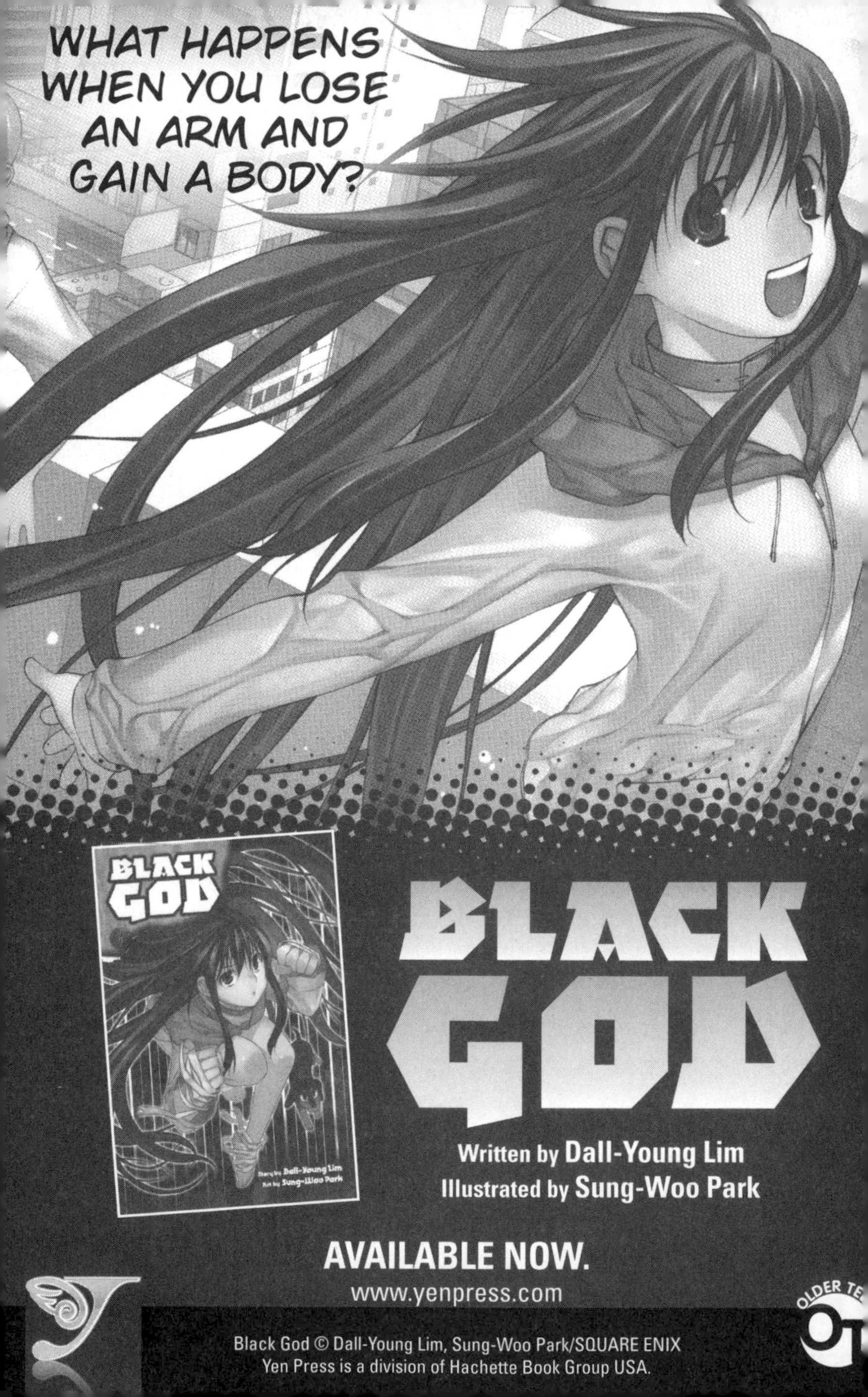
WHAT HAPPENS WHEN YOU LOSE AN ARM AND GAIN A BODY?
BLACK GOD
BLACK GOD
Story by Dall-Young Lim
Art by Sung-Woo Park
Written by Dall-Young Lim
Illustrated by Sung-Woo Park
AVAILABLE NOW.
www.yenpress.com
Black God © Dall-Young Lim, Sung-Woo Park/SQUARE ENIX
Yen Press is a division of Hachette Book Group USA.

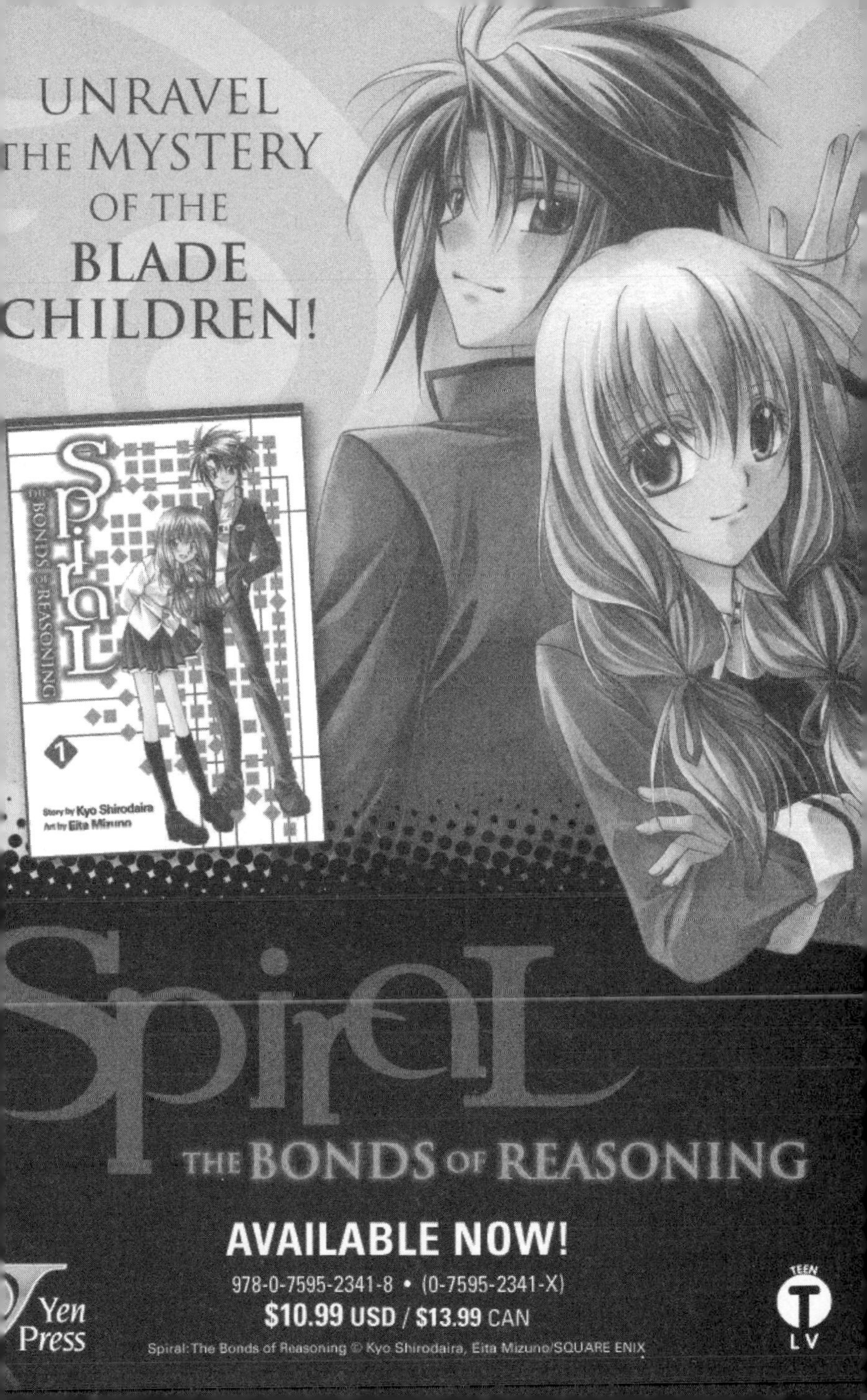
UNRAVEL
THE MYSTERY
OF THE
BLADE
CHILDREN!
Spiral
THE BONDS OF REASONING
1
Story by Kyo Shirodaira
Art by Eita Mizuno
Spiral
THE BONDS OF REASONING
AVAILABLE NOW!
978-0-7595-2341-8 • (0-7595-2341-X)
$10.99 USD / $13.99 CAN
Spiral: The Bonds of Reasoning © Kyo Shirodaira, Eita Mizuno/SQUARE ENIX
Yen Press
TEEN
T
LV

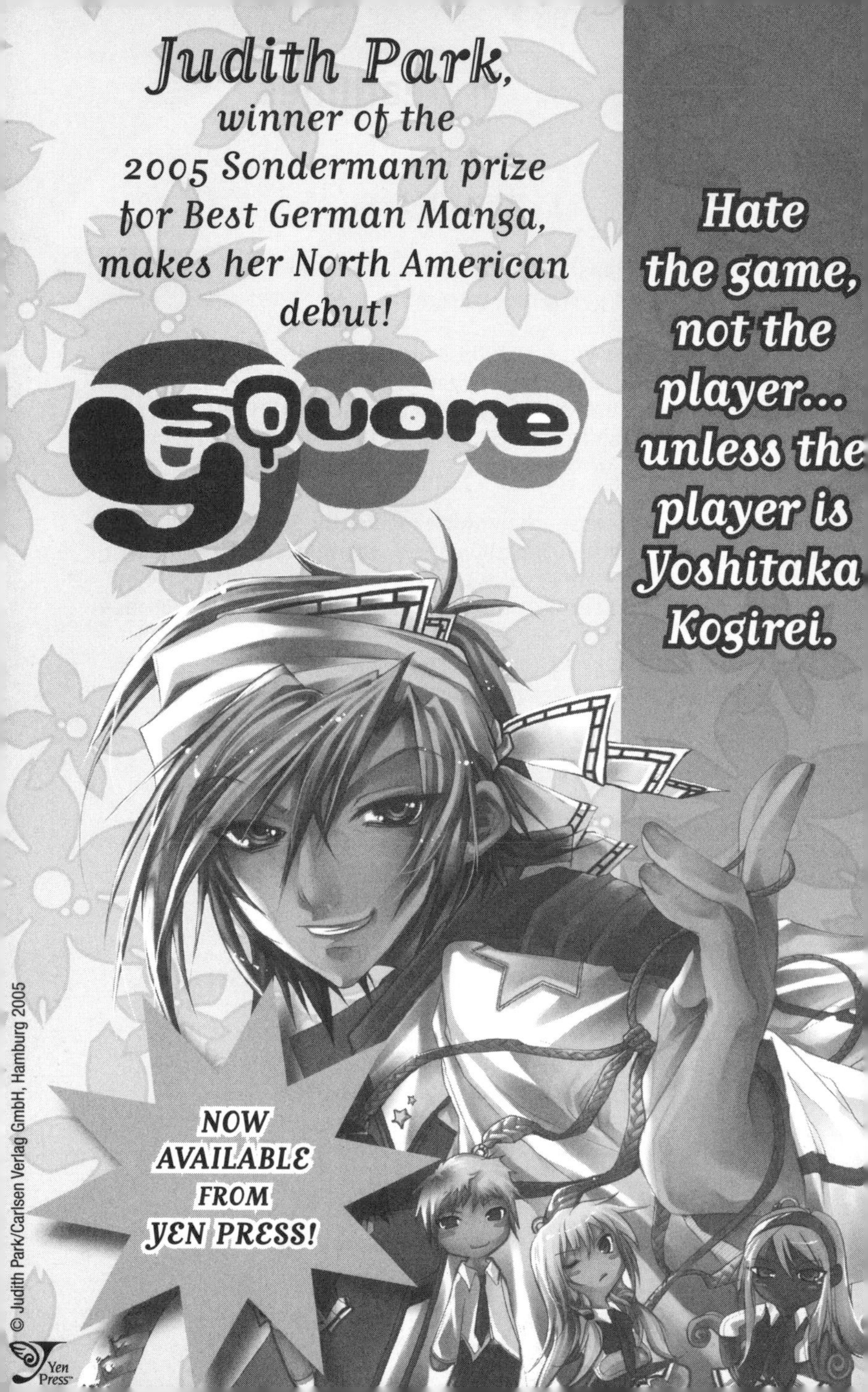
Judith Park,
winner of the
2005 Sondermann prize
for Best German Manga,
makes her North American
debut!
y square
Hate
the game,
not the
player...
unless the
player is
Yoshitaka
Kogirei.
NOW
AVAILABLE
FROM
YEN PRESS!
© Judith Park/Carlsen Verlag GmbH, Hamburg 2005
Yen Press

ALICE on D
2

by Shirō Ih

Translation: Christine Schilling
Lettering: Keiran O'Leary

ALICE on Deadlines Vol. 2 © 2005 Shirō Ihara / SQUARE ENIX. All rights reserved. First published in Japan in 2005 by SQUARE ENIX, CO., LTD. English translation rights arranged with SQUARE ENIX CO., LTD. and Hachette Book Group USA through Tuttle-Mori Agency, Inc. Translation © 2008 by SQUARE ENIX CO., LTD.

Yen Press
Hachette Book Group USA
237 Park Avenue, New York, NY 10017

Visit our Web sites at www.HachetteBookGroupUSA.com and www.YenPress.com.

Yen Press is an imprint of Hachette Book Group USA, Inc. The Yen Press name and logo is a trademark of Hachette Book Group USA, Inc.

First Yen Press Edition: March 2008

ISBN-10: 0-7595-2845-4 / ISBN-13: 978-0-7595-2845-1

10 9 8 7 6 5 4 3 2 1

BVG

Printed in the United States of America